"*Theological Foundations* deals with the BIG questions: 'Why am I here?' and 'What is worth living for?'—inviting college students to the approachability and necessity of theology and its relevance to real life. The perfect book for introducing the building blocks of theology!"

—Br. Armand Alcazar, FSC, associate professor of theology, Lewis University

Praise for the previous edition:

"This text fills a real need for a challenging introductory text in Catholic theology. It is beautifully conceived, well written, inviting, and full of splendid resources rarely, if ever, found in comparable texts."

—David Gentry-Akin, Saint Mary's College of California

". . . an excellent introduction to undergraduate theology. The reference librarian sections of each chapter are invaluable. If you need one text for an introductory course, this is the one."

—Daniel McGuire, University of Great Falls

Theological Foundations

Concepts and Methods for Understanding Christian Faith

REVISED AND EXPANDED

J. J. Mueller, SJ, editor

Created by the publishing team of Anselm Academic.

Cover image of Jesus and five apostles by © Fotowan / shutterstock.com

Printed in the United States of America

7035

ISBN 978-1-59982-101-6

ABOUT THE AUTHORS

J. J. Mueller, SJ
Fr. Mueller holds a PhD in historical and systematic theology from the Graduate Theological Union at Berkeley. His interests are Christology and social responsibility.

Ronald Crown
Dr. Crown holds a DPhil in theology (New Testament studies) from the University of Oxford and an MS in library science from the University of Kentucky.

Bernhard A. Asen
Dr. Asen holds a PhD in biblical languages and literature from Saint Louis University. His particular interests are the prophets and the Psalms.

James A. Kelhoffer
Dr. Kelhoffer holds a PhD in New Testament and early Christian literature from the University of Chicago. His interests are the New Testament and the early church.

Brian D. Robinette
Dr. Robinette holds a PhD in theology from the University of Notre Dame. His primary interests are Christology and theological anthropology.

Daniel Finucane
Dr. Finucane holds a PhD in historical theology from Saint Louis University. His interests include ecclesiology and foundational theology.

Jay M. Hammond
Dr. Hammond holds a PhD in historical theology from Saint Louis University. His interests include medieval Christianity, Franciscan thought, and sacramental theology.

Barbara W. Blackburn
Dr. Blackburn holds a PhD in historical theology from Saint Louis University. Her interests are moral theology and the theology of death and suffering.

J. A. Wayne Hellmann, OFM Conv
Dr. Hellmann holds his doctoral degree in historical and systematic theology from Ludwig-Maximilian Universität in Munich, Germany. His interests are the study of St. Francis of Assisi, the Franciscan spiritual tradition, and the application of theology to social justice.

Ronald Modras
Dr. Modras holds a doctorate in theology from the University of Tubingen in Germany. His interests include interreligious dialogue and Jewish-Christian relations.

John Renard
Dr. Renard holds a PhD in Islamic studies from the Near Eastern Languages and Civilizations Department of Harvard University. Since 1978, he has been teaching courses in Islam and other major non-Christian traditions as well as comparative theology at Saint Louis University.

Angelyn Dries, OSF
Dr. Dries holds a PhD in historical theology from the Graduate Theological Union at Berkeley. Dr. Dries is the Danforth Chair of Theology at Saint Louis University. Her areas of interest include world Christianity and the modern missionary movement.

Michael McClymond
Dr. McClymond holds a M.Div. from Yale University Divinity School and a PhD in theology from the University of Chicago. He has done field research on Pentecostalism in Brazil and Mozambique, and is co-chair of the Evangelical Theology Group in the American Academy of Religion.

ACKNOWLEDGMENTS

Thank you to the following people who advised the publishing team through discussion, class testing of the manuscript, student focus groups, or review of this work in progress:

Anthony Amodeo
Reference and Instruction Librarian, Loyola Marymount University, California

Jason Bourgeois
Quincy University, Illinois

Ulrike R. M. Guthrie
MA, independent scholar, Maine

Alan D. Krieger
Theology Librarian, University of Notre Dame, Indiana

Mari Heidt
Marquette University, Wisconsin

Harriet A. Luckman
College of Mount Saint Joseph, Ohio

Michael McClymond
Saint Louis University, Missouri

Ruben Rosario-Rodriguez
Saint Louis University, Missouri

Daniel Scholz
Cardinal Stritch University, Wisconsin

Paul Wadell
Saint Norbert College, Wisconsin

Maureen Walsh, graduate student,
Georgetown University, Washington, DC

CONTENTS

Part II

CHRISTOLOGY AND ECCLESIOLOGY: FOLLOWING CHRIST IN A COMMUNITY OF THE HOLY SPIRIT 103

Part III

THE CHURCH'S MISSION IN THE WORLD 217

Part IV

THE ABRAHAMIC FAITHS: CATHOLICISM AND RELATIONSHIPS WITH JUDAISM, ISLAM 275

Part V

CATHOLIC THEOLOGY IN A GLOBAL CONTEXT 327

THE STRUCTURE OF THE CONTENT AND ITS RELATIONSHIP

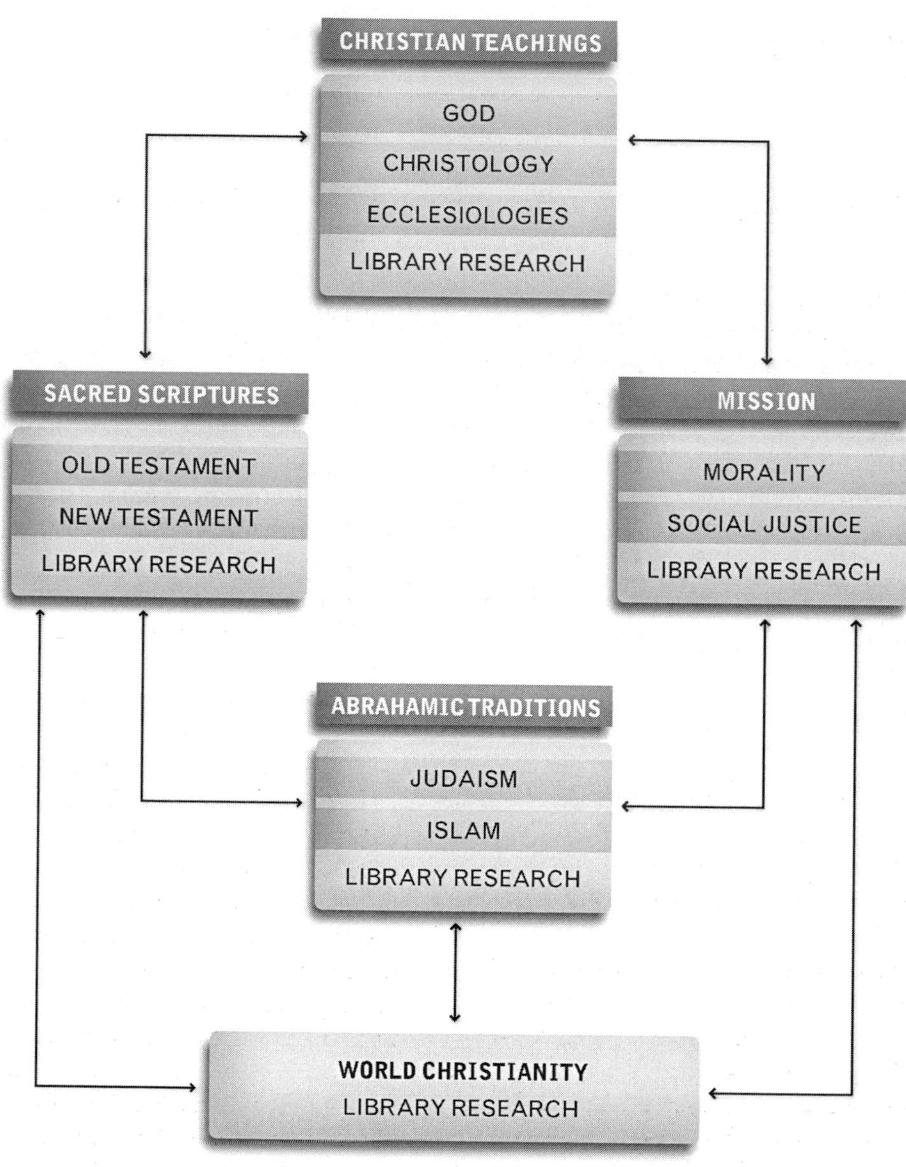

from the EDITOR

J. J. Mueller, SJ

PURPOSE OF THIS BOOK

This book is about how to successfully study theology. Nothing is foreign to the domain of theology and, because theology pursues the deepest questions of being authentically human in God, why should there be any limit? Absolutely everything is grist for the theological mill. As an academic discipline, theology is not insular, exclusive, or a foreigner in the academy; it is in conversation with the best results, discoveries, and methods of every academic discipline's pursuit of truth. Theology takes up the most important questions for every human being: who we are and who we want to be, the meaning and purpose of life, good and evil, death, suffering, love, family, humanity, society, our human differences, the role of governments and authorities, poverty and wealth, the marginalized and the vulnerable. Theology takes up cosmic questions as well: Why am I here? What is worth living for? Why is there a blue planet spinning in this galaxy among billions of other galaxies? What is it all about?

Theology above all addresses what it is to live in God's mystery, and that even though one cannot adequately answer all these questions there is purpose to being in this universe. The Christian believes what Jesus said and did and in what he asked of his followers: to love God above all things and one's neighbor as oneself. Christian theology teaches, to put it bluntly: God is love.

AUDIENCE

This book is intended primarily for college students; however, it is also for people of the Catholic faith and other Christian denominations in general; for people of other religious traditions; and for people of no particular tradition but who are seekers. All are welcome to sit at the theological table.

This book provides a solid foundation for this theological discussion. The text is designed both for people with little or no background in theology and those with quite a bit of background but who seek a solid explanation of the subdisciplines involved. *Theological Foundations* is designed as a "first book," to be read all at once or by individual chapters, selected to introduce theological material pertinent to a particular course. In reading each chapter, students will receive an overview of the subdisciplines of theology. They will come to understand terms, concepts, vocabulary, and the development of the tradition through the ages and across cultures. Students will build a basic understanding of the whole of theology through its parts. They will be capable of building upon this base immediately, as well as be able to relate new material to this foundation.

ORGANIZATION OF THE BOOK AND REVISIONS

This expanded edition of *Theological Foundations* has been revised to better reflect the diversity of the college classroom, whether that classroom is at a Catholic college or university, or one sponsored by another religious denomination, or one without a specific faith orientation. This text also is written with awareness that many schools have a diverse student body that is global and that includes many religious beliefs and practices (e.g. Islam, Buddhism, Confucianism, and so on). This revision respects the religious plurality of the college audience, regardless of where it is found. Our hope is to encourage religious dialogue.

The book begins with an important new introduction by Daniel Finucane, entitled "Religion, Spirituality, and the Question of God." The reader will want to read and respond to this introduction first in order to discover his or her inner questions, to engage the text, and to invest in the pursuit of answers. Christianity professes that God works in and through each person's humanness, and that belief is a presupposition and important starting point to engage the topics in this book.

Two new chapters have been added to this new edition, giving the book twelve chapters representing subdisciplines of theology. The first of these, chapter 1 by Brian D. Robinette and titled "Discerning the Mystery of God," places the "God Question" front and center as the ground of theology and necessary for talk about God. Because God is woven through the entire book and, Christian theology would argue, life itself, this chapter is key to all the other ones, and thereby a good way for students and teachers to begin the book. In fact, it might be eminently worthwhile for students to read this chapter at the beginning of the course and again at the end, noting how one has developed over the course of reading the text.

Also new in this edition is chapter 6, "Protestantism, Evangelicalism, Pentecostalism—Changing Contours of Christianity in the Modern Era." In this chapter, Michael J. McClymond explores these three historic paths of Christian belief and practice, and how and why they developed. His presentation is a necessary inclusion for a fuller consideration of churches and individuals that call themselves "Christian" and who participate in the Christian tradition. Catholic, Protestant, Evangelical, Pentecostal: all stem from the Judeo-Christian scriptures and belong to the Christian tradition.

Note: In further consideration of this broad understanding of the Christian tradition, this revised text has adjusted its approach to capitalizing the word *church*. In this text, *church* is used to mean a number of things: a local congregation or all Christians everywhere (e.g. the "universal church"), or a specific Christian denomination (e.g., "the Roman Catholic Church," "the Methodist Church"). Only in the last use is *church* capitalized in current accepted practice and in this text. In quotations, however, this book retains the use of capitals in quoted sources. We hope that by observing this convention we can avoid confusion between statements that refer to beliefs or practices common to the universal church and those that apply specifically to Roman Catholicism, for example, but not necessarily Christians of other denominations.

ARRANGEMENT OF EACH CHAPTER

Each chapter is set up the same way. It begins with an introduction from the editor, then the area specialty, or subdiscipline, in theology is presented, followed by questions about the text and also questions for discussion. The chapters conclude with an integrated research component, "From the Research Librarian." The research skills provided in this section are progressive and programmatic, so they are best done in order from chapters 1–12. These skills are summarized at the end of the text. In the course of these sections, the student will learn electronic research skills both for libraries and internet. Most importantly, this research component will build understandings regarding what the skills are, why they work, and how one might adjust when using a particular approach does not yield the desired results. The skills learned can be applied across other academic disciplines and will transfer to life situations during and after college as well.

Library Revision

Finding reputable and reliable electronic data is the difference between information and scholarship. Research librarian author Ron Crown has pioneered the integrated library skill component provided with each chapter in this text. A number of schools using this text have remarked on the effectiveness of this approach. With today's fast-paced reliance on electronic sources (and research at libraries today is primarily electronic, as few libraries use card catalogs), the methods provided in the library component are key to college research. Throughout this revised edition, Crown has further streamlined the research sections for easier use of resources, targeting needed skills to help students become "library literate for a lifetime."

from the REFERENCE LIBRARIAN

A Practical Guide to Doing Research

Ronald Crown

The purpose of this introduction is to acquaint you with some basic library research skills for the study of theology. Call it "Using the Library 101." Learning how to use a library is an important part of studying theology—or any other subject for that matter (and the library skills you will learn can be applied to any subject, not just theology). Part of becoming an educated person is not just learning things but *learning how to learn* things. Truly educated people not only know more than they did before they received an education, but also know how to continue learning after they have left school. Questions about the Christian faith—theological questions—are not likely to disappear just because you have taken a course in theology or graduated from college, so learning how to study a subject is just as important as learning the subject itself. Knowing how to use a library's resources is critical in this regard.

So how does the library fit into learning how to learn? And, more importantly, how does the library fit into learning *after* you have learned how to learn? While you are in college, the library supplements the expert knowledge communicated by your professors and gleaned from textbooks. After you leave college, a library can, in effect, replace professors and textbooks as your main, regular source of specialized knowledge on almost any subject. You will be fortunate indeed if, after leaving college or university, you live near a good library—assuming that you know how to use it.

All that we say about library skills and research techniques in this book boils down to two key elements:

SKILL KEY #1

Use the library's reference collection to begin your research.

SKILL KEY #2

Use the library's catalog to locate sources of information.

Everything you will learn in this book about using the library elaborates on one of these two key elements. These two elements relate closely because, as we shall see, knowing how to use the reference collection can make using your library's catalog a whole lot easier.

A third skill should also receive mention:

SKILL KEY #3

Use the library's collection of online databases and printed periodical indexes to identify articles in magazines and scholarly journals.

This is indeed an important library skill, but we will not be spending much time with it in this textbook for the following reasons:

1. The philosophy of library instruction (or "information literacy") underlying this book is a "curriculum-integrated" approach. Instead of trying to present all of the library skills you might possibly need or use, we are assuming your library skills will continue to develop as you proceed through the course of your studies. In particular, as your knowledge and expertise in a subject area increase, the library skills you will need will become more sophisticated as well. Learning the library skills presented here will provide you with a solid basis for the more advanced library skills you will need later on, much as an introductory course in a subject area provides a foundation for further study.
2. Because this text is an introduction to studying theology, the focus of the research discussions will be on the initial stages of research, which usually involve the use of the library's reference collection (Skill Key #1). By way of contrast, periodical indexes and databases often include material beyond the level and scope of an introductory course.
3. The main principle behind Skill Key #2, the distinction between a "keyword" search and a search using subject headings, also applies to searches in article databases. Instructors and librarians who wish to include Skill Key #3 as part of a course should be able to do so based on the foundations presented in this book.

STARTING WITH THE REFERENCE COLLECTION—SKILL KEY #1

So, you have a topic, and you want to learn more about it. Why start with the reference collection?

An academic library is divided into two main parts: a reference collection and a circulating collection; there may be other divisions as well, such as special collections, but we will ignore these for the time being. For many people, the distinction is simply the books you cannot check out and those you can, but there is more to it than that.

A reference collection, of course, contains reference books, i.e., books you use to look up something. Dictionaries are one example of a reference work. No one sits down to read a dictionary from cover to cover; one refers to it. Another obvious example of a reference work is an encyclopedia. You may be familiar with encyclopedias such as *World Book*, *Encyclopedia Britannica*, *Collier's*, and so forth. These are general-knowledge encyclopedias intended to cover the broad scope of human knowledge. They are alike in their aim to provide basic knowledge about the subjects covered. That gives us the first reason for starting research in the reference collection: reference works provide a basic orientation to your topic.

The vast majority of the encyclopedias, especially in academic libraries, are subject-specific encyclopedias. Note the following encyclopedia titles:

The Routledge Encyclopedia of Philosophy, ten vols.

The Encyclopedia of Ethics, three vols.

The Encyclopedia of Bioethics, five vols.

The Encyclopedia of Human Behavior, four vols.

The Encyclopedia of Psychology, eight vols.

The Freud Encyclopedia, one vol.

The Encyclopedia of the Enlightenment, four vols.

The Dictionary of American History, ten vols.

The Encyclopedia of the United States in the Nineteenth Century, three vols.

Each of these encyclopedias focuses on a particular subject to the exclusion of everything else. Subject-specific encyclopedias thus have two important advantages over general-knowledge encyclopedias: First, a subject-specific encyclopedia will often devote more space to a particular topic, providing you with a more detailed introduction to it. Second, a subject-specific encyclopedia will often include coverage of specialized topics for which a general-knowledge encyclopedia simply has no room. Not only can you often find more detailed information in a subject-specific encyclopedia, but you can also find information on topics not covered in a general-knowledge encyclopedia. As even introductory-level college courses involve technical subject matter beyond the level of "general" knowledge, the use of subject-specific encyclopedias is imperative.

Scan again through the list of encyclopedias. Notice that some of them cover broad subject-specific areas (philosophy, psychology, American history), while others cover a subset of those fields: ethics (a subset of philosophy), Freud (a subset of psychology), and (a subset of American history). This brings us to the important matter of the scope of an encyclopedia.

Look at the following three subject-specific theological encyclopedias:

The Encyclopedia of Christianity, five vols.

The Encyclopedia of Early Christianity, two vols.

Augustine through the Ages: An Encyclopedia

These three encyclopedias, beginning with the first, cover an increasingly narrow range of subject matter—from the entirety of Christianity to a particular historical period of Christianity (the early church) to a particular individual prominent in the early church (Saint Augustine).

The scope of subject-specific encyclopedias can vary in other important ways. For example, besides being limited chronologically to a particular period of history (e.g., the *Encyclopedia of Early Christianity*), an encyclopedia can be limited geographically (e.g., the *Dictionary of Christianity in America*). The scope of an encyclopedia also varies with respect to whether it includes biographical articles or not. For example, the *Oxford Dictionary of the Christian Church* includes articles on persons, but the *New Dictionary of Theology* does not. This is important to know because one of the ways of studying theology is to study theologians. Note, too, that entire encyclopedias can be biographical in that they are devoted to a single individual; see the previous examples on Freud and Saint Augustine.

The scope of an encyclopedia can also vary depending on the approach taken to the subject. Broadly speaking, theology can be approached either historically (i.e., the history of theology) or systematically (e.g., the study of theological concepts isolated from any historical context, often called "doctrinal" or "fundamental" theology), as illustrated by the following two titles:

Dictionary of Historical Theology

Dictionary of Fundamental Theology

Unfortunately, encyclopedia titles are not always so clear. The title *New Dictionary of Theology* does not give you much help when it comes to determining whether it treats theology historically or systematically or both.

REVIEW #1

Let's review what we have learned so far. The reference collection is a distinct part of the library, separated from the rest of the library collection in order to provide basic knowledge about a subject as compared to the mass of information contained in the library's general collection. The reference collection is comprised mostly of subject-specific encyclopedias whose scope can vary for any particular subject. Based on what we know now, we can elaborate on the first key element of using libraries

SKILL KEY #1

Use the library's reference collection to begin your research.

a) **Use a subject-specific encyclopedia to acquire specialized knowledge about a subject.**
b) **Use a subject-specific encyclopedia whose scope is appropriate for both your topic and the approach you want to take to that topic.**

But how are we supposed to know which subject-specific encyclopedia to use? And how can we tell if its scope is appropriate?

Part of the purpose of this textbook is to help answer such questions. Each chapter is about a particular subfield within the broad field of theology. Accordingly, the research section at the end of each chapter begins by introducing and discussing the use of reference tools whose subject matter and scope are appropriate for researching topics related to that chapter. In addition, the reference collection is based in what is usually called the "Reference Department" (or, more recently, the "Information Commons," "Public Services," or some similar designation), which is where you can find a reference librarian who can assist in locating appropriate encyclopedias or other resources to use. All academic libraries have such reference librarians. Their training includes library research methods and they have familiarity with the library's collections, especially the reference collection. Often reference librarians are themselves subject specialists with advanced degrees. Usually the librarian will be able to guide you quickly to the reference tool best suited to your specific request. Reference librarians may spend part of their working day at a reference desk, where they are available to anyone with a question about library research. They are usually available by appointment also. Check with your library to find out what specific research services it provides. As you become more familiar with library resources and research techniques, you will come to rely less on the reference librarian's assistance and more on your own knowledge and abilities; that is, you will become an independent learner.

However, just knowing you should start with an encyclopedia in the reference collection will not do any good unless you also understand how to make the best use of an encyclopedia. Suppose you have found a subject-specific encyclopedia of an appropriate scope for your topic. If you are like most people using an encyclopedia, you find an article on your topic, read it, acquire the basic knowledge you need as a foundation for further research, and move on. However, many encyclopedias (and most of the good ones) have other features that can be very useful, especially when beginning the process of research. Later chapters of this book examine such features of encyclopedias as cross-references, indexes, and synoptic outlines of contents. Right now, however, we will focus on the one feature of encyclopedias that will help take the research process beyond the encyclopedia: the bibliography that lists additional sources on a topic and appears at the end of the encyclopedia article. (If there is no bibliography at the end of the article, try a different encyclopedia.) The titles listed in the bibliography not only provide you with a list of potential resources but also can be used to discover additional titles not listed there. The use of encyclopedias as access points gives yet another reason to start research in the reference collection and explains why, in addition to being a repository of basic knowledge, the reference collection is separate from the rest of the library's collection. The reference collection provides the means by which you find your way into the rest of your library's collection.

How does it do that? Think about how you normally find out what is in a library. Likely you search the library's catalog using one of the three main types of library searches: by author, by title, or by subject. Searching by an author's name (usually in the form "last name, first name") or by book title is straightforward. However, if you are interested in a particular subject but do not know either the title of a book on that subject or the name of an author who has written on the subject, you are left with the third alternative: subject searching. Subject searching is somewhat more complicated than searching by author or title because it involves the use of a specialized vocabulary called "subject headings." Subject headings are assigned to books by catalogers for the precise purpose of enabling library users to find books on particular subjects. Most academic libraries in the United States use the specialized subject vocabulary developed by the Library of Congress and published in a multivolume, frequently revised and updated series called the *Library of Congress Subject Headings* (abbreviated *LCSH*). One reason it is frequently revised and updated is because books keep appearing on subjects that did not exist in the past, for example, books about computers or the Internet.

Look at the following sample adapted from the *LCSH* (29th ed.) that shows the beginning of the entry for the subject heading "Theology." Notice that not only is "Theology" a subject heading, it also appears with subdivisions ("Theology—Methodology") and even with sub-subdivisions ("Theology—History—20th Century").

Theology
UF Christian theology [note: "UF" means "used for"]
Theology—19th century
[Former heading] [***note: "Former heading" means the library may still have relevant books listed under this obsolete heading as well***]
Theology—20th century
[Former heading]
Theology, Christian
BT Christianity [***note: "BT" means "broader term," the broad category of which the subject "theology" is a part***]
God
RT Religion [***note: "RT" means "related term," a subject category that overlaps the current category***]
NT Apologetics [***note: "NT" means "narrower term," a subcategory of the present subject***]
Church
Natural theology
Negative theology
Theology, Doctrinal
Theology, Practical
[. . .]
—History
——Early church, ca. 30–600
UF Theology—Early church, ca. 30–600
[Former heading]
——Middle Ages, 600–1500
UF Theology—Middle Ages, 600–1500 [note: other historical subheadings would follow here]
—Methodology
UF Propaedeutics (Theology)
Theology—Propaedeutics
NT Storytelling—Religious aspects—Christianity

Subject headings can also be qualified by adjectives and appear in an inverted form ("Theology, Doctrinal"); this is so that other subject headings beginning with the word "Theology," referring to other types of theology (e.g., "Theology, Practical"), will appear in alphabetical sequence. Therefore, subject headings for something as simple and straightforward as "Theology" can be quite complex and not exactly intuitive. So how do you determine the correct form of subject heading, especially in those cases where the subject heading may be expanded with subdivisions or may simply not be intuitive? This is where the bibliography from your encyclopedia article becomes important.

Let's illustrate this with an example. After reading the chapter of this text that discusses Christology, you are interested in the rise of heretical Christological views in the early church. Instead of just guessing the subject heading for books on that topic, find a subject-specific encyclopedia whose scope is appropriate for the topic. Since you have not read the chapter on Christology yet, your reference librarian might direct you to the *Encyclopedia of Early Christianity*. After pulling the volume off the shelf, look up "Heresy" and then take note of the bibliography at the end of the article. An excerpt of such a bibliography follows:

> Bibliography
> H.E.W. Turner, *The Pattern of Christian Truth* (London: Mowbray, 1954); W. Bauer, *Orthodoxy and Heresy in Earliest Christianity* (Philadelphia: Fortress, 1971; orig. German ed., 1934); E.P. Sanders et al., eds. *Jewish and Christian Self-Definition*, 3 vols. (Philadelphia: Fortress, 1980–1982)
>
> (Adapted from the *Encyclopedia of Early Christianity*, 2nd ed., vol. 1.)

Because all the titles appear in the bibliography, you already know they are about your topic (even if the title of the book does not clearly indicate it), so it does not matter which one you choose to identify subject headings. Armed with this bibliographic information, you then search your library catalog using one of the titles from the bibliography. If, for example, you searched for *The Pattern of Christian Truth*, the catalog record would look something like this (if your library does not own this book, you could try another title from the bibliography):

Author	Turner, H. E. W. (Henry Ernest William), 1907–
Title	The pattern of Christian truth: a study in the relations between orthodoxy and heresy in the early church / H. E. W. Turner.
Published	New York: AMS Press, 1978.
Description	xvi, 508 p.; 23 cm.
Series	Bampton lectures; 1954.
Note	Reprint of the 1954 ed. published by A. R. Mowbray, London, which was issued as Bampton lectures, 1954.
Bibliography	Includes bibliographical references and indexes.
Subjects	Theology, Doctrinal—History—Early church, ca. 30–600. Heresies, Christian—History—Early church, ca. 30–600.

Note the two subject headings assigned to this book; one of them—"Heresies, Christian—History—Early church, ca. 30-600"—appears to be exactly what you need for this topic. This subject heading informs us that the book is about the history of heresy in the early church and that the period of the early church extends from approximately 30 CE to 600 CE ("ca." is an abbreviation for the Latin word *circa*, which means "approximately," and "CE" refers to Christian Era and replaces the familiar AD, Anno Domini or "Year of Our Lord").

In most library catalogs, you do not have to re-enter your search once you have a subject heading; you can simply click on the highlighted subject heading to produce a list of related subject headings:

Heresies Christian History Early Church Ca 30–600—24 Related Subjects	24
Heresies Christian History Early Church Ca 30–600	64
Heresies Christian History Early Church Ca 30–600 Historiography 2005	1
Heresies Christian History Early Church Ca 30–600 Sources	4

The first line indicates there are twenty-four other subject headings related to "Heresies, Christian—History—Early Church ca. 30–600" in this catalog, and the second line shows there are sixty-four books listed with that subject heading (results will obviously vary from library to library). Already, you have expanded the range of sources available to you far beyond those listed in the encyclopedia. What's more, you are also able to find books on the topic written after 1997, the publication date of the *Encyclopedia of Early Christianity*. Look at the publication dates of the following titles from the sixty-four listed:

1	A Companion to Second-Century Christian "Heretics"	2005
2	Irenaeus' Use of Matthew's Gospel in Adversus Haereses	1998
3	Lost Christianities: The Battles for Scripture and the Faiths We Never Knew	c2003
4	Pauline Christianity: Luke—Acts and the Legacy of Paul	2002

The other subject heading that appeared in the catalog record for *The Pattern of Christian Truth*—"Theology, Doctrinal—History—Early Church ca. 30-600"—represents a broader subject range than "Heresies, Christian"; for one thing, it will certainly encompass orthodox Christian thinking. For another, not just Christology but any theological topic, such as those considered in this text—ecclesiology, sacraments, and so on—could be included within the scope of a book with this subject heading. However, since the heading potentially includes Christian heresies within its range, a book with that subject heading could still be at least partly about Christian heresy. The only way to tell is to examine the book itself. Using a broader subject heading is one way to adjust your search strategy if your first attempt with a subject heading does not produce results (as in a smaller library with a less-extensive collection on the subject of heresy in the early church).

LIMITED RESOURCES

What if the library doesn't own the *Encyclopedia of Early Christianity*? You can always ask your librarian to help you find an appropriate encyclopedia for your topic, and there is one encyclopedia you can use as a "fallback" to research almost any theological topic, the *New Catholic Encyclopedia* (*NCE*), 2nd ed., published in 2003; some libraries may still have the first edition published in 1967, which will also work.

Let's see how researching the topic of early Christian heresy in the *NCE* compares with what we found in the *Encyclopedia of Early Christianity* (*EEC*). The *NCE* is a general encyclopedia in the sense that it covers a range of subjects, not simply theology or church history but also science, literature, public affairs, and so on. However, because it was produced by Catholic scholars for those with an interest in Catholic subjects specifically, the coverage of theological topics is more extensive than that normally found in a general encyclopedia. You will notice the difference in scope between the *NCE* and the *EEC* by observing that the article on heresy in the *NCE* includes not only a section on the "Patristic Era" (i.e., the early church) but also a section on the "Middle Ages and After." It contains additional articles on "Heresy (Canon Law)" and "Heresy, History of," with their respective foci on the Church-law aspects of heresy and the history of heresy and heretics, respectively. The amount of basic information in the *NCE* specifically on early Christian heresy may vary from that in the *EEC*, but you can use the bibliography in the same way to help you find your way through the library catalog. The following is an excerpt from the bibliography at the end of the *NCE* article on heresy:

> **Bibliography:** H. E. W. TURNER, *The Pattern of Christian Truth* (London 1954). K. RAHNER, *On Heresy* (New York 1964).
>
> (From the *New Catholic Encyclopedia*, 2nd ed., vol. 6.)

Notice that the title *The Pattern of Christian Truth* also appears in this bibliography. Also, there is no order to the way titles are listed in the bibliography (as was the case with the bibliography from the *EEC*). The listing of an encyclopedia bibliography may be alphabetical, chronological, or, as in the two bibliographies we have looked at, in no particular order. In addition, the most recent title listed in the *NCE* bibliography was published in 1964 (even though the encyclopedia was published in 2003). That should alert you to the need to use the titles from this bibliography to find more up-to-date books and not limit yourself to the titles in the bibliography.

REVIEW #2

Let's again take a moment to review. Catalogers assign subject headings to books to enable you to find books on the subject in which you are interested. This information is included in the catalog record and is searchable. All library catalogs (whether electronic or not) provide for this kind of subject searching, but being able to search the library catalog by subject depends upon knowing the correct subject heading. Although subject headings can be complicated or nonintuitive, the use of bibliographic information from an encyclopedia article on a subject makes it easy to identify the appropriate subject heading. In addition, because subject headings (like encyclopedias) vary in scope, it is possible to adjust a search strategy by choosing a broader or narrower subject heading.

We can now expand the two key elements of using libraries:

SKILL KEY #1

Use the library's reference collection to begin your research.

a) Use a subject-specific encyclopedia to acquire specialized knowledge about a subject.
b) Use a subject-specific encyclopedia whose scope is appropriate for both your topic and the approach you want to take to that topic.
c) **Use encyclopedia bibliographies to identify subject headings for your topic.**

SKILL KEY #2

Use the library's catalog to locate sources of information.

a) **Use subject headings to identify precisely books on your topic.**
b) **Use subject headings whose scope fits your topic as closely as possible, then adjust your search with a broader or narrower subject heading as necessary.**

Using Keyword Searching to Identify Subject Headings

In addition to using encyclopedia bibliographies, there is another way to identify subject headings: The advent of electronic library catalogs has made it possible to search the catalog by "keyword." Keyword searching is sometimes called "natural-language" searching because this type of search simply looks for words wherever they appear in the catalog record. Keywords are simply any words (or brief phrases) that may appear in a book title, in the author's name, in a subject heading, in notes added to the record by a cataloger, or in tables of contents. (Precisely which parts of a catalog record are included in a keyword search may vary from library to library.) Thus it is possible to search for a book on a subject simply by typing in some keywords related to that topic. You might get results with a word in the book's title, for example, or maybe even a subject heading. The problem is determining which keywords to use by thinking of terms you would expect to find in the title or table of contents (many electronic library catalogs now include tables of contents) of a book on a particular subject. If we continue our example using the subject of heresy in the early church, we might try a combination of keywords such as "early," "church," and "heresy." There are many other possibilities. Indeed, that is part of the problem: there are so many possibilities with a keyword search. We can type the following as our search statement (the use of "AND" ensures that all three words will be present in any record retrieved):

early AND church AND heresy

Keyword searching can complicate your search by bringing up irrelevant material. The following record (abbreviated here) was among those retrieved by such a search. All of the aforementioned keywords appear in this record, but the book has nothing to do with the topic of heresy in the early church. We have highlighted our search terms.

Author	Como, David R., 1970–
Title	Blown by the Spirit : Puritanism and the emergence of an Antinomian Underground in pre-Civil-War England / David R. Como.
Published	Stanford Calif.: Stanford University Press, 2004.

Table of contents

Subjects	Antinomianism—England—History—17th century. Puritans—England—History—17th century. England—**Church** history—17th century.

Compare that with the following catalog record (again, abbreviated). This book is actually about the topic of heresy in the early church (see part 2 in the Table of Contents) but would not have shown up in our keyword search. The keyword search requires that all the search terms be present; in the case of this record for *Lost Christianities*, "early" and "church" appear (both, as it happens, in the subject heading) but not "heresy" (although "heresies" does and is highlighted).

Author	Ehrman, Bart D.
Title	Lost Christianities: The Battles for Scripture and the Faiths We Never Knew/Bart D. Ehrman.
Published	New York : Oxford University Press, c2003.

Table of Contents

Subjects	Apocryphal books (New Testament)—Criticism, interpretation, etc. **Heresies,** Christian—History—**Early church,** ca. 30–600. Church history—Primitive and **early church,** ca. 30–600.

Of course, we could include both the singular and plural forms of "heresy" in our search, but then we should do the same for all the terms in our search. And how many other keywords must we use to find exactly what we want in the catalog?

Here is another record that would have been retrieved by a keyword search on "early," "church," and "heresy" (although it was necessary to scan through two or three dozen titles):

Title	Orthodoxy, **heresy,** and schism in **early** Christianity / edited with introductions by Everett Ferguson.
Published	New York : Garland, 1993.
Subjects	Church history—Primitive and early church, ca. 30–600. Theology, Doctrinal—History—**Early church,** ca. 30–600. Heresies, Christian—History—**Early church,** ca. 30–600.

After seeing that this book is indeed about the desired subject, we can now readily identify the precise subject heading to use. So, the problem with using keywords is that (1) it is highly likely that, although keyword searching can retrieve relevant material, it will also retrieve a large amount of irrelevant material (see *Blown by the Spirit* in the earlier example), which you then have to wade through to find what you want; and (2) it is equally likely that you will miss relevant material (such as *Lost Christianities*). Notice, however, the one thing that appears for all the books actually about the subject of heresy in the early church: the presence of the subject heading "Heresies, Christian—History—Early Church, ca. 30–600." Ultimately, a keyword search can lead to an appropriate subject heading and thus can be a useful way to identify such subject headings.

Whether you use an encyclopedia bibliography to identify subject headings in your library catalog or simply do a keyword search, *the use of subject headings remains the most precise way to ensure that you will find material about your subject.* Keyword searching can be a useful technique if you use it to identify subject headings in order to focus your search. The less time you spend sifting through irrelevant material, the more time you will have to spend on your research.

We can now add another point to the second key element of using the library:

SKILL KEY #2

Use the library's catalog to locate sources of information.

a) Use subject headings to locate precisely books on your topic.
b) Use subject headings whose scope fits your topic as closely as possible, then adjust your search with a broader or narrower subject heading as necessary.
c) **As an alternative to using encyclopedia bibliographies, use keyword searching to identify subject headings for your topic.**

Using "Concise" Dictionaries

Each specialized field of knowledge has its own technical vocabulary of words that appear only in the context of that field of study or that have a distinctive meaning when used in that field. You may have come across several unfamiliar terms as you read this chapter, for example, words like *patristic*, *Christological*, or *heresy*. The word *Christological* is usually found in a theological context, while the word *heresy* can be used in relation to other subjects. You could, of course, simply look up the meaning of unfamiliar terms in a standard dictionary, but just as there are subject-specific encyclopedias, there are also subject-specific dictionaries to help with understanding the specialized vocabulary of a field of knowledge. Such subject-specific dictionaries do what all dictionaries do: provide basic definitions (and sometimes, brief discussions) of the technical vocabulary of the field.

The following are the titles of three standard concise dictionaries for theology. If your library does not have at least one of these, ask the librarian to show you an alternative title.

Donald K. McKim. *Westminster Dictionary of Theological Terms*. Louisville, KY: Westminster John Knox Press, 1996.

Gerald O'Collins, SJ, and Edward G. Farrugia, SJ. *A Concise Dictionary of Theology*. Revised and expanded ed. Mahwah, NJ: Paulist Press, 2000.

Geoffrey Parrinder. *A Concise Encyclopedia of Christianity*. Oxford, UK: Oneworld, 1998.

COMPLETE REVIEW

Your repertoire of library skills has expanded as follows:

SKILL KEY #1

Use the library's reference collection to begin your research.

a) Use a subject-specific encyclopedia to acquire specialized knowledge about a subject.
b) Use a subject-specific encyclopedia whose scope is appropriate for both your topic and the approach you want to take to that topic.
c) Use encyclopedia bibliographies to identify subject headings for your topic.
d) Use a concise subject-specific dictionary to look up the specialized vocabulary of a particular field.

SKILL KEY #2

Use the library's catalog to locate sources of information.

a) Use subject headings to locate precisely books on your topic.

continued

continued

b) Use subject headings whose scope fits your topic as closely as possible, then adjust your search with a broader or narrower subject heading as necessary.
c) As an alternative to using encyclopedia bibliographies, use keyword searching to identify subject headings for your topic.

We will add to this list throughout the book. You might want to copy these onto a piece of paper or notebook for your next trip to the library.

As we proceed through the rest of this textbook, we will continue to build on the two key elements of using the library, which will help you become a lifelong learner. You know enough now to begin your journey of discovery in theology and in the library. Don't forget, if necessary, to ask the librarian for help.

THE INTERNET

The Internet is a wonderful thing. In fact, many library resources (such as library catalogs) are available on the Internet for searching by anyone. But there is an important distinction to be made between the electronic resources provided by your library (which may be available on the Internet), such as library catalogs, article databases, electronic books, and so on, and things that are simply "out there" on the World Wide Web. The electronic resources provided by your library have been selected specifically for the purpose of academic research. Therefore, they can be regarded as suitable for academic research, with no questions asked. Obviously, there is much on the Internet that has not been evaluated by any librarian or included in any library collection, so it is important that you learn to evaluate carefully the quality of any Internet source you may want to use or cite in academic work (that is another part of learning how to learn). We will have more to say on this in a later chapter. At this point, we only want to emphasize that the library has invested a great deal of expense and effort to provide high-quality sources of information for your use. Using the resources the library provides means you can spend less time asking yourself whether a source is sufficiently authoritative for academic research.

THE PROCESS OF RESEARCH

Research is not a series of mechanical steps to be followed. Doing research is, in part, a matter of knowing where to look for what you want to find, but before you know where to look, you must know where you can look, that is, what kinds of resources are available. That is why this book focuses on the basic library skills of using a reference collection and searching the library catalog. Exactly which library skill you employ in any given situation will depend on the precise nature of the question you are asking. Sometimes your research will begin and end with reading an encyclopedia article or simply looking up the meaning of an unfamiliar word or phrase. At other times, you will need to do more in-depth research and make use of several library skills. There will often be more than one way to approach researching a topic. The library skills you learn in this book will give you options. If one thing does not work, try an alternate approach. After all, it would not be called "research" if you knew exactly where you were going (and how you were going to get there) from the beginning. If you get stuck, the reference librarian is always there to assist you.

INTRODUCTION

Religion, Spirituality, and the Question of God

Dan Finucane

"I'm spiritual but not religious."

A lot of folks say that these days. Maybe you, reading this introduction, have said it. But what does it mean? Granted, there are plenty of reasons to avoid the label, "religious." Watching the imagery of some religious people in the media, in cable shows, and on line, it is not hard to find reasons to avoid being pegged as "religious." "Organized religion" is often unorganized, disorganized, or over-organized. Sometimes it just seems beside the point. Hypocrisy, violence, stupidity, shallowness, boring rhetoric (add your own observations and experiences here) can come in religious packages, carried by religious practitioners.

Then again, some people are spiritual *and* religious. They might still have questions, of course. They might still argue with aspects of their religion. They may feel pulled to explore, to step out of what they have been handed, to expand their religious world. They may be intrigued by aspects of other faiths, by other religious practices of people they know, or by mysterious (or just strange) things they have heard or seen connected to religion. Even deeply religious people have religious questions. But they may wonder whether it's okay to question what has been handed them. They may wonder whether it's okay to challenge religious beliefs.

If you are reading this introduction, the chances are pretty good that you are studying theology and that this is a textbook for a course. Maybe you have been forced to take a core requirement course for college. Maybe you are intrigued by the possibility of doing academic theology. But maybe you are suspicious of a theology textbook. You might feel that you have had enough theology, and can't believe you are taking more. Or maybe you have never studied religion or theology formally and think everyone else in the class already knows a lot more than you. The backgrounds, attitudes, and opinions of your classmates may be very different from yours, yet here you all are, stuck together in the same classroom. Then again, there could be value in having a diverse group of people with different experiences looking at theological questions together.

Wherever you are coming from, whether you are spiritual, or religious, or both, or neither, whether you are struggling to find God, or struggling with the idea of God, I would like to invite you to take a chance, to take the topics in this book seriously. You might be surprised by something new, by a new angle on some old religious themes, and maybe even something that helps you to ask better questions and find helpful insights to act on.

In this book, we invite you to consider several specific theological perspectives. The authors know religion can be corrupted by unspiritual influences. We also believe it doesn't have to be. If you are spiritual but not religious, the authors here will not ask you to be less spiritual. We ask that you take another look at what it can mean to be religious.

WHAT *IS* RELIGION?

We begin with a definition rooted in an etymology, a "root" meaning. (This is a textbook; what did you expect?) Religion comes from the Latin root *religio*: to bind or tie together. If we were asked to fill out a form that asked our religion, we might fill in "Christian" or "Catholic" or "Lutheran" or "Baptist." We might answer "Buddhist" or "Moslem" or "Hindu." Maybe we would write "Agnostic" or "Atheist" or "None" in the blank. We might just blow off the question and write something humorous (any Reformed Druids out there?). Maybe we would rather write "spiritual."

The etymology of "religion" invites a different approach than mere labeling. It invites a more subtle reflection. Maybe being a Hindu or Christian or agnostic is what ties my life together. That is my religion in name and in reality. But for some people the real thing binding my days into a life is something not ordinarily called a religion.

For some people *family* is the biggest thing in their lives. Do you know a grandmother who lives for her children and grandchildren? All of her time and energy are spent on them. Or maybe *work* ties a person together. If you go to law school, you may work for a couple of years afterwards, spending 80–90 hours a week, learning your trade, paying your dues, earning the respect of senior partners, making a place in a firm you were happy to be hired by. Even if you make it to church on Sunday, your real religion may be "Lawyer."

Power can hold a person's focus; power can hold one's life together. Accumulating and then protecting power can take all of one's time and energy. *Money* can be a religion. Money can draw us in, inspire us, surround us. Buildings erected with it and monuments created to it form as big an image on our cities' skylines today as medieval cathedrals ever did in the past.

A lot of things can tie our life together, forming a *de facto* religion.

Now notice the subtle point here. Family, work, power, money—these are not evil things. A loving family is where we are nurtured and grow, where we are safe, where we are *loved*. Work can be satisfying at a deep level; I have friends who are lawyers and they are terrific people. Power gets things done. Power can be used well or poorly. It can be shared, it can be used by those "on top" to create, to support, to infuse meaning into the lives of others. Money comes in handy when it is time to pay the bills or to open up new possibilities (*tuition* could even fit here).

The question is not whether these things are good. It is whether they can work as a *religion*. Sometimes it takes being successful in one of these areas, or in something else of central importance, for us to realize that they cannot be the whole picture. We end up asking, is that it? Is that *all*? We might then be tired enough, discouraged enough, in pain enough, or maybe creative or intrigued enough, to ask a different question. What *can* tie a life together?

WHAT IS SPIRITUALITY FOR?

Humans are spiritual beings. Human history illustrates a pervasive yearning and expression of that part of us that looks beyond, that seeks transcendence, that wants to go beyond our own experiences and ourselves. From cave paintings tens of thousands of years old to tens of thousands of sites on the Internet today, human expression shows that humans seek a depth and transcendence that is spiritual. Modern astronomy offers us tremendous views of the cosmos by the Hubble and Chandra telescopes. As we probe the expanse of the universe more deeply, we have reason to probe more deeply inside ourselves too. We may be haunted by the sense that we are part of something more.

Exercising our deepest spiritual potential is not easy. Ancient religious texts and modern efforts alike testify to spiritual frustrations, false attempts, failure, and practices that draw on religious discipline to further our efforts to be what we most want to be.

In addition to such internal challenges we face distractions and confusions from outside. The sheer plurality of beliefs and religious expressions around us can discourage us from consulting outside guides and resources. Given that some religious voices spend a great deal of time yelling at each other, the temptation is great to cut them all off. Quieter, wiser voices are harder to find. Trusting genuine, proven sources takes time and discernment, and a style of spiritual understanding that won't fit readily into a sound bite or a blog.

Much in the spiritual and religious landscape works to tear us up or throw us apart, rather than tie us together. If humans are capable of spiritual depth, we are also able to wreak violence on fellow human beings, other living creatures, and the earth itself. Natural disasters may make us wonder about what powers there might be above us, causing pain even while nature also reveals its striking beauty. Wars, pollution, and countless personal stories of tragedy make us wonder what is going on, and whether there are powers that might be able to help us.

Such obstacles raise a challenge for those of us who perceive ourselves as transcendent, spiritual beings, and who choose the spiritual path: will we put our *trust* in the spiritual, even in the face of dramatic challenges? Will we put our *faith* in transcendence and hope, or will we fall back into fear and doubt, settling for a lesser version of being human? Are we willing to *work* at being spiritual?

Independence and Interdependence

Few people would equate genuine spirituality with isolation, though we know if the reasons are strong enough and the situation important enough, we may have to stand alone at times. But that sort of strength is what makes us able, when we are at our best, to interact well with others too. Spirituality is not the ability to stand aloof, to ignore or avoid the fate of those around us.

What makes us genuine and what can lead us to a genuine sense of religion (what *can* tie us together) is an integrity that draws out our openness, our concerns, our talents, our understanding of the world and our desire to care for others, and that draws on our deepest self to grow and make an impact on those around us. Personal integrity and caring for others are linked in the deepest spiritual instincts.

People can experience this even in "small" ways. Have you ever volunteered your time to help someone? Ever tutored a kid? If you have ever worked with an eighth grader who is having trouble with math, you know it is a genuine spiritual experience. You are not going to have much opportunity to think about yourself while you are trying to explain what a variable is to a kid who is scared of equations. Chances are, if this student is this far along in school and is not a fan of algebra, there is more going on than mathematical ability or inability. Fear is big. Frustration is a habit. Are you a psychology major? You are now. You have to figure out how to use your relationship with this kid (and maybe you just met her) to try to pry open some little window where you can sneak in some self confidence, maybe a small math step or two, and maybe at least an hour spent on homework that she will not completely hate. Ever pull off something like that?

There is no greater feeling than helping someone. You don't mind not getting paid. You might feel like others should know you accomplished something (you might tell your friends), but that is beside the point. What really matters is that you know, and the kid knows, that you *helped*. And it was because you were selfless. You gave away time and energy. Even if you didn't turn the child into a math genius, you cared enough to work with her.

Specific attitudes, skills, commitments, and even discipline, go along with this sort of work. These overlap in a huge way with the spiritual life. They involve effort. They require a willingness to see what is front of us, to not be in denial. Our efforts can take time, and may lead to failure, causing us to question whether to keep at it. At some point they lead us to the realization that being satisfied is related to being comfortable, to being open to relating to others. Such experiences call us to tie together what is in us and what is in the world.

Spiritual integrity is a balance of internal and external elements. Certainly the spiritual life has subjective elements: we must interpret our own experience, follow our deepest insights. But are our subjective resources enough? Do we grow spiritually if we are isolated? We are drawn to relate to others. Spiritual honesty includes the need to guard against our ability to kid ourselves. Our deepest instincts and questions draw us out of ourselves to self-awareness, even self-criticism. Such questions come from the deepest centers of our souls and make us restless until we confront them. Not to face them is to lose our best humanity.

Our cultural identity is deeply rooted in independence. Our spiritual instincts invite us to interdependence. Put simply, interdependence is a good way to live life's challenges.

A Self Through Others

Have you ever felt part of something bigger than yourself? I recall vividly being on a football field decades ago. It was a bright, crisp, sunny Midwestern autumn afternoon. My team had the ball. We ran a screen play to the right. Each lineman picked up his block. The back read the field, cut, saw an opening, and made it into the end zone. We had practiced this screen play countless times. Each time we ran it we wanted to score. This time we did—and a few other times, too. What remains palpable in my memory is the feeling that in that moment I was part of something bigger than me. As a team we "came together." There was almost a slow-motion perception, a clearer level of realization of what was happening. Each person was needed, each person performed his role, and the touchdown was the work of the entire team. And I had an awareness during the play that I was part of something bigger than myself.

This sort of experience can happen in other places. Certainly it occurs on other fields and floors in sports. Something like it happens in theaters. Have you ever performed in a play? Have you ever felt the lines you had practiced flowing so naturally on stage that you weren't playing a part, you *were* the character? When a production "works," the audience is drawn into the scene, suspending their role as observers, entering the moment. Musicians, too, can experience such transcending the self. Several parts come together and each voice contributes to the song, but the result is more than different voices singing at the same time. It is no coincidence we use the word *harmony* to describe both this musical reality and other occasions when something big happens that joins people together as one. In these "zones" of experience, there is a deepened expression of what we are individually. We don't lose our identity; yet we are deepened as we become part of something else. There is a paradox here. We go beyond ourselves, in a sense we lose ourselves, to find ourselves in a deeper way.

Is this sort of tying together of selves the stuff of religion?

Who Can You Trust?

We are in this together.

We may experience this phenomenon in "peak" moments, whether we literally climb to the top of a mountain, or scuba dive in the depths of a coral reef; we feel ourselves coming together in exhilaration, when our individual efforts have succeeded. Or we may experience the rightness of not focusing on ourselves alone, when we help another. In experiences such as these we know that we are more truly ourselves when we don't isolate ourselves. But if we recognize the fulfillment in such interdependence, we still must face the fact that not every interaction is a peak experience. Not every play works. Not every song harmonizes. When does it work? Who can we trust? We need the skills to face that challenge, to face some very real questions. A big one is, if we wish to follow a spiritual path, who do we want to travel with?

The Value of Questions

It is healthy to ask questions. It is healthy to question companions in the spiritual life. Questioning people, and religion itself, is healthy. It is normal and important to do so; don't the best of friends do it continuously?

Depending on what we have been through, what we have been taught, what we have experienced, many of us realize we have to question, especially with regard to spiritual and religious realities. We may have been told not to question. This may have made sense at certain points in our development, for example, when we were young and learning the basics. But at some point we probably began to ask questions—and made our teachers uncomfortable.

Now we reach a crucial issue for adult believers, or nonbelievers, in religion. Is questioning a problem? Is questioning inconsistent with faith? Does questioning put one at odds with one's church, one's faith? More specifically, is questioning welcome or unwelcome in the Christian tradition, or within particular Christian churches? Is this theology text to be questioned? Is this a text that questions itself?

The answer on both counts is yes. Not only is it okay to question in the area of religion, it might be vital. It could even be one of the most important things you do. Compare the instinct to question with the experience of other relationships, perhaps with friends. How do you get to know someone? How do you deepen a relationship? How do you know how much to commit to someone?

Again, I will use myself as an example. After my wife and I met we knew each other from a distance for some months, because we worked at the same place. I knew a few things about her, because I knew some of her friends and I could ask. One weekend we had our first big "cosmic" date. We had lunch together. We talked. Then we had dinner together. We talked some more. We stayed up until 2 a.m. talking. We asked each other about where we went to school. We learned bits about what made us laugh, what we took seriously, and what our families were like (which, by the way, also fit the previous two categories of seriousness and laughing). After knowing each other for three decades we are still talking, still learning about each other. But somewhere in the first months, we knew enough to enter a serious relationship together. We answered questions about each other that led us to deeper places in our conversations, in our understanding of each other, and in the realization that we shared deep goals. Trust and love grow out of such deeper questions and realizations. We got married not because we knew each other completely, but because we knew each other well enough to know we wanted to spend the next five or six decades deepening our relationship, deepening what we knew about each other, deepening what we could be and do together.

There is a metaphor here for human relationships with God.

How can a person know God without questioning what God is like? What sort of relationship is it possible to have with anyone, God included, if we don't probe and question?

What if God loves us to explore, challenge, and ask questions as a step into better relationships? In human relationships questioning becomes more important the older we are, and the more we *choose* our relationships. Early on, we find ourselves in a family. Parents, siblings, relatives, and friends just show up around us as we realize we are here. When it's working right, the older we get, our parents open our world more and more, letting go of us more too, so that we can explore relationships ourselves. (As a parent. let me add that this process is tough on us too.) We learn, sometimes by trial and error, who to trust, who to spend more time with. Although we start out life being "handed" a family, home, safety, and love, eventually our own responsibility kicks in. We develop an openness: our own independence and interdependence.

The longer we live, the more we may ask questions. That includes asking questions about God. The more years and experiences accumulate, the more one is able to relate to other people—many people would say that their relationship to God has deepened over time as well. Many religious traditions assert that God made us; if that is true, then does it not logically follow that one's relationship to God can become as deep as one's own identity?

TRADITION

Here is another etymology. "Tradition" has the Latin root *traditio,* meaning "to hand on." Religions live by handing on traditions, just like every other human activity that lasts more than one lifetime or one generation. A lot of things are handed to us. "Tradition" may or may not be the word we use to describe what we learn about medicine, literature, the golden days of our school's sports teams, mathematics, geography, World War I history, genetics, or family stories about our great-grandfather who missed his ride on the Titanic, but these are all traditions if they are handed to us. Do we want to accept delivery? That may depend on what is on the list. There is a wise saying, "If you do not know history, you are bound to repeat it." We are not interested in merely repeating the business of life; we are moving on in the constantly changing circumstances of this world to create a life of our own.

Although we certainly should learn things for ourselves, much of what we know is interwoven with what we are given by others. We benefit from the experience and wisdom of others. And of course we will, in turn, offer what we know to others. Just as important, we should examine carefully what we are handed. Thinking critically, asking questions, is not necessarily to deny the importance of what we are being offered. It means we are taking it seriously. How else could the genuine wisdom of others become our own? How else could we improve on what others have learned, if not by adding our own experience to theirs? How else could we expect what is handed on to *live*?

If it is to be healthy, religion must be a *living tradition.*

When pursuing spirituality, we do well to listen to the depths of our own spiritual instincts. We do well to choose worthy companions and try to understand them. Following the spiritual path could take a while. There can certainly be distractions and pitfalls. We should look for good guides, for people who have a sense of depth, who have integrity, who are not manipulative. Do they have a sense of centeredness, even peace? We should seek companions and guides who have what Aristotle would call *phronēsis,* a word that means *practical wisdom*. We do well to look for companions who are serious and also have a sense of humor. A guide should be someone you can trust with the right sort of questions. Look for a guide who will listen. Look for a guide who knows something, who will challenge you, not just tell you what you want to hear. Are you being challenged to deeper integrity, to be more honest with yourself?

When we pursue spirituality, we will meet people who claim to know God. It is quite legitimate to question whether their claim is genuine. If it is, then it makes sense to ask them what they know!

The chapters that follow are meant to be challenging. One of those challenges is the invitation to look—maybe to look again—at some *traditional* religious resources from those who have gone before. The texts and practices, the experiences and beliefs, the revelations and the mistakes in religious traditions are a laboratory where we can question and learn. Question the authors here. Are they worthy guides? What are they handing on?

HOW BIG IS (MY) RELIGION?

My beliefs are unique to me, since I am a unique person. But can beliefs be shared too? In a study of American beliefs and culture, especially concerned with the theme we have here called "independence and interdependence," Robert Bellah and his coauthors describe a very individualistic form of religion. In the book, *Habits of the Heart: Individualism and Commitment in American Life* they relate how they met a practitioner of "Sheilaism." Sheila Larson has named her beliefs after herself. She chooses not to be a member of a religion. She describes her faith as rooted in her "own little voice" (p. 221). She believes in God, and lives out her concern for herself and others, rooted in that faith.

It would be intriguing to probe more into this type of religion, to consider what Sheila has been through that supports and challenges her Sheilaism. But I introduced her religion here for another, very specific reason: to suggest a thought experiment.

What is your reaction to hearing of her sort of religion? Do you wonder who Sheila Larson is? Are you intrigued by her, or by the notion of naming a religion after yourself? Do you feel a twinge of jealousy, thinking, "My name could be in that book, I could have been interviewed by Bellah?" In some sense, each of us could be there. If religion is tying our life together, each of us *is* there in a sense. But, unless we choose to focus solely on ourselves, there is more.

While there is integrity in taking responsibility for oneself, here we also pose the question: at what point should responsibility be shared? If we are in this together, how do we work on "tying things together" *together*? If I discover worthy ideas and practices on my spiritual path, wouldn't I want to share them with people I care about? Wouldn't I be excited if those I cared about made discoveries too? How wide should the path be? The world is a big place. If we're interested in spirituality at all, how big should our spirituality be?

Worldview

What is your worldview? What is your basic approach to the world? How do you organize and make sense of what you know about the world? How do you process new experiences, knowledge, and insights? How do you relate to science and art, music and politics? What tools connect you to world events? What connects you to your friends? What basic vision do you have that makes sense of your life?

Are you consistent? Are you the same person at work or school that you are at home? What sorts of things tend to cloud your vision? What does it mean for you to "think outside the box"?

What shapes your sense of what is dreadful, wonderful, humorous, or holy? What inspires you to act well? What pulls you down? What urges you to get involved in work that needs to be done? What do you do to relax and regain your energy? What do you enjoy doing with friends, with family? What do you want to accomplish today, or over the next few years? What do you want to accomplish over the span of your life?

Or course, creating a worldview that has depth and consistency does not happen all at once. The sheer depth and breadth of human knowledge is such that no human being can know everything. Even though we are "all in this together," the scope and plurality of what humans know and care about makes us pause; does the enormous variety of views mean that humans cannot possibly, really come together? Fortunately, even from a practical point of view, we can see that this is not the case. We can see people from different places, backgrounds, and faiths working cooperatively—not always, not enough, perhaps, but it does occur. The media show us disasters and human misery, but they also show us human courage. They show us examples of people who work cooperatively, even in a world of plurality. Not just challenges, but resources can be global and varied and powerful in their impact.

The challenge for each of us is to embrace a worldview that is open to others, and that also gives us the foundation to ask the right questions. The challenge is to live with a worldview that can understand and respect the views of others, even while connecting us solidly to our own roots.

Any worldview must face key questions. How can humans get along with each other? Can our life be lived well with those with whom we agree and disagree? Does our worldview address basic human hopes? Can I trust other people? How do I deal with evil? What needs do I have, if I am to be fully human? What resources can I draw on? Is there a God? Is God a Creator who is in relationship with creation? Will God help us? Who is wise enough for me to trust, or follow? Ultimately, are my hardest efforts worth it? Is the world a good place?

The modern world certainly provides a wealth of (sometimes mixed) blessings. The time we spend with television, radio, phones, and Internet tools that link us to our surroundings and our friends can make our heads spin. How can I keep up with all that I can access, that I can connect to? Modern cultural pluralism brings several temptations. At times we may want to dig in and not listen to others. We might want to give up when we feel washed over by an ocean of information. But we also want to find ground to stand on. Can we be embedded in a point of view that nurtures us but that remains open to challenge and growth? Where can we gain a foothold, a base from which to develop our view of things?

An Experiment

Try this. Tired of the rat race? Take thirty minutes alone, and step away from all the turmoil. Spend a half hour unplugged. Turn off the television, take out the ear plugs, set aside the phone and the pager, close down the computer . . . unplug everything. If you want to set a timer so that you will know when thirty minutes is up, okay. Now, sit with your self, with your own thoughts.

Go ahead, try it. Put this book down and come back to it later.

Depending on your lifestyle and your usual habits, this experiment could be very strange. I have had one or two students become angry when I assigned it: "How *dare* you put me out of touch with my friends?!" Most people have trouble adjusting at first, but then calm down. Maybe you found yourself going over your "to-do" list in your head. Maybe you thought about your family and friends, about people you miss. Maybe you are used to this sort of exercise, or are just good at this sort of thing, and found a small island of peace and even creativity within it. Maybe you prayed.

What enters our minds when we are not distracted? What if we take time to clear out the layers of things that keep us busy? There could be some challenges here. The "to-do" list, or the list of what I can *stop* doing, might need adjusting in the light of a different, quieter place.

Of course no exercise of this sort is sufficient to create a worldview. But it is a step that can offer perspective. And it can be repeated.

Another Exercise

Consider this question. When you die, what do you want in your epitaph, on your tombstone? This might seem like a strange, even rude question. We are not comfortable with the notion that we will die, yet each of us will. So what do you want on your tombstone? If you are planning to be cremated and won't have a gravesite, imagine someone will want to put up a plaque somewhere. What do you want on the plaque? In asking you to think about what you want said about you when you die, am I being ghoulish or macabre? No, but I am serious.

I have asked my students to write their epitaph on the first day of class in two different courses: a beginning theology course and a course on western civilization. It is the first thing I say to them on the first day, right after telling them my name and the name of the course so they know they are in the right room. Actually, I ask them to respond to two questions, each to be answered on one side of a 3 x 5 card. Not too much room there to get verbose. The first question is, "What does it mean to be human?" The second is what they want written on their tombstone. I explain that doing this at the very start of the course obtains what social scientists see as baseline data. (Probably when I ask the questions, some students still wonder if they are in the right room.)

The value in posing these questions is that they force us to focus (and for these students the challenge comes quickly and out of the blue) on what our values are. Once we are done with our time here, how would we like to be known? What is the meaning of that one human life: ours? At the end of the course, three months later, I give the cards back.

A decent course in the humanities should help us work on the answer to both questions. My favorite course in college was a year-long look at art history. Each day, through the paintings and sculptures of different artists, our professor would ask us, "What does this work say about what it means to be human?" For the test we had to know names and dates; we had to be able to identify who painted what. But this professor was far more concerned that we wrestle with what it means to be a human being. Some art helps with this. Some seems to avoid the issue. Every time I left class I was arguing, either with other students or with myself, about what it means to be human. The professor told us we should be asking these questions every day for the rest of our lives. We should be thinking about western art on our death beds.

Asking students to answer the two questions on the first day is an idea I stole—perhaps I should say, "handed on"—from my art history professor. The two questions on the index card are related for me. To be human is to be finite. We have only a certain number of days. What we do with them matters. This fact can be sobering; it may make us anxious. Our finiteness is also what ennobles us. On each day, what we do matters. If it is possible to waste time, time we can never get back, it is also possible to fill our time well, to live well. It is possible to live well each day.

A TRIP TO TUSCANY

One of my favorite places is a spot that I have visited only once; the Basilica of Santa Croce (Holy Cross) in Florence. I had read about it before going there. When I stepped inside I felt a strange connection, a familiarity, walking around the nave. On one side near the back of the church is the tomb of Galileo. Across the way is the burial place of Michelangelo. Up further are the bones of Machiavelli. Entering this church, on a day in late spring a few years ago, I stepped into the world of the Renaissance and the early stages of the modern world in Europe. I felt the challenges that are still with us. Even more importantly, I felt the strength, the resources that are still with us. In Santa Croce, I felt immersed in an incredible heritage of art and poetry, science and politics, deep traditions to which we now add our modern resources, our problems, and our technologies.

Where do *you* go to meditate, to get perspective?

Where can you return to in your mind, or visit by actually travelling, to connect to the people who nourish and enrich your world?

If you haven't done so already, why not try the index card exercise. Leave your music on this time while you think about the answers. Where would you like your plaque or gravesite to be located? Who would you like your life to inspire?

THIS BOOK HAS A WORLDVIEW

The authors of this textbook are writing from a point of view. It may or may not resemble yours. Is it possible to take them seriously? Will they take you seriously? I believe they will be honest with you. Also, they will try to challenge you. In the imagery used by the editor of this book, J. J. Mueller, SJ, the following chapters are inviting you to "come to the table," to look, listen, and discuss the issues these authors present. There is real content here, and some of it is technical. This may surprise some readers, who have not experienced theology as a rigorous discipline. Digging for historical, philosophical, linguistic, and spiritual connections in the pursuit of theological understanding is hard work. It is also worth the trouble. Real theology will not fit well in the vehicle of a blog. Some topics cannot be covered in a talk show or a news story.

What This Textbook Will Present

A major challenge for any of us is to create an honest, consistent worldview, a worldview that touches the entirety of our lives, loves, successes, failures, losses, and triumphs. A major goal of this book is to present a consistent worldview. The authors of this text believe in God. If you also believe, there may be food for thought to deepen and enrich your faith. The authors may challenge you too.

What if you are not sure if you believe there is a God, or if you are convinced God doesn't exist? Is studying theology then a waste of time for you? A fruitful exercise might be to pursue the question, how do you *know* there is not a God? Is this a matter of proof? Of assurance? Trust in God is not a matter of proving God exists. Is *not* believing subject to proof? Can you prove God does not exist?

Some modern proponents of atheism argue that religious belief is dangerous. Is it? Why? If you are open to the possibility of God being real, what clues might you expect to be worth taking seriously? Which questions would you ask?

At the root of the Christian faith, there is a foundational theological question about Jesus himself. Who *is* this man? As the chapter on the New Testament here will describe, this is the central theme of the Gospels. In this book several authors will pursue a set of questions that are all ways of getting at that central question: Who is this Jesus?

Here we will address questions of how we can read Christian Scriptures *critically*. This is necessary because people interpret the Bible in a variety of ways. Do these Scriptures therefore mean anything we want them to mean? What issues does the text itself present to us? What did the early witnesses to Jesus' life think of him? A chapter on Christology here will probe what happened when the Christian message entered a new culture. What happens when an Aramaic message encounters the language and thought patterns of Greeks?

In modern society, we still ask, "Who is this man, Jesus?" In novels, movies, and television specials we see different debates and claims. What happens when an Aramaic and Greek and Roman message encounters our contemporary wealth of languages and thought patterns? What questions matter to us? Did Jesus marry Mary Magdalene? Are there missing manuscripts that can tell us what he really was like? We are not so different from the people who created the Christological controversies of the first centuries. Academic theology engages these questions and others that are raised in each historical era. What can we take from earlier attempts to understand? What intellectual tools can we bring to such questions today?

While this text is written by Christians, they are Christians who know they live in a rich, pluralistic world. How did the church interact with the world in its first generations? How does it interact with people today, with the variety of cultures and faiths on this global stage?

We cannot understand the Christian message without understanding its mother religion, Judaism. In this text we find authors who probe the creation of the Jewish Scriptures and the experiences of a living Judaism today. Can we also come to understand another child of Judaism: Islam? Can we listen to the heart of Islam, and understand it on its own terms? Can we avoid the caricatures that too often are presented about it?

Regardless of your spiritual or religious beliefs or understandings, the chapters here will invite you to examine the workings of an ancient worldview, a worldview that has encountered many historical questions and that still engages modern conversation partners. We are inviting you to this table, believing that the discussions you find here will be valuable.

The spiritual quest cannot help but raise questions about our relationships to others, and to the Other. This book addresses such questions. It sees God as relational. Christian theology talks about God as Trinity. The doctrine of the Trinity asserts that, at the most foundational level of being, God is *relational*, even as God is *One*. As we seek meaning, do we find we are "in this together"? The worldview presented here is not surprised by that. It is the conviction of the authors that we are relational because God is relational: we are made in the image of God.

Do we seek the Other? In this book you will find authors who believe the Other seeks us. In the Jewish and Christian Scriptures we find not just an encounter with the Source of human transcendence; we find humanity's Creator, initiating a relationship with human beings. Christianity embraces a God who enters into God's own creation, and meets humanity as one of us; through Jesus Christ the human and divine are joined. Christians also assert that, in the ongoing life of the church—in its sacraments, in its concerns for justice, in its concern for moral living—the living reality of Christ himself is handed on.

Christian tradition is no stranger to persons who seek meaning and spiritual depth. The questions and quest of Christianity are echoed in the words of Saint Augustine: "You made us for yourself and our hearts are restless until they rest in you" (*Confessions* 1.1).

Why Take a Theology Course?

One of my presuppositions and core insights into human beings is this: everyone does theology. We all think about spirituality, religion, and the big questions. Many of us do it at 2 a.m., maybe in small conversations between two or three friends.

How many places are there to talk about such things? If you tell people you want to set aside a couple of hours over the next few weeks to talk about the "meaning of life," chances are they will laugh at you. But who doesn't, at some time, wonder where their life is going? Who doesn't wonder what their life *means*? The reason I walk into a classroom every semester is to find out if we can take up those 2 a.m. conversations at 10 a.m., in groups that are a bit bigger, in a place where we can draw on other people, and where we can draw on resources that have proven to be helpful in the past. We can find wisdom in others. And we are in this together.

Too often, religious worship and, sorry to say, classes on religion are dull and static. That's crazy. Everyone faces the task of figuring out how to tie his or her life together; how can we let this stuff be boring? Maybe we can work on *that* together. Others have done some of the work, some of the discovering before us. This does not mean just swallowing whole what they are serving up, but they do have insights we can work with. At its best, religion should mean grappling with meaning and meaningfulness. Religions were all originally created by acting and living, by not settling for unfulfilling answers, but desiring to live more authentically. Religion is more a verb than a noun. If it is done right, religion, like the spiritual life, will also at times be a struggle. But through struggle it will make us more alive.

Our wisest predecessors knew this. Socrates wasn't trying to become a famous philosopher when he walked into the agora. He argued with anyone who would listen because he wanted to understand what was true. Paul of Tarsus wasn't posing for a painting or church sculpture when he preached. He wanted to present the message of Christ. He *had* to preach (see 1 Cor 9:16). In writing to his followers, he challenged them to find a more sophisticated form of faith: "When I was a child, I spoke like a child, I thought like a child, I reasoned like a child; when I became an adult, I put an end to childish ways. For now we see in a mirror, dimly, but then we will see face to face. Now I know only in part; then I will know fully, even as I have been fully known" (1 Cor 13:11–12).

It is good to question. It is good to probe deeply, to use our minds as well as we can, to put into words what we can understand. "Theology" comes from two Greek roots; *theos*, meaning "god," combined with *logos*, meaning "word" or "understanding." Is theology possible? Can one put God into words? Theologians assert that we can never come to a final understanding of God. We are finite. But we can know enough of God to enter the relationship where we will learn more and more.

Theology is seeking: faith seeking understanding.

Wrestling with God

I want to offer an image for doing theology, to bring to a close these introductory reflections and as a way of opening to the chapters that follow. I invite you to think about a passage from the Jewish Scriptures.

This will work best if you read the story first: Genesis 32:22–32. You might want to read this story in context too. Earlier material on Jacob can be found in Genesis 25:19–34; 27:1–32:21.

It is the middle of the night. Jacob's family, everyone he has traveled with, is gone. He is alone. He is in the dark. It is not clear who he is wrestling with.

Jacob wrestles well; he holds his own until dawn is coming, and the foe has had enough. "Let me go for the day is breaking!" (Gen 32:26). Jacob will not quit. Is the opponent fair? He puts Jacob's hip out of joint. Still Jacob does not let go; he will not let go unless he receives a *blessing*.

Now the opponent has a question. *Who are you?* Does Jacob know? He answers correctly, doesn't he? *Jacob.* Not anymore, Jacob. "You shall no longer be called Jacob, but Israel, for you have striven with God and with humans, and have prevailed" (Gen 32:28). Now he is someone new; this new name says who he really is. The people who will come from him will carry this new name, this new identity. They will struggle too, and limp as Jacob did.

Have you ever wrestled in the middle of the night? A decision has to be made. Which job? What direction of study? Am I headed for a breakup in this relationship? What am I supposed to do with my life? The hardest part can sometimes be forming the right question, let alone answering it. The image of wrestling is a powerful metaphor here. "Wrestling" well describes our down-to-earth, "hands-on" questioning. We struggle to *come to grips* with the next steps that face us. We understand what Jacob is dealing with. We wrestle too, to connect, to tie things together.

Jacob is returning to his home after decades away from his father, whom he has deceived, and his brother, who wanted to kill him. Jacob has returned to face his past, to face his decisions, to face the need to move ahead; he must return to be whole. He must sort things out. This one night it all comes to a head. He wrestles with the One who gives him life. He will not let go.

Is Jacob having a religious experience?

Religio has its own roots in another Latin word: *ligare*. From this we get the word "ligament." With his hip put out of joint, Jacob knows the pain of torn tissue, of destroyed connections. Is Jacob having a *religious* experience? He is being torn limb from limb. Is the opponent cruel or ironic? Why does Jacob become someone new? Even with a past torn by distrust and fear—he stole his brother's birthright, and his *blessing*—he comes back. He wrestles. And he will not stop unless he is blessed.

Who can give Jacob the thing that he could not steal? Who can give Jacob a new self? At the crisis point of the story, as light starts to seep into the scene, Jacob/Israel asks his opponent, "Please tell me your name" (Gen 32:29). And he doesn't get an answer. Everything in the story gets named. Jacob calls the place "Penuel," because there he struggled with God, face to face, and lived. He limps past Penuel. He has been to the Jabbok as Jacob and leaves as Israel. But he never gets the name of the one who *blesses* him.

So what is Jacob doing? Theology?

We cannot control the Other. But when we struggle to come to grips with ourselves and the One who meets us in our greatest depths, even in our darkest nights, we become someone new. We are blessed.

Discerning the Mystery of God

Brian D. Robinette

from the EDITOR

Imagine a student wants to attend your university and asks you to explain how it works. You might say, "A president runs the school, teachers provide training and knowledge in different disciplines, and administrators help with course advising, counseling, that sort of thing."

The newcomer nods; he now understands in a generic way how your school functions, but as yet knows nothing of the people themselves, who will be crucial for one's education. You might further explain, "I like and know the president and the goals we have set as a school and how we are treated." Or, "You have to take Dr. Smith, she is so great and has taught me so much. I am going to major in her subject area now." Or, "You should consider this fraternity and its moderator. They do service for others, are involved in school activities, and have a great spirit. I've made good friends there." Now the potential student knows something about the personal side, the heart and soul of your university. As a result, the student gets more enthused about this school as a good place to grow and to attain life's goals.

The word *God* is a generic statement of a divine deity, a word used by most anyone who believes in a higher power or transcendence in life. In this sense God can seem abstract, even generic, revealing little more than the above organizational summary describes a school. What matters about God is God's involvement in life, heart, and spirit, as well as how one can experience this God. The introduction by Daniel Finucane showed many examples of how God may encounter one's life.

In the Christian tradition, a long history of God's revelation connects with Judaism, beginning with Abraham (about 1500 BCE), and culminates in a new revelation in Jesus' life, death, and Resurrection for the salvation of all people. Jesus' revelation discloses a new way of knowing God in personal terms. God as "Father," "Son," and "Holy Spirit" shows God's love, truthfulness, forgiveness, goodness, graciousness, and compassion for all people. This revelation is "personal" because through it God enters the deepest self and the world surrounding the self. For Christians, Jesus' words in sacred scripture reflect the obligation such relational love entails: "Love God above all things and your neighbor as yourself."

Just as Christian tradition believes that God begins and ends humanity itself, so it is appropriate that this text begin with Brian Robinette's chapter exploring this "God of Love and Love of God," breaking into and sustaining one's life and one's world.

WONDERMENT AND PERPLEXITY: WAYS TO GOD, WAYS TO THEOLOGY

Chances are you are already a theologian—yes, a theologian. Here is why: you are capable of wonderment and perplexity, of surprise and doubt, of astonishment and anxiety, and no less importantly, of reflecting upon and giving expression to the ultimate significance of these things.

The fourth-century Egyptian monk Evagrius Ponticus (d. 399) famously described the theologian as "one who truly prays." Such a definition might seem a bit quaint today, perhaps too pious. If so, it might be that we have a deficient appreciation of what prayer is. If we imagine prayer as "talking" to God, whether out loud or quietly "in our heads," we will not be wrong, but our understanding will be limited. Prayer, on Evagrius's account, is much more attitudinal than verbal, far more an orientation of the heart and mind than recitation of words, however helpful formal prayers may at times be. At its most distilled, prayer is the opening of the whole human person in simple and sustained attention to that which most astonishes and perplexes, namely, the unfathomable mystery of God.

This mystery is not unfathomable because God cannot be thought or talked about. Theology is, after all, "God-talk," from the Greek *theos* ("God") and *logia* ("discussion"). More formally, theology is "faith seeking understanding," as the twelfth-century Anselm of Canterbury put it. As we begin to reflect upon and speak about the unfathomable mystery that we name "God"—even if we dispute that any such God exists!—we are engaged in a more deliberative (i.e., theoretical or interpretive) act of theology. This is obviously very important to the present text, since, whether we are attempting to understand the sacred scriptures (chapters 2 and 3) the meaning of Jesus Christ (chapter 4), the role of the church, Christian traditions, and the sacraments (chapters 5, 6, and 7), Christian morality and social justice (chapters 8 and 9), the relationship between world religions (chapters 11 and 10), or the mission of the church in our global context (chapter 12), we are using our intellectual capacities to interpret, analyze, and form judgments, however tentatively and open to revision, in ways that exhibit all the rigors of any academic discipline. And like any academic discipline, doing theology means imparting knowledge and a variety of skills to those who would interact with its major sources, figures, and themes. And yet what is most distinctive about the discipline of theology is that, in the midst of this often heady enterprise of "faith seeking understanding," one can never finally comprehend the reality from which theology gets its name. That is, precisely in one's effort to achieve a basic mastery over the concepts and methods of theology, God's infinite mystery remains elusive, which therefore makes it impossible for theology to reach definitive, final conclusions. Rather, theology remains a continuous process of inquiry and discovery. Because the reality of God is inexhaustible, the work of theology is in principle never done. Indeed, the work of theology is always beginning anew.

The realization that we might not finally be able to comprehend the ultimate "object" of theology may be a disconcerting one, at least initially. Perhaps it will be disheartening (and not a little shocking) to learn that a theologian no less learned than Thomas Aquinas (d. 1274) could make this statement towards the beginning of his *Summa Theologica*: "Now, because we cannot know what God is, but rather what He is not, we have no means for considering how God is, but rather how He is not." This is an astounding admission of ignorance, not least because it comes so early in a text whose length and scope is virtually without parallel in the history of Christian theology. How is it that theology intends to be a legitimate area of human inquiry if its chief object is in fact no "object" at all, i.e., not a discrete "thing" among other things, not a "part" of the world, not even its best or highest part? And why (we might want to ask Thomas) does it take so many words to say as much? Wouldn't it be better to say, along with the twentieth century philosopher Ludwig Wittgenstein, that "what can be said at all can be said clearly, and what we cannot talk about we must pass over in silence"? If we can only say how God is not, why say anything at all?

Such questions highlight the central paradox of all theological inquiry, namely, that it seeks to say something intelligible, meaningful, and even practical about a reality whose depth and breadth is infinite, and therefore beyond our capacities finally to comprehend. We can even deepen this paradox by saying that all theological inquiry springs from and abides in God's inexhaustible mystery. Even when at its most lucid and technical, theology is a form of discourse that, if done well, points language beyond itself to the infinite Silence from whom all words spring, and in whom they have their rest.

Wonderment as Way to God

With all this talk about paradox and mystery, theology might begin to seem too remote, too abstract, perhaps too otherworldly to have much grip on ordinary life. Such a concern is understandable, though nothing could be further from the truth. To paraphrase Saint Augustine (d. 430), the chief difficulty here is not that God is so remote; it is that *we* are remote. It is *we* who are so often inattentive to the awe-inspiring mystery that lies just beneath our noses. It is *we* who, as a result of our many distractions, preoccupations with routine and excessive self-consciousness, remain dulled to the inner vitality of things, and thus closed off from the secret wellspring of our lives. Perhaps there are moments, though, when the scales seem to fall off our eyes so that we can perceive the world in a fresh light, and with a spontaneous and renewed sense of gratitude. A quiet exhilaration may overtake us as we become awakened to the simple *thereness* of things, the fact that there is anything at all rather than nothing. Though we might not often formulate it in quite this way—"Why is there something rather than nothing?"—it is likely we all sense from time to time how wonderfully strange this world is, how awesome it is to be alive, to be sensing, feeling, thinking flesh, to be a part (albeit, a very small part) of a universe whose vastness, age, and complexity strains the imagination. It is no mere wordplay to say that what is most extraordinary is the ordinary. We only have to be sufficiently awake to perceive it.

If we find ourselves astonished by the immensity of the universe we inhabit, no less astonishing are the most simple and delicate of things that fill it. The English poet William Blake famously captured something of the enchantment of the particular in his poem "Auguries of Innocence":

> To see a world in a grain of sand,
> And a heaven in a wild flower,
> Hold infinity in the palm of your hand,
> And eternity in an hour.

No religion, no philosophy, no culture has a monopoly on this childlike sense of wonderment. It is no one's to possess; for surely the moment one tries to possess it, the spontaneity of gratitude it inspires vanishes. In fact, we may lose something of its immediacy and freshness as we grow older, as we slip into deeply engrained patterns of activity and thought, as we become absorbed in our projects and self-estimations, or as we suffer experiences in life that make us barricade ourselves for protection from hurt, perhaps to the point of despair. Even so, we might think of our capacity for wonderment as something constantly to renew and cultivate, even a fundamental spiritual practice to accompany all that we do, think, and say. Not to undertake this practice is to risk premature death, or a kind of living death. Albert Einstein spoke of this very risk when he wrote that "the most beautiful experience we can have is the mysterious. It is the fundamental emotion which stands at the cradle of true art and science. Whoever does not know it and can no longer wonder, no longer marvel, is as good as dead, and his eyes are dimmed." Einstein further spoke of this "mystery" as forming the basis of "true religiosity," which for him meant a basic reverence for all life.

To be attentive to the extra-ordinary in this way is, I suggested earlier, nothing less than the heart of prayer, even if we might be unaccustomed to naming it as such. To open oneself to the world as though for the very first time is to become a person of wonder. Long before we have uttered a "religious" word, if somehow we have said "yes" to our very existence in gratitude and responsibility, we have already made the first and most primitive gestures towards prayer. Wonderment thus lies at the basis of all theology, even as theology will go on to inquire further about this wonderment, about its source and fullest realization, about its meaning and implications for how we are to live in its midst.

Perplexity as Way to God

If one of the fundamental characteristics of being human is the capacity for wonderment, surely another is the capacity for asking questions—big questions. Of course, we can ask questions of a factual or practical sort to assist in getting on with the business of life. The ability to do so, to be "problem solvers," makes humans especially clever animals. But these are not the questions I mean. We can grow perplexed by things in a more comprehensive sense, in a way that sets us on a quest to discover the meaning of life itself. We can ask questions of an *existential* sort, by which I mean those that lead one to explore the possibilities and significance of human existence. "What does it *mean* to be a human person?" we might ask. Given that there *is* something rather than nothing—a truly astonishing fact too easily taken for granted—is there a purpose to this something? Why is it all here, and why are *we* here as its witnesses, as self-aware and self-directing participants? Is there a transcendent origin and goal to this universe of which we are a part, and which might allow us to speak of a shared destiny with all things; or is the expansion of this bewildering universe, along with its ever-emergent properties and myriad forms, without any intrinsic and enduring worth? Is there a direction and aim to life, perhaps even a final fulfillment to its dramatic unfolding; or is the universe simply here in magnificent indifference to the hopes and sufferings of its creatures, leaving us with no more meaning, no more purpose than what we choose to create for ourselves?

The very fact that we can ask questions like these highlights just how peculiar human beings are. Though we obviously share the common lot of finite creatures, insofar as we are subject to the natural laws and evolutionary processes that give it shape, we human beings are unique in our capacity and constant need for asking questions of the most varied and expansive sort, including those about life's ultimate significance. "Man is only a reed, the weakest in nature," wrote the seventeenth-century philosopher Blaise Pascal, "but he is a thinking reed." By "thinking," Pascal does not mean the ability to solve problems. He means the ability and felt urgency for reaching out towards things beyond our ability to presently imagine or grasp, for inquiring about life and death as a whole—in a word, for reaching out towards infinity. We are finite creatures who have a taste for transcendence, a yearning for limitless reality; and it is just the propulsive force of asking questions, of casting our very existence in the form of open-ended inquiry, that manifests such infinite thirst.

This paradoxical unity of smallness and greatness, of finitude and boundless desire, of being a tiny creature in a vast universe that we nevertheless seek to comprehend and transcend: this paradoxical unity is what makes us human. It is a paradox memorably expressed in the Hebrew Bible:

> When I look at your heavens [God], the
> work of your fingers,
> the moon and stars that you have established;
> what are human beings that you are mindful
> of them,
> mortals that you care for them?
> Yet you have made them a little lower than
> God,
> and crowned them with glory and honor
>
> (Ps 8:3–6)

Compared to the immensity of creation, and, in the psalmist's view, the everlastingness of the creator God, we are as nothing, mere creatures of dust whose days are like grass, as Psalm 103 starkly puts it. And yet our nature as human creatures is to reach out for what surpasses us, to become open to the limitless mystery that forms the milieu of our lives. A theologian might express the matter along these lines: we are made *by* God, and made in a way that exhibits a capacity *for* God. We are creatures who are utterly dependent *upon* God for our very being, yet we bear in our finitude a fundamental openness *toward* the infinite reality of God, in whose "image and likeness" we are made (Gen 1:26).

There are at least three main points we can take away from this preliminary exploration of divine mystery and the theological work of its discernment. The first concerns the *intimate relationship between God and humanity in all theological activity*. Although it is crucial to stress the fundamental difference between God and creation—a point whose further significance we shall explore momentarily—it is no less crucial to appreciate that inquiring after God is also (and necessarily) inquiring into the meaning of the human condition. If it is true that we are made by and for God, as Jewish, Christian, and Islamic traditions all affirm, then it is also true that any further discovery into the reality of God entails a deeper discovery of ourselves, since God is the ultimate fulfillment of human desire. The human being is structured, so to speak, in such a way as to be open to the inexhaustibly rich reality of God. This insight can help us appreciate why theology is, as the twentieth-century theologian Karl Rahner characterizes it, a process of "awakening and interpreting the innermost things in [human] existence." Theology should not be thought of as acquiring information that is alien or extraneous to human life, but a further plunging into the "ultimate depths" of that life.

Second, we should also understand that *when we are asking questions of ultimate significance, even when (and perhaps especially when) we are not sure of the answer, just then we are asking questions about God*, at least indirectly. When we grow perplexed about our lives and our worlds, perplexed about what constitutes the good life, perplexed about whether ultimate truth and justice exist, perplexed about why our world is filled with so much beauty and creativity as well as evil and decay, perplexed about the worth of human life in the face of suffering and death—when we find ourselves moved by such questions, even if sometimes we work to ignore or suppress them, we are, in fact, being moved by theological questions. This is why earlier I wagered that you are a theologian.

Third, one of the best ways to understand *the nature of the theological enterprise*, at least in the more formal terms that animate the present text, is to see it as *an activity that makes these questions more explicit and rigorous.* To join in the work of theology is to engage a conversation that has already been taking place, a conversation with a tradition (or traditions) filled with sacred texts, historical events, rituals, legal codes, ethical practices, and peoples who have contributed diversely to discerning the shared mystery of our lives. Though engaging the work of academic theology will entail the acquisition of basic skills and a basic familiarity with major texts and concepts, to participate in such an effort is to take up a simple invitation to help you make what you already do, as a person of wonder and questioning, more reflective and articulate.

DISCERNING THE MYSTERY: THE GOD OF ISRAEL

Perhaps we are now better able to appreciate how wonderment and perplexity are ways to God, and thus points of entry into the diverse tasks of theological inquiry. One reason why this is important to highlight is that it reminds us that as we engage the richly diverse traditions of the Judeo-Christian heritage, we are engaging peoples who have been similarly moved. This is too easily forgotten. With the accumulation of history, texts, and doctrines over many centuries, we might be led to believe that when these traditions speak of God, what "God" refers to remains a fairly settled matter. So when, for example, the Nicene Creed (325 CE) of the Christian faith declares, "We believe in one God, the Father, the almighty, maker of heaven and earth, of all things seen and unseen," we might assume that the reality of which this confession speaks is made fully comprehensible to those who confess it. This is hardly the case.

Recall the quote from Thomas Aquinas above: "Now, because we cannot know what God is, but rather what He is not, we have no means for considering how God is, but rather how He is not." What this statement means to emphasize is that in all our efforts to imagine or speak of God, whether we say God is "one," a "father," "almighty," or a "creator," we will fundamentally distort that reality if we do not simultaneously insist on the limitations of our imaginations. Every affirmative statement about God ("God is 'x'"), Thomas asserts, no matter how subtle or sublime, no matter how long revered in our theological traditions, will lead to serious distortions and false confidences if not accompanied by a robust negation ("God is *not* 'x', at least not in any way we can finally grasp"). Lest we reduce God to a mere object of comprehension, in which case God would not truly be God, we must learn to un-say all that we say; or better, we must deny that our images and ideas fully coincide with what they signify. The reason for such intellectual humility is not because God is *un*intelligible. Theology is not a brand of anti-intellectualism. Rather, it is because God is *inexhaustibly* intelligible, an infinite and dynamic reality who, while inviting the utmost capacities of our hearts and minds, nevertheless exceeds and saturates those capacities. Like a light whose intensity is perceived as darkness by unadjusted eyes, so is the infinite actuality of divine presence perceived as a kind of absence to finite minds. Thomas puts the matter this way: "Since everything is knowable according as it is actual, God, Who is pure act without any admixture of potentiality, is in Himself supremely knowable. But what is supremely knowable in itself may not be knowable to a particular intellect [such as a human being], because of the excess of the intelligible object above the intellect; as, for example, the sun, which is supremely visible, cannot be seen by the bat by reason of its excess of light."

If Thomas's manner of expression adopts some technical language with which you may be unfamiliar ("pure act" and "potentiality," for example), we need not look very far in the Jewish and Christian Scriptures to find the same basic sentiment.

WHAT'S IN A NAME? THE TRANSCENDENCE AND NEARNESS OF YHWH

Consider the example of Moses. In one of the most important and frequently cited passages in the Old Testament (Exod 3), Moses, whose personality as prophetic leader and lawgiver looms large in Israel's history, encounters the sight of a burning bush (a symbol of divine presence) while tending a flock of sheep at Mount Horeb (also known as Mount Sinai) in the Sinai desert. What made the sight so arresting was that the bush was ablaze yet unconsumed. Drawn towards the spectacle out of curiosity, and perhaps some trepidation, Moses hears a voice calling, "Moses, Moses!" "Here I am," the future leader of Israel responds (v. 4). Told to come no further, Moses is instructed to remove his sandals out of reverence for the holy ground he has unexpectedly approached. Filled with a sense of astonishment—the "holiness" of God is described here as inspiring unspeakable awe—Moses covers his face as the voice self-identifies as the God of the Hebrew people. Such divine self-manifestation, of which there are numerous instances in the Old Testament (though none more significant than this), is called a *theophany*, which literally means a "showing" of God (from the Greek *phainein*, "to show").

While this "blinding light" does not grant Moses immediate comprehension, something crucial about God's character is nonetheless communicated in the encounter. What we discover in the narrative's unfolding is that, so far from being a remote and indifferent deity, this God of Abraham, Isaac, and Jacob is a compassionate presence who seeks to liberate the Hebrew people from their captivity. In a dramatic exchange between God and Moses, God first acknowledges the unjust treatment of the Hebrew people by the Egyptians, under whose dominion they were currently serving as slaves. "I have observed the misery of my people who are in Egypt; I have heard their cry on account of their taskmasters. Indeed, I know their sufferings" (v. 7). This link between divine mystery and compassion, or between God's transcendent freedom and loving regard for humanity, makes clear that any affirmation of God as "almighty" in scripture, as with the later Nicene Creed, has nothing to do with the brute force of a capricious cosmic tyrant; it has to do with God's will and ability to redeem human beings from bondage and non-identity, to restore humanity to its original dignity and blessedness.

Evidently perplexed about this God now summoning him to lead the Hebrew people out of Pharaoh's Egypt, Moses inquires further: "If I come to the Israelites and say to them, 'The God of your ancestors has sent me to you,' and they ask me, 'What is his name?' what shall I say to them?" (v. 13). With a response that only deepens the mystery, yet in a way emphasizing faithful presence, God declares, "I am who I am." And again: "This is what you shall tell the Israelites: 'I am has sent me to you.'" And yet again: "Thus you shall say to the Israelites: The Lord (Yahweh), the God of your ancestors, the God of Abraham, the God of Isaac, and the God of Jacob, has sent me to you. This is my name forever; and this my title for all generations" (vv. 14–15).

The name "Yahweh" is in fact a form of the verb "to be" in Hebrew, thus the variations "I AM" and "I am who am." While the name Yahweh (written YHWH, and thus also known as the *tetragrammaton*, or "four letters") has given rise to much philosophical and theological speculation throughout history, we can modestly underscore two interrelated aspects for its continuing significance in Jewish and Christian theology.

The first is that the name highlights divine *transcendence*. That God is "I AM" (or "I am who am") means, at the very least, that divine reality is not determined by anything other than God. In contrast to creatures whose existence is finite and dependent, divine reality is not dependent on anything but itself. Later in Latin theological tradition this will be described as God's *aseity*, which means that God exists from God's own self (from *a*, "of," and *se*, "self"). God does not depend on the world in order to be God, though the world depends entirely upon God for its very being. Divine aseity is another way of affirming God's radical otherness. God is wholly other than the world, not something "alongside" or a "part" of the world of finite creatures. To speak of God this way—which is hard to do consistently—requires us to deny that any of our images or concepts, or even the sum of them, manages to grasp the reality of God. Though we may affirm many things about God, and indeed theological speech can at times be a riot of words, we will also need to say that God is *not* this and *not* that; God is not a creature, not something we can add up among the items in the universe, not anything we can fully imagine or comprehend. Divine aseity is therefore closely related to divine *ineffability*, which means that God is "inexpressible." The transcendent reality of God draws human language to itself while remaining beyond all expression. Like a bush aflame yet unconsumed, the holy mystery of God resists all domesticating thought and speech.

Secondly, the name Yahweh signifies that God is present and active in history. While "I am who am" may suggest something abstract and static, as though divine transcendence implies airy indifference to the world, on the contrary, the Hebrew verb "to be" (which here strongly suggests "being *for*") signifies God's faithfulness to Israel, a faithfulness materialized through Yahweh's deliverance of the Hebrew people from their captivity. Yahweh is the one who calls new things into existence, the one who makes the impossible possible, the one who "brings out" (through the event of "exodus") those enslaved and left for dead. If "I am who am" highlights divine transcendence, then this transcendence is also a drawing near in profound intimacy, a compassionate being-with and being-for, a faithful presence working within history for its redemption. Indeed, this is the central point of the narrative as it continues to tell the story of Moses' return to Egypt and his confrontation with the imperial power of Pharaoh. As the Hebrew people flee their captors in the dead of the night, they pass through the waters of the Red Sea, escape into the Sinai desert, and eventually arrive at the mountain where Moses first encountered Yahweh. Through the further mediation of Moses, Yahweh establishes a covenant (a formal bond of mutual commitment) with the Hebrew people requiring of them a pattern of life uniting right conduct with right worship, as decreed by Yahweh's commandments (the Law). And so, through the transcendent agency of God the Israelites are freed *from* bondage and non-identity (exodus) and freed *for* new identity and responsibility in relationship to each other and to their God (covenant). From within this bond of relationship the Israelites will embark upon a long journey through the desert and enter the land of Canaan, or the "Holy Land," where they will begin to settle and prosper as a nation. Exodus, covenant, Law, and land: these are the concrete means by which Israel will discern and inhabit the divine mystery, a mystery whose transcendence and compassionate nearness is expressed by the name "Yahweh."

CREATION AND THE ONE GOD: FROM NARRATIVE TO CONFESSION

With the story of exodus and covenant we have the most central of Israel's narratives. This narrative, as well as the lived experience it enshrines, shapes imagination and discourse in the biblical traditions, and from it the later confessional and doctrinal statements about God in Jewish and Christian theology will emerge. We might call the story of exodus and covenant the "primary narrative" of Israel. That is not to say that the events to which it refers are prior to all other events in Israel's history—though, to be sure, the events associated with the exodus and covenant are quite early (approximately mid-thirteenth century BCE). Rather, this narrative is primary in the sense that it, and its ongoing retelling through a variety of oral and textual traditions coalescing in the Old Testament, provides a grounding sense of identity and meaning, a narrative focus for understanding who God is and who the people of Israel are in relationship to God. From inside this narrative world, so to speak, the Jewish people will constantly interpret former and subsequent events in their history, its triumphs as well as its disasters. As they grow perplexed about events, as they look gratefully to God during times of prosperity and stability, as they question God's faithfulness during periods of trial and even catastrophe, as they consider the origin and final purpose of creation as a whole—through such theological stirrings, which by no means are irrelevant to us many centuries later, the people of Israel will look through the lens of their primary narrative to discern patterns of meaning, purpose, and promise. Such a process tells us a great deal about the nature of theological inquiry more generally, namely, that it entails a constant interweaving of present experience, historical remembrance, narration, and critical reflection.

We see this interweaving at work in the biblical understanding of God as creator. Consider the way the creation stories in Genesis take shape. Although it is quite natural to assume that these stories were composed first, in fact they were not composed until fairly deep into Israel's history. For example, what scholars call the "Priestly narrative" (Gen 1:1–2:4) was not composed until some six centuries after the time of Moses, during or after the Babylonian Exile (586 –539 BCE). (For more on the history and authorship of Genesis, as well as the rest of the Pentateuch, see chapter 2.) What this means, among other things, is that although the Bible opens with "In the beginning, God made the heavens and the earth," such words already reflect many centuries of Jewish history and experience. No wonder, then, that we can hear echoes of the exodus and covenant in the creation stories. For example, as God is described as drawing forth dry land from a watery chaos on the third day of creation, we might be reminded of the Israelites being freed from their Egyptian captors and delivered through the waters of the Red Sea into a land of their own. Similarly, the creation account depicts God's creative act as a word of command ("Let there be . . ."), for not only does this highlight God's sovereignty over the chaos of the pre-creational void, but it is this very word that called Israel to covenantal relationship and provided commandments for its corporate life. Just as God "speaks forth" the being and identity of the Hebrew people through exodus and covenant, so does God speak all creation into being from non-being. Creation and covenant are, within the Hebrew imagination, internally linked.

This link helps to explain why the creation story in Genesis 1 exhibits important differences amid similarities with parallel creation stories of its time, particularly the *Enuma Elish*, a Babylonian creation story dating from the late third millennium BCE. Like the *Enuma Elish*, the order of creation is said to emerge from the formless void of the waters. Unlike its Babylonian counterpart, however, which characterizes the act of creation as the result of a violent rivalry among the gods (reflecting the polytheism of the broader Mesopotamian culture), the Priestly narrative emphasizes the transcendence and unity of God, as well as the primordial goodness of creation. God is not simply *a* god among other gods, but *the* creator God who brings all things into existence. Moreover, God's creative activity has nothing to do with rivalry, either with other gods or with creatures. Rather, God creates freely, without compulsion, without external necessity, without calculated motive, and endows creation with an original blessing: "God looked at everything he had made, and he found it very good" (v. 31). "To be" is to be blessed. Scripture would tell us that creation is, at its very root, a free gift of the one God, who takes delight in it. Such gratuitous creation, such unexpected and felicitous excess, is the wellspring of all astonishment. None of this has to be, not a single thing; and yet here it all is, a free gift of the creator God who artfully brings into existence that which had not previously existed.

Here, then, we have some appreciation of how the particular historical experience of God as Yahweh—as the one who liberates, the one who makes impossible things possible, the one who brings forth identity from non-identity and establishes relationship out of alienation—opens up a rich perception about God as creator. From the encounter with God as the one who redeems, the Israelites gain a distinctive understanding of the God who creates, and vice versa. This mutuality between creation and redemption is therefore key for understanding the significance of Jewish monotheism.

Although, to be sure, the emergence of monotheism in Jewish tradition reflects a long and ambiguous history—the numerous temptations to idolatry recounted in the Old Testament attest to this—the story of creation, as we find in Genesis 1, provides unambiguous (if poetic and hymnic) affirmation of God's sovereign unity. Such insistence, which obviously lies at the heart of all three "Abrahamic faiths" (Judaism, Christianity, and Islam), finds another memorable and frequently referenced formulation in the Book of Deuteronomy. Composed to represent Moses' final discourses to the people of Israel before his death, this condensed statement, known as the *Shema* of Israel, functioned like a primitive creed, i.e., a formal confession of the people's faith. It is a confession that the Christian Nicene Creed will later echo ("We believe in one God"): "Hear [*Shema*], O Israel: The Lord (YHWH) is our God, the Lord alone! You shall love the Lord your God with all your heart, and with all your soul, and with all your might. Keep these words that I am commanding you today in your heart" (Deut 6:4–6). Notice here that the affirmation of God's oneness is not merely a reasoned philosophical position, however philosophically significant such an affirmation might be; it is a testimony of personal and corporate commitment to the God who liberates and creates. It is *this* God, and not any other, who delivers the captives and reestablishes relationship; and it is *this* God, and not any other, that the ancient Israelites (and modern heirs of their faith) confess as the creator and Lord of all things. The monotheism this confession represents, then, is trustful and loving, not merely a speculative proposition. It is a confession that was to be "lived into," to be deepened through a pattern of life, as the rest of the passage makes clear: "Recite [these words] to your children and talk about them when you are at home and when you are away, when you lie down and when you rise. Bind them as a sign on your hand, fix them as an emblem on your forehead, and write them on the doorposts of your house and on your gates" (6:7–9). In other words, in all one's departures and arrivals, in one's rest and activity, in one's relationships and times alone, the mind and heart ought to be orientated to the living mystery of the one God. Such is the life of prayer.

LIVING THE TRIUNE MYSTERY: THE GOD OF CHRISTIAN FAITH

Thus far we have been unpacking, gradually and through appeal to scripture, the meaning of the first lines of the Nicene Creed: "We believe in one God, the Father, the almighty, maker of heaven and earth, of all things seen and unseen." As is hopefully clear by now, to say "we believe" is a confession of faith. (The word "creed" comes from the Latin *credo*, which means, "I believe.") Though a formal doctrine (or official teaching) of the Christian church, this creedal statement, like the *Shema* of Israel, is a corporate testimony rooted in historical experience and articulated through narrative and conceptual reflection that concisely expresses devotion to the one God who brings all things into being, and whose creative and regenerative capacities are without limit ("almighty"). The Creed asserts that God is not *a* creature among other creatures—God is neither this nor that—but the infinite, transcendent Source of all things ("maker of heaven and earth"). It is from this mystery that all things flow, and it is in this mystery that all things live, move, and have their being (Acts 17:28).

One aspect of the above creedal statement we have yet to examine is the affirmation of God as "Father." Doing so requires that we make more explicit the Trinitarian character of Christian discourse. As we shall see, Christian discourse about the one God takes on a threefold pattern as a result of the historical encounter with Jesus Christ—his life, death, and Resurrection—and the indwelling of the Holy Spirit, who draws creation into the dynamic life of the self-giving God. Trinitarian language about God is not concerned with a logical puzzle about how "one" can also be "three," but a framework for making sense of and speaking competently about God's self-communicating reality in history. As with our sketch above, in which the character of the transcendent God is revealed in and through the particulars of history and interpersonal relationships, so too will we see how the doctrine of the Trinity emerges from lived experience and narrative reflection to articulate in conceptual terms the relational and dynamic nature of the one God. Importantly, the significance of this doctrine is not to issue abstract statements about God that have little relation to concrete human existence. It is, rather, a language that articulates in a rich and vibrant way our conscious and active participation in divine life. In short, the doctrine of the Trinity is concerned with *theōsis*, or what the ancient church called the "divinization" of creation.

PARTICIPATION IN DIVINE LIFE: SCRIPTURAL WITNESS AND CREEDAL FORMULATION

Irenaeus of Lyons, who is widely regarded as the most important theologian of the second century, summarized the Christian theology of the Incarnation by saying that "God became what we are in order to make us what He is." Echoing Saint Paul's affirmation that through Christ we are "adopted" as sons and daughters of God (Eph 1:5), Irenaeus's simple formulation finds frequent and various reformulation throughout succeeding generations of early church theologians, including the well-known instance of fourth-century theologian Athanasius of Alexandria, whose work on the divinity of Christ was important to the First Council of Nicea (325). (It was the Council of Nicea that ultimately led to the Nicene Creed under consideration.) As Athanasius puts it in his *On the Incarnation*, the eternal Word (or *Logos*) of God "was made man so that we might be made God." It is a radical statement to make, though it should be properly understood. To be "made God" (the Greek term for this is *theopoiēsis*) is not to be taken in the sense that human beings become God as such, for only God is God by nature. Rather, the idea is that human beings might, through invitation and cooperation with grace, "participate" in God's nature, i.e., might become more and more like God, in whose image and likeness they are made; might live more deeply into the infinite mystery through the ongoing practice of the faith. This is possible, observe Irenaeus and Athanasius, because God has become one of *us*, has accommodated God's own reality to our human situation in a supreme act of self-giving love. From a Christian point of view, this act of condescension (or *kenōsis*, which means in Greek, "self-emptying") is the definitive moment of divine revelation.

Scriptural Witness

As will be further discussed in chapter 4 in relationship to the study of Christology, numerous passages in the New Testament, and indeed the entire structure of the Nicene Creed, exhibit a *descent-ascent* pattern to account for God's self-bestowal in Jesus Christ and the ongoing activity of the Holy Spirit in history and in the church. Specifically, God's Word (or *Logos*) is described as "entering into" or "descending into" our world in the person of Jesus Christ, whose life and death express in historically concrete form the compassion and humility of God. Obviously this spatial imagery is metaphorical, and yet it means to convey that the invisible, transcendent God has become "visible" or "manifest" in our world in an unprecedented way. As Saint Paul puts it in his letter to the Colossians, Jesus is the "image of the invisible God," the one in whom "the fullness of God was pleased to dwell" (Col 1:15, 19). Here too we have of an instance of theophany, though now in the person of Jesus Christ. (Scholars sometimes substitute the term *christophany* to speak of an "appearance" of Christ.) The corollary to this descent pattern is the imagery of Christ's "Resurrection" and "ascension" after his death. Having entered into the depths of our human condition in order to take on our suffering and alienation, even to the point of death on the cross, Jesus is raised from the dead and "greatly exalted" by God the Father, who gives him "the name that is above every name" (Phil 2:5–11).

In other key passages Paul speaks of Jesus' Resurrection and exaltation as a work of God's Spirit who now indwells believers so that they too might be "raised" to new life, both now and in the future. Consider this classic passage from his letter to the Romans: "If the Spirit of [God] who raised Jesus from the dead dwells in you, [God] who raised Christ from the dead will give life to your mortal bodies also through his Spirit that dwells in you" (Rom 8:11). Although here we do not yet have the formal doctrine of the Trinity, at least not in the way that subsequent generations will make more conceptually precise, we nevertheless see a threefold pattern to Paul's characterization of salvation. The (Holy) Spirit of God (the Father) raises Jesus from the dead, and now this Spirit dwells within believers so as to transform them in and through divine life. As Paul puts it in the same letter, the Spirit of God lives within believers and cries out "*Abba*, Father!" so as to make them "children of God" (8:15–17). We should note here that this cry of "Abba!" (or "Father") is the Aramaic name Jesus frequently used to speak of God throughout his life and ministry, and therefore a decisive factor for the language of "Father" in Christian language about God. This passage therefore makes the daring claim that God's Spirit draws us (through "adoption") into the relationship Jesus himself had with his Father.

We see similar patterns of descent and ascent in other New Testament writings as well. In the conclusion of the Gospel of Luke, for example, God the Father is said to raise Jesus from the dead, while the risen Christ sends the Holy Spirit to his followers as promised by the Father (Luke 24:49). Luke's sequel, the Book of Acts, depicts the Apostle Peter as speaking of this fulfilled promised as follows: "This Jesus

God raised up, and of that all of us are witnesses. Being therefore exalted at the right hand of God, and having received from the Father the promise of the Holy Spirit, he has poured out this that you both see and hear" (Acts 2:32–33). Notice again the imagery of the risen Christ's ascent, as well as the threefold pattern in characterizing divine activity: God raises Jesus from the dead, and from this "exaltation" the Holy Spirit is "poured out" within the community—that is, the church—which it then animates. The Spirit of God is therefore described as extending Christ's historical mission in the world through the work of the church. In the conclusion of Matthew's Gospel, this work of "sending" is crystallized in the Great Commission, as the risen Christ proclaims, "Go therefore and make disciples of all nations, baptizing them in the name of the Father and of the Son and of the holy Spirit, and teaching them to obey everything that I have commanded you. And remember, I am with you always, until the end of the age" (28:19–20). Now given a new identity, and incorporated into the body of the risen Christ through the regenerating waters of baptism—baptism, within Christian practice, is a sacramental sign of participation in Christ (see chapter 7)—the members of the church are bonded together to share in and extend new life to others.

Creedal Formulation

Looking, finally, at the overall structure of the Nicene Creed, one sees just this descent-ascent movement at work. This is significant to observe, for although the creed bears within it doctrinal content that specifies what the church confesses and believes, it exhibits a narrative shape that characterizes the creative, redeeming, and sanctifying activity of God in a threefold way, as the work of Father, Son, and Holy Spirit. The Nicene Creed tells a compact drama, one whose confessants are thoroughly self-implicated as subjects of and respondents to God's triune activity.

In the first section, already detailed in this chapter, God is affirmed as one, as Father, as almighty, and as creator. In the second section, the creed affirms that this one God, through the eternal Word (or *Logos*), enters into human history by becoming human. Jesus Christ is, for Christians, the definitive revelation of God in the world, showing precisely in the warp and woof of creation the infinite compassion of God. There is no limit to God's self-emptying love, not even the horror of death through crucifixion. ("For our sake he was crucified under Pontius Pilate" highlights the historical specificity of the divine gesture.) God's creativity cannot be squelched by death, but overcomes even that which would separate people from God and each other through the gift of Jesus' Resurrection, the "new creation," as Saint Paul often puts it. The risen Christ is "ascended into heaven"—that is, he opens up the whole of creation to new and eternal life in God—and is now the definitive standard by which all human life is judged. Jesus Christ is therefore not only the fullest revelation of God's love for humankind (this is the "kenotic" movement of God towards us by assuming our humanity) but is also the fullest realization of human existence as made in the image and likeness of God (this is the "transcendent" movement of humanity towards God). And so, the self-giving of God to humanity and the self-giving of humanity to God utterly converge in the person of Jesus Christ. This convergence is what makes possible redemptive "participation" in divine life, namely, *theōsis*.

The third section of the creed speaks of the Holy Spirit and the ongoing life of the church in the world. By saying that the Holy Spirit "proceeds from the Father and the Son, with whom [the Spirit] is worshipped and glorified," the creed affirms that it is truly God who indwells and animates the church in its worldly mission. The Spirit who hovered over the waters at the dawn of creation ("the author and giver of life"); the Spirit who stirred the holy prophets of Israel; the Spirit who raised Jesus from the dead to renew all of creation from sin and death: this same Spirit draws the diverse members of the church into reconciliation with each other so that together they may become agents of transformation in the world. The "indwelling" of the Holy Spirit therefore does not imply a self-enclosed or exclusionary form of life, but opens up human belonging to an "outward" and self-giving mission of connectivity and embrace.

The entire drift of the creed affirms that Christian life, to the extent it is energized and shaped by divine life, is dynamic, relational, and self-giving. And as will become clearer in later chapters, such a life, insofar as it is lived well, has little to do with withdrawing into the backwaters of an elite club; it is a challenging, even risky way of life that entails two movements at once: ongoing spiritual formation with others in community, and a commitment to fostering reconciliation and justice in a world that desperately needs it.

CONCLUSION: TRINITARIAN THEOLOGY TODAY

This chapter has traced a path of discovery that began with a consideration of divine mystery in terms of wonderment and perplexity. To follow wonderment and perplexity is a process of discernment, or what is called "theology." Divine mystery is never exhausted by human discernment, which therefore makes us always beginners in its undertaking. Theological reflection is at its best when it continually rediscovers the original impulses of wonderment and perplexity that stimulate it. It is also at its best when it engages rich traditions of those who have lived and discerned the mystery throughout history. Theology can therefore be thought of as an ongoing conversation, extending over many centuries and always broaching new experiences, questions, and insights, so as to assist its practitioner in the task of living the mystery in the present and towards the future.

As has been shown, the Old Testament gives distinctive shape to that task through, among other things, the elaboration of its primary narrative, which emphasizes the historical dialogue between God and the people of Israel through the themes of creation, exodus, and covenant. The Christian Scriptures are thoroughly steeped in this primary narrative, though they reframe its central features in response to the life, death, and Resurrection of Jesus Christ, whom Christians affirm as God's definitive self-manifestation to human beings. The church understands such self-emptying on the part of God as simultaneously the fulfillment of human existence, whose transformative (or "divinizing") effects are extended in the church and the world through the work of the Holy Spirit. Christians therefore discern and live according to the infinite mystery of God in a triune way, as Father, Son, and Holy Spirit. This language takes on a narrative shape, as both the New Testament and Nicene Creed show, though it is possible also to specify aspects of that language in more conceptually explicit ways. This close relationship between story and doctrine is crucial to remember, since too often doctrines can become detached or even isolated from the lived experience that first nourished them.

Significantly, this insistence on the close relationship between experience and concept, history and doctrine, narrative and theory, is a central feature of many contemporary theologies of the Trinity. Numerous theologians today continue to argue for the need to reconnect our sometimes abstract formulations of doctrine with lived experience and narrative reflection. This chapter concludes, then, by briefly indicating four ways contemporary theology commonly seeks to make this connection more explicit and thorough.

1. The unity of transcendence and immanence in talk about God.

This chapter has stressed two seemingly contrary things at once, but which are not contrary at all when properly understood. On the one hand, it has spoken of God's otherness, or transcendence, and consequently the limits of human images and concepts in the attempt to apprehend divine mystery. Insofar as humans are creatures, we cannot grasp God like we might some common object of experience. Returning to the quote from Thomas Aquinas, the infinite actuality of God cannot be absorbed or comprehended by finite minds, and so in some sense God's excessive "light" appears to humans as a kind of "darkness." The influential, fifth-century mystical theologian Pseudo-Dionysius the Areopagite spoke of God's "dazzling darkness" to emphasize just this paradox. On the other hand, such insistence on transcendence in no way denies that God might be able and willing to enter into dialogue and relationship with creatures. On the contrary, many theologians would assert, it is just God's transcendence that makes it possible for God to be intimately near or involved with creation, which is what we mean by "immanence." This is one of the crucial implications of the doctrine of the Trinity. It affirms at once God's transcendence and immanence, God's otherness and nearness, God's infinity and loving compassion in becoming finite "for us and for our salvation." Trinitarian discourse means to keep these (apparent) opposites in creative tension. The transcendent God *becomes* human to share divine life *with* humans, to draw all creation more profoundly into God's infinite mystery. Such "outpouring" and "returning" is the rhythm of life in God, which the Holy Spirit continuously makes possible. Only by keeping transcendence and immanence in closest unity is one able to avoid thinking of God as a remote and indifferent deity, or, conversely, as indistinguishable from creation. As presented in the creed, God is infinitely "more than" creation, yet this "more than" keeps creation in its triune embrace.

2. The relational reality of God, and the communal character of Christian life.

Another key point of emphasis in contemporary theology is the relational character of God. Christians most certainly affirm God as one ("We believe in one God"). However, Christians should not think of divine unity as somehow opposed to relationship. Here too Trinitarian discourse means to keep apparent opposites in creative tension. In God perfect relationship *is* perfect unity. God is not an isolated, static, and supremely self-satisfied "ego" that surveys all things from an unapproachable perch; rather, the Christian tradition understands God as a relational, dynamic, and self-giving reality who freely wills to create out of superabundance. As Pseudo-Dionysius is also famous for asserting, "The Good is self-diffusive," meaning that God is an infinite fullness of relationship that is most itself when it gives itself away. God the Father eternally expresses the Word in the unity of the Holy Spirit, and so is an eternally dynamic flow of relationship. This is truly profound in its implications. If people are made in the "image and likeness of God," this means that humans are most truly themselves when they are self-giving with and for others. Concretely this means that the Christian lives more richly into his or her vocation insofar as it is lived in community. As many contemporary theologians argue, such an insight cuts at the heart of modern individualism. The human person is a thoroughly porous creature, one born out of and for participation in a broad array of interpersonal and social relationships. Though living in relationship makes Christians vulnerable to one another, the vocation of the Christian is to heal damaged relationships, to bring reconciliation where there is hurt, and to bring justice and wholeness where there is suffering and alienation. To be so engaged is, in fact, to draw creation more richly into the heart of the triune God. By stressing this point, contemporary theology seeks to recover the practical, social, and even political implications of Trinitarian theology.

3. The awareness of metaphor in gendered language about God.

Recent decades have witnessed significant reflection and debate among theologians regarding gender-specificity in language about God. For many centuries masculine-based metaphors and pronouns were dominant, even "normative" when speaking of God, as is obviously true for the use of Father and Son in Trinitarian discourse, although the Holy Spirit has sometimes been thought of as gender-neutral or even feminine. But since the latter half of the twentieth century, increasing numbers of men and women have questioned the normativity of masculine God-language since it seems to imply that men are more "representative" of God than women. Citing the social inequality this allocation of language seems to reflect and underwrite, a growing number of Christian theologians argue that God language must become more "inclusive," either by supplementation with feminine imagery and pronouns or, alternatively, through avoidance of gender-specification when possible. There are, as one might suspect, many possible stances to take on this highly complex and sensitive issue, which goes to show just how important social and cultural change is in how we imagine and talk about God. No doubt the question has arisen, and even become urgent, as a result of rapid and profound changes in gender relations over the last century or so. The issue is particularly challenging for Christians since Jesus himself, obviously a man living in a patriarchal society, used the term *Abba* ("Father") to address God—though, as is also pointed out by numerous feminist theologians, Jesus challenged many patriarchal sensibilities in his day, not least through his close association with women in his ministry. In any case, no matter where one finally stands on this issue of ongoing debate, the problems it raises require discernment about the limits of human imagination and language when it comes to the mystery of God. If, on the one hand, the ultimate vocation of language is to speak out of and to the reality of God, on the other hand, one must always do so knowing that no language, whether masculine, feminine, or gender neutral, manages to capture the transcendence of God.

4. The importance of engaging other views of God creatively and dialogically.

Finally, and related to the above point, contemporary theologians are intensely engaged in reflection over the unique challenges that arise when encountering persons from other religious and cultural traditions, and therefore when encountering differing (and sometimes radically alternative) views of divine mystery, including those who are indifferent or even hostile to notions of God. What makes our pluralist age unique is not that people now have so many differing views of God—such has always been the case—but that today we live in such close proximity with such differences due to the massive mobilization of populations made possible by advances in communication and transportation. More now than ever, we are aware of how distinctive histories and cultures shape the ways humans imagine their place in the world, and thus how context-sensitive one's view of ultimate reality is. Faced with such ambiguity, people may buckle down and cling to their cultural and religious heritage; we might think of fundamentalism as one kind of response to growing pluralism. On the other hand a sense of futility or even cynicism regarding the search for truth can set in, making the very notion of discussing "ultimate reality" seem hopeless or arbitrary. Relativism can be another kind of response to pluralism. Between rigid fundamentalism and ephemeral relativism, however, is the more challenging (though creative) path of seeking unity *in* difference. Without reducing all religions to an abstract unity in a way that ignores or falsifies legitimate differences, it is possible to be committed to a particular religious tradition while also remaining open to the truth, goodness, and beauty of other religious traditions. (See chapters 10 and 11 for more on Christianity's relationship to other religions of the world.) If, for example, a Christian is convinced that Jesus Christ is the definitive self-disclosure of God in history, this will not mean therefore that the mystery of God cannot be found richly and compellingly in other religious traditions. Indeed, to remain hospitable to the mystery of God no matter where it is found is essential to any truly theological undertaking. For the Christian, the understanding of God as Trinitarian actually inspires and informs this openness to otherness, since the God it affirms is relational and dialogical. The idea of the infinite mystery of God has a corollary: people will always be able to discover more about God. For the Christian, the triune character of that mystery means that one will discover more about God in the context of relationship, even when (and perhaps especially when) one encounters persons very different from oneself.

Questions about the Text

1. What is the central paradox of all Christian theology?
2. What three major points characterize the discernment of divine mystery in theological activity?
3. What is a *theophany*, and what two aspects are closely associated with its instance in Exodus 3?
4. What is Israel's "primary narrative" in brief, and how does it shape Israel's understanding of God as liberator and creator?
5. What is the meaning of *theōsis*, and how is it central to the doctrine of the Trinity? Explain your answer by referring to the "ascent-descent" pattern in key passages from scripture, as well as the structure of the Nicene Creed.
6. What implications follow from the Christian understanding of God as "relational" and "self-giving," especially in terms of the church's role in the world?

Questions for Discussion

1. Have you ever thought of the question, "Why is there something rather than nothing?" What sort of feelings or thoughts does such a question elicit from you?
2. Do you think theological reflection is compatible with doubt? Why or why not?
3. What are some other examples of a theophany in scripture, or perhaps in other religious contexts? How do people today typically speak of encounters with the divine, and are such accounts similar or different from celebrated instances in the past?

4. Do you think it important to maintain a balance between transcendence and immanence in one's understanding of God? In what ways do you think the doctrine of the Trinity might assist in this? Do you agree with the author that the doctrine of the Trinity, by its emphasis on relationship and self-giving, presents a strong challenge to the individualism of much modern life? Explain. Might such a doctrine promote a more open and dialogical attitude toward people of other religions? Again, explain your thinking in this regard.
5. Is gender-specific language inevitable or appropriate in theological discourse? Why? Christians debate whether they should maintain or change language about God in light of gender equality in society and the church. What are your thoughts on this issue?

For Further Study

Downey, Michael. *Altogether Gift: A Trinitarian Spirituality*. Maryknoll, NY: Orbis Books, 2000.

Eck, Diana. *Encountering God: A Spiritual Journey from Bozeman to Banares*. Boston: Beacon, 2003.

Edwards, Denis. *How God Acts: Creation, Redemption, and Special Divine Action*. Minneapolis: Fortress Press, 2010.

Gutierréz, Gustavo. *The God of Life*. Trans. Matthew J. O'Connell. Maryknoll, NY: Orbis Books, 1991.

Haught, John. *God after Darwin: A Theology of Evolution*. Boulder, CO: Westview Press, 2007.

Hunt, Anne. *Trinity: Nexus of the Mysteries of Christian Faith*. Maryknoll, NY: Orbis, 2005.

Johnson, Elizabeth A. *Quest for the Living God: Mapping Frontiers in the Theology of God*. New York: Continuum, 2007.

_____. *She Who Is: The Mystery of God in Feminist Theological Discourse*. New York: Crossroad, 1992.

LaCugna, Catherine Mowry. *God for Us: The Trinity and Christian Life*. San Francisco: HarperSanFrancisco, 1991.

Lane, Dermot A. *The Experience of God: An Invitation to Do Theology*. New York: Paulist Press, 2005.

Ratzinger, Joseph Cardinal (Pope Benedict XVI). *"In the Beginning . . .": A Catholic Understanding of the Story of Creation and the Fall*. Trans. Boniface Ramsey. Grand Rapids, MI: Eerdmans, 1995.

from the REFERENCE LIBRARIAN

Researching "God"

God—what a topic! As Brian Robinette's discussion makes plain, "God" encompasses a wide range of thoughts, concepts, images, responses, etc. How do you research such a manifold topic as "God"? Let's go back to Skill Key #1 as outlined in "A Practical Guide to Doing Research" at the beginning of this book.

SKILL KEY #1

Use the library's reference collection to begin your research.

a) Use a subject-specific encyclopedia to acquire specialized knowledge about a subject.
b) Use a subject-specific encyclopedia whose scope is appropriate for both your topic and the approach you want to take to that topic.
c) Use encyclopedia bibliographies to identify subject headings for your topic.

The first thing to do (Skill Key #1a) is to identify a subject-specific encyclopedia, i.e. an encyclopedia likely to include an article on "God." Of course, "God" is such a broad concept and of such great significance throughout human history that you will find a "God" article in many encyclopedias, including general encyclopedias such as *World Book.* In the initial stage of an introductory theology course, you will want to consult an encyclopedia on theology *(theologia*—conversation about God), that is, an encyclopedia that covers the field of theology broadly conceived, rather than more specialized areas of theology such as will be covered in subsequent chapters in this book. In other words, you are also using Skill Key #1b by finding a subject-specific encyclopedia whose scope is appropriate for what you are researching—which, at this point, is simply general background information about "God" relevant to an introductory course. Here is a list of some encyclopedias offering this kind of coverage (note that the words *dictionary*, *handbook*, and *companion* in these titles are essentially equivalent to the word *encyclopedia*). Most libraries are likely to have at least one of these; if not, your reference librarian can suggest an alternative.

Wolfgang Beinert and Francis Schüssler Fiorenza, eds. *Handbook of Catholic Theology.* New York: Crossword, 1995.

Adrian Hastings, ed. *The Oxford Companion to Christian Thought.* Oxford; New York: Oxford University Press, 2000.

Joseph A. Komonchak, Mary Collins, and Dermot A. Lane, eds. *The New Dictionary of Theology.* Wilmington, DE: Michael Glazier, 1987.

Ian McFarland et al., eds. *The Cambridge Dictionary of Christian Theology.* New York: Cambridge University Press, 2011.

Each of these titles contains at least one article on "God" providing an overview of this vast topic. The word "God" covers such a wide range, in fact, that some reference works offer several articles on various aspects of the subject. For example, the *Handbook of Catholic Theology*, besides an article on "God," includes the following articles: "God: Acts of," "God: Attributes of," "God: Contemporary Issues," "God: Fatherhood of," "God: Mystery of," "God: Names of," "God: Possibility of Knowledge of," "God: Proofs of Existence of," and "God: Theology of." Such a collection of articles can actually be quite helpful if you are considering writing a research paper on "God" (much too large a topic for a single research paper); by merely observing the names of the articles, you can become aware of a number of aspects of "God" as a subject, one of which might help define a topic for research.

But for now, let's stay with the general subject "God." After reading the article from whatever encyclopedia you have chosen, you are ready to take another step in acquiring additional information about your topic: finding books relevant to the subject. As you have seen in "A Practical Guide to Doing Research," at this point, Skill Key #1c comes into play. You can use the bibliography appearing at the end of the article to identify subject headings used in your library's catalog pertaining to "God." These subject headings will be useful for finding more books about the same topic.

Let's see how this might work in practice. (You might try this exercise in your own library's catalog.) The bibliography appearing at the end of the article on "God" in the *New Dictionary of Theology* includes the following titles:

Langdon B. Gilkey, *Naming the Whirlwind: the Renewal of God-Language.*

John Macquarrie, *In Search of Deity: An Essay in Dialectical Theism.*

John Courtney Murray, *The Problem of God, Yesterday and Today.*

Following Skill Key #1c, go to your library catalog and do a title search (your librarian can show you how if you are unsure) on the first of these titles, *Naming the Whirlwind.* You might discover the following subject headings assigned to this book:

LANGUAGE AND LANGUAGES—RELIGIOUS ASPECTS.

LANGUAGE AND LANGUAGES—RELIGIOUS ASPECTS—CHRISTIANITY.

THEOLOGY.

THEOLOGY certainly covers the subject of God but as you can easily see just from the table of contents for this textbook, "theology" covers a number of other things as well. In other words, THEOLOGY is not likely to be a useful subject heading to focus precisely on "God." The other two headings seem to be even further away from your desired topic. So, let's try the second title from the bibliography, *In Search of Deity.* Among the subject headings for this book appear the following:

GOD.

NATURAL THEOLOGY.

THEISM.

Besides the variant NATURAL THEOLOGY (how is this different from THEOLOGY?), the other two subject headings are both of possible use, especially, of course, GOD. Using GOD as a subject heading for books about God certainly makes sense. But as indicated above, "God" is a very large topic. Is there a way to focus a search more narrowly; in other words, is there a way to find books on a *manageable* topic?

To answer that question, try the third title from the encyclopedia bibliography, *The Problem of God, Yesterday and Today,* by which you discover yet another subject heading relevant to "God."

GOD (CHRISTIANITY)—HISTORY OF DOCTRINES

This subject heading moves you further along the path you want to travel, that is, it includes the subject "God" while narrowing the focus by adding a subdivision to the main subject heading. In this case, you can research "God" by studying how ideas about God ("doctrines") have developed historically. That is still a fairly large topic but you are moving in the right direction.

Since you know now that the subject heading GOD can be subdivided, you might ask yourself what other ways the subject can be divided. There is a simple way to do this. Most library catalogs now make it possible for you to view an alphabetical list of subject headings (usually by doing a SUBJECT search; ask your librarian how to do this if you don't know how). You should be able to discover that the simple subject heading GOD has a number of different subdivisions by which you may be able to focus your research on "God." Note the following subject headings:

GOD—ATTRIBUTES

GOD—ATTRIBUTES—HISTORY OF DOCTRINES

GOD (CHRISTIANITY)—HISTORY OF DOCTRINES—EARLY CHURCH

GOD (CHRISTIANITY)—HISTORY OF DOCTRINES—MIDDLE AGES

GOD—FATHERHOOD

GOD—GOODNESS

GOD IN LITERATURE

GOD—KNOWABLENESS

GOD—LOVE

GOD—MOTHERHOOD

GOD—NAME

GOD—OMNISCIENCE

GOD—PROOF

GOD—WORSHIP AND LOVE

As you work your way through the catalog (or, perhaps, discover by using other titles gleaned from an encyclopedia bibliography), you will discover that there are other related subject terms (see p. 50) which do not begin with the word "God." Here are a few of these:

DEATH OF GOD THEOLOGY

FEAR OF GOD

FEMINITY OF GOD (compare the heading GOD—MOTHERHOOD listed above)

GLORY OF GOD

HOLY SPIRIT

IMAGE OF GOD

MONOTHEISM

POLYTHEISM

TRINITY

So there are certainly a number of ways of approaching the subject of "God" through the library catalog, including many others not listed above. Whatever subject heading(s) you finally use, you are more likely to have greater success by employing the skill keys we have been describing. Use an encyclopedia of appropriate scope in order to find an article that matches your topic as closely as possible (Skill Keys #1a and #1b). This, in turn, means that the books listed in the bibliography of that article are more likely to have subject headings that will lead you to similar books through the library catalog (Skill Key #1c). You should also keep in mind that, sometimes, there is more than one appropriate subject heading and that you may need to use more than one heading to find what you are looking for. For example, note the two headings from the lists above: FEMINITY OF GOD and GOD—MOTHERHOOD.

At this point, you should be in good position to employ Skill Keys #2a and 2b, using appropriate subject headings in the library catalog to discover more information about your topic.

As Robinette suggests, theology—God-talk—really pertains to all the various matters covered throughout this textbook, whether scripture, Christology, the sacraments, morality and social justice, world religions, and forms of Christianity found either in the United States or anywhere in the world. Each of these more specific subject areas (as you will see) also presents an aspect of "God-talk." One way of studying one of these other subject areas is by studying how the concept of God pertains to that subject. For example, you might be particularly interested in biblical notions of God (see chapters 2 and 3). At this point, you should know enough to begin by finding an article on "God" (or whatever aspect of the subject of God you want to research) in one of the encyclopedias listed in the research sections of chapters 2 and 3. When you do, you will discover that there is another subject heading we have not yet encountered: GOD—BIBLICAL TEACHING. This will help find books on biblical ideas about God. If you are interested in ideas about God found in other religions such as Judaism or Islam, you can research the notion of God found in those religions by using the encyclopedias listed in chapters 10 and 11. If you are observant, you may have already figured out how to do that (does the heading GOD (CHRISTIANITY) listed above give you a hint?).

In this section, we have reinforced most of the basic library research skills outlined in "A Practical Guide to Doing Research." In subsequent chapters, you will have the opportunity to practice these skills further and to enhance your skills by additional refinements to what you have already learned.

PART I

THE SACRED SCRIPTURES AND CHRISTIAN THEOLOGY

The Old Testament

Bernhard A. Asen

from the EDITOR

Have you seen movies, read books, or heard stories about people who lost their memory and, as a result, also lost their identity? Who we are is unveiled in time by our earliest environment of family, then by what we do, experiences we have, choices we make, and their consequences. Each of us is born in the middle of the human story, not the beginning. Before people wrote, they told stories about themselves and the meaning of life as they experienced it. At some point, they began to record their memories and what they believed about how to live and what was important. Many of those memories were based on religious experiences. First transmitted orally and then in writing, the record provided an identity for those people. In the major religious traditions of the world, we refer to the most significant oral traditions and written records as sacred texts. Such texts are handed down to help shape the people of current and future generations. Sacred texts therefore hold a special place in a community because they talk about the God–human relationship and who one is, why one is here, and what one is about.

Theology (lit., "talk about God") is faith seeking understanding; it is the "memory" of a faith community seeking God, finding God, and handing down that knowledge and wisdom, so others can know the truth of this encounter with God and its essential role in being human. A text is not simply repeated; it is alive in a community as a resource to find God, point to God, live in God, and be formed by God.

We begin this section at the beginning, with the sacred texts that form Christianity's collective memory, in order to understand who, what, and why this community of believers has come to be. We look at why Christianity has incorporated Jewish sacred texts as part of the Christian sacred texts—an important part of the tradition not only for Christians but, as we shall see later, also for Muslims in their sacred texts, called the Qur'an. And as we explore what theology is and does, we do not want to lose sight of the great theme of theology: you, me, humanity, creation, and God together. No one and nothing is left behind.

THE HEBREW BIBLE, CALLED BY CHRISTIANS THE "OLD TESTAMENT"

My maternal grandfather was a great storyteller. Over the years, I have told and retold many of his stories to family and friends. He was fond of talking about his youth and his life on the farm. He sang songs and recited poetry, told riddles, and recited limericks. I have also found out from my mother and other family members that many of Grandpa's stories were precisely that—stories. "Some of them had a kernel of truth," my mother once told me, "but most of them were greatly embellished!"

Sometime in the second century BC, a man named Jesus, son of Eleazar son of Sirach of Jerusalem, wrote an introduction to a book he says was written by his grandfather, Jesus Ben Sira.

> Many great teachings have been given to us through the *Law and the Prophets and the others [i.e., other books]* that followed them, and for these we should praise Israel for instruction and wisdom. . . . So my grandfather Jesus, who had devoted himself especially to the reading of the *Law and the Prophets and the other books* of our ancestors, and had acquired considerable proficiency in them, was himself also led to write something pertaining to instruction and wisdom so that by becoming familiar also with his book those who love learning might make even greater progress in living according to the law.
>
> You are invited therefore to read it with goodwill and attention, and to be indulgent in cases where, despite our diligent labor in translating, we may seem to have rendered some phrases imperfectly. For what was originally expressed in Hebrew does not have exactly the same sense when translated into another language. Not only this book, but even the *Law itself, the Prophecies, and the rest of the books* differ not a little when read in the original. [emphasis added]

This introduction to the book of Sirach (also known as the Wisdom of Jesus son of Sirach, and Ecclesiasticus) gives us some valuable information about the collection of books that circulated among the Jewish community some two-hundred years before the beginning of the Christian era. Three times, Ben Sira's grandson tells us his grandfather was devoted to reading the "Law and the Prophets and the other books." Here we may have the earliest reference to the division of the Hebrew Bible into three parts: the Law, the Prophets, and the Writings. When referring to these three parts of their Bible, the Jewish people, who are often referred to as the "People of the Book," use the Hebrew words for Law (Torah), Prophets (Nebiim), and Writings (Ketubim). By adding the vowel "a" between the initials of these words (TNK) they form an acronym—TaNaK. Even today, Jews still refer to their Bible by this acronym. The Tanak is also known as the Jewish Testament, the First Testament, and, by most Christians, the Old Testament (OT). The word "old" is to be understood in the sense of "prior, first, or venerable," not "outdated" or "superseded" by the New or Christian Testament.

Ben Sira's grandson tells us further that he translated his grandfather's book from Hebrew into Greek and warns that even the best translations "differ not a little" from the original texts. The Tanak was originally written in Hebrew, although some small portions (e.g., Dan 2:4b–7:28) are written in Aramaic.

Also beginning around the second century BC, the Tanak was translated into Greek. This translation is known as the Septuagint (meaning "seventy") and is frequently abbreviated by the

Roman numerals for seventy, LXX. According to an ancient tradition, seventy-two scholars translated the Tanak in seventy-two days. The number was rounded off to seventy.

It is important to note that while Sirach's grandson refers to the "Law, Prophets and other [books]," the Jewish people do not consider the Book of Sirach to be part of the Tanak. The book was included, however, in the LXX. By the time Sirach was translated, Greek had become the dominant language of the ancient world. The leaders of the Jewish community at that time did not consider books written in Greek to be inspired by God. Consequently, some books that were part of the LXX were not included in the Tanak. Jews and Protestants refer to the following books, or parts of books, as *apocryphal* (their meaning is "hidden" or obscure), but Roman Catholics refer to them as *deutero-canonical* (added later to the collection or canon of inspired writings):

1 and 2 Esdras

The Wisdom of Solomon (follows Song of Songs)

1 and 2 Maccabees

The Letter of Jeremiah (chapter 6 of Baruch)

Tobit (follows Nehemiah)

Sirach (or Ecclesiasticus: follows The Wisdom of Solomon)

Susanna (chapter 13 of Daniel)

The Prayer of Manasseh

Baruch (follows Lamentations)

Judith (follows Tobit)

The Prayer of Azariah and the Song of the Three Jews (follows Daniel 3:23; verses 24–90)

Bel and the Dragon (chapter 14 of Daniel)

Additions to Esther (follows Esther)

As stated, the Jews did not include these writings in the Tanak, not only because they were written in Greek but also because they were not widely read or used. But why do Protestants refer to these books as apocryphal, while Roman Catholics refer to them as deuterocanonical? In order to answer this question, we need to move forward in history to the fourth century AD, when Latin became the dominant language of the Roman Empire. From approximately 390–405 AD, Saint Jerome (342–420), a great scholar and linguist, moved to the Holy Land and translated the Christian Scriptures from their original languages into the growingly popular Latin, the language of the people of the fourth-century Roman Empire; his translation is called the Vulgate. For the Old Testament he relied on both the Hebrew and Greek texts but placed a higher value on the Hebrew language and decided to follow the order of books in the Tanak rather than in the LXX. The books not included in the Tanak he considered apocryphal.

Centuries later, when Martin Luther (1483–1546) translated the Bible into German, he also followed the order of books in the Tanak and placed these writings in a separate section still known today as the Apocrypha. Luther, following the lead of Jerome, considered these books important for history and spiritual edification but not canonical, inspired, or appropriate for establishing church doctrine. In response to Luther and the Reformation, the Council of Trent (1545) officially declared for the Roman Catholic Church that these books were not apocryphal but deuterocanonical.

You may have noticed that the division of Law, Prophets, and Writings referred to in the introduction to Sirach places the prophetic books in the middle of the collection. However, if you look at your English translation of the Bible, you will no doubt find that the prophets are not in the middle but at the end of the Tanak. The last book of the Tanak is Second Chronicles, but the last book of most English translations of the Bible is the book of the prophet Malachi, which ends with the words, "Lo, I will send you the prophet Elijah before the great and terrible day of the Lord comes. He will turn the hearts of parents to their children and the hearts of children to their parents, so that I will not come and strike the land with a curse" (4:5–6).

In order to understand this arrangement, we once again need to jump ahead hundreds of years into the Christian era. Whereas the Jewish people saw the prophets as the prime interpreters of the Torah, Christians saw the prophets as foreshadowing or hoping for the future coming of Jesus. In the New Testament (NT) Gospels, John the Baptist is referred to as "Elijah who is to come" (Matt 11:14; 17:9–13; Mark 6:14–15; Luke 1:17), mentioned by the prophet Malachi. According to the Gospel writers, John the Baptist prepared the way for Jesus, whom Christians confess as the Christ. Christ is not Jesus' last name but a Greek translation of a Hebrew word *meshiah* ("messiah"), which means "anointed one." In 1 Samuel 10:1, we read that "Samuel took a vial of oil and poured it on [Saul's] head, and kissed him; he said, 'The Lord has anointed you ruler over his people Israel.'" From that time on, when kings ascended to the throne of Israel, they were considered "anointed ones" (messiahs). As we will see later, it was with Saul's successor, David, that the word *messiah* took on special, even technical, meaning.

The ancient Israelites believed that the kingship of David's descendants would last forever, and traditional Jews continue to expect the coming of the new and final David, the Messiah. Christians, however, believe that Jesus is the "Messiah, the Son of David, the son of Abraham" (Matt 1:1).

Though the Jewish people may have great respect for the New Testament, the Tanak is complete and sufficient in itself; they do not need the New Testament in order to live out their faith. Christians, however, must never lose sight of the fact that without "the Old Testament, the New Testament would be an incomprehensible book, a plant deprived of its roots and destined to dry up and wither" (The Pontifical Biblical Commission, 2002, p. 211). For example, Christians need the Tanak to properly understand Jesus because the concept of the messiah (*Christos* in Greek) is thoroughly grounded in the history and tradition of the Tanak.

An influential Jewish scholar named Martin Buber (1878–1965) once addressed a group of priests and said, "What is the difference between Jews and Christians? We all await the Messiah. You believe He has already come and gone, while we do not. I therefore propose that we await Him together. And when He appears, we can ask him: were You here before?" Then he paused and added: "And I hope that at that moment I will be close enough to whisper in his ear, 'For the love of heaven, don't answer'" (Wiesel, 354–55).

As we proceed now to look at the various divisions of the Tanak, we need to keep in mind that, like my grandfather's stories, the stories contained in the Law, Prophets, and Writings are diverse kinds of literature. Many of the stories record actual events that can be corroborated by extrabiblical history and literature, but many of them are based on legends, remnants of ancient myths, songs, and hymns that may never have actually happened but that contain important and enduring "kernels of truth."

TANAK DIVISION 1—TORAH: WORDS OF INSTRUCTION

The first division of the Tanak is the Torah. Torah is often translated into English as "law" but more properly means "teaching" or "instruction." In the broadest sense, the entire Tanak is teaching and instruction. More narrowly defined, the Torah refers to the books of Genesis, Exodus, Leviticus, Numbers, and Deuteronomy. These books are known as the *Pentateuch* ("five scrolls"). The Jewish tradition also calls them the "Five Books of Moses" because, according to that tradition, Moses was the author of these books.

However, through many centuries, it has become clear to Jewish and Christian scholars that the Pentateuch was not the work of Moses or of any one particular author but is rather a compilation of a variety of authors and literary sources.

Already in the seventeenth century, Jewish scholar Baruch Spinoza (1632–1677) and Christian scholar Richard Simon (1638–1712) began to question the Mosaic authorship of the Pentateuch. However, it was not until the nineteenth century that a formal hypothesis developed concerning the formation of the Pentateuch. A German scholar, Julius Wellhausen (1844–1918), developed what has come to be known variously as the "Documentary," "Source," or "JEDP Hypothesis," which argues that the Pentateuch is a compilation of four primary anonymous sources. Though the hypothesis has been and continues to be questioned and refined, it is now widely accepted by contemporary scholarship as a valuable analytical method for studying the Pentateuch. The anonymous sources are as follows:

J This author prefers to refer to Israel's God by the name Yahweh ("Lord"). The Yahwist's literary style is down-to-earth, picturesque, and fond of what are known as anthropomorphisms (placing human qualities on God). For example, the Lord walks "in the garden at the time of the evening breeze" and "made garments of skins for the man [Adam] and for his wife, and clothed them" (Gen 3:8, 21).

E Known as the Elohist source, this author prefers to use the name Elohim ("God"). In the Hebrew language, Elohim is plural in form but singular in meaning. The Elohist sees God as more transcendent than does the Yahwist and emphasizes God's communication through dreams (Gen 28:10–22).

D The Deuteronomist (from the book of Deuteronomy, meaning "second law") is concerned with issues relating to Israel's law code and the importance of Israel's covenant relationship with Yahweh. Most scholars today consider the book of Deuteronomy to be the heart of the Pentateuch.

P The Priestly source emphasizes God's holiness, the importance of worship, the sacrificial system, times, seasons, and genealogies (Gen 1:1–2:4; 5:1–32).

Precisely when these sources were written is still the subject of considerable debate. Many of the stories were first passed on orally from generation to generation. Various redactors (editors) along the way provided additional information and commentary until finally, sometime after the Babylonian exile (586 BC), the sources came together into the form we have today.

Genesis: Origins and Ancestry

The first book of the Torah (Pentateuch) is Genesis. It can be divided into two major sections: Chapters 1–11 are known as the Primeval History (the word primeval refers to "origins," "beginnings") because they deal with the creation of the cosmos and human beings, the alienation of human beings from God, and the destruction of the world through the great flood, followed by a new beginning and the start of civilization. Chapters 12–50 were once referred to as the Patriarchal History (a patriarch is a man who is head of a family or group). However, more recently—and more accurately—these chapters have been called the Ancestral History because men and women played equally crucial roles in Israel's history and tradition.

The Tanak contains two accounts of the creation of "the heavens and the earth" (Gen 1:1).

The first (Gen 1:1—2:4) probably comes from the Priestly (P) writer of the Pentateuch. As you read it, you will discover that it is progressive and repetitious and that the transcendent God "speaks" the world and humanity out of chaos into existence. It is as though the author wanted to provide people with a creation creed or a confession that could be used in worship or in teaching.

When God says, "Let us make humankind in our image, according to our likeness" (Gen 1:26), God is addressing all the heavenly beings, inviting them to become involved in the creative process. Christians believe that the fullness of the Godhead (Father, Son, and Holy Spirit) was involved in creation. However, the Trinity was not on the mind of the Priestly writer.

Other nations around Israel also had creation stories filled with gods, goddesses, and heavenly beings. One of these stories, the *Enuma Elish*, or Babylonian creation story, dates as far back as 2300 BC and has some interesting parallels to the P creation story. For example, both stories speak about chaos, and both follow a similar pattern of the creative process. The major and decisive difference between the two stories is that the *Enuma Elish* involves many gods (polytheism), while Israel's God acts alone.

This transcendent God also created male and female human beings simultaneously. When you read Genesis 1:26 carefully, you will observe that one gender is not created before the other. God first creates human beings and then differentiates them according to gender. The Hebrew word used here for "human being" is *'adam* and includes both male and female.

In the second creation story (Gen 2:4b—3:24), the J writer of the Pentateuch sees the Lord God (Yahweh Elohim) as very down-to-earth. In fact, the man (*'adam*) is formed from "the dust of the ground" (*'adamah*) (Gen 2:7). There is a Hebrew play on words here (*'adam, 'adamah*), where God is imaged as a potter who shapes clay. Later (2:21–22), the woman is "built" or "constructed" from the man's rib. Though the man was created first, the woman, we are told, was to be a "helper," a "partner" (2:18), not a subordinate. They were created in relation, not in competition, to one another.

The man and the woman lived in a primeval garden where they had access to all the fruit of the trees except the fruit of the tree of the knowledge of "good and evil" (Gen 3:5) that was in the middle of the garden (3:3). Created in relationship but also with the freedom to choose, the man and the woman both decided to eat from the forbidden tree. In so doing, they overstepped the bounds of being creatures. They wanted, rather, to become "know-it-alls"—gods themselves. Theologians refer to this as the "Fall" and to the couple's decision as the "originating" or "original sin," which led to God's decision to expel them from the garden lest they "take also from the tree of life, and eat, and live forever" (3:22).

Like the P creation story, another ancient text sheds some interesting light on J's Fall narrative. In one version of a document known as the Mesopotamian (Babylonian) Gilgamesh Epic (720–612 BC), the hero, Gilgamesh, searches for a plant that will give him everlasting life. However, on his return home after he finds the plant, a snake steals it and then the snake sheds its skin. The ancients saw this as a sign of immortality.

From here on, the primeval history of humanity becomes increasingly estranged from the creator God. Brotherly rivalry (Cain and Abel) leads to violence and finally to murder (Gen 4:1–16). The world's violence and corruption increase to the point where God decides to send a great flood to destroy the earth (Gen 6—8:19). Just as there were other accounts of creation in the ancient world, so also there were other flood stories. The Babylonian Gilgamesh and Atrahasis epics share a number of similarities with the biblical flood account. The primary difference is that the biblical account is set in a monotheistic, rather than a polytheistic context. The "Lord sits enthroned over the flood; the Lord sits enthroned as king forever" (Ps 29:10). God then makes a covenant with Noah promising that the world will never again be destroyed by the mighty waters (Gen 8:20—9:17) and places the rainbow in the sky as the sign of that promise. Civilization begins anew, but human corruption and alienation from God continue (Gen 9:18–28). The primeval history ends with the story of the Tower of Babel (Gen 11:1–9), where human beings once again attempt to become like God by building a tower that reaches to heaven. God confuses their speech into babbling, however, which means that they cannot understand one another and have to stop the construction of their tower. Thus Genesis explains the beginning of many languages and nations. This biblical word for confusing speech (Babel) has entered the English language as the word babble, often referring to the nonsense speech of babies.

The Ancestral History

Genesis 12–50 recounts the stories of the founders of God's people, especially Abraham, Isaac, Jacob, Joseph, and their wives and families. The three major themes in the ancestral history all revolve around the word promise:

- Promise of land
- Promise of many descendants
- Promise of a continuing relationship with God (covenant)

However, the ancestors repeatedly face what seem to be insurmountable obstacles to the fulfillment of these promises.

In Genesis 12:1–3, Abram ("mighty father") is told by the Lord, "Go from your country and your kindred and your father's house to the land that I will show you. I will make of you a great nation, and I will bless you, and make your name great, so that you will be a blessing. I will bless those who bless you, and the one who curses you I will curse; and in you all the families of the earth shall be blessed."

The obstacle, however, is that we are told in Genesis 11:30 that Abram's wife, Sarai, "was barren; she had no child." Fearing that the promise of many descendants (Gen 15:2) will not be fulfilled, Sarai decides to help the promise along, so she gives Abram her slave-girl, Hagar, so as to produce an heir. Hagar gives birth to Ishmael (which means "God has heard"), but Ishmael will not be the heir. God tells Abraham (Abram) that Sarah (Sarai) will bear a son and his name will be Isaac (Gen 17:19). With names changed from Abram and Sarai to Abraham ("father of a multitude") and Sarah ("princess") (Gen 17:5, 15), the birth of Isaac is announced in Genesis 18. Sarah laughs at the prospect of bearing a child at age 90, but God has the last laugh when Isaac ("laughter") is born (Gen 21:1–7).

While Genesis 16 and 21 are the only accounts in the Tanak concerning Hagar and Ishmael, it is important to point out that God also promises Hagar (Gen 21:18) and Abraham that Ishmael will be blessed, fruitful, exceedingly numerous, and the father of twelve princes and a "great nation" (Gen 17:20). According to the Islamic tradition, which traces its religious heritage back to Abraham, Abraham and Hagar are buried near the Ka'aba in the Grand Mosque in Mecca, and Ishmael, not Isaac, is Abraham's number-one son. Furthermore, when Abraham dies at age 175, we are told that both his sons, "Isaac and Ishmael buried him in the cave of Machpelah" (Gen 25:9).

After Abraham passes the supreme test of faith through his willingness to offer his "only son" (Gen 22:2), the Lord once again reaffirms the promise to Abraham to make his offspring "as numerous as the stars of heaven and as the sand that is on the seashore" (Gen 22:17). Abraham obeyed the Lord's command because he submitted himself to God (the word Islam, by the way, means "submission") and trusted that the Lord would "provide" (Gen 22:8, 14).

The realization of this promise of many descendants, however, requires now that Isaac and his beautiful wife, Rebekah, also have children. However, the same obstacle that confronted Sarah confronts Rebekah; she is unable to bear children. Isaac prays to the Lord, who responds by allowing Rebekah to conceive not one but two children, Esau and Jacob, who represent two nations: Israel (Jacob) and Edom (Esau) (Gen 25:23).

Esau is the firstborn and, according to ancient custom, should receive his father's blessing, as well as the lion's share of the family inheritance. During their birth, however, Jacob (which means "the one who supplants") grabs his brother Esau by the heel and tries to pull him back into the womb so that Jacob will be the firstborn (Gen 25:26). Jacob is unsuccessful, but it will not be his last attempt to gain the right of the firstborn. Rivals from the beginning, Jacob manages to swindle Esau out of his birthright in exchange for a bowl of stew (Gen 25:29–34) and later, with his mother Rebekah's help, tricks Esau out of father Isaac's blessing (Gen 27).

At odds with Esau, Jacob then embarks on a series of journeys that include several encounters with the Lord. The first encounter comes through a dream at Bethel ("house of God"), where the Lord introduces himself to Jacob as the "God of Abraham your father and the God of Isaac" (Gen 28:13) and then reiterates the ancestral promise to Jacob that "the land on which you lie I will give to you and to your offspring; and your offspring shall be like the dust of the earth . . . and all the families of the earth shall be blessed in you and in your offspring" (Gen 28:13–14).

Jacob meets and falls in love with Rachel, daughter of his uncle Laban, and works seven years for her hand in marriage (Gen 29:20) but is tricked into marrying Leah instead and then has to work another seven years before marrying Rachel (Gen 29:27–28).

Rachel, like Rebekah and Sarah before her, was barren, but "God remembered Rachel, and God heeded her and opened her womb. She conceived and bore a son . . . and she named him Joseph" (Gen 30:22–24).

Jacob's next decisive encounter with the Lord occurs at a place called Peniel ("face of God"), where a "man" (perhaps an angel, perhaps the Lord) wrestled with Jacob until daybreak (Gen 32:24). Refusing to let the "man" go, Jacob says, "I will not let you go, unless you bless me" (Gen 32:26). Jacob is asked his name, responds, and is then told, "You shall no longer be called Jacob, but Israel, for you have striven with God and with humans, and have prevailed" (Gen 32:27–28). And so Jacob becomes Israel ("the one who strives with God"), the father of the twelve tribes that will make up the nation known as Israel.

Jacob next meets his estranged twin, Esau, and upon seeing him is so moved that he says, "For truly to see your face is like seeing the face of God" (Gen 33:10). At the end of the Jacob story, the rival brothers are reconciled and, like Ishmael and Isaac before them, together bury their father, Jacob (Gen 35:29).

The final chapters of the ancestral history (Gen 37–50) recount the story of Joseph and his rivalry with his brothers. Not only do the brothers resent that Joseph is their father Jacob's favorite, but also they are put off by Joseph's dreams and, on first reading, his superior attitude. The brothers initially plot to kill Joseph but instead decide to sell him into servitude in Egypt, where, ironically, through his ability to interpret dreams, Joseph will rise to power, be reconciled with his brothers, and eventually save his entire family from famine. In the end, Jacob journeys to Egypt and settles in the land of Goshen. The book of Genesis ends with Joseph's words to his broth-

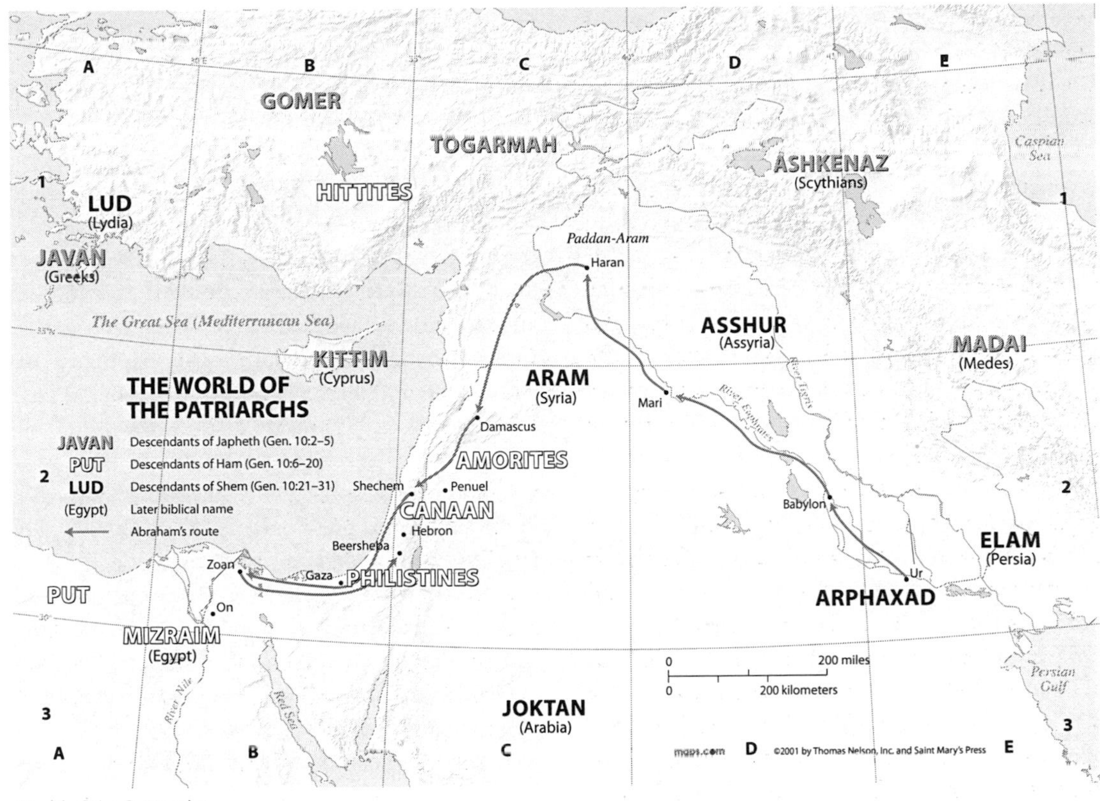

World of the Patriarchs

ers, restating the promise to Abraham that "God will surely come to you, and bring you up out of this land to the land that he swore to Abraham, to Isaac, and to Jacob" (Gen 50:24). Joseph dies and is "placed in a coffin in Egypt." The very last word of Genesis, "Egypt," prepares the way for the remaining books of the Torah.

Covenant and Law

Whereas the ancestral history emphasizes the promise of children and becoming a great nation, the books of Exodus, Leviticus, Numbers, and Deuteronomy emphasize the promise and importance of the land and the ongoing relationship between the God of the promise and the children of the promise.

The dominant figure in Exodus is Moses. When the book of Exodus opens, we read that "a new king arose over Egypt, who did not know Joseph" (Exod 1:8). This Egyptian king, or *Pharaoh*, thought that he was divine; indeed, the Nile River was considered the birthplace of the Egyptian gods. Fearful that the "Israelite" people were becoming too numerous, the Pharaoh overworks the people but finds that they continue to multiply. The Pharaoh then embarks on a program of genocide, demanding, "Every boy that is born to the Hebrews you shall throw into the Nile, but you shall let every girl live" (Exod 1:22). The scene is set for a struggle between Israel's God and the Pharaoh of Egypt, who thinks he is a god. We will see a somewhat similar struggle in the NT when King Herod responds to Jesus' birth with what has been called the "Slaughter of the Innocents" (Matt 2:16–18).

Moses, rescued as a baby by Pharaoh's daughter from certain death in the Nile (Exod 2:1–10), will rise to become, along with Abraham and David, one of the three most revered figures in Israel's history. In what is frequently referred to as Moses' "call narrative," God reveals himself as the "God of your father, the God of Abraham, the God of Isaac, and the God of Jacob" (Exod 3:6) and also as Yahweh (Exod 3:13–15). In the Hebrew language, Yahweh is actually a form of the verb "to be" (thus "I am who I am," Exod 3:14). This emphasizes that Israel's God is a dynamic, active, "verbal" God who intervenes on behalf of his people.

Though reluctant, Moses accepts Yahweh's call, repeatedly confronts the Pharaoh and demands that he let the Israelite people out of Egypt, and finally, through a series of plagues beginning with turning the Nile to "blood" (Exod 7:14–25) and ending with the death of the first-born of the Egyptians (Exod 12:29–32), where the angel of death passes over God's people (Passover, Exod 12:1–28), they leave Egypt and bondage. This depiction of exodus from bondage to freedom brought about by God has remained a strong image and motivating force for many peoples, cultures, and religious traditions.

The next major event in the journey to the promised land is known as the Sinai Covenant. Like the covenants with Noah and Abraham, this covenant contains a promise from God, but it also contains a promise of the people to God. When Moses and the people arrive at Mount Sinai, God says: "Now therefore, if you obey my voice and keep my covenant, you shall be my treasured possession out of all the peoples. Indeed, the whole earth is mine, but you shall be for me a priestly kingdom and a holy nation" (Exod 19:5).

This covenant is conditional. It involves keeping God's law as set forth in the Decalogue, or Ten Commandments (Exod 20:1–17; Deut 5:6–21). These commandments were not understood as clubs hanging over people's heads but as tokens of love. If you love me, God is saying in the Ten Commandments, there are certain things that you will and will not do for me and for others. The descendants of Abraham, like Abraham himself, are called to obey (trust) that the Lord will provide.

There were two basic kinds of law in the ancient world, apodictic (absolute) and casuistic (case) law. Apodictic law is expressed in the formula, "You shall not," and casuistic law in the formula, "If you do *x*, then *y* will be the consequence." With the exceptions of the casuistic commands to keep the Sabbath day (Exod 20:8) and honor one's parents (Exod 20:12), the remaining commandments are apodictic.

In addition to the Ten Commandments, which are referred to as moral or ethical law, the Tanak also contains other law codes that pertain to matters of worship, sacrifice, and the observance of important festivals, especially the festivals of Unleavened Bread and Passover.

The entire book of Leviticus is devoted to laws that concern holiness. What is known as the Holiness Code (Lev 17–26) emphasizes what the people are to do to be that "holy nation" that God called them to be in Exodus 19:6.

The Book of Numbers recounts the journey of God's people through the wilderness and prepares them for their entrance into the land. Numbers contains many fascinating stories about encounters with other people and nations, among them the story of Balaam and his talking donkey (Num 22).

Many scholars today would consider the Book of Deuteronomy to be the heart of the Torah. It emphasizes the importance of the covenant and how Moses was a "prophet in Israel . . . whom the Lord knew face to face. He was unequaled for all the signs and wonders that the Lord sent him to perform . . ." (Deut 34:10–11).

TANAK DIVISION 2—NEBIIM: WORDS OF JUDGMENT AND SALVATION

The second major division of the Tanak is known as the "Prophets." It includes the books called the Former Prophets (Joshua, Judges, 1–2 Samuel, 1–2 Kings), the Major Prophets (Isaiah, Jeremiah, Ezekiel), and the Book of the Twelve or Minor Prophets (Hosea, Joel, Amos, Obadiah, Jonah, Micah, Nahum, Habakkuk, Zephaniah, Haggai, Zechariah, Malachi). These books are called "minor" not because they are less important but simply because they are shorter. The books of the Former Prophets, together with Deuteronomy, are known as the Deuteronomistic History (DtrH). Taken as a whole, these books narrate the history of Israel from the death of Moses to the Babylonian Exile in 586 BC. The DtrH centers on and expands the continuing covenant relationship between God and the people.

The books of Joshua, Judges, Samuel, and Kings recount the Israelites' entrance into and settlement of the land of Canaan. Once settled on the land, the people become increasingly convinced that in order to become a "great nation" (Gen 12:2), they need to be "like other nations" (1 Sam 8:5). Consequently, they demand to have a king to rule over them. Though reluctant, and not before warning the people what they are asking for, God grants their request (1 Sam 8:4–22).

Israel's first king, Saul, is anointed (remember that the Hebrew word for "anointed one" is *meshiah*) by Samuel (1 Sam 10:1). Popular and well intentioned, Saul is rejected by God because of disobedience (1 Sam 13:8–15; 15) and replaced by a man after God's "own heart" (1 Sam 13:14). That man is David, who, along with Abraham and Moses, numbers among the three most important figures in the Tanak. David is also popular and well intentioned, and he, too, is disobedient. However, unlike Saul, David is not rejected but given a promise that his dynasty will last forever.

David is anointed king of all Israel, makes Jerusalem the capital, and defeats the Philistines (2 Sam 5). He then decides to build the Lord a "house" (i.e., a temple) for the Ark of the Covenant, the ancient symbol of the Lord's presence with Israel (2 Sam 7). In return, the Lord tells David, through the prophet Nathan, that the Lord will make David a "house" (i.e., a dynasty).

> The Lord will make you a house. When your days are fulfilled and you lie down with your ancestors, I will raise up your offspring after you, who shall come forth from your body, and I will establish his kingdom. He shall build a house for my name, and I will establish the throne of his kingdom forever. I will be a father to him, and he shall be a son to me. When he commits iniquity, I will punish him. . . . But I will not take my steadfast love from him, as I took it from Saul. . . . Your house and your kingdom shall be made sure forever before me; your throne shall be established forever. (2 Sam 7:11b–16)

In these words, we have what is known as the Davidic covenant or succession narrative. David's kingly line will continue in perpetuity. From this point on in Israel's history, it is believed that the anointed one (messiah) will come from David's line. Even though David commits adultery with another man's wife (Bathsheba) and then has the man (Uriah) killed, David is not rejected as king (2 Sam 11).

Once again the prophet Nathan comes to David. However, this time he comes with a story that exposes David's sin. David then admits what he did and repents (2 Sam 12:7–15). Thereafter, while David is never rejected by the Lord as was Saul, his "house" is constantly plagued by sibling rivalry, rebellion, dysfunction, and death.

David's successor, Solomon, builds the temple that David wanted to build (1 Kings 6:1–38) and becomes known for his wisdom and wealth. However, Solomon's love for building leads to overtaxation, and his marriages to foreign women lead to idolatry and apostasy. When Solomon's son, Rehoboam, ascends the throne, the people ask him to "lighten the hard service of your father and his heavy yoke that he placed on us" (1 Kings 12:4). Rather than relent, however, Rehoboam responds, "My father disciplined you with whips, but I will discipline you with scorpions" (1 Kings 12:11).

The people of the north, led by Jeroboam (922–901 BC), rebel against Rehoboam, and the once-united monarchy of David and Solomon splits into two. From then on, the north, with its capital in Samaria, was known as Israel, and the south, with its capital in Jerusalem (the City of David), was known as Judah. Israel continued as a separate nation until it was defeated by the Assyrians in 722 BC. Judah fell to the Babylonians in 586 BC.

During the history of these two separate kingdoms, we have a succession of individuals known as prophets whose messages contain both judgment and salvation:

a) The prophets of the Assyrian period include Amos, Hosea, Micah, Isaiah of Jerusalem, Joel, Nahum, and Zephaniah.
b) The prophets of the Babylonian and later Persian periods include Jeremiah, Habakkuk, Obadiah, Ezekiel, Second and Third Isaiah, Haggai, Zechariah, Malachi, and Jonah.

Though sometimes understood as predictors of the future, these prophets were much more proclaimers of God's covenant responsibilities for specific times and places—just as in our own era we can mention certain religious and political leaders who speak out on behalf of social justice and the preservation of the environment. While there are some predictive elements in prophecy, they are not primary. For the prophets, the future was not one hundred or five hundred years down the road but tomorrow, next week, next year. For the Jewish people, the prophets are the prime interpreters of the Torah. Because God had chosen Israel, the people had a special responsibility to be that "holy nation" mentioned in Exodus 19:5.

Prophetic oracles are usually introduced by what is known as the prophetic messenger formula: "Thus says the Lord. . . ." The oracles often proclaimed judgment not only on the nations but also on Israel and Judah. In the prophet Amos are a series of oracles against foreign nations that charge them with what we today might refer to as "war crimes" (Amos 1:1—2:3). However, in the oracles against Judah and Israel (Amos 2:4–8), the crimes are not war crimes but crimes against God's own people that, among other things, include rejection of the Torah (2:4), selling the "righteous for silver, and the needy for a pair of sandals" (2:6), and trampling the "head of the poor into the dust of the earth" (2:7).

According to Amos, it was precisely because Israel was God's people and should have known better that they would be judged harshly: "You only have I known of all the families of the earth; therefore I will punish you for all your iniquities" (Amos 3:2). All of the worship and sacrifice in the world are insufficient if the poor and downtrodden are not cared for or, worse, are pushed aside.

For Amos, and for the prophets as a whole, perhaps no two words are more important than justice and righteousness. While the precise meaning of these words must be defined in the specific context of each prophet, Amos sums it up well when he says:

> I hate, I despise your festivals, and I take no delight in your solemn assemblies. Even though you offer me your burnt offerings and

> grain offerings, I will not accept them; and the offerings of well-being of your fatted animals I will not look upon. Take away from me the noise of your songs; I will not listen to the melody of your harps. But let justice roll down like waters, and righteousness like an ever-flowing stream. (Amos 5:21–24)

As important as worship and sacrifice are, they cannot replace taking care of the most marginalized and least powerful in the community. This also includes care for the land itself and is the basis of our contemporary concern for the environment.

But there were also those times when the prophets spoke oracles of salvation. Stern and firm as he was, even the prophet Amos looked forward to a time of salvation:

> The time is surely coming, says the Lord, when the one who plows shall overtake the one who reaps, and the treader of grapes the one who sows the seed; the mountains shall drip sweet wine, and all the hills shall flow with it. I will restore the fortunes of my people Israel. . . . I will plant them upon their land, and they shall never again be plucked up out of the land that I have given them, says the Lord your God. (Amos 9:13–15)

Isaiah of Jerusalem looked forward to a time when the Lord would "judge between the nations, and shall arbitrate for many peoples; they shall beat their swords into plowshares, and their spears into pruning hooks; nation shall not lift up sword against nation, neither shall they learn war any more" (Isa 2:4).

This same oracle is found also in Micah 4:3 and, sarcastically, in Joel 3:10, where the prophet tells them to go ahead, "beat your plowshares into swords, and your pruning hooks into spears," it will not matter if you do because in the end it is the Lord who will judge the nations. It is the Lord who is "a refuge for his people, a stronghold for the people of Israel" (3:16).

In a series of poems found in Isaiah 40–55, the prophet speaks about a "servant" who will suffer great sorrow (Isa 53) but whose "anguish . . . shall make many righteous, and he shall bear their iniquities" (Isa 53:11). It is not clear whether the servant is an individual or the people as a whole—though Christians have traditionally interpreted this servant as referring to Jesus. What is clear is that this servant was wounded for the people's transgressions and crushed for their iniquities and that by the servant's bruises, the people would be healed (Isa 53:5).

And in Judah's darkest hour, the prophet Jeremiah looked forward to a new covenant with the house of Israel and the house of Judah:

> The days are surely coming, says the Lord, when I will make a new covenant with the house of Israel and the house of Judah. It will not be like the covenant that I made with their ancestors when I took them by the hand to bring out of the land of Egypt—a covenant that they broke, though I was their husband, says the Lord. But this is the covenant I will make with the house of Israel after those days, says the Lord: I will put my law [torah] within them, and I will write it on their hearts; and I will be their God, and they shall be my people. (Jer 31:31–33)

TANAK DIVISION 3—KETUBIM: WORDS OF WISDOM

The third and final division of the Tanak is the Ketubim, or the "Writings." The material in this division is more varied than that found in the Torah and Nebiim. The Writings contain history (1–2 Chronicles, Ezra, Nehemiah), songs (Psalms), proverbs (Proverbs), love poetry

(Song of Songs), laments, praise (Lamentations, Psalms), hero/heroine stories (Ruth, Esther, Daniel 1–6), and what is known as "wisdom literature" (Job, Ecclesiastes).

While poetry can be found throughout the Tanak, the Writings contain some of Israel's most elegant and prayerful poetry. Hebrew poetry, like poetry generally, has some defining characteristics. One important characteristic of Hebrew poetry is what is known as parallelism. In synonymous parallelism, a similar, complementary statement in the second line follows a statement in the first line. For example, "The heavens are telling the glory of God; and the firmament proclaims his handiwork" (Ps 19:1). Antithetical parallelism occurs when a second line makes an opposite statement from the first line: "The Lord watches over the way of the righteous, but the way of the wicked will perish" (Ps 1:6). In synthetic parallelism, the thought of the first line is expanded in the second line: "O Lord, do not rebuke me in your anger, or discipline me in your wrath" (Ps 6:1).

The Book of Psalms contains 150 poems that give God praise, lament, extol the Davidic monarchy, and thank God for many acts of individual and communal deliverance. Well over one-third of these 150 songs are laments, either of individuals or of the community. Because the Israelites did not formulate a specific belief in an afterlife until the post-exilic period (after 586 BC), it was important for God to come to help individuals and the community now, not in some future life beyond this one.

This life was to be lived fully but also wisely. The wise are those whose "delight is in the law of the Lord" and who "meditate" on that law "day and night" (Ps 1:2). The words of wisdom found in the Writings emphasize that the just will be rewarded and the unjust punished. "The Lord watches over the way of the righteous, but the way of the wicked will perish" (Ps 1:6). "Therefore walk in the way of the good, and keep to the paths of the just. For the upright will abide in the land, and the innocent will remain in it; but the wicked will be cut off from the land, and the treacherous will be rooted out of it" (Prov 2:20–22).

At the same time, however, Job, who was said to be "blameless and upright, one who feared God and turned away from evil" (Job 1:1), suffered the devastating loss of his seven sons, three daughters, and all his wealth and possessions. Later, struck with "loathsome sores" over his entire body (Job 2:7), Job cannot understand why he suffers. In the midst of his pain and distress, three "wise" friends (Eliphaz, Bildad, and Zophar) come to visit him and offer the traditional words of wisdom that Job must have done something wrong to deserve such punishment. "Think now," asked Eliphaz, "who that was innocent ever perished? Or where were the upright cut off?" (Job 4:7). Nevertheless, Job persists in his innocence and in the end is invited by the Lord to consider the mystery of creation, where Job comes to a realization: "I have uttered what I did not understand, things too wonderful for me, which I did not know" (Job 42:3). When Job then "repent[s] in dust and ashes" (Job 42:6), he receives "twice as much as he had before" (Job 42:10). A further challenge to traditional wisdom is found in the Book of Ecclesiastes (Qohelet, meaning "the preacher," in Hebrew), where the author says:

> When I applied my mind to know wisdom, and to see the business that is done on earth, how one's eyes see sleep neither day nor night, then I saw all the work of God, that no one can find out what is happening under the sun. However much they may toil in seeking, they will not find it out; even though those who are wise claim to know, they cannot find it out. (Eccl 8:16–17)

In the end, similar to Job, Qoheleth concludes that the meaning of life is to "fear God, and keep his commandments; for that is the whole duty of everyone. For God will bring every deed into judgment, including every secret thing, whether good or evil" (Eccl 12:13–14).

While many factors contributed to Job and Qoheleth's challenge to traditional wisdom, surely the most important factors were the loss of the land, the Temple, and the Davidic monarchy after 586 BC. Though Cyrus the Persian allowed the Jews to return to their homeland in 539 BC, things would never be the same again, and further, even greater, suffering was on the horizon.

After Alexander the Great (356–323 BC) conquered the Persians, the Jews came under the power and influence of Hellenism (Greek culture and religion). Hellenism fascinated many Jews, especially the young. Many others, however, saw it as a threat to their traditions and to their faith. The first six chapters of Daniel are stories of how Daniel and his three friends remained loyal to the Lord even though they served in a foreign court. In this "time between," often called the intertestamental period, it was important to serve "the living God" (Dan 6:20, 26) and not idols of metal, wood, or stone.

Alexander's successors became increasingly ruthless in their attempts to force the Jews to assimilate. In 167 BC, a tyrannical ruler named Antiochus IV Epiphanes tried to wipe out the Jewish faith by banning people from having copies of the Torah, preventing worship on the Sabbath, and forcing people to worship Zeus.

In an act that has come to be known as "the abomination of desolation," Antiochus sent his soldiers into the Temple in Jerusalem in 167 BC, where they slaughtered a pig (considered an "unclean" animal by Jews) on the altar and erected a statue of Zeus (1 Macc 1:41–64). These abominable acts led to the Maccabean revolt, where Judas (known as Maccabeus, "the hammer") and his brothers zealously fought off the merciless Hellenizers. In December of 164 BC they triumphed over Antiochus's soldiers and cleansed the Temple. This cleansing is known to this day in Judaism as Hanukkah (Dedication).

During this period of intense persecution, the Jews needed assurance once again that the promises made to Abraham would be fulfilled. A new kind of literature, known as "apocalyptic," appeared during this period. Its primary purpose was to provide people hope in the midst of despair. The word *apocalyptic* comes from the Greek word for "reveal" or "uncover." What apocalyptic literature reveals is how God will ultimately be victorious over evil and establish his kingdom forever.

Daniel 7–12 provides us with the only complete example of apocalyptic literature in the Tanak. Written during the dark days of the Maccabean struggle against Hellenism, the author has a night vision:

> I saw one like a human being [literally, "son of man"] coming with the clouds of heaven. And he came to the Ancient One and was presented before him. To him was given dominion and glory and kingship, that all peoples, nations, and languages should serve him. His dominion is an everlasting dominion that shall not pass away, and his kingship is one that shall never be destroyed. (Dan 7:13–14)

The "one like a human being" is a heavenly figure to whom God would give everlasting rule. This figure would become very important as history moved closer to the beginning of the Christian era.

In the Christian NT, the expression "Son of Man" is one of a number of Christological titles applied to Jesus. In the NT Gospels, the phrase "Son of Man" occurs over eighty times and, importantly, is used only by Jesus. The words are also found in Acts 7:56 (Stephen's martyrdom) and in Revelation 1:13, where the author, similar to Daniel, sees "one like the Son of Man." The NT Book of Revelation is Christian apocalyptic literature. In order to understand this often misused and abused book, it is important to read it against the background of its Jewish apocalyptic roots, where previous ideas and language are drawn upon and established: for example, visions (heavenly court convened), images (beasts, angels, plagues, harvest), phrases (names for God, horns of animals, seals, books, cities), numbers ("seven" as perfect number), and colors ("white" is heavenly). Once again, we can see the need to understand the OT in order to understand the NT.

Another reason the period between the Tanak and the NT is so important is because many ideas developed that were not present previously in the tradition. For example, the only explicit reference we have to a belief in life after death in the Tanak is found in Daniel 12:2: "Many of those who sleep in the dust of the earth shall awake, some to everlasting life, and some to shame and everlasting contempt." Prior to this time, it was believed that when people died, they went to Sheol, the place of the dead. Furthermore, in this intertestamental period, there is an increasing interest in angels and demons not present elsewhere in the Tanak. The deuterocanonical Book of Tobit is an angelophany where the angel Raphael ("God heals"), disguised as a man, Azariah ("the Lord heals"), accompanies a young man named Tobias on a fascinating journey that involves exorcism of a demon (Asmodeus) and a miraculous healing of blindness.

Belief in life after death, angels, and demons, along with many other beliefs, became increasingly important and had enormous impact on the writers of the NT. As we said at the beginning of this chapter, Christians must never lose sight of the importance of the Tanak for understanding the NT, for without the Tanak, the NT would be an incomprehensible book, "a plant deprived of its roots and destined to dry up and wither."

My grandfather often said, "I should write a book." He never did. I could have written a book as well but had only a few brief pages to introduce you to the "People of the Book," their incredible stories, and enduring faith that God, "will swallow up death forever. . . . wipe away the tears from all faces, and the disgrace of his people he will take away from all the earth, for the Lord has spoken. . . . This is the Lord for whom we have waited; let us be glad and rejoice in his salvation" (Isa 25:8–9).

Christians, too, are "People of the Book." They believe that God's Messiah was enfleshed in the life, death, and Resurrection of Jesus the Christ, and they too wait "with eager longing" (Rom 8:19) for the time when God "will wipe every tear from their eyes. Death will be no more; mourning and crying and pain will be no more, for the first things have passed away" (Rev 21:4; cf. Isa 25:8–9).

Questions about the Text

1. What does Tanak mean? What are its three divisions?
2. What does Torah mean?
3. What do the sources J-E-D-P mean?
4. Explain the Sinai Covenant and its conditions.
5. Who were the first three kings of Israel?
6. To what historical event does the feast of Hanukkah refer?
7. What does the word *apocalyptic* mean?

Questions for Discussion

1. How might the threefold arrangement of the books of the Tanak influence one's understanding of the concept of the Messiah?
2. What are some of the important theological themes of the Torah? Why do you consider them important?
3. If prophecy is primarily proclamation and not prediction, how can people be "prophetic" in today's world?
4. What do you think it means to live life not only fully but also wisely?
5. Why do you think apocalyptic literature is sometimes used to frighten people rather than to provide them with hope?

For Further Study

General

Berlin, Adele, and Marc Zvi Brettler, eds. The *Jewish Study Bible: Jewish Publication Society; Tanakh Translation*. New York: Oxford University Press, 2004.

This translation reflects contemporary biblical scholarship as well as the richness of the Jewish tradition. It contains excellent notes and informative essays on the history of Jewish interpretation of the Tanak.

Brown, Raymond, E., SS, Joseph A. Fitzmyer, SJ, and Roland E. Murphy, OCarm, eds. *The New Jerome Biblical Commentary*. Englewood Cliffs, NJ: Prentice Hall, 1990.

This one-volume commentary on the entire Bible is compact and comprehensive. It is highly respected by biblical scholars from various Christian denominations.

Lysik, David A., ed. *The Bible Documents: A Parish Resource*. Chicago: Liturgy Training Publications, 2001.

This is a handy collection of some of the Catholic Church's most important documents concerning the interpretation of scripture.

Miller, John, W. *How the Bible Came to Be: Exploring the Narrative and Message*. New York: Paulist Press, 2004.

This book is an exploration of the formation and history of the biblical canon.

The Pontifical Biblical Commission. *The Jewish People and Their Sacred Scriptures in the Christian Bible*. Boston: Pauline Books & Media, 2002.

Wiesel, Elie. *Memoirs: All Rivers Run to the Sea*. New York: Alfred A. Knopf, 1995.

Introductory

Anderson, Bernhard W., and Katheryn Pfisterer Darr. *Understanding the Old Testament*. Abridged 4th ed. Englewood Cliffs, NJ: Prentice Hall, 1998.

This one-volume introduction complete with photos, maps, and chronologies can be read by all those interested in the OT, regardless of religious persuasion.

deSilva, David A. *Introducing the Apocrypha: Message, Context and Significance*. Grand Rapids, MI: Baker Academic, 2002.

This book introduces the OT apocrypha and shows how many of these Jewish writings were used by the authors of the NT.

Wisdom Literature

Schüssler Fiorenza, Elisabeth. *Wisdom Ways: Introducing Feminist Biblical Interpretation*. Maryknoll, NY: Orbis Books, 2001.

This volume is an introduction to feminist biblical studies and interpretation using wisdom as the departure point.

Murphy, Roland E. *The Tree of Life: An Exploration of Biblical Wisdom Literature*. 2nd ed. Grand Rapids, MI: Eerdmans, 1996.

An accessible, clear, and concise introduction to the wisdom books of the OT.

The Prophets

Miller, John W. *Meet the Prophets: A Beginner's Guide to the Books of the Biblical Prophets*. New York: Paulist Press, 1987.

This introduction to the biblical prophets attempts to bridge the gap between the meaning of the message then and now.

Jewish Apocalyptic Literature

Collins, John J. *The Apocalyptic Imagination: An Introduction to the Jewish Matrix of Christianity*. New York: Crossroad, 1987.

This is an introduction to Jewish apocalyptic literature in its historical context.

from the REFERENCE LIBRARIAN

Researching Bible Topics—Old Testament

There are many possible topics of research for the Old Testament; let's try to categorize them. One category of topic is biographical. Is there a particular figure (Abraham, Moses, David, etc.) that you would like to study in depth? Another category would include subjects related to the Bible's "world of thought" and would include researching such biblical and theological concepts as "righteousness," "faith," or "covenant," or such biblical phenomena as "prophecy," "wisdom literature," "apocalyptic," and so on. Yet another category might be topics relating to the historical world of the Bible. This would include the study of the geographical setting of scripture, including archaeological investigation, daily life and customs, and so on. There is much more, but perhaps this is enough to get you started.

Whatever your topic is, remember your starting point is as follows:

SKILL KEY #1

Use the library's reference collection to begin your research.

a) Use a subject-specific encyclopedia to acquire specialized knowledge about a subject.

b) Use a subject-specific encyclopedia whose scope is appropriate for both your topic and the approach you want to take to that topic.

What subject-specific reference sources should you use to study the Old Testament? A number of reference works are devoted entirely to the Bible. The most comprehensive are the two multi-volume encyclopedias listed below.

David Noel Freedman, ed. *The Anchor Bible Dictionary*. 6 vols. New York: Doubleday, 1992.

Katherine Doob Sakenfeld, ed. *The New Interpreter's Dictionary of the Bible*. 5 vols. Nashville: Abingdon Press, 2006–2009.

Don't let the word *dictionary* in the title throw you off. These are exhaustive encyclopedias containing articles on almost any topic imaginable relating to the Bible (both Old and New Testaments). Most articles have bibliographies, often listing both books and journal articles.

Some reference sources focus even more narrowly on the OT alone or on parts of it. For example, your library may own the following title devoted entirely to the five books of Moses:

T. Desmond Alexander and David W. Baker. *Dictionary of the Old Testament: Pentateuch*. Downers Grove, IL: InterVarsity Press, 2003.

Another type of reference tool, usually called a Bible dictionary or handbook, may also be useful. Bible dictionaries are usually one volume, so the articles will be shorter than those you will find in the *Anchor Bible Dictionary*. The following titles are representative of this type of reference tool; your librarian can suggest alternatives if your library does not own either one.

> Mark Allan Powell, ed. *The HarperCollins Bible Dictionary*. 3rd ed. New York: HarperCollins Publishers, 2011.
>
> David Noel Freedman, ed. *Eerdmans Dictionary of the Bible*. Grand Rapids, MI: Eerdmans, 2000.

Since, as you have already learned, study of the Bible entails the use of a number of technical terms (Tanak, Torah, Pentateuch, etc.), the following example of a concise dictionary, as described in the introductory chapter, will be helpful for quickly looking up the meaning of an unfamiliar term or expression:

> Richard N. Soulen and R. Kendall Soulen. *Handbook of Biblical Criticism*. 3rd ed., rev. and expanded. Louisville, KY: Westminster John Knox Press, 2001.

The one-volume Bible dictionaries may also be helpful for definitions.

Although almost all of the reference tools just listed will be helpful with specifically theological topics, some reference tools (including the three listed next) focus entirely on the theology of the Bible. Such reference tools usually contain articles on terms actually appearing in the Bible and theological concepts based on those terms.

> Donald E. Gowan. *The Westminster Theological Wordbook of the Bible*. Louisville, KY: Westminster John Knox Press, 2003.
>
> Carroll Stuhlmueller, ed. *The Collegeville Pastoral Dictionary of Biblical Theology*. Collegeville, MN: Liturgical Press, 1996.
>
> Kevin J. Vanhoozer et al., eds. *Dictionary for Theological Interpretation of the Bible*. Cambridge, UK: Baker Academic, 2005.

Finally, another type of useful reference tool is a Bible atlas. Understanding the geographical setting of the biblical story is crucial to grasping the significance of the overall biblical narrative. Many atlases of the Bible have been published. If your library does not own one of the atlases listed below, ask the librarian if there is something similar available.

> Yohanan Aharoni *et al.*, eds. *The Carta Bible Atlas*. Jerusalem: Carta, 2002.
>
> Marcus Braybrooke and James Harpur. *Collegeville Atlas of the Bible*. Collegeville, MN: Liturgical Press, 1998.
>
> Adrian Curtis, ed. *Oxford Bible Atlas*. 4th ed. Oxford, New York: Oxford University Press, 2009.

Remember also that it is possible to begin research on almost any topic, including the Bible, using the *New Catholic Encyclopedia* (described in the introductory chapter). You can find articles for all three types of topics mentioned, including OT figures (such as Abraham, Moses, or David) or other aspects of the OT that you have read about in this chapter (e.g., see "Pentateuchal Studies," 11:88–100, for a much lengthier discussion of the documentary hypothesis) or about important theological topics (such as righteousness, prophecy, etc.).

Researching Individual Books of the Bible

One more way of studying the Bible is to study each individual book, asking appropriate questions: Who wrote it? When was it written? Why was it written? What situation was being addressed? What were the historical circumstances behind the writing of the book? What does the book (or certain sections of it) mean?

We will use this type of topic to illustrate the second of the key elements of using the library.

SKILL KEY #2

Use the library's catalog to locate sources of information.

a) Use subject headings to locate precisely books on your topic.

You can, of course, find articles on individual books of the Bible in almost all of the reference sources listed previously. The bibliographies from these reference sources as described in the introductory chapter will lead you to the appropriate subject heading(s) for a biblical book, but subject headings for the Bible have a unique format, so it will be worthwhile to see how they are formed.

Subject headings for OT books always begin with the root "Bible O T" (the "O T" stands for "Old Testament") and follow the pattern given below. (Be sure to put a space between the "O" and the "T.")

Search format:

Subject heading "root"	*Name of Book*
Bible O T	Genesis
Bible O T	Isaiah

As you will discover in the next chapter, the format for books of the NT is the same, with the difference that "N T" (for "New Testament") is used instead of "O T." We will have more to say about subject headings for biblical books in the next chapter. For now, you should have a good grasp of the importance of using a subject-specific encyclopedia.

Student Tasks

1. Ask your reference librarian to show you where the Bible encyclopedias are located.
2. Select a book from the OT and use the correct form of subject heading to search your library catalog for books about it.

[Note: Most college and many public libraries allow electronic access to their catalog through the Internet. That convenience allows a student to work from home, dorm, or other places. This makes your computer a terminal connected to the library resources.]

The New Testament and Other Early Christian Literature

James A. Kelhoffer

from the EDITOR

Imagine a favorite beautiful lake, where the water is fresh, fish abound, and gentle streams empty in and out. For all the change and motion, somehow the lake seems always the same. That's much the way the Christian Bible is. It is a resource that gives life, changes and flows into people's lives, yet seems to remain the same. The sacred scriptures are a living resource that informs, dwells in, and challenges the lives of Christians.

Christianity's sacred texts are contained in the Bible. For Christians, the heart of the Bible is the revelation of God in Jesus the Christ, by his words and actions, which are contained in the New Testament (NT). Just as different types of writings make up the Old Testament (OT), so too the NT consists of different writings, especially Gospels and letters to communities by various authors. Why some writings were included in the Bible and others were not is an interesting theological topic—we will see some discussion of it in the following chapters.

The role of the Christian Bible as a source for theology is central because Jesus is the center of the Christian revelation in God. "God-talk" (*theology*) for believing Christians relies on the historical event of Jesus that is alive today. The NT describes Christian experiences of God's revelation of Christ. For Christians, the sacred texts provide a resource to nourish the soul, to celebrate religious moments and events, to understand their relationship with God, and many other purposes. Theology brings its sacred texts to bear on its best understanding of God and God's ways and how to respond. Theology, through scripture scholars, continually seeks to better understand the sacred texts, especially in their language, time, place, and context. That said, the focus is still on the lived experience of Christians throughout the world. Christians believe that only when the sacred scriptures as the revelation of God come alive through living Christians, in word and deed— in relationships, self, and creation—is the relationship with God alive and active.

This third chapter will explore the relationship of the NT and other Christian literature to theological investigation. It will also conclude the section on sacred texts and pave the way for the remainder of the book. The significance of this chapter will become more evident as we see how the scriptures are used in the rest of the book.

OVERVIEW: THE EARLY CHRISTIANS AND THEIR WRITINGS

Four Gospels, One Jesus, and Luke's "Many" Witnesses

The author of the Gospel according to Luke begins by telling us that he consulted with "many" earlier writings and eyewitness accounts about Jesus:

> Since many have undertaken to set down an orderly account of the events that have been fulfilled among us, just as they were handed on to us by those who from the beginning were eyewitnesses and servants of the word, I too decided, after investigating everything carefully from the very first, to write an orderly account for you, most excellent Theophilus, so that you may know the truth concerning the things about which you have been instructed. (Luke 1:1–4)

Sometimes I wonder what happened to all those "many" other writings and witnesses. Doubtless, some of them are reflected in the writings that comprise our New Testament (NT). Early Christians, such as the author of Luke, would eventually produce quite a number of narratives about Jesus and the early church, letters, and other writings as witnesses to their faith, their experiences as followers of Jesus, and their attempts to form nurturing communities. Several of these writings came to be included in the NT; others were not.

This short introduction to the NT has three main parts. Part 1 briefly mentions the twenty-seven writings included in the NT, as well as several other early Christian writings that date to the first or early-second centuries. Part 2 considers the four NT Gospels (Matthew, Mark, Luke, and John) and what these four authors emphasize in their accounts of Jesus' public ministry and death. Part 2 also discusses where written Gospels came from and introduces a comparative approach to the Gospels and their sources. Part 3 looks at early Christian letters and focuses on the Apostle Paul's letter to the Galatians. Because most of the NT writings are letters, this section offers some guidelines on how to read early Christian letters.

What Is the New Testament (and What Is It Not)?

The NT is a collection of twenty-seven of the earliest Christian writings. Christians today (whether Roman Catholic, Orthodox, or Protestant) receive these twenty-seven writings as their Second or New(er) Testament of scripture.

In the chapter on the OT, we saw that the Hebrew Bible/Tanak/OT includes different kinds (or genres) of literature: the Law, the Prophets, and the Writings. The NT likewise contains different literary genres. In addition to the four narratives about Jesus (commonly referred to as "Gospels"), there is one narrative about the earliest church (Acts), twenty-one letters (or writings with at least some characteristics of an ancient Greek letter), and one apocalypse. These writings were composed between approximately 50 CE and 120 CE and may be summarized as follows:

1. Historical narratives: Five writings (the four Gospels and Acts). The first three Gospels—Matthew, Mark, and Luke—are oftentimes referred to as the Synoptic Gospels because of the large amount of overlapping materials. (In Greek, *synoptic* means "seen together.") The Fourth Gospel, or Gospel according to John, is distinguished from the Synoptic Gospels by its theological emphases and extensive sections on Jesus' discourses and

miracles. In addition to these four narratives about Jesus, the Acts of the Apostles offers a selective history of the earliest church. The author of the Gospel of Luke also wrote the Acts of the Apostles. These two volumes together are commonly referred to as Luke-Acts and in terms of their length comprise approximately one-fourth of the NT.

2. Letters: Twenty-one writings total. Thirteen of the NT letters are attributed to the Apostle Paul. Of these thirteen, seven are known today as the undisputed Pauline letters (Romans, 1 Corinthians, 2 Corinthians, Galatians, Philippians, 1 Thessalonians, Philemon) because virtually all scholars are persuaded that Paul did in fact write them. The undisputed Pauline letters date to the 50s CE and are the earliest surviving Christian writings. The other six NT letters attributed to Paul are commonly called the deuteropauline letters (a "second" [= *deutero*] group of Pauline letters), since many scholars doubt that Paul himself wrote them (2 Thessalonians, Colossians, Ephesians, 1 Timothy, 2 Timothy, Titus). The last three deuteropauline letters are oftentimes called the Pastoral Epistles. The eight other NT letters (or letter-like writings) were either written anonymously or attributed to other apostolic figures, such as Peter. They are the book of Hebrews and the seven Catholic or General Epistles (James, 1 Peter, 2 Peter, 1 John, 2 John, 3 John, Jude).
3. Apocalypse: The Revelation of John is the only NT example of this genre. In the chapter on the OT, you read about apocalypses, including the OT book of Daniel, and both the similarities and differences of this genre to the OT prophets.

So, in terms of the number of writings, most of the NT is comprised of letters (twenty-one out of twenty-seven) from a church leader such as Paul to an early Christian community. Since the NT includes the works of different authors and different literary genres, you may find it helpful to think of the NT as a *library* of early Christian writings rather than as a single "book."

In addition to these twenty-seven writings, we either possess or know something about numerous other writings by the first generations of Christians. The following list offers other examples of early Christian historical narratives, letters, and apocalypses.

1. Other early Christian historical narratives include the *Gospel of Thomas*, the *Gospel of Peter*, the *Infancy Gospel of Thomas*, the *Protevangelium of James*, the *Gospel of the Ebionites*, the *Gospel of the Nazarenes*, the *Gospel of the Hebrews*, one writing (possibly two) known as the *Gospel of Truth*, the *Acts of Paul and Thecla*, the *Martyrdom of Polycarp*, and the recently discovered *Gospel of Judas*.
2. Other early Christian letters include a lost letter of Paul to the church at Corinth (mentioned in 1 Cor 5:9); *3 Corinthians* (a second-century writing known not to be written by Paul); seven letters of Ignatius, a bishop and martyr from Antioch in Syria; *1 Clement*; the *Didache* or *Teaching of the Twelve Apostles*; Polycarp's *To the Philippians*; and *Barnabas*.
3. Two other early Christian apocalypses are the *Shepherd* of Hermas and the *Apocalypse of Peter*.

When did the church decide upon the NT as a collection of (only) twenty-seven particular writings? This was a complicated process that took several centuries. In fact, the earliest surviving document listing the NT's twenty-seven writings (and no others) as comprising the authoritative Christian NT comes from a single (albeit influential) bishop in Egypt, Athanasius of Alexandria, in the year 367 CE. What this means is that if you were a follower of Jesus in the early centuries of the church, you may well have heard some—but most likely not all, or even many—NT writings read in your church community. You may also have come into contact with any number of other early Christian writings as well.

Why Is the New Testament Written in Greek?

All the NT writings were written in ancient Greek—not Hebrew (the primary language of the Jewish Scriptures), Aramaic (the mother tongue of most Palestinian Jews, including Jesus), or Latin (the main language in the western parts of the Mediterranean, such as Italy, North Africa, and Spain). More specifically, the writings of the NT are in the *Koine* ("common") dialect of ancient Greek. After the conquests of Alexander the Great (who died in 323 BCE, more than three centuries before the birth of Jesus), Koine Greek had become the standard language for commerce in most cities in the eastern parts of the Mediterranean, including Syro-Palestine. Koine Greek remained a common language in the Greek East even after Roman rule spread to these regions during the second and first centuries BCE. The ancient Mediterranean world included numerous different languages, cultures, and ethnic groups. Within this multicultural milieu, the writers of the NT, like so many of their non-Christian neighbors, chose the "common" dialect of Koine Greek for their written communications.

In addition, most citations of the Jewish scriptures in the NT are from the OT in a Greek translation known as the Septuagint (LXX). You read about the Septuagint in the last chapter. The "Bible" of many early Christian communities was the OT in Greek.

What Does "New Testament" Mean?

The term *New Testament* can also be translated as "new covenant." Three NT writers—the author of Luke, the Apostle Paul, and the author of Hebrews—refer to the "new testament/covenant" to differentiate between the relationship that God established with the Jewish people, as related in the Torah, and the extension of that relationship to all humanity in Jesus Christ (Luke 22:20; 1 Cor 11:25; 2 Cor 3:6a; Heb 7:22, 8:6–13, 9:15, 12:24). For example, the Apostle Paul writes that God "has made us competent to be ministers of a new covenant[/testament]" (2 Cor 3:6a). Paul also mentions "the old covenant[/testament]" (2 Cor 3:14), and the author d of Hebrews refers to "the first covenant[/testament]" (Heb 9:1, 15, 18). As we read in the last chapter, the possible connotation that the Jewish Scriptures are somehow "old(er)" need not suggest to us today that the "new covenant/testament" has superseded the first covenant/testament or rendered it outdated. Although this is apparently the view of certain early Christian writings, such as Luke-Acts (e.g. Luke 2:34–35; Acts 28:28), early Christian literature reflects a variety of views toward Jews and the Jewish Scriptures.

EARLY CHRISTIAN GOSPELS

Each of the four Gospels offers distinctive information about Jesus, his public ministry, death, Resurrection, and significance. We shall first survey the main emphases in Matthew, Mark, Luke, and John, and then consider how these writings about Jesus came about. When we look at the sources the Gospel authors used and examples of how they edited their sources, we can learn much about these authors' theology, as well as recognize the points about Jesus that they especially wished to emphasize to their communities.

What Are the Main Themes of Mark, Matthew, Luke, and John?

Mark

Each of the NT Gospels deserves to be read for its distinctive characterization of Jesus. In each Gospel, you will notice certain themes that are not emphasized as much—or at all—in the other Gospels. For example, the earliest of the three Synoptic Gospels, the Gospel of Mark, follows three prominent themes:

1. Secrecy about Jesus' messianic identity
2. The disciples' lack of understanding about Jesus and his teachings
3. The suffering of Jesus

Here is an example of the first theme in connection with a miracle of Jesus:

> He [Jesus] took her by the hand and said to her, "Talitha cum," which means, "Little girl, get up!" And immediately the girl got up and began to walk about (she was twelve years of age). At this they were overcome with amazement. He strictly ordered them that no one should know this, and told them to give her something to eat. (Mark 5:41b–43)

Next follows an example of the second theme, namely the disciples' lack of understanding:

> But when they saw him [Jesus] walking on the sea, they thought it was a ghost and cried out; for they all saw him and were terrified. But immediately he spoke to them and said, "Take heart, it is I; do not be afraid." Then he got into the boat with them and the wind ceased. And they were utterly astounded, for they did not understand about the loaves, but their hearts were hardened. (Mark 6:49–52)

It is not until the middle of Mark's narrative that Jesus starts to reveal that he will suffer and die, the third theme:

> Then he [Jesus] began to teach them that the Son of Man must undergo great suffering, and be rejected by the elders, the chief priests, and the scribes, and be killed, and after three days rise again. He said all this quite openly. And Peter took him aside and began to rebuke him. But turning and looking at his disciples, he rebuked Peter and said, "Get behind me, Satan! For you are setting your mind not on divine things but on human things." (Mark 8:31–33)

You may have noticed that this last passage ties together two different themes in Mark: Jesus' suffering and the obtuseness of one prominent disciple, namely Peter.

Matthew

Although the Gospel of Matthew shares many points in common with the Gospel of Mark, it gives its own particular presentation of Jesus. One theme we may not expect to find in Matthew is Jesus' affirmation of the Mosaic Law (Torah) to his followers:

> Do not think that I have come to abolish the law or the prophets; I have come not to abolish but to fulfill. For truly I tell you, until heaven

ASSIGNMENT

I encourage you to read all of Mark in a single sitting, looking for the three themes of secrecy, misunderstanding, and suffering. Ask yourself how the author of Mark weaves them together to offer his audience an overall picture of Jesus' healing ministry, interactions with disciples, and death. While reading Mark, you may notice additional, less-prominent themes in this Gospel and find it helpful to consider how these complement Mark's main themes. Of these three main themes of secrecy, misunderstanding, and suffering in Mark, only the suffering of Jesus emerges as a prominent theme in the other NT Gospels.

> and earth pass away, not one letter, not one stroke of a letter, will pass from the law until all is accomplished. Therefore, whoever breaks one of the least of these commandments, and teaches others to do the same, will be called least in the kingdom of heaven; but whoever does them and teaches them will be called great in the kingdom of heaven. For I tell you, unless your righteousness exceeds that of the scribes and Pharisees, you will never enter the kingdom of heaven. (Matt 5:17–20)

At the end of this passage, the scribes' and Pharisees' "righteousness" is regarded positively as a goal that Jesus' true followers must achieve and then surpass, in order to "be called great in the kingdom of heaven." This points to an element of conflict or competition between Matthew's community and (other) Jews who either do not follow Jesus or do not follow Jesus in the way that the author of Matthew prescribes. Such conflict is further underscored by Matthew's depiction of Jesus as entering "*their* synagogue" (Matt 12:9, emphasis added) to heal a man who had a withered hand. Compare the parallel passage in Mark 3:1, which reads "*the* synagogue." Mark does not explicitly distinguish, as Matthew does, between Jesus' followers and those associated with a synagogue.

Such differentiation from the synagogue can likewise be seen in two of Matthew's references to the disciples' missionary activities. During his lifetime, the Matthean Jesus commands a limited outreach only toward Jews: "Go nowhere among the Gentiles, and enter no town of the Samaritans, but go rather to the lost sheep of the house of Israel" (Matt 10:5b–6). By contrast, at the very end of this Gospel, Jesus sanctions a universal mission to all nations:

> Go therefore and make disciples of all nations, baptizing them in the name of the Father and of the Son and of the Holy Spirit, and teaching them to obey everything that I have commanded you. And remember, I am with you always, to the end of the age. (Matt 28:19–20)

In Matthew's community, making disciples and "teaching them to obey everything" Jesus commanded apparently included keeping the Mosaic Law (Torah), which according to Matthew 5:17–20 will never pass away. We therefore find in Matthew's narrative an attempt to bring together several disparate themes and emphases, including missions to Jews and Gentiles and the importance of the Torah.

Luke

The third Synoptic Gospel, Luke, also has its own distinctive themes and emphases. Most scholars agree that, different from the other three Gospels, the Gospel of Luke displays a special interest in establishing his version of Jesus' story among other ancient Greco-Roman and Jewish historical narratives. Luke makes this aim evident in his prologue (Luke 1:1–4, discussed above), where he claims that his account will start at the beginning, be based on eyewitness reports, and investigate with accuracy. These four claims can be found at the beginning of many Hellenistic and early Roman histories. Luke wanted readers like Theophilus (Luke 1:3; Acts 1:1), the person to whom his book is addressed, not just to learn miscellaneous interesting details concerning Christian origins but also to be persuaded that his version of the events offered the "truth" about what actually took place. For Luke, earlier written sources (such as Mark and the common source known as Q, discussed below) were extremely valuable but required the skillful hand of a trusted historian for ordering and interpretation.

In addition to supplementing Mark with numerous fascinating stories about Jesus' birth and childhood and the birth and teachings of Jesus' role model, John the Baptist, Luke also highlights, among other things, the inclusion of women among early followers of Jesus and a concern for the poor. Much more so than Matthew or Mark, Luke's Gospel highlights women who traveled with Jesus. Yet despite the additional attention women receive in this Gospel, scholars today debate whether Luke's depictions of women are actually more positive than those in Matthew or Mark. Two passages in particular inform this debate:

> Soon afterwards he went on through cities and villages, proclaiming and bringing the good news of the kingdom of God. The twelve were with him, as well as some women who had been cured of evil spirits and infirmities: Mary, called Magdalene, from whom seven demons had gone out, and Joanna, the wife of Herod's steward Chuza, and Susanna, and many others, who provided for them out of their resources. (Luke 8:1–3; cf. Mark 15:41)

■ ■ ■

> Now as they went on their way, he entered a certain village, where a woman named Martha welcomed him into her home. She had a sister named Mary, who sat at the Lord's feet and listened to what he was saying. But Martha was distracted by her many tasks; so she came to him and asked, "Lord, do you not care that my sister has left me to do all the work by myself? Tell her then to help me." But the Lord answered her, "Martha, Martha, you are worried and distracted by many things; there is need of only one thing. Mary has chosen the better part, which will not be taken away from her." (Luke 10:38–42)

In particular, Luke 10:38–42 seems to imply Jesus' rejection of the notion that a woman must assume a subordinate, servile role within the household.

Concerning the rich and the poor in this Gospel, Jesus warns about those who "store up treasures for themselves but are not rich toward God" (Luke 12:21) and about the future punishment awaiting such people: "But woe to you who are rich, for you have received your consolation. Woe to you who are full now, for you will be hungry. Woe to you who are laughing now, for you will mourn and weep" (6:24–25). Likewise, only in Luke does Jesus instruct the "very rich" ruler to sell "all" that he owns (Luke 18:22–23, cf. Matt 19:21–22; Mark 10:21–22).

John

The author of the Gospel of John acknowledges that he writes in order to inspire faith in Jesus: "Now Jesus did many other signs in the presence of his disciples, which are not written in this book. But these are written so that you may come to believe" (John 20:30–31a). The author of the Fourth Gospel also provides figurative "I am" sayings of Jesus:

> I am the bread of life. Whoever comes to me will never be hungry, and whoever believes in me will never be thirsty. . . . I am the living bread that came down from heaven. Whoever eats of this bread will live forever; and the bread that I will give for the life of the world is my flesh. (John 6:35; 51)

In his prologue (1:1–18), John emphasizes the role of Jesus the Word in creation:

> In the beginning was the Word, and the Word was with God, and the Word was God. He was in the beginning with God. All things came into being through him, and without him not one thing came into being. (John 1:1–3a)

You may find it helpful to read the entire Johannine prologue and reflect on how this passage compares with the presentations of Jesus in the Synoptic Gospels, especially the genealogies (Matt 1:1–17; Luke 3:23–38; cf. Mark 1:2–4).

By now you may agree that a person reading, for example, Mark in light of Matthew's narrative (or vice versa), would likely miss many important details in Mark (or Matthew). It is important to approach each Gospel individually in order to gain an appreciation for its author's overall theological concerns. Having surveyed each of these Gospels separately, in the following sections we shall consider the origin of written Gospels about Jesus and the oral and written traditions behind the NT Gospels.

From Jesus to the Gospels: Where Did the Gospels Come From?

The four narratives about Jesus' life, ministry, and passion attributed to Matthew, Mark, Luke, and John were originally written anonymously and were, moreover, not called "gospels" by their authors. NT authors consistently use the Greek term for *gospel* for oral proclamation of the "good news." By the middle of the second century, the term *gospel* was added to gospel manuscripts as a literary designation for these writings, characterizing them as a written summary of the "good news" of Jesus. Also in the second century, names were attached to these writings, presumably to distinguish between different written Gospels in Christian communities that possessed more than one Gospel. Although the Gospel authors chose not to indicate much about themselves in their writings, from careful study of these writings we can learn much about what they thought about Jesus and his significance.

Concerning *when* the Gospels were written, we can work forward from an approximate date for the crucifixion of Jesus (30 CE). You have already read that the earliest surviving Christian writings are the Apostle Paul's seven undisputed letters, which date to the 50s CE. Most scholars date Mark's Gospel to around 70 CE because of its likely reference to the first Roman-Jewish War (66–73 CE), which culminated in the destruction of Jerusalem and the Jewish temple:

> Do you see these great buildings? Not one stone will be left here upon another; all will be thrown down. . . . But when you see the desolating sacrilege set up where it ought not to be (let the reader understand), then those in Judea must flee to the mountains. (Mark 13:2, 14)

The Gospels of Matthew and Luke were written after Mark and might be dated between 75 CE and 85 CE, and John, probably toward the 90s or early in the second century. One thing this means is that four decades passed between the lifetime of Jesus (30 CE) and the earliest surviving written Gospel about Jesus (Mark, 70 CE). This is one reason that the author of Luke, in the passage with which this discussion began, acknowledges having made use of "many" written sources and eyewitness testimonies (Luke 1:1–4). What Luke explicitly acknowledges was most probably true for the other three NT Gospels as well.

The circulation of oral traditions about Jesus for decades prior to—and, indeed, after—the emergence of written Gospels can explain a number of the similarities among these four Gospels. For example, we read in all four accounts that Jesus was crucified under Pontius Pilate (the Roman Prefect of Judea, 26–36 CE) on a Friday at the time of the Jewish festival of Passover, the celebration of the exodus and subsequent covenant with Yahweh in Sinai (Matt 26:2; Mark 14:16; Luke 22:15; John 19:14). Despite these similarities, the Synoptics and John have developed these details into different narratives. Mark and the other two Synoptic Gospels present Jesus celebrating the Passover on Thursday evening with his disciples the day before the crucifixion (for example, Mark 14:12–25). Yet in the Fourth Gospel, Jesus does not celebrate the Passover with his disciples because he is arrested prior to the Passover, which in John's account falls on Friday evening (not Thursday evening, as in the Synoptics). Another disparity concerns the timing of the crucifixion: Did it commence in the morning or the middle of the day? According to Mark 15:25, it begins around 9:00 a.m., but in John 19:14–16, it starts shortly after 12:00 p.m. The telling and retelling of stories about Jesus by his followers over several decades prior to the writing of Gospels about Jesus can account for many such similarities and differences.

The Synoptic Problem (I): What Is It, and Can It Be Solved?

The Synoptic Problem addresses the need to account for both the similarities and the differences among the Gospels of Matthew, Mark, and Luke. How can there be so much overlapping material about Jesus' life, ministry, and death, yet such distinctive and even contradictory points in each Gospel? The most widely accepted solution to the Synoptic Problem has two main parts. Acknowledged by nearly all scholars today, the first part posits that the author of Mark wrote first and was used as a source by the authors of Matthew and Luke. Building on this hypothesis of Markan priority, we can learn much about the theology of Matthew and Luke by looking at what they chose to incorporate, edit, or leave out from Mark. Let's consider representative examples from Matthew and Luke. To see the differences, we will start with the Markan source.

You have read that secrecy is a prominent theme in Mark. Mark 6:47–52 relates how Jesus' disciples were in a boat on the sea when they saw Jesus walking on water. Earlier, this chapter touched upon the disciples' reaction:

> They thought it was a ghost and cried out; for they all saw him [Jesus] and were terrified. But immediately he spoke to them and said, "Take heart, it is I; do not be afraid." Then he got into the boat with them and the wind ceased. And they were utterly astounded, for they did not understand about the loaves, but their hearts were hardened. (Mark 6:49b–52)

Matthew includes some of this material from Mark 6:47–52 but takes it in a decidedly different direction:

> They were terrified, saying, "It is a ghost!" And they cried out in fear. But immediately Jesus spoke to them and said, "Take heart, it is I; do not be afraid." Peter answered him, "Lord, if it is you, command me to come to you on the water." He said, "Come." So Peter got out of the boat, started walking on the water, and came toward Jesus. . . . When they got into the boat, the wind ceased. And those in the boat worshiped him, saying, "Truly you are the Son of God." (Matt 14:26b–29, 32–33)

Notably, Matthew passes over in silence Mark's depiction of the disciples' hard-heartedness and instead presents the apostle Peter as joining Jesus in walking on water. Matthew's Jesus does not censure the disciples for their obstinacy. Instead, the disciples acknowledge Jesus as God's Son (Matt 14:33). One thing that Matthew's editing of this Markan passage reveals is that Matthew is not merely a passive recipient of earlier gospel traditions. Rather, Matthew is an active author who finds his own creative theological voice through editing Markan (and other) materials available to him.

Let's consider another example of editing, this time from the Gospel of Luke. Luke subtly edits material from Mark concerning the end of the world. In both the Markan and Lukan versions, Jesus speaks about what will happen in "this generation," that is, during the lifetime of Jesus' contemporaries. Let's look at the two texts together:

Mark 13:30	Luke 21:32
Truly I tell you, this generation will not pass away *until all these things* have taken place.	Truly I tell you, this generation will not pass away until *all things* have taken place.

With the exception of omitting one Greek word (*tauta*, a demonstrative pronoun meaning "these"), the Lukan version is essentially the same as that in Mark. But do the two verses in Mark and Luke mean the same thing?

In Mark 13:30, the occurrence of "all these things" within a generation of Jesus' death includes colossal and observable changes in the heavens and the appearance of the Son of Man:

> But in those days, after that suffering, the sun will be darkened, and the moon will not give its light, and the stars will be falling from heaven, and the powers in the heavens will be shaken. Then they will see "the Son of Man coming in clouds" [cf. Dan 7:13–14] with great power and glory. Then he will send out the angels, and gather his elect from the four winds, from the ends of the earth to the ends of heaven. (Mark 13:24–27)

You may recall from the beginning of this chapter that the author of Luke made use of eyewitnesses for his Gospel and, by implication, was not an eyewitness or a follower of the earthly Jesus. Luke wrote at some time after Mark, when the expectation of Mark 13:24–30 had not been realized. Luke eliminates this difficulty by removing a single word, *these*, from Mark 13:30. In Luke 21:32, "all things" is less specific than "all these things" (Mark 13:30) and need not be taken as a reference to Jesus' prediction of the End, as in the Gospel of Mark.

We find a similar example of Luke's editing of Mark to teach about the end of the world in Mark 9:1 and Luke 9:27:

Mark 9:1	Luke 9:27
There are some standing here who will not taste death until they see that the kingdom of God *has come with power.*	There are some standing here who will not taste death before they see the kingdom of God.

In Mark's narrative, the "coming" of God's kingdom may be interpreted in light of Mark 13:24–30, which predicts the coming of the Son of Man within "this generation." By deleting "has come with power" (Mark 9:1), Luke 9:27 makes no such claim. In Luke's theology, seeing "the kingdom of God" (Luke 9:27) and "all things" taking place (21:32) is open to any number of interpretations and does not denote that the time of the End is near, as Mark 9:1 and 13:24–30 do. To be sure, Luke does expect Jesus to return at some future point (see, for example, Luke 12:35–48; Acts 1:11), just not as soon as Mark's narrative implies.

The Synoptic Problem (II): What Is the Sayings Source "Q"?

The last section introduced the first part of the solution to the Synoptic Problem accepted by most scholars today: the hypothesis of Markan priority posits that Mark wrote first and that his Gospel was used as a source by Matthew and Luke. The second part of the solution to the Synoptic Problem builds on the hypothesis of Markan priority and notes that the authors of Matthew and Luke made use of Mark differently. Because neither Matthew nor Luke reflects the other's particular editing of Markan materials, most scholars infer that Matthew and Luke wrote independently of one another.

Despite the independence of Matthew and Luke, these two Gospels share in common approximately two hundred thirty-five verses that do not occur in Mark. More than two hundred verses is a substantial amount of material that most likely would not have survived for decades in independent oral traditions until the writing of Matthew and Luke. Since Matthew and Luke wrote independently of one another and share so much non-Markan material in common, most scholars are persuaded that in addition to Mark's Gospel they made use of one or more other written sources. In German-language NT scholarship, the word *Quelle* ("source") designates this non-Markan source material preserved in Matthew and Luke. The existence of this other source material ("Q") in Matthew and Luke is the second part of the most commonly accepted solution to the Synoptic Problem. Matthew's and Luke's extensive borrowing from Mark and Q accounts for many of the similarities among the three Synoptic Gospels.

In addition to materials from Mark and Q, it is likely that at least some passages contained only in Matthew came from pre-Matthean sources (M) and, likewise, that Luke made use of written sources not reflected in Mark or Matthew (L). The four-source hypothesis—encompassing Mark, Q, M, and L—offers the most complete explanation for why the Synoptic Gospels contain so much overlapping material and also how each of these three Gospels offers distinctive materials.

The following chart summarizes the four-source hypothesis:

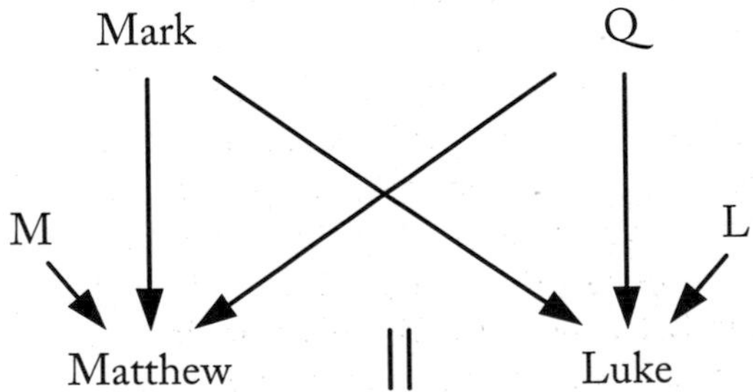

Why Are Only Three of the Gospels "Synoptic"? The Synoptics and John

One thing that this short introduction to the NT will not attempt to resolve is the relation of the Fourth Gospel to the Synoptics. Scholars are not of one mind on this issue. If one posits that John borrowed from one or more of the Synoptic Gospels, it is necessary to explain why this author offers such a different characterization of Jesus, as compared with those in the Synoptics. On the other hand, maintaining the independence of John vis-à-vis the Synoptics runs into the difficulty of explaining points where John overlaps with the Synoptics. Examples of similar gospel materials in John and one or more of the Synoptics include Jesus' feeding of the five thousand (John 6:1–14; Mark 6:30–44); the healing of a Roman official's son (John 4:46–53; compare the healing of the centurion's child or slave in Q/Luke 7:1–10 and its parallel in Q/Matt 8:5–13); and especially numerous parts of the passion of Jesus in John 18–19. Whereas nearly all scholars study the Synoptics within the framework of Markan priority and a strong majority accept the "Q" hypothesis, there is as yet no consensus concerning a possible literary relationship between the Synoptics and John.

KEEPING IN TOUCH: EARLY CHRISTIAN LETTERS

This chapter's third and final section focuses primarily on early Christian letters. We will present this section in two parts. Part 1 will consist of the following:

1. Some principles for reading an early Christian letter
2. Applying these principles to the Apostle Paul's letter to the Galatians

Building on the discussion of Galatians, in part 2 we will consider:

1. How the book of Acts depicts Paul's opponents and the unity of the church
2. Understandings of faith and works in Paul and two other NT authors
3. Three NT authors' perspectives on living as a Christian within the Roman Empire

Part 1: Principles of Interpretation

Principles for Reading Early Christian Letters

Think about the last time you received a letter. Was it from a parent, a boyfriend or girlfriend, a friend from high school, or someone else? What prompted the person to write to you at this particular point in time? The following are questions you ask intuitively when a letter (or some other form of communication, such as an e-mail or an instant message) arrives:

a) Author: Who wrote it? What do I know about this person that will help me understand his or her communication?
b) Audience: To whom did they write? What is my relationship to the author? Is this a personal letter to me or an advertisement, mass mailing, or "spam" email that others receive as well?
c) Opponents: What persons, practices, or beliefs does the author oppose? (In the case of a NT letter, you will want to know whether the author's opponents are non-Christian Jews, Greco-Roman polytheists, or Christians with a different theology or understanding of Jesus.)
d) Purpose (Occasion): What led the author(s) to write this letter to me (us) now? What response does the author encourage or expect from me?

You can learn much about the twenty-one NT letters—and, indeed, all of the NT writings—by studying them with these questions in mind. Before you read further, let me invite you to read the NT book of Galatians, which is one of the Apostle Paul's undisputed letters. Make a list of what Galatians reveals about its author, audience, and occasion (purpose), as well as Paul's opponents. After you have done this for Galatians, you can pose the questions outlined in this section to other NT letters. The following paragraphs offer a few remarks concerning each of these four areas in Galatians.

Application of Principles

Paul the Author. As was standard practice in ancient Greek letters, Paul's letter to Christians living in Galatia, territory in what is now Turkey, begins by identifying its author: "Paul an apostle—sent neither by human commission nor from human authorities, but through Jesus Christ and God the Father, who raised him from the dead—and all the members of God's family who are with me" (Gal 1:1–2). In this letter's opening statement, Paul assumes his authority as an apostle sent by God. Later in Galatians, we will learn that Paul's Christian opponents disputed whether God had in fact commissioned Paul to proclaim the good news to the Gentiles.

Paul also recalls an earlier time in his life when his zealousness for his Jewish faith led him to persecute the church:

> You have heard, no doubt, of my earlier life in Judaism. I was violently persecuting the church of God and was trying to destroy it. I advanced in Judaism beyond many among my people of the same age, for I was far more zealous for the traditions of my ancestors. But when God, who had set me apart before I was born and

> called me through his grace, was pleased to reveal his Son to me, so that I might proclaim him among the Gentiles, I did not confer with any human being, nor did I go up to Jerusalem to those who were already apostles before me, but I went away at once into Arabia, and afterwards I returned to Damascus. (Gal 1:13–17)

Paul was not one of Jesus' original twelve disciples (cf. Acts 7:57–8:1; 9:1–31; 22:1–21; 26:2–23). Scholars today debate whether Paul's first encounter with the risen Jesus represents a particular "calling" within Paul's Jewish faith or a "conversion" to a different religion. This question is part of a larger debate about when Judaism and Christianity became separately defined religions.

Later in this letter, Paul recalls that he was the one who led the Galatians to faith in Jesus and that they received God's Spirit and beheld miracles that Paul performed when they came to believe (Gal 3:1–5). From Galatians and Paul's other letters, we also learn something about Paul's ministry as a traveling evangelist. Paul used letters as a way to stay in touch and address problems in those congregations he was not able to visit as often as he may have wished.

Galatian Audience. Throughout this letter, Paul expresses concern that the Christians in Galatia have rejected—or are about to reject—the good news (gospel) that Paul had earlier proclaimed to them:

> I am astonished that you are so quickly deserting the one who called you in the grace of Christ and are turning to a different gospel—not that there is another gospel, but there are some who are confusing you and want to pervert the gospel of Christ. (Gal 1:6–7)

In particular, Paul worries that the Galatians may have believed that becoming circumcised was required for all male converts to Christianity. Although circumcision for men was prescribed in the Jewish Law (Torah) and common in Judaism and in several other cultures in the ancient Near East, the practice was quite unpopular in Greco-Roman society. At the time Paul wrote Galatians, his Greco-Roman audience appears to have been pulled in three different directions: Should they continue to affirm Paul's teaching; embrace a different version of the good news from other Christian missionaries, including circumcision; or return to their former polytheistic religion(s)? In the following passage, Paul reflects concern about the last of these possible reactions:

> Formerly, when you did not know God, you were enslaved to beings that by nature are not gods. Now, however, that you have come to know God, or rather to be known by God, how can you turn back again to the weak and beggarly elemental spirits? How can you want to be enslaved to them again? You are observing special days, and months, and seasons, and years. I am afraid that my work for you may have been wasted. (Gal 4:8–11)

Elsewhere in this letter, Paul uses the metaphor of a mother's pain in childbirth to describe his anguish and concern for this congregation's spiritual well-being (Gal 4:19–20).

Paul's Christian Opponents. Early in this letter, Paul offers the hypocrisy of the Apostle Peter, referred to as Cephas, as an example of his current opponents' untenable theology:

> But when Cephas came to Antioch, I opposed him to his face, because he stood self-condemned; for until certain people came from James, he used to eat with the Gentiles. But after they came, he drew back and kept himself separate for fear of the circumcision faction. And the other Jews joined him in this hypocrisy, so that even Barnabas was led astray by their hypocrisy. But when I saw that they were not acting consistently with the truth of

> the gospel, I said to Cephas before them all, "If you, though a Jew, live like a Gentile and not like a Jew, how can you compel the Gentiles to live like Jews?" (Gal 2:11–14)

In Paul's theology, there is only one people of God made up of Jews and Gentiles, whether circumcised or uncircumcised, men or women, enslaved or free (Gal 3:27–28).

Yet the early church included some followers of Jesus who believed that the covenant of circumcision given to the patriarch Abraham in Genesis 17 had created divisions in humanity—divisions that remained even after the time of Jesus. In Galatians, Paul claims that those who embraced this position and, accordingly, opposed his theology included the Apostle Peter and James (Jesus' brother, not an apostle and mentioned in Mark 6:3). It is important to underscore that Galatians reflects an *intra-Christian* debate over the relationship of the good news of Jesus Christ to the OT. From this letter, we do not learn about a conflict between Christianity and Judaism. Instead, we see sincere followers of Jesus with different understandings struggling to work out important theological positions some twenty years after the death of Jesus. Such conversations continue in the Church today as well, for example, on matters like euthanasia, abortion, divorce, sexuality, women, and money.

Purpose (Occasion). Now that we understand something about the author, audience, and opponents in Galatians, Paul's purpose for writing this letter to this particular congregation at this point in time becomes clear: Paul responds to the theology of his Christian opponents in an effort to reassure the Galatians of the legitimacy of their belief in the good news (gospel) that Paul had proclaimed to them. It is easy to understand why Paul's tone is so urgent in this letter. Rival Christian missionaries had come to Galatia, undermined Paul's authority, and challenged certain aspects of Paul's theology, including the notion that God accepts people because of their faith, or belief, in Jesus regardless of whether they keep the Mosaic Law (including, for men, circumcision). Paul's opponents would have agreed with him concerning the importance of faith in Jesus but responded that faith should lead Jesus' followers to respect the continued validity of the covenant of circumcision that the Lord made with Abraham in Genesis. Paul's opponents would likely have found common ground with the author of Matthew, who you will recall assumes that followers of Jesus will keep the Law (Matt 5:17–20; 28:19–20).

Part 2: Placing Paul in Conversation

Acts of the Apostles: Paul's Opponents and the Unity of the Church

The preceding pages have examined Paul's letter to the Galatians and given attention to what this letter reveals about its author, audience, occasion, and opponents. The remaining sections of this chapter build on this discussion of Galatians by examining three related topics. These are (1) Paul's opponents and the unity of the church in Acts; (2) understandings of faith and works in the NT letters of Ephesians and James; and (3) the Christian as a part of the Roman Empire, according to Paul's letter to the church at Rome, the epistle of 1 Peter, and the Revelation of John. Giving attention to these three topics helps us to see to what extent these theological discussions, like the matter of circumcision, remained living and unresolved issues in the early church during, and after, the time of Paul.

Although in Galatians Paul identifies his opponents as rival Christian leaders, another early Christian author would portray differently this same crisis over circumcision. Writing several decades (or more) after Paul, the author of Luke-Acts presents Paul's primary opponents not as church leaders but as non-Christian Jews. Luke's selective history of the early church, the Acts of the Apostles, characterizes Jewish antagonists to the Pauline mission as follows:

> But when the Jews saw the crowds, they were filled with jealousy; and blaspheming, they contradicted what was spoken by Paul. . . . Thus the word of the Lord spread throughout the region. But the Jews incited the devout women of high standing and the leading men of the city, and stirred up persecution against Paul and Barnabas, and drove them out of their region. So they shook the dust off their feet in protest against them, and went to Iconium. (Acts 13:45, 49–51)

You can find additional allegations of persecution of the Pauline mission by Jews in Acts 17:5–7,13; 18:12–17; 21:27–28; 23:12–15; 24:1–2; 25:2b–5. In contrast to Galatians, the Acts of the Apostles never mentions that Paul had to defend himself against the accusations of Christian opponents, let alone rival Christian leaders. Most scholars regard the earlier witness of Paul as the more reliable account.

In the understanding of the author of Acts, the church was unified and dealt with the question of circumcision rather easily. In Acts, it is the Apostle Peter (not Paul) who first converts Gentiles and allows the male converts to remain uncircumcised (Acts 9:32–11:18). When church leaders meet to discuss the matter, James, the Lord's brother, affirms Peter's and Paul's labors among the Gentiles (Acts 15:13–21). How does this picture of a unified, harmonious church compare with Galatians 2:11–14, where Paul opposes Peter (Cephas) to his face after James had sent spies to Antioch to report on Paul's missionary work among the Gentiles? Such differences between Acts, on the one hand, and Galatians and Paul's other undisputed letters, on the other hand, support the inference that Acts was likely written a generation or two after Paul by an author who had not personally known Paul or read Paul's letters.

The maps shown here chart the journeys of Paul as related in the Acts of the Apostles. While scholars argue that the chronology and details of the journeys as told in Acts are questionable or inaccurate (as will be discussed in the pages that follow), the images shown here provide a visual reference to Luke's telling of the history.

Faith and Works in Paul, Ephesians, and James

In Galatians, Paul responds to his opponents' accusation that not requiring the Mosaic Law (Torah), including circumcision, will lead to lawless conduct by followers of Jesus. The rationale for this accusation seems to be that if the Law is set aside as a guide for human behavior, there will be no limits or absolute ethical requirements governing the Christian life—much like some today believe that if a strict or narrow interpretation of the Bible is not followed (e.g., based on particular scriptures about women's rightful behavior or corporal punishment), our society will go "to hell in a hand basket." In response, Paul offers freedom in Christ as an opportunity to serve one's fellow believers and thereby govern ethical conduct: "For you were called to freedom, brothers and sisters; only do not use your freedom as an opportunity for self-indulgence, but through love become slaves to one another" (Gal 5:13). For Paul, works of the Mosaic Law are entirely unnecessary:

> Yet we know that a person is justified not by the works of the law but through faith in Jesus Christ. And we have come to believe in Christ Jesus, so that we might be justified by faith in Christ, and not by doing the works of the law, because no one will be justified by the works of the law. (Gal 2:16)

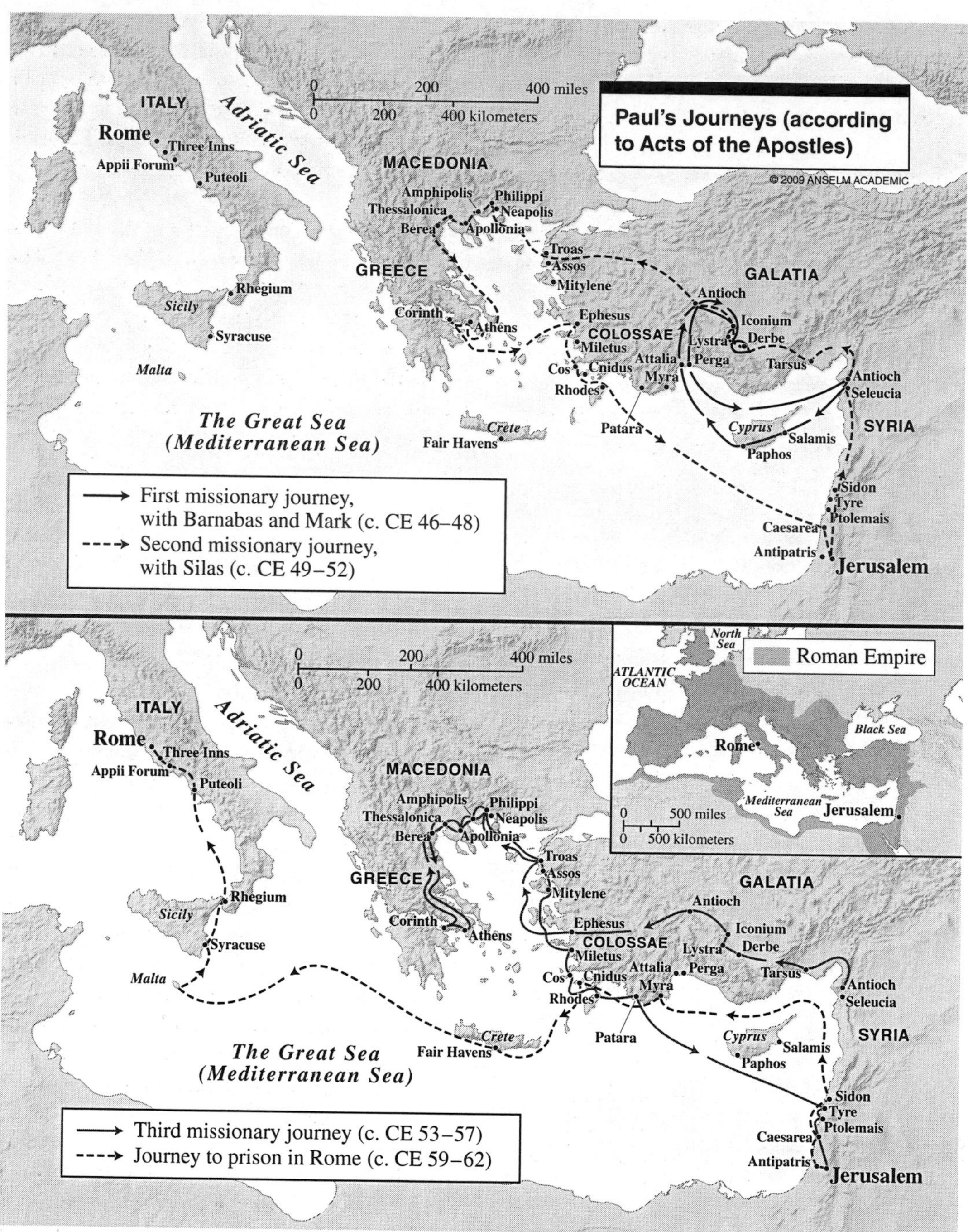

The maps shown here chart the journeys of Paul as related in the Acts of the Apostles. While scholars argue that the chronology and details of the journeys as told in Acts are questionable or inaccurate (as is discussed in this chapter), the images shown here provide a visual reference to Luke's telling of the history.

Another of Paul's undisputed letters, Romans, likewise states: "For we hold that a person is justified by faith apart from works prescribed by the law" (Rom 3:28).

Paul's teachings on faith and works in response to a particular crisis did not put an end to the issue in the early church. The subject comes up, for example, in the letter to the Ephesians. The theology of Ephesians differs at several points from that reflected in the seven undisputed letters of Paul. For this reason, nearly all scholars believe that a later student or admirer of Paul wrote Ephesians. That is why Ephesians is classified among the NT's six deuteropauline letters. An example of the distinctive theology in Ephesians concerns faith and works:

> For by grace you have been saved through faith, and this is not your own doing; it is the gift of God—not the result of works, so that no one may boast. For we are what he [God] has made us, *created in Christ Jesus for good works*, which God prepared beforehand to be our way of life. (Eph 2:8–10, emphasis added)

The Apostle Paul could have agreed with the statement that salvation is God's gift to humanity and is "not the result of works." Yet the notion that believers are "created in Christ Jesus for good works" is not a part of Paul's theological vocabulary in Galatians or the other undisputed Pauline letters. At the time of the Galatian crisis, Paul was too busy confronting works of the Law (Torah) to reflect on the importance of works in general for followers of Jesus.

Another NT letter, James, likewise reflects an interest in faith and works. James is one of the Catholic (meaning "general") Epistles. Different from Ephesians but like Galatians, James reflects a polemical context and criticizes the position of certain other Christians:

> What good is it, my brothers and sisters, if you say you have faith but do not have works? Can faith save you? If a brother or sister is naked and lacks daily food, and one of you says to them, "Go in peace; keep warm and eat your fill," and yet you do not supply their bodily needs, what is the good of that? So faith by itself, if it has no works, is dead. (Jas 2:14–17)

Like Ephesians, the Epistle of James refers to "works" but not specifically to works prescribed in the Mosaic Law. More than anything, James addresses how the faithful should live in a manner consistent with what they believe.

These three early Christian authors—Paul, the author of Ephesians, and the author of James—tell us about conversations and, at times, debates over the relative importance of faith and works in the Christian life. Such conversations are a necessary part of forming any religious community and continue today among Christians and people of other religions.

Living as a Christian within the Roman Empire

The previous section mentioned Paul's concern about the allegation that his theology could lead to lawlessness or immorality (Gal 5:13). In his later letter to the church at Rome, Paul again addresses this concern:

> I appeal to you therefore, brothers and sisters, by the mercies of God, to present your bodies as a living sacrifice, holy and acceptable to God, which is your spiritual worship. Do not be conformed to this world, but be transformed by the renewing of your minds, so that you may discern what is the will of God—what is good and acceptable and perfect. (Rom 12:1–2)

The metaphor of a "living sacrifice" envisions believers who voluntarily limit their freedom because they have received God's mercy and now wish to offer themselves to God's service. In the following chapter of this letter, Paul expands upon this teaching about the believer's ethical conduct to include principles for living within the (totalitarian) Roman Empire:

> Let every person be subject to the governing authorities; for there is no authority except from God, and those authorities that exist have been instituted by God. Therefore whoever resists authority resists what God has appointed, and those who resist will incur judgment. For rulers are not a terror to good conduct, but to bad. Do you wish to have no fear of the authority? Then do what is good, and you will receive its approval; for it is God's servant for your good. . . . Pay to all what is due them—taxes to whom taxes are due, revenue to whom revenue is due, respect to whom respect is due, honor to whom honor is due. (Rom 13:1–4a, 7)

Likewise, 1 Peter, one of the Catholic Epistles, offers a similar exhortation to live as peaceful citizens under the authority of Rome:

> For the Lord's sake accept the authority of every human institution, whether of the emperor as supreme, or of governors, as sent by him to punish those who do wrong and to praise those who do right. For it is God's will that by doing right you should silence the ignorance of the foolish. As servants of God, live as free people, yet do not use your freedom as a pretext for evil. Honor everyone. Love the family of believers. Fear God. Honor the emperor. (1 Pet 2:13–17)

According to Paul and the author of 1 Peter, then, Christians are expected to make every effort to live within the constraints of the Roman Empire. Both authors maintain that the faithful must seek to live within that society without conforming to it.

By contrast, the NT's only apocalypse, the Revelation of John, views Rome as fundamentally hostile to the people of God:

> I saw a woman sitting on a scarlet beast that was full of blasphemous names, and it had seven heads and ten horns. The woman was clothed in purple and scarlet, and adorned with gold and jewels and pearls, holding in her hand a golden cup full of abominations and the impurities of her fornication; and on her forehead was written a name, a mystery: "Babylon the great, mother of whores and of earth's abominations." And I saw that the woman was drunk with the blood of the saints and the blood of the witnesses to Jesus. (Rev 17:3–6)

John thus identifies Rome with Babylon, the enemy of the ancient Israelites. Interestingly, the author of 1 Peter can likewise refer to Rome as "Babylon" (1 Pet 5:13) without expressing alarm about the danger that, according to Revelation, Rome poses to the church.

Cultural and other differences have led sincere believers to variant experiences within a particular society. Such was clearly the case for Paul and the author of 1 Peter, who accepted life within Roman society, and the author of Revelation, who viewed Rome as fundamentally corrupt and looked forward to the time of her downfall (Rev 18:1–3). In the centuries following these writings, numerous Christian authors attempted to address what it meant to live within Roman society, which at times could be hostile toward the church. Following the rise of the first Christian emperor Constantine in the early fourth century, the question would have to be redefined to consider whether the Empire, now led by a Christian emperor, was too friendly toward certain expressions of Christianity and too severe toward others, not to mention Jews and polytheists as well.

SUMMARY

In this chapter, we have learned that early Christians wrote historical narratives about Jesus (gospels) and the early church, apocalypses, and letters. Twenty-seven of these writings, composed between approximately 50 CE and 120 CE, came to be included in the NT. The NT is written in Koine Greek, which was the common language in most cities in the eastern parts of the Mediterranean after the conquests of Alexander the Great. Each of the four NT Gospels presents a distinctive picture of Jesus. One reason for the differences among these Gospels is that their authors borrowed from various oral and written traditions and wrote decades after the crucifixion.

Twenty-one of the NT writings are letters. When reading an early Christian letter, it is helpful to ask what the letter reveals about the author, audience, opponents, and purpose. Despite their many points of agreement, the NT writings also highlight differences and even divisions in the early church on matters such as circumcision, the relative unity of the earliest church, the importance of faith and works, and living as a Christian within the Roman Empire.

Questions about the Text

1. How many writings are there in the NT? What are the three main literary categories?
2. What are the two classifications for the authorship of the Pauline letters, and why are there two?
3. What are the main themes in Mark's Gospel? In Matthew's? In Luke's? In John's? Why are they important?
4. What is the "Synoptic Problem"? Describe the hypotheses used by most scripture scholars to explain it.
5. What are the four principles for reading an early Christian letter? Why are they important to follow?
6. What is the tension between faith and good works in Paul and other NT authors? How do you evaluate this tension today?

Questions for Discussion

1. Why does it or does it not make sense to refer to the NT as a single "book"? How might the metaphor of the NT as a library of much of the earliest surviving early Christian literature be more helpful and accurate?
2. Scholars today debate whether Paul's encounter with the risen Jesus represents a particular "calling" within Paul's Jewish faith or a "conversion" from Judaism to a different religion. What do you think? If you have had religious experiences, do you generally regard them as more of a calling or a conversion? Or have you experienced elements of both?
3. Galatians and Acts offer two different pictures of the early church—one divided and the other unified. If you grew up in the church (or some other religious community), which of these resonates with your experience of your religious community?
4. How important is faith to your understanding of God? How important are works as an expression of your faith?
5. Romans 13 and 1 Peter 2 instruct the early Christians to submit to the governing Roman authorities. Can you think of a time when you would be unwilling to submit to your government? Can you think of any circumstances under which you would agree with the Revelation of John and characterize a totalitarian regime as worthy of God's judgment and destruction? What happens when Christians today have different views about how to respond to the policies of a particular government?

For Further Study

Ehrman, Bart D. *The New Testament: A Historical Introduction to the Early Christian Writings*. 4th ed. New York: Oxford University Press, 2008.

This book provides an excellent introduction to the NT and some two dozen other early Christian writings.

Holmes, Michael W., ed. *The Apostolic Fathers*. Grand Rapids, MI: Baker, 1989.

This affordable volume offers short introductions and English translations of fifteen of the earliest extracanonical Christian writings, known today as the "Apostolic Fathers" (*Barnabas*; the *Didache*; the seven letters of Ignatius of Antioch; Polycarp, *To the Philippians*; the *Martyrdom of Polycarp*; *1 Clement*; *2 Clement*; the *Shepherd* of Hermas; and *Diognetus*).

Jefford, Clayton N. *Reading the Apostolic Fathers: An Introduction*. Peabody, MA: Hendrickson, 1996.

This volume offers helpful chapter-long introductions to the Apostolic Fathers.

Koester, Craig R. *Revelation and the End of All Things*. Grand Rapids, MI: Eerdmans, 2001.

In providing commentary on the NT's apocalypse, the Revelation of John, this author engages certain popular contemporary approaches to Bible prophecy and interpretations of apocalyptic literature, such as in the *Left Behind* novels.

Powell, Mark Allan. *Fortress Introduction to the Gospels*. Minneapolis, MN: Fortress, 1998.

This text includes chapters on the historical Jesus and the origins of written gospels, the four NT Gospels, and other early Christian gospels.

Roetzel, Calvin. *The Letters of Paul: Conversations in Context*. 4th ed. Louisville, KY: Westminster John Knox, 1998.

This is a survey of the Apostle Paul's Hellenistic and Jewish cultural contexts, the thirteen NT letters attributed to Paul, and models of interpreting Paul's theology, legacy, and significance.

from the REFERENCE LIBRARIAN

Researching Bible Topics—New Testament

As you continue to develop your research skills from the foundation of chapter 1, remember the basic starting point and Skill Key #1 to unlock research:

SKILL KEY #1

Use the library's reference collection to begin your research.

a) Use a subject-specific encyclopedia to acquire specialized knowledge about a subject.
b) Use a subject-specific encyclopedia whose scope is appropriate for both your topic and the approach you want to take to that topic.

What reference tools are available for studying the New Testament?

Many of the reference tools mentioned in the library research section at the end of the previous chapter, such as the *Anchor Bible Dictionary* and *The New Interpreter's Dictionary of the Bible*, can be used for researching NT topics since they cover the entire Bible, both Old and New Testaments. However, several reference tools are devoted entirely to the NT, including:

Craig A. Evans and Stanley E. Porter, eds. *Dictionary of New Testament Background*. Downers Grove, IL: InterVarsity Press, 2000.

Joel B. Green and Scot McKnight, eds. *Dictionary of Jesus and the Gospels*. Downers Grove, IL: InterVarsity Press, 1992.

Gerald F. Hawthorne and Ralph P. Martin, eds. *Dictionary of Paul and his Letters*. Downers Grove, IL: InterVarsity Press, 1993.

Ralph P. Martin and Peter H. Davids, eds. *Dictionary of the Later New Testament and Its Developments*. Downers Grove, IL: InterVarsity Press, 1997.

The first three titles focus on specific NT writings: the four Gospels, the Pauline Epistles (including the deuteropauline letters), and the remaining writings of the NT. These volumes contain articles on each of the NT writings covered as well as important theological topics (e.g. "kingdom of God," "messianic secret," "eschatology") raised by the content of those writings. The fourth title in the list is not tied to particular writings of the NT but is "concerned with archaeology, geography, historical figures, political institutions, historical events, peoples and culture."

Another type of reference tool commonly used in Scripture study is a concordance. A concordance lists all the occurrences of a particular word in the order in which they appear in the Bible. For example, if you are interested in the use of the word *hope*, you might encounter a list such as the following one (here abbreviated) in a concordance.

HOPE‡ (187) [HOPED, HOPEFUL. HOPELESS, HOPES, HOPING]

Ru	1:12	Even if I thought there was **h** for me.
2Ki	6:33	Why should I **h** in the LORD any longer?
1Ch	29:15	on the earth are like a shadow, and there is no **h**.
Ezr	10:2	but even now there is **h** for Israel in spite of this.
Job	3:9	let it **h** for light, but have none;
	4:6	and the integrity of your ways your **h**?
	5:16	So the poor have **h**, and injustice shuts its mouth.

(From *NRSV Concordance Unabridged*, ed. Kohlenberger, Grand Rapids, MI: Zondervan, 1991.)

Note that you may need to take alternate forms of a word into consideration (hoped, hopeful, etc.); some are listed at the beginning of the list, but not all concordances do this. Also, make sure that you use a concordance that matches the English version of the Bible you are using (the reference librarian can help you find the right concordance). This is because different English translations may use different English words to translate the same Hebrew or Greek word.

Refining the use of Library of Congress subject headings

The second key element of using the library is this:

SKILL KEY #2

Use the library's catalog to locate sources of information.

a) Use subject headings to locate precisely books on your topic.

continued

continued

b) Use subject headings whose scope fits your topic as closely as possible, then adjust your search with a broader or narrower subject heading as necessary.

In the previous chapter, you learned that subject headings for OT books follow a particular format: Bible O T [name of book]. Subject headings for NT books follow the same format, but "N T" is used (for "New Testament") in place of "O T" as the "root" of the subject heading. (Again, make sure to put a space between the "N" and the "T.")

Search format:

Subject heading "root"	*Subdivision*
Bible NT	[name of book]
Bible NT	Matthew
Bible NT	Romans
Bible NT	Corinthians 1st

These are very broad subject headings and, in fact, may be too broad for the particular topic you want to pursue. Remember, you want to use subject headings to locate precisely books on your topic. One way of focusing a subject search more precisely is by adding subdivisions to the basic "root" subject heading for any particular biblical book (this applies to OT books also). Two of these additional subdivisions are standard and often useful. Examine the following subject headings that include the subdivisions "Criticism, interpretation, etc." or "Commentaries."

Search format:

Subject heading "root"	*Subdivision 1*	*Subdivision 2*
Bible N T	Matthew	Criticism, interpretation, etc
Bible N T	Matthew	Commentaries
Bible O T	Genesis	Criticism, interpretation, etc
Bible O T	Samuel 1st	Commentaries

Let's explore what these headings mean, beginning with the "Criticism, interpretation, etc." addition to the Library of Congress subject heading root. Look at the following catalog record in which the subject heading "Bible NT Matthew—Criticism, interpretation, etc." appears. Note that "Sermon on the Mount" has been assigned as an additional subject heading because that is the aspect of "criticism, interpretation, etc." on which this particular book focuses. If you are interested in the Sermon on the Mount in particular, you have an additional subject heading by which to refine your research.

Author	Weber, Gerard P., 1918–
Title	*Breaking open the gospel of Matthew: the Sermon on the Mount / Gerard P. Weber and Robert L. Miller.*
Published	Cincinnati, Ohio : St. Anthony Messenger Press, c1998.
Subjects	Bible. NT Matthew—Criticism, interpretation, etc. Sermon on the mount.

Here is another example.

Author	Brown, Jeannine K., 1961–
Title	*The Disciples in narrative perspective: the portrayal and function of the Matthean Disciples / Jeannine K. Brown.*
Published	Atlanta, GA : Society of Biblical Literature, c2002..
Subjects	Jesus Christ—Disciples. Bible. NT Matthew—Criticism, interpretation, etc. Apostles.

Because this book focuses on the disciples in Matthew, the book has been given two subject headings to indicate this—"Jesus Christ—Disciples" and "Apostles." If you are interested in the portrayal of the disciples in Matthew (and Matthew alone), you now know that you can search for similar books by combining these two subject headings in one search. (How would you search for a book on the portrayal of the disciples in the Gospel of Mark?)

Here is a final example. This book covers the topic of salvation in the Gospel of Matthew, as noted in the subject heading. (How would you search for a book on salvation in the Gospel of John?)

Author	Luomanen, Petri, 1961–
Title	*Entering the kingdom of heaven: a study on the structure of Matthew's view of salvation / Petri Luomanen.*
Published	Tübingen : Mohr Siebeck, c1998.
Subjects	Bible. NT Matthew—Criticism, interpretation, etc. Salvation—Biblical teaching.

You can see that the subject heading "Bible NT Matthew—Criticism, interpretation, etc." encompasses a variety of topics related to the Gospel of Matthew, including specific themes (the disciples, salvation) or a specific passage (Sermon on the Mount in Matthew 5–7). Using the subdivision "Criticism, interpretation, etc." allows you to view a variety of topics related to the biblical book you want to study and to identify more precise subject headings, which you can then use alone or in combination with the "criticism, interpretation, etc." heading.

The other subdivision mentioned is "Commentaries," and it refers to a specific format. Commentaries on Scripture are simply explanations of the meaning of the biblical text that follow the order of the text, beginning with chapter 1, verse 1 and proceeding to the last verse of the last chapter. This type of book is useful for studying specific passages or even individual verses within a book.

Commentaries come in all varieties. Some are aimed at a popular audience, some are aimed at biblical scholars (and require a knowledge of ancient languages such as Greek or Hebrew), and others fall somewhere in between. You will probably have to look at a particular commentary to determine whether you can use it.

One kind of commentary that is often very useful, especially for undergraduates, is called a "one-volume commentary." This simply means that commentaries on all of the books of the Bible are contained in one volume. Such commentaries are, obviously, not as detailed as an entire commentary written on just one book—but for that very reason they are less technical and easier for nonspecialists to use. The following one-volume commentary was produced by Roman Catholic biblical scholars, but your library may own several others that are just as useful.

The New Jerome Biblical Commentary. Englewood Cliffs, NJ: Prentice Hall, 1990.

Unlike most one-volume commentaries produced by Protestant scholars, this volume also contains a commentary on the deuterocanonical books. (What does *deuterocanonical* mean? How can you find out?)

Another type of subject search is a search for books on a specific person, an individual mentioned in the Bible. The format usually followed when searching for persons as subjects is the same as that used when searching for persons as authors, "last name, first name." However, since persons mentioned in the Bible do not have "last names," at least not in the usual sense, a descriptive phrase, as illustrated by the examples for both Old and New Testament persons that follow, is often added to the name to make clear to whom the search is referring.

Search format:

Name	*Descriptive phrase(s)*
Abraham	Biblical patriarch
Moses	Biblical leader
Isaiah	Biblical prophet
Saul	King of Israel
Matthew	The apostle, Saint
Luke	Saint
Paul	The apostle, Saint

By now, you should have a good grasp of the basics of library research, including using the reference collection both to obtain basic information about your topic and as a way to lead you into the rest of the library collection. You should also understand how using subject headings in the library catalog enables you to search with precision for books in your library. In subsequent chapters, we will further elaborate on these techniques.

Student Tasks

For each of the following tasks, look for books published within the last fifty years.

1. Go to your library and locate a dictionary of the NT.
2. Select a book from the NT and use the correct form of subject heading to search your library catalog for books about it.
3. Find a commentary on the book you have selected.
   Format = Bible NT [name of book] Commentaries
4. Find a book that deals with a particular topic or aspect of the NT writing.
   Format = Bible NT [name of book] Criticism, interpretation, etc.
5. Find books about a person in the NT, using the Library of Congress format: [Name Descriptive phrase]. What subdivisions appear with the subject heading for that person?

CHRISTOLOGY AND ECCLESIOLOGY: FOLLOWING CHRIST IN A COMMUNITY OF THE HOLY SPIRIT

Christology—"Who Do You Say That I Am?"

Brian D. Robinette

from the EDITOR

To confirm our identity, we are often asked for photo identification, typically a driver's license. I have yet to come across anyone who likes his or her photo. One reason is that the camera takes a three-dimensional image and changes it to two dimensions, which distorts and flattens the real person. Successful painters and film and television directors and cinematographers, among others, learn to convincingly communicate through flat, two-dimensional mediums. A second reason for not liking the ID photo is that it says nothing really important about *who* the person is. If I know the person, I might cite as most important that she is lovable and loving, generous, thoughtful, and kind; has a great sense of humor; is sensitive, caring, peace-filled, honest, intelligent, insightful, and dedicated—a wonderfully unique individual.

The same can be said about Jesus the Christ. Though one cannot sit down with Jesus and learn from him in person because time and history create distance, "flattening" Jesus like a photo, one can draw upon a great deal of material about him in the Bible. This material comes from those who knew him, followed him, and experienced him; it tells of those who met him and whose plans changed radically after encountering him.

Theology tries to "thicken" or flesh out these sources and resources, allowing one the knowledge and freedom to encounter this same Jesus of Nazareth today. This has been part of the legacy of Christianity from the start: people asking questions in order to deepen their faith, or as Anselm might say, practicing "faith seeking understanding." Christology is at the heart of finding the answer to the identity question: Who is Jesus? This chapter examines three sources to thicken that understanding of who this Jesus really is and how he was perceived by others in his time and history. It begins with the source of that knowing, which is a narrative or story, and explores its purpose of telling something Christianity considers crucially important, namely Jesus' call to salvation in God.

THE QUESTION

In a turning point in his ministry, Jesus asks his disciples a question that seems innocent enough yet has remained the fundamental question for Christology ever since. Jesus and his ministry had developed quite a reputation by this point. He had numerous followers, both near and far, and perhaps just as many enemies. The question probably seemed a matter of information gathering, an attempt to discern the "beat on the street": "Who do people say that I am?" (Mark 8:27). Jesus' disciples reply with a variety of answers: some say "John the Baptist; and others, Elijah; and still others, one of the prophets" (8:28). Jesus follows up with a more pointed and personal question, one that, like many of his questions, discloses not only something fundamental about himself but also something fundamental about the one whom he addresses: "But who do *you* say that I am?" (8:29a, emphasis added).

Peter ventures a reply that seems to represent the thought of the gathered disciples: "You are the Messiah" (Mark 8:29b). Peter seems to know quite well the meaning of his statement. Jesus is the "anointed one" of Israel (derived from the Hebrew *meshiah*), the one who will deliver God's covenanted people from exile and bondage, the one elected by God to finally reestablish the unity and independence of Israel from Roman imperial domination, a leader like King David, who, 1,000 years earlier, was also hailed as God's "anointed one" for his legendary religious, political, and military leadership. But Jesus never confirms Peter's reply. Imagine the disciples' surprise, then, as Jesus tells them not to tell anyone about him. Imagine their puzzled looks as he proceeds to tell them that the "Son of Man" will suffer and be rejected by Israel's leaders, that he will be killed and rise after three days. No wonder Peter "took him aside and began to rebuke him" (8:32b). How could Jesus possibly be Israel's messiah if he was to endure rejection and humiliation? What kind of bizarre liberation could come from such demonstrable defeat? Indeed, what has messiahship to do with suffering and death? Now imagine the disciples' shock when Jesus responds to Peter's rebuke with his own: "Get behind me, Satan! For you are setting your mind not on divine things but on human things" (8:33b).

Christology begins with a question—"Who do you say that I am?"—and is the attempt to answer the question of Jesus' ultimate identity and purpose. In more precise terms, Christology is the systematic study of Jesus of Nazareth, the one called the "Christ" (*christos* is Greek for the Hebrew *meshiah*): his mission and person, his relationship to God, his ultimate significance for humanity. As the story in Mark's Gospel so poignantly reveals, thinking Christologically often challenges our assumptions. It requires attention to paradox and surprise. The fact that one no less than Peter, Jesus' closest disciple and leader of the primitive Christian movement, could get it wrong (while getting it right) indicates the challenge before us. For Peter was correct: Jesus is the messiah, the "anointed one" of God, but *not* in the way Peter and so many of his contemporaries imagined the messiah to be. Like the blind man who is healed just before this startling exchange (Mark 8:22–26), Peter is blind to Jesus' true messianic mission. In fact, Jesus regards Peter's vision as a dangerous illusion and temptation, hence the strong rebuke. What Jesus wants Peter and his disciples to "see" is a reversal of assumptions and values: "For those who want to save their life will lose it, and those who lose their life for my sake, and for the sake of the gospel, will save it" (8:35).

In this chapter, we shall learn to think Christologically and to discover how the story of Jesus' life, death, and Resurrection provides the basic theological framework for understanding his identity and mission. We will begin by examining the life-story of Jesus of Nazareth and how, in light of their powerful Easter experiences, the disciples and other early Christians began a process of interpreting that story in daring theological terms. We shall also explore how the later Christological doctrines, or official teachings of the church, particularly those of the fourth and fifth centuries CE, continue to provide indispensable "grammatical rules" to assist Christians as they speak about Jesus, his relationship to God, and his significance for humanity. Throughout our study, we shall identify three touchstones that structure all Christological reflection:

1. All Christology derives from *story*.
2. All Christology is rooted in an experience of *salvation*.
3. All Christology springs from the conviction that in Jesus Christ the *presence of God* has been revealed and has taken hold of the world in an unprecedented way.

THE STORY BEGINS: JESUS OF NAZARETH AND THE KINGDOM OF GOD

Election and Eschatology

Jesus was a storyteller. He told fantastic stories, strange stories, stories that liberated and enlightened, stories that confused and upset. As a first-century Palestinian Jew living in a storytelling culture, Jesus lived by stories. Most of all, he lived (and died) by Israel's primary narrative.

As we have seen in the previous chapters, the people of Israel told and retold the story of exodus and the covenant. Their self-understanding was shaped by a faith that God had acted decisively in history to liberate their Hebrew ancestors from slavery and Egyptian imperial domination, establishing them as a free people now beholden to their liberator God in mutual fidelity. As God promised to love and protect the Hebrew people, so they promised proper worship and ethical activity as codified in the Law (Torah). Freedom *from* slavery and bondage (exodus) implied a freedom *for* a committed community of faith and justice (the covenant). Throughout their subsequent history, from the time of the united kingdom under kings Saul, David, and Solomon (1022–922 BCE) to the time of devastation and exile during the Babylonian period (587–537 BCE), the people of Israel, and especially the prophets, viewed their fortunes as tied to their faithfulness to the covenant. In times of crisis, the prophets proclaimed messages of grief, judgment, and conversion, calling upon their people and leaders to return to the covenant with God in order to avert disaster. Often, the prophets cited social and economic injustices as reasons for their internal hardships and vulnerabilities to outside forces, for example, the Assyrians, the Babylonians, and, during Jesus' time, the Romans. And often, with their messages of judgment and radical critique came messages of hope for a future when God, just as in the time of exodus, would bring an end to all that afflicted them.

If we are to understand how the larger pattern and the individual stories of Jesus' life make sense, we must see them as reflecting this broader historical and narrative context. There are two structural features about this context. The first is a theology of election. The people of Israel, including Jesus, resolutely believed that God had a unique destiny for them, a belief that in and through their specific history as a people, God's character was revealed and the original purposes for humanity disclosed. As part of God's covenant with Israel, the people were also God's "elect," marked with a distinctive responsibility to be a "light to the peoples" (Isa 51:4). The second structural feature is a particular theology of history, or what we call "eschatology." *Eschatology* literally means the "study of the last things," that is, the study of history's ultimate future. Jesus passionately believed, as did many of his contemporaries, that God would soon bring about a fulfillment of Israel's history, a decisive resolution to the all-too-present realities of suffering, alienation, brokenness, and oppression. Theirs was an "eschatological imagination"—a worldview that imagined and yearned for a final future fulfillment of creation and history, for human well-being, for lasting peace and justice. The God of life and death, of past, present, and future, would soon bring about a new and final exodus in a way that would not just involve Israel, but because of Israel's special role in salvation history, it would also be a fulfillment for *all* people. It is important that we keep these two aspects in mind, particularly as we consider Jesus' specific focus on the people of Israel in his mission. Unquestionably, his mission is for Israel, but because it is for *Israel*, it is also for all humanity. Election (particularity) and eschatology (universality) go hand in hand.

As one might expect, this eschatological imagination was especially robust during times of historical crisis. During Jesus' time, Israel lived under the oppressive rule of the Romans. The once-independent nation of Israel was occupied by the external and "pagan" forces of an empire that seemed to many Jews very much like the Egyptians who had enslaved their ancestors more than twelve hundred years earlier. While the Romans allowed the Jews to practice their religion, run their Temple, and keep many of their customs, the burdensome taxation, ubiquitous military presence, and overall powerlessness to function as an independent nation with its own king provided more than enough evidence to any Jew that God's deliverance was needed. Consequently, several Jewish groups yearned for, spoke of, and, in some cases, fought for a future in which Israel would be internally healed of religious and social divisions and freed from the external forces of oppression.

For many, these were necessarily linked. For example, there were those who imagined that what Israel needed most of all was an internal reformation and purification so that God would deliver Israel from its enemies. The Pharisees held this view, as did John the Baptist, Jesus' immediate predecessor and mentor, though he differed from the Pharisees in many ways. As the requirements for God's coming rule and solution to Israel's desperate circumstances, John preached total moral conversion and purification, ritually enacted by water baptism. Other groups, such as the Zealots, openly spoke of a military solution, in which Israel would throw off the yoke of oppression by force. Still others, like the Sadducees, the priestly and aristocratic class who ran the Temple in Jerusalem, and who had much at stake in keeping the peace with Rome so that the Temple might continue to function as Israel's religious and symbolic center, tended to maintain the status quo and compromise with Roman authorities. As we shall see, sometimes they actively cooperated with Roman leaders to identify and remove potential threats of religious and political unrest as a matter of security.

As should be clear by now, during Jesus' time there was little distinction between religion and politics. Whereas we tend to separate these terms, in the ancient world, religious practice was rarely a private matter but instead was bound up with all dimensions of human life, including the social, economic, and political. Only if we keep this in mind will we be able to fully grasp why Jesus was so threatening to so many parties, why he was killed, and why his message and ministry continue to be a powerful force for religious and social transformation today. However, we will not understand the particular mission and person of Jesus unless we also understand his historical context, his eschatological imagination, and the way he emerges as a distinctive voice in the diverse landscape of first-century Judaism. Jesus' message of the "kingdom of God" will resonate with all that we have examined thus far, but it will also provide a strikingly different alternative to the solutions just outlined. His is a story with an unexpected twist.

Proclamation of the Kingdom of God

"The time is fulfilled, and the kingdom of God has come near; repent, and believe in the good news" (Mark 1:15). These words in Mark's Gospel inaugurate Jesus' public ministry. We need to examine several features of this bold proclamation to gain a better appreciation of Jesus' mission.

"*The time is fulfilled.*" Jesus' imagination was eschatological, possessed by the singular idea that Israel's story was coming to fulfillment. The future is now; God is doing something new and groundbreaking under our very noses. "*The kingdom of God has come near.*" God's rule is overtaking human history in an unprecedented way to bring about final healing and liberation, that is, "salvation." The kingdom of God is an event that is happening. It is "at hand," in the immediate future, but it is also, in a very real sense, "now." It is both present and future, or as theologians commonly put it, "already and not yet."

If we can keep these two aspects in a state of tension, we will be able to grasp something of the dramatic character of Jesus' stories, actions, and mission. "*Repent, and believe in the good news.*" The coming kingdom of God demands a decision, a reaction—conversion. This call to repentance quite literally means to "turn about-face," to go the opposite direction. Whereas we tend to think of repentance as a matter of apologizing for personal sins, repentance meant for Jesus the changing of one's entire worldview: how one perceives, thinks, speaks, and acts. Jesus is summoning people to a new and radical way of life, one convicted by and committed to the "gospel" or "good news" that God is presently doing and will soon complete.

But what is this "kingdom of God," and what makes it "good news"? While it is the central symbol of his ministry, Jesus never strictly defines the "kingdom of God" in the way one might a philosophical category or scientific principle. The reason for this is at least two-fold. First, the "kingdom of God" is symbolic: it cannot be defined any more than "God" or "love" or "beauty" can be adequately defined. One must use multiple metaphors and analogies to even begin disclosing something of the richness of what is meant. For this reason, Jesus constantly uses stories, and most often parables, to speak of this extraordinary reality. He says, for example, that the kingdom of God is like the tiny mustard seed that grows beyond anyone's imagination to become larger than other bushes. The kingdom of God is a gift and a fullness of God encountering us in ways that may initially seem humble but will eventually exceed our expectations.

Second, the "kingdom of God" for Jesus is not merely an "idea" but a concrete reality that comes about through action, divine and human. It is something that is performed, something to be realized or made real in and through the cooperative activity of God and humanity. Jesus does not merely preach this reality; he lives it, enacts it, and summons others to do likewise, and this is exactly why it is "good news." For in his ministry of physical, spiritual, and social healing, of establishing peace and justice among people, he is seeking to bring about God's ultimate plan of well-being or salvation for humanity. Story alone is capable of capturing something of the dramatic revolutions in human affairs that the kingdom of God would bring about.

But what is "good news" for some may seem challenging and even offensive to others. Jesus' Sermon on the Mount, for example, is a bold proclamation of liberation for the poor and oppressed, for those who are meek, who mourn and hunger, who are merciful and make peace, "for theirs is the kingdom of heaven" (Matt 5:1–7:29). What is presently the situation of despair and alienation for many will soon be flipped upside down and turned inside out. Things are *not* what they are supposed to be, and God is doing something about it, says Jesus.

Along with this emancipatory message comes a message of confrontation and judgment. Those who maintain social and religious distinctions of "insider" and "outsider," and those who stand to benefit from the way things are—the privileged, the elite, the powerful, and the persecutors—stand under judgment and a call to total conversion. It is perfectly understandable that Jesus' ministry attracted just as many enemies as it did followers. His was a polarizing ministry in many ways, though he ultimately sought reconciliation between groups of people who stood in opposition to each other as part of a religious, social, and political system binding them in interminable conflict. One of Jesus' best-known parables (the Good Samaritan) illustrates the point.

Asked by a scholar of the law what he must do to inherit eternal life, Jesus in turn asks the scholar to summarize the law. The scholar responds, "You shall love the Lord your God with all your heart, and with all your soul, and with all your strength, and with all your mind, and your neighbor as yourself" (Luke 10:27). Jesus responds, "You have given the right answer; do this, and you will live" (v. 28). Apparently unsatisfied, the scholar further pursues the question and asks Jesus, "And who is my neighbor?" (v. 29). With this question, Jesus has the opportunity to drive his point home. The question about "neighbor" has everything to do with the kingdom of God, so Jesus tells a story that begins quite conventionally. (Parables often begin with an ordinary scene, only to suddenly explode into paradox and surprise.)

A man falls victim to robbers and is left half-dead. A priest happens to be walking by. Here we might expect the priest to do something magnanimous. A priest is surely our model of holiness, but the priest passes by on the opposite side, as does the Levite after him. (Levites were subordinate Temple officials.) At this point in the story, the listener might actually suspend judgment about this ostensible breach of justice because the priest and Levite were required by the law not to touch the body of a corpse (and the man surely must have appeared dead). According to ritual purity laws, touching the body of a corpse would make them ritually impure to carry out their religious duties in the Temple.

The next to come along is the Samaritan. The Samaritan people, situated between Jerusalem to the south and Galilee to the north, were considered an "outsider" group, Jewish by ethnicity but heretical in their practices. They had become independent from mainstream Judaism about four hundred years earlier and had developed their own scriptures, worship practices, and sacred spaces. Often vilified for their heterodox ways, they were a ritually "unclean" people. Yet this Samaritan, despite whatever unorthodox beliefs he may have held, actually performs the reality of the kingdom. As the parable puts it, he is "moved with pity" at the sight of the wounded, naked man (Luke 10:33). In Hebrew, the word *compassion* refers to that "gut feeling" one has when deeply moved by a feeling of care and love. Importantly, it is just this kind of reaction metaphorically ascribed to God prior to the exodus: "I have observed the misery of my people who are in Egypt; I have heard their cry on account of their taskmasters. Indeed, I know their sufferings" (Exod 3:7). Moved by God's own compassion for the dispossessed, the Samaritan performs the very thing one would expect from the priest and Levite. He pours oil and wine over the wounds, bandages them, and takes the man to a place of rest, even promising the innkeeper he will come back to pay whatever is further needed in restoring the man's health (Luke 10:34–35). There is surprising excess to the gift. The kingdom of God comes by way of reversing and even overflowing expectations.

"Which of these three, do you think, was a neighbor to the man who fell into the hands of the robbers?" Jesus asks (Luke 10:36). Jesus turns the tables, and now the questioner is the one questioned. The legal scholar, faced by the parable, responds in the only sensible way: "The one who showed him mercy" (v. 37a). "Go and do likewise," says Jesus (v. 37b), concluding a repartee that, with a few swift verbal strokes, dismantles the questioner's assumptions about demarcating lines of ritual purity and the groups distinguished by them. It is not that Jesus rejects the Law, for he seeks to fulfill it (Matt 5:17). Jesus is outraged by how the Law had been used as a weapon and source of division, when its original purpose was to bring reconciliation between people. The Law, and many of Israel's central symbols, especially the Temple, as we shall see, had been co-opted by the powerful and elite for self-aggrandizement. "Do not judge, so that you may not be judged. . . . How can you say to your neighbor, 'Let me take the speck out of your eye,' while the log is in your own eye?" (Matt 7:1, 4). Woe to those who occupy places of privilege. Woe to those who place heavy demands (religious and economic) on the people. Woe to the hypocrites obsessed with obtaining personal purity by way of separating themselves from sinners (see Matt 23:1–36). "The greatest among you will be your servant. All who exalt themselves will be humbled, and all who humble themselves will be exalted" (Matt 23:11).

Miracles

Along with the sayings of comfort and judgment recorded by the Gospels, we also find many deeds whereby Jesus symbolically enacts something of the reality of God's kingdom. All four Gospels relate numerous episodes of Jesus healing persons bearing physical and spiritual affliction. While modern people may have difficulty with these stories, consigning them to an archaic or "mythological" way of thinking long superseded by modern science, there is little question that acts of a miraculous character were ascribed to Jesus during his lifetime.

If we are to fully appreciate the miracles in the Gospels, we cannot simply view them as a suspension of nature's laws in a kind of holy magic show or as proof of Jesus' divinity. Rather, the miracles disclose God's kingdom in a unique way, for by them God brings about healing for people in the reality of their concrete situation, in their bodies and private suffering, and often openly giving them dignity by restoring them to their community (for example, lepers, sick, blind, deaf). Jesus' ministry is all-encompassing and holistic, transforming ordinary people in the socially isolating experience of suffering. Often, people who suffer from some kind of physical infirmity also suffer from it socially and spiritually. Perhaps you have personally witnessed or even experienced how a chronic disease or disability can isolate a person from social groups, even those that are supposed to be the most inclusive and nurturing. The conventional wisdom of Jesus' time tended to view physical infirmity as a visible sign of impurity, as though disease and disability were manifestations of personal sin. Consequently, those suffering from chronic disease and dysfunction were often excluded from participating fully (if at all) in Jewish religious life. Jesus rejected this arrangement outright. "As [Jesus] walked along, he saw a man blind from birth. His disciples asked him, 'Rabbi, who sinned, this man or his parents, that he was born blind?' Jesus answered, 'Neither this man nor his parents sinned; he was born blind so that God's works might be revealed in him'" (John 9:1–3).

As Jesus touches and heals the "untouchables"—the leper, the woman with a hemorrhage, the demoniac boy, the man with a withered hand—he simultaneously restores to them those social and spiritual relationships that in many cases had been denied them from birth. Jesus does not explain evil; he simply confronts it. The leper is healed and told to present himself to the Temple (Mark 1:40–45). The paralytic's sins are forgiven, just as he is given his health (Mark 2:1–12). The Gerasene demoniac condemned to roaming night and day among the tombs is healed and told to return to his family (Mark 5:1–20). The crippled woman stands up and praises God (Luke 13:10–13). The mute person is given the capacity of speech (Matt 9:32–34). "Great crowds came to him, bringing with them the lame, the maimed, the blind, the mute, and many others. They put them at his feet, and he cured them, so that the crowd was amazed when they saw the mute speaking, the maimed whole, the lame walking, and the blind seeing. And they praised the God of Israel" (Matt 15:30–31).

The New Testament (NT) describes such events as "acts of power" (*dynameis*) or "signs" (*sēmeia*), whereby Jesus directly confronts the palpable forces of evil in its diverse and mysterious manifestations. A miracle, theologically understood, is the dramatic in-breaking of God's rule into the world in order to restore human beings to that physical, social, and spiritual wholeness intended for them from the beginning of creation. Evil and suffering represent the antikingdom and are emphatically not God's will for humanity. Miracles are therefore filled with eschatological significance: they are fragmentary realizations of God's ultimate future of well-being for human beings, and thus part of the overarching narrative that Jesus is proclaiming and manifesting in his ministry.

Table Fellowship

In addition to his proclamation and miracles of healing, Jesus symbolically enacts the reality of the kingdom through his inclusive "table fellowship." Though it might be difficult to grasp this in our contemporary context of supermarkets, microwaves, and "fast food," in the ancient world, and in ancient Judaism in particular, eating and sharing a meal was an intimate act charged with wide-ranging social and religious significance. Indeed, the table functioned as a kind of microcosm of Jewish society and practice. For a first-century Jew, an array of purity laws and customs regulated all aspects of eating—what one ate and when, how it was to be eaten and with whom, and so on. While such laws and customs can promote an appreciation for the sacredness of meal, they could also (and frequently did) become a source of division between those regarded ritually "clean" and "unclean."

As we have already noted, for certain prominent groups in first-century Judaism, and here we may point to the Pharisees as an example, a conception of holiness prevailed that fostered a sense of distinction and even separation from other (ritually impure or "unclean") groups through the rigorous adherence to laws and ancestral customs. However, it is just this comprehensive "purity system" that Jesus consistently challenges as a false path for Israel, and nowhere more forcefully than in his table fellowship of shocking hospitality to and inclusivity of the sinner and outsider. "When the scribes of the Pharisees saw that he was eating with sinners and tax collectors, they said to his disciples, 'Why does he eat with tax collectors and sinners?' When Jesus heard this, he said to them, 'Those who are well have no need of a physician, but those who are sick; I have come to call not the righteous but sinners'" (Mark 2:16–17).

Just as in the parables of the lost sheep, the lost coin, and the prodigal son (see Luke 15),

Jesus' mission is not intended primarily for those who imagine they are already righteous before God but for the outcast and unclean. By including sinners at the table, Jesus is quite deliberately enacting a story alternative to the one told by those who anticipate Israel's deliverance through the heroic and self-justifying adherence to a purity system. "Listen to me, all of you, and understand: there is nothing outside a person that by going in can defile, but the things that come out are what defile" (Mark 7:14–15).

To be sure, Jesus is passionately interested in moral and spiritual conversion. One need only survey the difficult sayings and precepts scattered throughout the Gospels to become aware of the true demands of discipleship, but the kind of conversion Jesus envisions is one that, instead of resulting in opposition between groups according to degree of purity, results in lasting reconciliation between them. God's coming kingdom precisely means the dismantling of "insider" and "outsider" suspicion and rivalry. Jesus' meal practices therefore anticipate God's ultimate future for humanity, where all are welcome to the eschatological banquet, even (and especially) those who appear to have received no formal invitation. Importantly, it is just this understanding of inclusion and reconciliation at the table that informs the early church's practice of Eucharist.

Confrontation at the Temple and the Question of Jesus' Authority

While much more could be said about Jesus' public ministry, we must now turn our attention to the culminating developments of Jesus' life that led to his death—and the apparent failure of his mission.

It should be obvious by now that Jesus was a dangerous man—dangerous because he preached empowering messages of hope to the marginalized and oppressed; he was reputed to heal persons of physical affliction, even forgiving them of their sins; he boldly challenged many of Israel's religious leaders to radical conversion; he was associated with John the Baptist, who had recently been beheaded by the local Roman ruler Herod; and some publicly hailed him as the "messiah" who would deliver Israel from Roman domination. As if all this were not enough to lead to a tragic end, like so many prophets before him, Jesus did something that, perhaps more than any other single act, sealed his fate. To more fully grasp the dramatic significance of this act, both historically and theologically, an understanding of its context is crucial.

The time was the annual Passover celebration, and the place, Jerusalem. The Passover celebration commemorated Israel's primary narrative, the exodus. As thousands of Jews streamed into Jerusalem for this central religious holiday, the atmosphere was electric and volatile. As might be expected, the Roman military presence in Jerusalem during this religious/national holiday was greatly intensified, for the exodus was not merely a memory of the distant past but a live hope among Jews for future emancipation from their Roman occupiers. Therefore, as all manner of pilgrims entered David's city, including those groups like the Zealots who openly spoke of a military overthrow of their oppressors, the slightest gesture of revolution was swiftly met by Rome's brutally efficient military. That Jesus and his followers entered Jerusalem under these combustible circumstances probably made him a marked man, but then Jesus engages in a provocative act at the very epicenter of the Jewish world:

> Then they came to Jerusalem. And he entered the temple and began to drive out those who were selling and those who were buying in the temple, and he overturned the tables of the money changers and the seats of those who sold doves; and he would not allow anyone to

> carry anything through the temple. He was teaching and saying, "Is it not written, 'My house shall be called a house of prayer for all the nations'? But you have made it a den of robbers." And when the chief priests and the scribes heard it, they kept looking for a way to kill him; for they were afraid of him, because the whole crowd was spellbound by his teaching. (Mark 11:15–18)

The Temple area was the public square of Jerusalem, the place where pilgrims would have first arrived to exchange currency and buy animals for sacrifice. In this symbolic act, Jesus challenges the Temple system as such and in particular, its aristocratic and priestly administrators, the Sadducees. Jesus was certainly not alone in criticizing the Temple system. Numerous Jewish groups were deeply troubled by how the Sadducees compromised with Roman authorities for the sake of self-preservation and privilege, not to mention the heavy taxation for the Temple's upkeep. As Jesus overturns the money-changing tables and disrupts the buying and selling in the Temple's perimeter, he forces to a halt the entire apparatus surrounding this central symbol. In effect, Jesus is saying the Temple no longer effectively mediates the presence of God for Israel. It is thoroughly corrupt, a "den of robbers."

Though Jesus' authority was frequently questioned throughout his ministry, this striking elevation in prophetic rhetoric especially provoked his opponents. As Mark relates in a succeeding passage, "The chief priests, the scribes, and the elders came to him and said, 'By what authority are you doing these things?'" (11:27–28). Who is this Jesus who challenges the Temple in this way, who presumes to authoritatively interpret the Law, who dares to forgive sins, who recklessly associates with the unclean, thus confusing what ought to be meticulously distinguished? Who is this who draws disciples unto himself—twelve, no less, to symbolize the number of Israel's tribes? What manner of man is this who would speak on behalf of Israel's God in this way?

Although Jesus (as portrayed in the Synoptic Gospels) rarely speaks of his own person in any explicit or formal way—Jesus does not, for example, describe himself as the "Second Person of the Trinity" or "one in being with the Father," as later church doctrines will—it becomes progressively clear in the converging pattern of his sayings and deeds that Jesus presumes to personally embody the reality of God in a unique and powerful way, as though the message of the kingdom of God were directly and inseparably related to him, its messenger. He speaks and acts with an unprecedented authority. As scandalous as it may be, particularly within a monotheistic context, it becomes increasingly difficult to avoid identifying the person of Jesus with the God he reveals. With this move in our reflection, we are beginning to discover from the "ground up," that is, from the history and life-story of the man from Nazareth, who he ultimately is. That is to say, we are now thoroughly engaged in a process of Christological discovery, one that with the ensuing events of his death and Resurrection will reach its decisive point of departure.

Crucifixion, Death, and Resurrection

In the passage previously cited, we read that following the incident at the Temple, various Jewish authorities sought to have Jesus killed. The provocation proved too much, especially given the context of Rome's zero-tolerance policy toward potential insurgency. Jesus is arrested and brought to stand trial before the Sanhedrin, a formal judicial assembly of chief priests, elders, and scribes. Various allegations are made against him, including blasphemy, messianic ambition, and threats against the Temple (Mark 14:53–65). Whatever the ultimate motivation for the Sanhedrin's handing over of Jesus to the Romans, perhaps foremost among them was the desire to quell any potential uprising that would result in a devastating response by Rome—not unlike what eventually happened forty years later when the Temple was destroyed (70 CE) to suppress a civil war. Assigning blame for Jesus' death is a delicate matter, but about this we can be quite clear: both Jewish and Roman authorities were involved in Jesus' brutal execution. If Jesus had already aroused significant opposition among the powerful and elite within Israel, enough that some of them wanted Jesus dead, the fact that he was crucified indicates Roman involvement because crucifixion was a specifically Roman form of torture and execution reserved for non-Roman citizens. It was intended to be gruesome theatre, orchestrated to instill terror and compliance among an occupied populace.

With cruel irony, Jesus died on a cross with a plaque above his head inscribed with these words, "The King of the Jews." The so-called "anointed one" of Israel died a criminal's death. The kingdom of God had not come, it seemed, but suffered demonstrable defeat as its chief messenger hung naked from a cross. Panic and fear set in among the disciples as they fled, leaving only the women to mourn at the tomb.

Now, had the story ended here, the man from Nazareth would be little more than a footnote in history. Jesus was certainly not the only Jew to be crucified, nor was he the only one hailed as Israel's "messiah." But Jesus' story does not end here, for not only will his once-dispersed and despairing group of disciples continue to tell the story of his life and death, but they also will begin proclaiming with boundless enthusiasm a most unlikely twist in its telling: that God raised this crucified Jesus from the dead, vindicated him in his messianic mission, and revealed him as "Lord." What is more, his death and Resurrection grant salvation—the forgiveness of sins, a new freedom from the power of violence and death, and a sure hope in the future that all creation will attain its ultimate destiny. A passage from Acts 2 concisely and powerfully frames the essence of the early church's proclamation. Here, as Peter addresses the people of Israel, he is able to "see" what was only obscure to him during Jesus' public ministry:

> "You that are Israelites, listen to what I have to say: Jesus of Nazareth, a man attested to you by God with deeds of power, wonders, and signs that God did through him among you, as you yourselves know—this man, handed over to you according to the definite plan and foreknowledge of God, you crucified and killed by the hands of those outside the law. But God raised him up, having freed him from death, because it was impossible for him to be held in its power. . . . This Jesus God raised up, and of that all of us are witnesses. . . . Therefore let the entire house of Israel know with certainty that God has made him both Lord and Messiah, this Jesus whom you crucified." . . . Peter said to them, "Repent, and be baptized every one of you in the name of Jesus Christ so that your sins may be forgiven; and you will receive the gift of the Holy Spirit." (Acts 2:22–24, 32, 36, 38)

At the beginning of this chapter, we observed that "thinking Christologically" requires an imagination open to paradox and surprise. That which appears to be utter failure becomes God's victory. This Jesus, who died not out of some masochistic death wish but because of his solidarity with the outsider, the unclean, and the sinner, becomes himself an outsider and a victim, one cursed as a common criminal. In other words, Jesus dies very much as a consequence of the life he led, and to the very end, even as he breathes his last, he offers peace and reconciliation to those who accuse and murder him: "Father, forgive them; for they do not know what they are doing" (Luke 23:34).

In this pattern of total self-giving love, even unto death, Jesus enacts a life-story that entails the reversal of conventional values. Authority comes not from domination but from humility; power is not manipulative but empowers others; authentic life results not from pursuing self-interest but dying to self. "Whoever wants to be first must be last of all and the servant of all" (Mark 9:35). Jesus' messianic vocation is not, therefore, a pursuit of a military revolution or the establishment of mighty fortresses but a vocation whose fundamental characteristic is living life wholly for the Other. "'You shall love the Lord your God with all your heart, and with all your soul, and with all your mind, and with all your strength' . . . [and] 'You shall love your neighbor as yourself.' There is no other commandment greater than these" (Mark 12:30–31). "No one has greater love than this, to lay down one's life for one's friends" (John 15:13).

Jesus' Resurrection from the dead is not a kind of reward for a life well lived, nor is it merely a happy ending to an otherwise tragic story. It is an event filled with tremendous significance for understanding who God is and the destiny God has for human beings. By raising Jesus from the dead, God is revealed as one who sides with the outsider and marginalized, as one who provides an ultimate hope for the victimized and oppressed. God is the God of life and death, and no power or threat can vanquish the divine will of well-being for humanity. However, just as God is revealed as a God for the oppressed, the Resurrection of Jesus is also an offer of forgiveness and grace. In the passage from Acts 2 previously cited, Peter declares that by raising Jesus from the dead, those who crucified him (and by extension, all who say "No" to God's kingdom) are given the opportunity to be fully reconciled to God. Having become victim to the violent rejection of God's will for humanity, Jesus is raised victorious as God's ultimate "Yes." God's love for humanity is so excessive and tenacious that even though Jesus, commended by God to Israel, is rejected and crucified as a criminal, God raises him from the dead as the ultimate gift of life. As Saint Paul puts it, "And he died for all, so that those who live might live no longer for themselves, but for him who died and was raised for them. . . . So if anyone is in Christ, there is a new creation: everything old has passed away; see, everything has become new!" (2 Cor 5:15, 17).

How did the disciples come to believe in this "newness," and what specific meaning does Resurrection language possess for Christians? This early Christian proclamation stands upon two pillars. The first was the discovery of the empty tomb by the women followers of Jesus. By itself, the empty tomb does not necessarily imply Jesus' Resurrection. It remains an ambiguous sign, as there are many possible reasons why it might have been empty, including the possibility that the disciples stole Jesus' body (see Matt 27:62–66). The second pillar is the tradition of Resurrection appearances in which Jesus reveals himself to his disciples as one who has triumphed over death. The accounts are varied, as a cursory examination of the Gospels demonstrates.

Despite their diversity, however, they all agree on two basic points. First, the risen Jesus who appeared to the disciples is the self-same Jesus of Nazareth, not some apparition or hallucination. The Gospels insist that Jesus, after his death and by the power of God, manifests himself in a way that is not the result of human imagination. The encounter comes from "beyond" them. Second, while this is the self-same Jesus of Nazareth the disciples knew and loved before his death, he is also transformed into a state of existence that is different from ordinary space–time existence. Jesus does not simply come back to life, as though he returns to his premortem life. Resurrection does not mean resuscitation; it means transformation—transformation into a manner of life that exceeds our capacity to imagine.

We may put it this way: Jesus' Resurrection is both in full continuity with his historical existence and in discontinuity to the extent that he has passed through death and been given a life no longer susceptible to corruptibility. Jesus' total human existence has reached its final and eternal fulfillment in God, and it is just this fulfilled life with God for which human beings are made. Jesus' Resurrection is the future of all creation, a future already present. The kingdom has come in the very person of Jesus.

THE STORY CONTINUES: THE CHRISTOLOGY OF THE NEW TESTAMENT CHURCH

Understandably, the early Christian proclamation was met with resistance and misunderstanding. The Gospels relate that even the disciples only gradually understood the nature and significance

Ministry of Jesus

of this event. Nevertheless, once the conviction set in, it completely revolutionized their imagination. As the disciples continued to tell and retell the remarkable events they witnessed, they began to see Jesus' life, death, and Resurrection as the ultimate revelation of God to humanity. This process of telling the story is an act of Christology. Recalling the definition provided at the outset of this chapter, Christology is the attempt to formally articulate Jesus Christ's mission and identity, his relationship to God, and his significance for humanity. In the NT, several Christological statements and patterns attempt to say something important about his identity and mission. Let us briefly examine three.

Jesus as "Lord" (*Kyrios*)

Early on in the primitive Christian movement, Jesus was hailed as Israel's "Messiah" and "Lord." In Greek, these words are *christos* and *kyrios* respectively. Importantly, Christians attributed to Jesus titles such as these in the context of worship: while they gathered in community to remember Jesus' deeds, death, and Resurrection; as they prayed through and rediscovered the scriptures; as they ritually enacted Jesus' Last Supper with his disciples before his death, and so on. The earliest Christians very much experienced the presence of the risen Christ among them, even singing hymns to him in a way that, from an outsider's point of view, might seem as though they regarded him as God. This is not to say that the earliest Christians had yet developed a specific vocabulary to speak of Jesus as "God," but the evolution of early Christian language and practice shows an unmistakable and steady process of coming to precisely this conclusion.

By hailing Jesus as "Lord," the earliest Christians were not just acknowledging Jesus' authority as God's true emissary in the world, and thus one to whom his disciples owed allegiance. They were also saying something about Jesus' exalted status after his death. By raising him from the dead, God has triumphed over chaos, violence, and death. Jesus is "Lord" of creation, sovereign in human history, sovereign among the world's powers, be they social, political, or religious. Paul summarizes this conviction in one of his letters as he writes that, although many people allege and worship other gods, "for us there is one God, the Father, from whom are all things and for whom we exist, and one Lord, Jesus Christ, through whom are all things and through whom we exist" (1 Cor 8:6). One cannot help but notice the closest relationship between "God" and "Jesus" in this passage. Though explicitly monotheistic, both the "Father" and the "Lord Jesus Christ" *together* are sovereign over creation and human history.

Death and Resurrection/Exaltation Christology

In his letter to the Philippians, Paul quotes an early hymn that epitomizes a second Christological pattern. It too tells a story but does so in a condensed narrative format, rich with meaning and mystery:

> Let the same mind be in you that was in Christ Jesus, who, though he was in the form of God, did not regard equality with God as something to be exploited, but emptied himself, taking the form of a slave, being born in human likeness. And being found in human form, he humbled himself and became obedient to the point of death—even death on a cross. Therefore God also highly exalted him and gave him the name that is above every name, so that at the name of Jesus every knee should bend, in heaven and on earth and under the earth, and every tongue should confess that Jesus Christ is Lord, to the glory of God the Father. (Phil 2:5–11)

Notice here the pattern of descent and ascent. Jesus first "descends"; though in the "form of God," he empties himself (*kenōsis*) and becomes the lowliest of the lowly, taking on a life of complete self-expenditure for others, even unto death on a cross. In Jesus, God's shocking humility is expressed. God's "power" is of the sort that it identifies with the powerless, itself becoming utterly vulnerable to the violent resistance of God's own creation. The "descent" is one of love. Yet, precisely because of this self-expenditure for others, God "highly exalted him" and gave Jesus the "name that is above every name." He ascends to the very honor of God the Father so that all should acknowledge Jesus Christ's lordship over creation. The pattern here echoes the very subversion and paradox we find in so many of Jesus' parables. Powerlessness becomes true power; humility becomes might; lowliness and service become transcendence and eminence. As Paul puts it elsewhere, "For God's foolishness is wiser than human wisdom, and God's weakness is stronger than human strength" (1 Cor 1:25). Jesus is God's living parable, his life, death, and Resurrection the very embodiment of divine wisdom and love.

Wisdom and Logos Christology

A third Christological pattern exhibits what is sometimes described as "high Christology." Its counterterm is "low Christology." These spatial images are helpful when talking about Jesus as divine (high) and human (low). This Christological pattern begins by characterizing Jesus' ultimate identity and mission in relationship to the eternal wisdom of God, even before Jesus' historical existence. Let us look briefly at two notable examples.

> He [Jesus] is the image of the invisible God, the firstborn of all creation; for in him all things in heaven and on earth were created, things visible and invisible, whether thrones or dominions or rulers or powers—all things have been created through him and for him. He himself is before all things, and in him all things hold together. . . . For in him all the fullness of God was pleased to dwell, and through him God was pleased to reconcile to himself all things, whether on earth or in heaven, by making peace through the blood of his cross. (Col 1:15–20)

Much could be said about this dense passage, but we must limit ourselves to just a few observations. First, this passage, also an early Christian hymn, draws deep from the well of Israel's wisdom tradition, as can be found in such OT writings as Proverbs, the Wisdom of Solomon, Sirach, Job, and many of the Psalms. What is distinctive about this Christological pattern is the way it speaks of Jesus as the personal embodiment of God's wisdom: the same wisdom originally bringing forth creation, the same wisdom responsible for order and beauty in the cosmos, the wisdom that inspires all human wisdom. As the "image of the invisible God," Jesus is the earthly and historical manifestation of divine transcendence. In Jesus, the fullness of God dwelt, reconciling humanity to God through the self-sacrifice of Jesus on the cross. Divine solidarity and forgiveness are together offered to humanity in his life, death, and Resurrection. Because Jesus so thoroughly manifests God's original plan for creation, it is possible to say that all things were created in, through, and for him. Jesus is the completion of all creation. The future of creation is eschatologically realized *in* him.

Second, as an instance of "high Christology," this passage speaks of Jesus' ultimate identity by highlighting his preexistence. The exalted status of Jesus as "Lord" of creation revealed to his disciples after his Resurrection is the identity Jesus always possessed, not only throughout his life but even prior to his historical existence, prior to creation itself. What God accomplished in and through Jesus Christ was God's plan for humanity all along. Jesus' ultimate identity and origin are not afterthoughts to creation but found in the heart of the eternal God.

This style of Christological reflection is even more explicit in the prologue of John's Gospel:

> In the beginning was the Word [*Logos*], and the Word was with God, and the Word was God. He was in the beginning with God. All things came into being through him, and without him not one thing came into being. . . . He was in the world, and the world came into being through him; yet the world did not know him. He came to what was his own, and his own people did not accept him. But to all who received him . . . he gave power to become children of God. . . . And the Word [*Logos*] became flesh and lived among us, and we have seen his glory, the glory as of a father's only son, full of grace and truth. (John 1:1–3, 10–12, 14)

The Greek word *Logos* used here, translated as "Word," bears important philosophical and theological implications for the history of Christology. John's Gospel consciously weaves Jewish and Greek philosophical thought to describe Jesus as both the decree of God's will for humanity and the incarnation of the divine intelligence. In Stoic philosophy, the *Logos* is the intelligent and creative power bringing forth and sustaining creation. By poetically portraying the *Logos* as "becoming flesh" and "dwelling among us," John's Gospel articulates a mature theology of Incarnation, where the divine and preexistent Son of God enters into the world out of love in order to save it from sin, disorder, and darkness. As such, we find here a bold ascription of divinity to Jesus Christ, the same sort of ascription found later in John's Gospel as it relates the Apostle Thomas's reaction to encountering the risen Jesus: "My Lord and my God!" (John 20:28).

In answer to the question "Who is Jesus?" the Gospel of John weaves poetry and narrative, Jewish and Greek thought, to say something that marks both the culmination of a process of Christological reflection in the NT and the indispensable foundation for all later Christian doctrine: He is the Son of God; the preexistent Wisdom of God become human; God's eternal Word who entered the world, was crucified, and rose to reveal God's saving love and glory.

FAITHFULLY INTERPRETING THE STORY: THE CHRISTOLOGICAL COUNCILS

Our final task in thinking Christologically is to understand something of the nature and purpose of the later Christological doctrines of the church, particularly from the fourth and fifth centuries CE. To do so, let us review where we are now with the three touchstones that are our "grammatical rules" for properly speaking about Jesus, his relationship to God, and his significance for humanity.

The Three Christological Touchstones

All Christology derives from story.

Christian revelation is not primarily concerned with the production of abstract propositions about the nature of reality but with the telling and retelling of a story of salvation. God reveals God's self in the dramatic unfolding of historical events—in the story of Israel and, in a more focused and definitive way for Christians, in the life, death, and Resurrection of Jesus Christ. Jesus' life is not just a parable lived out in the context of Israel's story but also one that reshapes and fulfills that context.

All Christology derives from an experience of salvation.

In Jesus, the earliest Christians encountered the liberating and forgiving love of God in a way that surprised and overwhelmed them. In the particulars of Jesus' life-story, God broke through the power of death with new life, overcame violent rejection with peace, and met sin with an unexpected offer of forgiveness. Formal reflection upon this experience of salvation is what Christian theology calls "soteriology" (from the Greek word *sōtēria*, meaning "deliverance"). As we have seen in our study, soteriology and Christology are closely related, and both are rooted in the story of Jesus' life, death, and Resurrection. It is from the experience of salvation that the earliest Christians came to worship Jesus and more clearly understand his relationship to God. As Christians called to mind all that Jesus had said and done and what God had done for Jesus by raising him from the dead, they experienced the presence of the risen Christ among them. From this communal context of worship emerged a reflective process that would produce oral traditions, hymns, titles, epistles, prayers, and textual portraits that together form the basic linguistic and conceptual materials for all subsequent Christology.

All Christology derives from the conviction that in Jesus, God's presence in the world has taken hold in an unprecedented way.

This presence was so powerful that the earliest Christians felt compelled to ask this fundamental question: Who must Jesus be if in him salvation has come about? Put somewhat differently: If, in Jesus, God has been revealed in a new and decisive way, who, in the final analysis, is this Jesus? This line of questioning proceeds from what Jesus "does" to his "person," or his "being." To employ a technical term, we are moving here from a functional consideration to an *ontological* one. (*Ontology* in philosophy is the study of "being.") In the former case, we reflect upon Jesus' work of proclaiming and bringing about the good news of salvation, that is, the kingdom of God. In the latter case, we reflect upon the "being" or "person" who in fact mediates this salvation. The fundamental logic of all Christology, one whose development we can trace in the NT, moves toward the affirmation of Jesus as God in human form. In Jesus, it is God who personally enters into human affairs.

The Council of Nicea (325 CE)

Such a conclusion creates a host of challenging questions, particularly within the context of monotheistic belief. For example, how is it possible to affirm that Jesus is somehow God while avoiding the undesirable conclusion that there are two gods? If we adopt John's language, namely that Jesus is the *Logos* become flesh, is this *Logos* to be thought of as God properly speaking or some lesser divinity? And how is it possible, if at all, for Christians to affirm that God "becomes" something when Christians also affirm that God is eternal and unchanging? Though these questions seem technical and perhaps unimportant, they actually created conflict and confusion within the Christian movement as it spread across the Mediterranean world and increasingly interacted with Greco-Roman culture and thought. Such confusion ultimately led to the need for Christian theologians and bishops to provide a conceptual framework to speak properly and consistently about Jesus' identity. This occurred at the Council of Nicea in 325 CE, a council convoked by the Emperor Constantine near his new city of Constantinople (Istanbul), and only twelve years after he declared Christianity a legal religion in the empire.

Precipitating this important council was the controversy sparked by the priest and theologian Arius (d. 336 CE). Arius argued that the only philosophically respectable and consistent position for Christians to hold was that the *Logos* is not eternal like the Father but created. While it is true that the Gospel of John describes the *Logos* as preexisting the creation of the world, this does not preclude claiming that the *Logos* was created by God the Father as the first and greatest of all creations. Only the Father is eternal; everything else is by definition a creature. In point of fact, argued Arius, God is utterly simple in being and unchanging. If, as Christians say, the *Logos* "became" human, we have already admitted that the *Logos* is not eternal and unchanging like the Father. In the end, the *Logos* is created, even though it is the greatest of all creations. As Arius was fond of putting it, "There was a time when the *Logos* was not."

If, from one point of view, Arius's position could claim a certain degree of philosophical coherence, it could not quite account for the way in which Christians actually encountered God (and not some lesser divinity) in Jesus Christ. By saying that the *Logos* was not God properly speaking but only a creature, Arius could not adequately explain how the "fullness of God" dwelt in Jesus, to refer to the previous passage from Colossians, or how the *Logos* was both "with God" in the beginning and "was God," as John's prologue reads. The need to clarify matters in view of Arius's public and influential campaign became increasingly evident, so a council of bishops and theologians in Nicea addressed the matter in a way that would produce a formal confession of faith, one still recited today in the form of the "Nicene Creed" among the vast majority of Christians around the world. Couched in the middle section of this creed, we find a series of statements that directly respond to Arius's challenge. In particular, the creed states that Jesus is not created but eternally flows from the inexhaustible creativity of the Father (he is "eternally begotten of the Father"). Moreover, Jesus Christ, as the eternal Son of the Father, shares in the Father's very divinity. He is "one in being" (*homoousias*) with the Father.

While these statements are indeed technical, let us understand what they ultimately mean. By saying that Jesus Christ is "true God from true God" and "one in being" with the Father, the Nicene Creed is saying that in Christ, the very reality of God is available in a remarkably intimate and personal way. Jesus is God's self-expression in the world. The difference between the positions of Arius and the Council of Nicea might be illuminated by means of an analogy. If, on my wedding day, I sent someone close to me to stand at the altar with my bride, let us say my best friend who knows more about me and is closer to me than anyone else, someone I trust implicitly and for whom I have the deepest respect, still his presence would be only a substitute for mine. Though he may speak for me and have authorization to stand in my place, his presence would still not be me. And just imagine the reaction of my bride—assuming I still had a bride! The difference between Arius and the Council of Nicea is analogous in this respect. The council is claiming that God's very self is encountered in Christ, not just a creature of elevated status, not a proxy. Jesus is the personal manifestation of God in the world in such a way that we can exclaim, as did Thomas, "My Lord and my God!"

From the Council of Constantinople (381 CE) to the Council of Chalcedon (451 CE)

Perhaps understandably, this ascription of divinity to Jesus Christ led to an opposite problem, one that existed as early as the first century but would eventually require the church to make a clarifying and corrective doctrinal statement almost 125 years after Nicea. In the decades following the council, debate raged over how to understand the relationship between the humanity and divinity in Jesus Christ himself. If the church believes that he is "one in being with the Father," does this mean he is still human? If so, in what way? Such questions became pressing because some so emphasized Jesus' divinity that it became difficult to account for his humanity. Bishop Apollinaris (d. ca. 390) of Laodicea, just south of the major Christian city of Antioch on the Mediterranean coast of Syria, intended to be faithful to the Nicene definition but ended up claiming that Jesus was a kind of "mixture" of humanity and divinity. Though Jesus possessed the body of a human, Apollinaris argued, his soul and mind were totally divine. To put it somewhat crudely, the *Logos* essentially inhabited the shell of a human body, somewhat like a driver sitting inside and operating a car.

The chief problem with this approach, however, is that it makes Jesus no longer fully human. He only possesses the appearance of being human when in fact his inner makeup and consciousness are divine. Such a view would hardly satisfy the NT's insistence that Jesus was in every way like a human being, except sin (Phil 2:5–8; Heb 4:15). Moreover, it contradicts an axiom that had prevailed in Christian theology for some time, an axiom that flows out of a fully developed theology of the Incarnation: "What has not been assumed is not saved." What this phrase means is that God saves humanity by assuming (or personally taking on) all aspects of the human condition with the purpose of transforming and elevating humanity toward its ultimate fulfillment. If Jesus were without a human soul, then we are left with the absurd conclusion that the human body has been saved but not the human soul. Salvation is the transformation of the whole person, so the logic goes, not just a part of the person.

Such were the counterarguments of Apollinaris's opponents. And, in fact, Apollinaris's position was formally rejected by the Council of Constantinople in 381. However, among those who opposed Apollinaris in order that Jesus' full humanity might be protected, some quite publicly introduced other kinds of errors that would eventually require clarification. For example, a bishop from Constantinople named Nestorius (d. ca. 451) so emphatically insisted on distinguishing Jesus' divine and human natures that he could not properly account for the unity of Jesus' person. This became particularly evident as Nestorius argued that Mary, the mother of Jesus, was not the "mother of God" (*Theotokos*), as she was celebrated to be in Christian hymns at the time, but only the mother of Jesus' humanity. For Nestorius, this distinction was necessary to safeguard the integrity of each nature. Unfortunately, this solution only created the opposite problem of suggesting that in Jesus Christ there are two distinct persons, one divine and one human. The confusion this unseemly conclusion produced required yet another definition for the church to debate and finally articulate, which it soon did. The initial debate took place at the Council of Ephesus in 431, with a subsequent debate taking place at the Council of Chalcedon in 451.

The formal definition of the Council of Chalcedon reads as follows:

> [We teach believers] to acknowledge one and the same Son, our Lord Jesus Christ,
>
> at once complete in Godhead and complete in manhood, truly God and truly man, consisting also of a reasonable soul and body;
>
> of one substance ["one in being"] with the Father as regards his Godhead,
>
> and at the same time of one substance ["one in being"] with us as regards his manhood;

like us in all respects, apart from sin;
as regards his Godhead, begotten of the Father before the ages,
but yet as regards his manhood begotten, for us and for our salvation, of Mary the Virgin, the God-bearer [*Theotokos*]. . . .
The distinction of natures being in no way annulled by the union,
but rather the characteristics of each nature being preserved and coming together to form one person.

This statement affirms that Jesus Christ is fully human and fully divine, not partly one or the other, contrary to Apollinaris. Moreover, the human ("manhood") and divine natures are united in one person, the one Jesus Christ, so that it is proper to say, contrary to Nestorius, that Mary is the God-bearer, or *Theotokos*. She does not just bear the humanity of Jesus but the whole person of Jesus Christ. The implication of Nestorius's position would lead to an intolerable split between Jesus' humanity and divinity. Chalcedon stresses the unity of his person.

In sum, then, in Jesus Christ, the fullness of God is expressed in human form. He not only most fully and definitively reveals God to human beings, but he also reveals the fulfillment of the human person. He is humanity at its most actualized, precisely *because* he is united with God. As a human person, he is "God-with-us," *Emmanuel* (Matt 1:23).

CONCLUSION: THE NEVER-ENDING QUESTION

The councils of Nicea and Chalcedon provided an enduring conceptual framework for Christology for over fifteen-hundred years. As a summary expression of the church's mature faith in Jesus Christ, they function like a set of grammatical rules to assist Christians in properly understanding and speaking of the mission and identity of Jesus Christ. As doctrines, they do not replace the story of Jesus found in the NT; rather, they serve to establish the parameters by which Christians may continue to read, interpret, and reflect upon that story without falling into critical errors.

Yet "thinking Christologically" is an ongoing and dynamic activity. Although these conciliar statements are fundamental to Christian faith, they should not replace the activity of actually doing Christology. Every generation of Christians is charged with the task of asking the question, "Who do you say I am?" Whether asked in the first or twenty-first century, this question invites new insights and unexpected perspectives upon God and humanity. As we have seen, it is just the sort of question that may radically challenge and even transform a person's perception of the world and way of life. Perhaps appropriately, then, we end this chapter with a series of questions that ask students new to theology to continue thinking Christologically in their own context.

Questions about the Text

1. What are the three touchstones that structure Christological reflection?
2. What does the word *Christ* mean?
3. What does the word *eschatological* mean?
4. What does the "kingdom of God" mean?
5. What word and its meaning are conveyed in the image at the beginning of John's Gospel?
6. What was the theological concern at the Council of Nicea? At the Council of Chalcedon? Explain the development that lead from Nicea to the conclusions at Chalcedon.

Questions for Discussion

1. This chapter argues that "thinking Christologically" frequently challenges one's assumptions about Jesus and God. As you read this chapter, what aspects of Jesus' ministry and his revelation of God most challenge your own assumptions?
2. Who are today's "Samaritans"?
3. Why, historically speaking, did Jesus die? Why are these historical factors theologically significant?
4. After reading the section on miracles, do you think miracles happen today? Have you experienced or do you know about anything along this line of human experience?
5. Do you think people today have a harder time appreciating Jesus' humanity or his divinity? Why?
6. What are some of the ways Jesus' life-ministry can continue to be a powerful force for social transformation today?

For Further Study

Alison, James. *Knowing Jesus*. London: SPCK, 1993.

Borg, Marcus J. *Meeting Jesus Again for the First Time: The Historical Jesus and the Heart of Contemporary Faith*. New York: HarperSanFrancisco, 1994.

Brown, Raymond E. *An Introduction to New Testament Christology*. New York: Paulist Press, 1994.

Johnson, Elizabeth A. *Consider Jesus: Waves of Renewal in Christology*. New York: Herder & Herder/Crossroad, 2002.

Kasper, Walter. *Jesus the Christ*. Translated by V. Green. New York: Paulist Press, 1976.

Lane, Dermot. *The Reality of Jesus*. New York: Paulist Press, 1976.

Loewe, William P. *The College Student's Introduction to Christology*. Collegeville, MN: The Liturgical Press, 1996.

Norris, Richard. *The Christological Controversy*. Philadelphia: Fortress Press, 1980.

Pelikan, Jaroslav. *Jesus through the Centuries: His Place in the History of Culture*. New Haven: Yale University Press, 1985.

Senior, Donald. *Jesus: A Gospel Portrait*. New York: Paulist Press, 1992.

Thompson, William M. *The Jesus Debate: A Survey and Synthesis*. New York: Paulist Press, 1985.

Wright, N. T. *The Challenge of Jesus: Rediscovering Who Jesus Was and Is*. Downers Grove, IL: InterVarsity Press, 1999.

The passages from the Councils of Nicea and Chalcedon are taken from *Documents of the Christian Church*, ed. Henry Bettenson, 2nd ed. (Oxford: Oxford University Press, 1963).

from the REFERENCE LIBRARIAN

Researching Theological Topics—Christology

Once again, we start at the beginning.

SKILL KEY #1

Use the library's reference collection to begin your research.

a) Use a subject-specific encyclopedia to acquire specialized knowledge about a subject.
b) Use a subject-specific encyclopedia whose scope is appropriate for both your topic and the approach you want to take to that topic.

Let's begin this time by addressing further the matter of the scope of an encyclopedia. In this chapter, you have encountered the names of several persons who figured prominently in the development of Christological views in the church. Therefore, you may want to conduct further research on a particular person, such as Athanasius or Apollinaris. One important way that encyclopedias vary in scope is the inclusion (or not) of biographical articles. Because not all encyclopedias include such articles, you will obviously want to use one that does for this kind of research. Conversely, if you are researching a concept or idea, you should know that some reference works contain only biographical articles and are therefore of no use to you in this case. If you are researching an event (such as a church council), then the reference tool you use must include historical coverage; not all reference works do. Finally, some comprehensive reference works try to include all these types of entries; often (but not always), these are multivolume encyclopedias.

Let's start with research on a person. The first question in determining the appropriate encyclopedia to use is simply "What person am I researching?" If your interest is in the Christological views of Paul or one of the NT Gospel writers, for example, you could use one of the reference tools listed at the end of the chapter on the NT. However, if you want to research a figure from the early church, such as Athanasius or Apollinaris, you must turn to some other tool, one whose scope extends beyond the NT. Here are some examples:

Patrick W. Carey and Joseph T. Lienhard, eds. *Biographical Dictionary of Christian Theologians*. Westport, CT: Greenwood Press, 2000.

As indicated by the title, this is limited to biographical entries only and covers all eras of church history.

Trevor A. Hart. *The Dictionary of Historical Theology*. Grand Rapids, MI: William B. Eerdmans, 2000.

The title offers a hint about the scope of this reference work; it offers coverage of persons and events (history) but not much on concepts (there are no entries on *homoousias*, *kenōsis*, or *Logos*, for example).

Adrian Hastings, ed. *The Oxford Companion to Christian Thought*. Oxford: Oxford University Press, 2000.

This "companion" includes coverage of all the types of subjects mentioned previously: persons, events, concepts. In this case, *companion* is synonymous with *dictionary* or *encyclopedia*; however, the use of *companion* in the title may also indicate a collection of longer essays on broader topics as opposed to a dictionary-type collection of shorter, more focused entries that are alphabetically arranged.

E. A. Livingstone, ed. *The Oxford Dictionary of the Christian Church*. 3rd ed. rev. Oxford: Oxford University Press, 2005.

This dictionary also includes coverage of all types of subjects.

As it happens, three out of these four reference works have entries for both Athanasius and Apollinaris. However, *The Oxford Companion to Christian Thought* has an entry for Athanasius but none for Apollinaris—remember, in a one-volume work that tries to cover the entire range of church history, sometimes something has to be left out.) So, if your interest is in Apollinaris, what can you do if there is no article specifically about him? Here we will further expand our repertoire of basic library skills as follows:

SKILL KEY #1

Use the library's reference collection to begin your research.

a) Use a subject-specific encyclopedia to acquire specialized knowledge about a subject.

b) Use a subject-specific encyclopedia whose scope is appropriate for both your topic and the approach you want to take to that topic.

continued

continued

c) Use encyclopedia bibliographies to identify subject headings for your topic.

d) Use a concise subject specific dictionary to look up the specialized vocabulary of a particular field.

e) Use an encyclopedia's index to locate information on subjects (including person) for which there is no separate article.

Never give up on a reference work if you do not find an article specific to your topic on your first attempt. Information on your subject may be "buried" somewhere in an article on some other subject. The editors of the *Companion to Christian Thought* have thoughtfully prepared for such an eventuality by providing an index of names at the back of the book that "contains only the names of people who do *not* [emphasis added] have their own entry, and is intended to supplement the full list of articles." Browsing through this index, you would find an entry for "Apollinaris (of Laodicea)" with cross-references to six other articles in the volume.

Apollinaris (of Laodicea)

Chalcedon, Council of

Docetism; Greek

Theology; Incarnation

Monophysitism

Nestorianism

(From *Oxford Companion to Christian Thought*, edited byAdrian Hastings. Oxford: Oxford University Press, 2000.)

The articles on "Chalcedon, Council of," "Docetism," "Incarnation," and "Monophysitism," would all be relevant to the topic of Christology. This underscores the importance of digging a little deeper when you do not find what you are looking for right away. The point is this: *Always check to see if an encyclopedia has an index (and what kind of index it has).*

Say you are looking for books on Athanasius and his views of Christology. After using an encyclopedia bibliography to provide an access point to the catalog, you may have discovered a book with a subject heading like the following (note again the descriptive phrase added to the name):

Search format:

Last Name	*Descriptive phrase*	*Subdivision 1*
Athanasius	Patriarch of Alexandria, d. 373	Contributions in Christology

Such "Contributions in . . ." subdivisions often appear after the names of persons as subject headings and indicate the contributions made by those individuals in whatever field is then specified. Obviously, the subject heading shown would indicate a book precisely on your topic of interest—the Christological views of Athanasius—and a book devoted entirely to that topic, so this subject heading certainly fulfills the recommendation we have made to "use subject headings whose scope fits your topic as closely as possible."

Note that the Library of Congress has recently started to do away with the "Contributions in . . ." subdivision. However, many libraries, especially those with a significant theology collection, continue to use this subdivision because it enables researchers to locate specific books about theologians who have a large number of books written about them, for example, Thomas Aquinas or Martin Luther. If your library catalog does not use the "Contributions in . . ." subdivision, you can accomplish the same thing by combining two or more subject headings in a single search. This search technique will be presented in chapter 7.

Remember that another part of the recommendation is to "adjust your search with a broader or narrower subject heading as necessary." One example of why that may be necessary is that a book does not have to be entirely about Athanasius's views on Christology in order to contain information on that subject. Look at the following titles located by a subject search on Athanasius, Saint, Patriarch of Alexandria, d. 373, none of which has the "Contributions in Christology" subdivision.

Khaled Anatolios. *Athanasius: The Coherence of His Thought*. London: Routledge, 1998.

Michael E. Molloy. *Champion of Truth: The Life of Saint Athanasius*. Staten Island, NY: Alba House, 2003.

Alvyn Pettersen. *Athanasius*. Milwaukee, WI: Morehouse Publishing, 1995.

Now I have to let you in on one of those little secrets your professors do not want you to know. Did you ever wonder how they have time to read all those books and articles they list in bibliographies of the works they write? The truth is they do not read everything in those lists. (Maybe a few have, but they are rare.) Rather, they try to find the parts of books that are relevant to what they are writing. They do that using one of two features every book intended for use by serious students should have—a table of contents and a subject index.

For example, the book *Champion of Truth*, by Molloy, lists the following two chapters in its table of contents:

Chapter 2: The Arians

Chapter 3: The Council of Nicea

Based on what you have read in this chapter, you should recognize that you are likely to find out most of what the author has to say on the topic of Athanasius and Christology in these two chapters. Molloy also includes a bibliography at the end of the book, providing you with more potential source material. However, the fact that there is no index in this book should tell you something about its intended audience—namely, an audience not interested in using an index. This, plus the fact that the book is only 136 pages and the publisher specializes in "popularized" treatments of theological subjects (you will learn to notice these kinds of things, or the librarian will often know), should tell you that the book is aimed at a general, not a scholarly, audience. There is nothing wrong with that, but it may be important to know, especially if your instructor wants you to use more scholarly works. On the other hand, such "popular" treatments are often easier to understand and helpful for the beginning theology student.

In another example, the book *Athanasius: The Coherence of His Thought*, by Anatolios, lists only four chapters in its table of contents. Each chapter title includes the phrase "the Relation between God and Creation." None of the four chapter titles makes it clear where in the book Athanasius's Christological views are discussed. Fortunately, this book was published by an academic publisher and is equipped with an index. (You are not expected to know which publishers are academic, popular, or some mixture of the two; if you want to know, the librarian can help.)

In Anatolios's index, you will find numerous page references under "Christ, doctrine of" in the index. You will also find subdivisions under "Christ, doctrine of," such as "'appropriation' model," "human body of," "human soul of," and "*Logos-sarx* model." You will also see cross-references to other entries in the index, such as "incarnation" or "redemption." The point is that you want to make the most efficient use of your time by using the index to focus precisely on your topic.

(From Khaled Anatolios, *Athanasius: The Coherence of His Thought*. London: Routledge, 1998.)

If you are interested in a more modern understanding of Christology, you would need to start with an encyclopedia whose scope encompasses a modern systematic treatment of Christology. The following standard reference titles all include such treatment and are likely to be found in Catholic college and university libraries.

Joseph A. Komonchak, Mary Collins, and Dermot A. Lane, eds. *The New Dictionary of Theology*. Wilmington, DE: Michael Glazier, Inc., 1987.

Wolfgang Beinert and Francis Schüssler Fiorenza. *Handbook of Catholic Theology*. New York: Crossroad, 1995.

The following reference work combines both historical and systematic coverage. Note that what is distinctive of this reference tool is that most articles have the same five-fold structure: (1) biblical background, (2) history of theology, (3) church teaching, (4) ecumenical perspectives, and (5) systematic reflections.

René Latourelle and Rino Fisichella, eds. *Dictionary of Fundamental Theology*. New York: Crossroad, 1994.

The scope of an encyclopedia can vary in yet other ways. For example, one important aspect of the scope of an encyclopedia that includes historical coverage is the range of periods covered. Most of the reference tools mentioned to this point cover the entire range of church history, but note the chronological limitation indicated by the following title:

Everett Ferguson, ed. *Encyclopedia of Early Christianity*. 2nd ed. 2 vols. New York: Garland Publishing, 1997.

To determine the precise dates covered by the period termed "early church," you need to read the preface or introduction to the encyclopedia.

Another encyclopedia might cover all periods of church history yet focus on one particular aspect of the history:

Leslie Houlden, ed. *Jesus in History, Thought, and Culture: An Encyclopedia*. 2 vols. Oxford, UK: ABC-CLIO, 2003 (also published as *Jesus: The Complete Guide*. New York: Continuum, 2005).

Such titles as these, by narrowing the scope of coverage, offer treatment of more subjects and more-detailed treatment of those subjects than a reference work encompassing all of Christian history and theology. Both of these more narrowly focused encyclopedias would be appropriate for studying Christology.

By now, you should have a good grasp of not just the importance of an encyclopedia's scope but also the kinds of questions involved in determining that scope. Does an encyclopedia include biographical coverage? Historical coverage? Coverage of systematic concepts? Is it limited chronologically or in some other way?

Student Tasks

1. Find an encyclopedia article on a theologian who was important for the development of Christology. Identify a particular theological idea or concept associated with that theologian and find an encyclopedia article on it (you may have to use a different encyclopedia).
2. Find an encyclopedia article relevant to some aspect of Christology (for example, one of the Christological titles such as "Lord" or "Son of God," or background articles such as "kingdom of God," "election," "eschatology," "wisdom," or "Logos"). Find an article on one theologian whose name you come across in the article (you may have to use a different encyclopedia).
3. Find an encyclopedia article on one of the ecumenical councils where Christological issues were discussed in the early church. Identify and find an additional article on either an important theological concept (other than Christology in general) discussed during the council or a theologian who was prominent at the council (you may have to use a different encyclopedia).
4. Locate one book on Christology with an index and browse through it, examining the way it presents various topics in the book. What topic, from all those included, would you like to pursue? Can you find an encyclopedia article on it?

The People of God: The Church

Daniel Finucane

from the EDITOR

When a child comes into the world, she usually receives a family name. The child belongs, is family, and shares in its reality, and without the child, the family may not exist someday. This child will carry the family forward into the future. Parents, siblings, grandparents, aunts, uncles, and the communities that surround them assume a necessary responsibility and obligation to nurture, care for, provide for, and love this child, as well as instruct her in the ways of living.

Being a member of a faith community is analogous. It means belonging to a family, being truly identified as one of the family—one belongs. For the Christian, this person now belongs to God through Jesus with the rest of the Christian family and is responsible and obligated to love God and neighbor and do all this implies.

Ecclesiology is the area of theology that studies living in the church as a member of the church's family—its history, variety, structures, and decisions; its past, present, and future. Christianity teaches that the source of it all, like a stone thrown into a still pond that sends ripples in every direction, is God, who sent Jesus Christ, gave the Holy Spirit, and invited all people into this familial love relationship as disciples.

To examine two thousand years of Christian tradition, even briefly, cannot be done here fully. What can be done is to provide understanding of some key foundational theological concepts. This chapter will go back to the early sources of the church in scripture, with an eye on its structures and strategies for living in the world and proclaiming the gospel. Also examined will be important understandings of some of the decisions in history and their ramifications for today and perhaps tomorrow.

One lesson that will be demonstrated throughout this text is the belief that the church is always in motion, alive and seeking to follow Christ in true discipleship; thus, its theological investigation is never finished. To put it simply, because theological knowledge is an investigation that is always seeking understanding, the more that theologians know, the more there is *to* know.

AN IMAGE

Imagine sitting at the edge of a large, peaceful pond. Into the water drops a stone. From the spot where it enters, ripples slowly spread out across the surface. Expanding waves swell to lift whatever is in their path. On the water, floating twigs and living things react and move. Fish and other creatures in the pond feel the effects. As the ripples touch objects on the surface, new ripples form and spread along their own courses. Expanding circles carry the record of an unexpected event that moves both the water and the things that live in its depths.

The event that we find at the beginning of the Christian church is a person—the Christ event (life-death-Resurrection). In the earliest description we have of the church, we hear Christ's followers preaching, proclaiming news of Jesus of Nazareth alive and then risen. This event/message is called the *kerygma* (Greek for "proclamation" or "announcement"). In a striking turnaround, the same people who ran away to save their lives when Jesus was arrested and killed are described in Jerusalem shortly after, calling Jesus the Christ (*Messiah* in Hebrew) and the Lord of all creation. Looking back on their own scriptures, they describe Jesus Christ as a stone rejected by other builders who has become a cornerstone for a new living building—a gathering together of people (see Ps 118:22, Mark 12:10, 1 Pet 2:4–8). In the pond metaphor, the risen Jesus is the stone that enters the waters of human history and sends ripples through the centuries.

Each person who joins himself or herself to Jesus Christ in baptism (from the Greek word *baptismo*, "to immerse") adds new ripples. Saint Paul writes that believers become part of Christ himself (1 Cor 12:12–13). As Jesus draws people into a living body, richer, larger, more complex waves of movement are created. Christ's ongoing presence and message grow in depth and strength.

What Then Is the Church?

We begin with the etymology of the root word for the insights it gives us. Originally, the Christians borrowed from the Hebrew word *kahal*, which meant "those gathered or assembled." The Greek word used by early Christians was *ekklēsia*, which also meant "assembly" and which became *ecclesia* in Latin. This word is still heard in the Romance ("Roman" or Latin-based) languages of Spanish (*iglesia*), French (*eglise*), and Italian (*chiesa*). When the Christian faith spread to northern Europe, emphasis was placed on assembling "in the Lord's (house)" (Greek = *kyriakon*), which became in German, *kirche*; and in English, *church*. In these etymologies, the key point is that it is an assembly that continues to gather for the purpose of worship of the Lord. In the academic discipline of theology, the study of the church is called "ecclesiology."

We now move to the traditional definition of *church*, which is offered in the *Catechism of the Catholic Church*: "In Christian usage, the word *church* designates the liturgical assembly, but also the local community or the whole universal community of believers. These three meanings are inseparable" (#752). But why this gathering? What is it called to do? How are these people connected to each other and to later generations? As we follow the story of the church, we will concentrate on its basic roots. A full look at church history would include discussion of the way the church leadership follows a hierarchy of offices. We would find too that many Christian communities have expressed their identity as a community of disciples. As Saint Paul reminds us, there are many gifts in this body of Christians (1 Cor 12:4–11).

How the Ripples Started

As we reflect on how the Christ event sends ripples through history, we can find no better place to begin than the scriptural passage in Acts (2:1–47) that has since ancient times shown the church, those who are immersed with Christ, what their common birth looked like and what it meant. In first-century Jerusalem, after Jesus ascends into heaven the Holy Spirit is poured out upon the disciples on the feast of Pentecost, the Jewish holy festival of the first fruits of the grain harvest in the spring, sometimes called the feast of "weeks" (Exod 23:14–17). The Greek name for the feast is "Pentecost," meaning "fifty," and refers to the fact that the feast falls fifty days after Passover. Filled with the Spirit, the Apostle Peter emerges from the upper room and addresses a crowd made up of people from all over the known world, telling them of God's breathtaking work, how it is described by the prophets, and how it is meant to spread. When Peter is asked by his hearers, "What happens next?" we can see how the impact of the *kerygma* begins to play out in their lives:

> Now when they heard this, they were cut to the heart and said to Peter and to the other apostles, "Brothers, what should we do?" Peter said to them, "Repent, and be baptized every one of you in the name of Jesus Christ so that your sins may be forgiven; and you will receive the gift of the Holy Spirit. For the promise is for you, for your children, and for all who are far away, everyone whom the Lord our God calls to him." And he testified with many other arguments and exhorted them, saying, "Save yourselves from this corrupt generation." So those who welcomed his message were baptized, and that day about three thousand persons were added. They devoted themselves to the apostles' teaching and fellowship, to the breaking of bread and the prayers. Awe came upon everyone, because many wonders and signs were being done by the apostles. All who believed were together and had all things in common; they would sell their possessions and goods and distribute the proceeds to all, as any had need. Day by day, as they spent much time together in the temple, they broke bread at home and ate their food with glad and generous hearts, praising God and having the goodwill of all the people. And day by day the Lord added to their number those who were being saved. (Acts 2:37–47)

Waves of later generations will be moved by the gospel; they too will be shaped by arguments and exhortations. They too will be challenged by corruption and shaped by communal life. When they succeed in handing on what they have received, it will be because they devote themselves together to the breaking of the bread. The foundations for the church are in place early on, developing in structures and forms we recognize today.

The Church Is a Paradox

As an ongoing event related to the Christ event, the church is always a combination of stability and movement. It is a place for believers to recognize each other and take strength from coming together. It is also where believers gather so they can be sent out. The church is where the Spirit of God creates Christian believers and moves them. Vatican Council II teaches:

> When the work which the Father gave the Son to do on earth (cf. Jn 17:4) was accomplished, the Holy Spirit was sent on the day of Pentecost in order that he might continually sanctify the Church, and that, consequently those who believe might have access through Christ in one Spirit to the Father (Eph 2:18). He is the Spirit of life, the fountain of water springing up to eternal life (cf. Jn 4:47; 7:38–39). . . . Guiding the Church in the way of all truth (cf. Jn 16:13) and unifying her in communion and in the works of ministry, he

> bestows upon her varied hierarchic and charismatic gifts, and in this way directs her; and he adorns her with his fruits (cf. Eph 4:11–12; 1 Cor 12:4; Gal 5:22). (*Lumen Gentium* 4)

This description of the Holy Spirit in the church is nothing more than a modern expression—the latest ripple—of the early insight of Saint Paul:

> Now there are varieties of gifts, but the same Spirit; and there are varieties of services, but the same Lord; and there are varieties of activities, but it is the same God who activates all of them in everyone. To each is given the manifestation of the Spirit for the common good. (1 Cor 12:4–7)

An Ongoing Vision for the *Ekklesia*

The event of the pouring out of the Holy Spirit of God at Pentecost sets out a vision and a mandate; from the start, the church gathers diverse people. Central to this story is the message that unity is built in diversity. Saint Paul writes that Christians need each other in order to be the Body of Christ. All members of the church have gifts or *charisms* (from the Greek word for "grace"). These gifts are given for all who embrace Christ and are given the Holy Spirit. What is rippling in the church? It is the presence of the Spirit of God, to enliven, to inspire different talents, and yet, to unify.

The Second Vatican Council takes up the root meaning of *ekklēsia* when it emphasizes the biblical image of the church as the people of God. It is tempting to think of the Roman Catholic Church in terms of its leaders, to see the Church as the pope and the bishops, but the council asserts that the Church is everyone gathered. Recalling the words of 1 Peter 2:9–10, the council describes followers of Christ as "a chosen race, a royal priesthood, a holy nation . . . who in times past were not a people, but now are the People of God" (see *Lumen Gentium* 9).

This is a people who live in and change the world with the gospel message. Vatican II captures that activity with another image: a pilgrim church (see *Lumen Gentium* 48). Pilgrims are people who are going somewhere. They seek a destination. They travel a certain way. The less baggage they carry, the better. The better their sight and sense of direction, the better they understand their journey, and the better they know their companions, the more effective they are in meeting challenges and arriving at their new home.

Starting with the apostles, the group that Jesus chose to follow him and sent to spread the good news of the reign of God coming near, the church has had to face a paradoxical challenge. In order to be true to the apostolic message, it has had to adapt and reexamine its structures and practices. In the unfolding generations, bishops, understood as successors to the apostles, preached the gospel and brought unity to the church by rehearsing its story. Over the years, the church has gathered these leaders into councils to respond to new controversies and deepen the church's understanding of the gospel. When it traveled to new lands and learned to speak new languages, Christianity remained true to its mandate to preach to all nations, and in doing so, it became inculturated. The church expresses the face of Christ in the features and manner of each group that embraces the gospel. In baptism, the Eucharist, the leadership of bishops, the basic creeds, and the canon of scripture, the identity of the church is preserved and at the same time evolves and moves as a living tradition. Pope John XXIII expressed this basic way of life in the Roman Catholic Church when he opened the Second Vatican Council in 1962 with the words, "The substance of the ancient doctrine of the deposit of faith is one thing, and the way in which it is presented is another" (Abbott, 1966,

715). He challenged the council fathers to take up the work of *aggiornamento* (to bring "up to date") to bring the gospel to the modern world. To do so, he wanted to throw open the doors to the world. The council soon invited Catholic women to attend, as well as people of other Christian denominations and other experts from around the world. Pope John's successor, Pope Paul VI, and other council leaders worked to deepen the Roman Catholic Church's cooperation with other Christians, as well as with women and men from other religious traditions. This bore fruit most notably in the council's document on ecumenism (*Unitatis Redintegratio*) and its document on the Church and non-Christian religions (*Nostra Aetate*).

We will take up Pope John's challenge again in this chapter. Our first task is to understand how the church has "rippled" through history as a living tradition and how the church can continue and deepen those ripples today.

AFTER THAT FIRST DAY

How has the church adapted and grown in Christ? Two significant challenges faced the first generations of Christians.

In the church's earliest years, the followers of Jesus were a subgroup of Judaism. Jesus, his apostles, and his other early followers were Jewish. After experiencing Jesus alive in the Resurrection, his followers continued to worship God in the Temple and obey the Jewish Law. They kept kosher and observed the Sabbath on the last day of the week. They also believed Jesus was the Christ—the Messiah—the fulfillment of God's promise; he was Lord over death, and the fulfillment of the Law. On the first day of the week, they met in their homes to break bread and experience Jesus present with them. Eventually, Gentiles were attracted to the new group. The question arose, "Did these people need to become Jews to be followers of Christ?" After significant turmoil (see Acts 15:1–29, Gal 5:2–12), the young Christian community, led by the arguments of Saint Paul, accepted the fact that baptism, rather than circumcision (the male rite of entrance into the Judaic covenant), made a Christian person a son or daughter of God (Gal 3:26–29). The book of Acts describes how the apostles met in Jerusalem in 49 CE, in what is the first recorded council, to argue the issue. In the process, the Jewish subgroup developed a new sort of relationship to its mother religion, Judaism, and stepped out into the world as a new way of following God. (Early on, the movement was, in fact, called "the Way"; see Acts 9:2; 22:4.)

As the first generation of Christians gave way to the next wave of believers, another challenge met them. The early church believed Jesus was going to return soon to complete the work of the reign of God. The first letter of Paul to the Thessalonians, arguably the oldest text of the New Testament (NT), illustrates how sure they were that Jesus' return would be in their own lifetimes (see 1 Thess 4:13–5:11). Yet many Christians began to die. The apostles, the foundational witnesses to the Resurrection, began to pass away before the return of the Lord. Eventually, the community realized it was going to be around for a while. With this shift in expectation about the time of Jesus' return, the community developed a new strategy for passing on the teachings of Jesus. Written gospels were compiled that carried the parables, healings, and sayings of Jesus, along with the narrative of his life, death, and Resurrection. A new strategy for carrying the tradition was created.

A HISTORICAL RESOURCE

In this chapter, we cannot take on every important challenge Christians have faced over twenty centuries or look at every development that has helped create the contemporary church, nor can we go into all the new questions that arise in every age where "faith seeks understanding." An ancient and yet ongoing example of how the church expresses a living tradition is found in the creeds, said weekly at the Sunday services of many different Christian communities. (Later, we will suggest more topics from church history that those who are interested in further study can pursue.)

Christians from a wide variety of denominations recite a creed (Lat., *credo* = "I believe"). The one Catholics pray after the scriptural readings of the Mass is called the Nicene Creed. It is named for the Council of Nicea (325 CE). It would probably be more accurate to call it the Niceno-Constantinopolitan Creed because the Council of Constantinople in 381 was still working on it. The Council of Ephesus (431) (the third council, held in the Greek seaboard city where Paul labored and the traditional home of Saint John the Evangelist) and the Council of Chalcedon (451) (the fourth council, nearly opposite Constantinople in Asia Minor) met later to handle other key issues.

We should point out that some changes in the Catholic version of the Nicene Creed came even later, in the Middle Ages. The "filioque" phrase (the addition of the words "and the Son") is one of the causes in the split between the Catholic and the Orthodox Church in 1054. This phrase remains both a source of tension and theological discussion between these churches.

All this illustrates the point that the Nicene Creed was written in a concise way to clarify what the church believed and to unite the people in that belief. Creeds functioned therefore less like a sermon and more like an archeological treasure site. Different layers of the past are preserved in

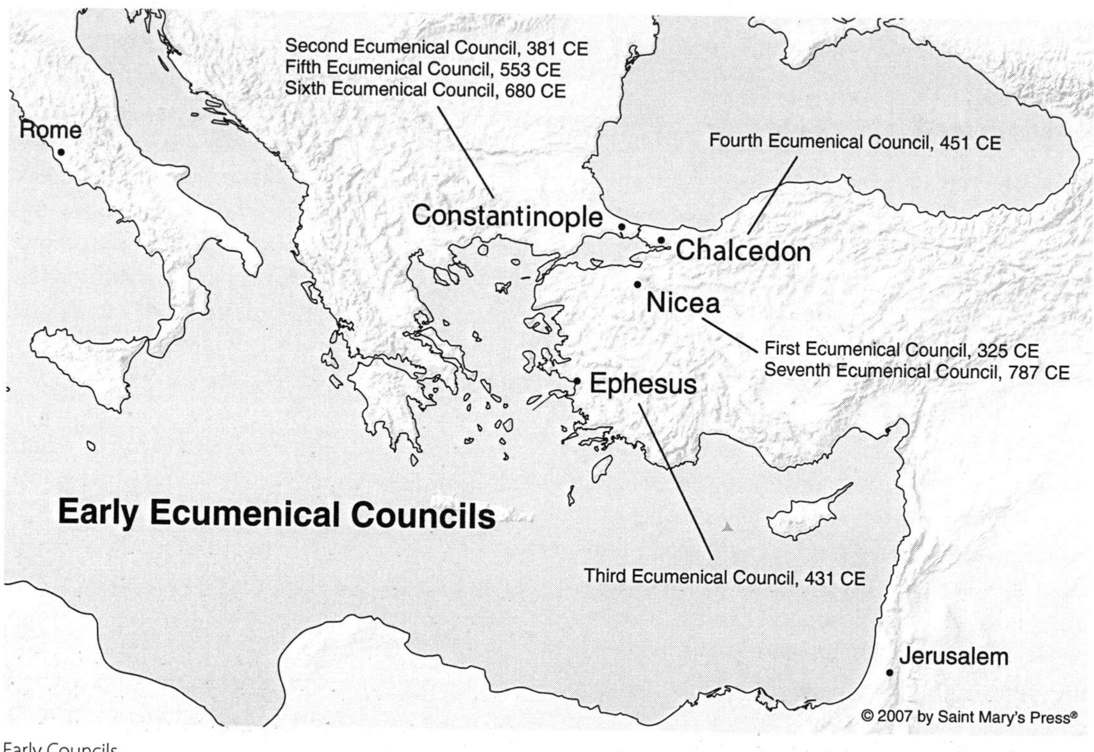

Early Councils

them, and we find pieces of events and arguments embedded in them. The church has used and adapted many different forms of creeds through the centuries. From the beginning, these statements of belief were proclaimed when the Christian service called "Eucharist" was celebrated and when the community came together for baptisms. The church's unity in Christ was thus expressed in many places and voices.

The odd thing is that though we may have heard this creed often and even recited it recently, we may not actually listen to the words. We now focus on the text itself as an example of living tradition. Try to read it as if it were the first time:

The Nicene Creed

I believe in one God,
the Father almighty,
maker of heaven and earth,
of all things visible and invisible.
I believe in one Lord Jesus Christ,
the Only Begotten Son of God,
born of the Father before all ages.
God from God, Light from Light,
true God from true God,
begotten, not made, consubstantial with the Father;
through him all things were made.
For us men and for our salvation
he came down from heaven,
and by the Holy Spirit was incarnate of the Virgin Mary,
and became man.
For our sake he was crucified under Pontius Pilate,
he suffered death and was buried,
and rose again on the third day
in accordance with the Scriptures.
He ascended into heaven
and is seated at the right hand of the Father.
He will come again in glory
to judge the living and the dead
and his kingdom will have no end.
I believe in the Holy Spirit, the Lord, the giver of life,
who proceeds from the Father and the Son,
who with the Father and the Son is adored and glorified,
who has spoken through the prophets.
I believe in one, holy, catholic and apostolic Church.
I confess one Baptism for the forgiveness of sins
and I look forward to the resurrection of the dead
and the life of the world to come. Amen.

(*Roman Missal* © 2010, ICEL.)

Using the archaeological image, a good place to start our investigation is to ask what elements strike us as odd or interesting. What sticks out? What sounds unusual? What differs from our usual expectations or expressions? What is said in a way we do not normally say things?

Digging Around in the Creed

Several phrases might be strange. "Visible and invisible" is not the way we usually talk. We are dealing with beliefs, though, with spiritual claims, so the idea behind it might make sense. We do know realities (love, trust, character) that are not visible in the same way as loaves of bread or a flowing river.

Statements about Jesus stand out too. Several are strung together: "Born of the Father before all ages, God from God, Light from Light, true God from true God, begotten, not made, consubstantial with the Father." Peter did not use this language in Acts 2. This is philosophical and theological language. It is language that early Christians wrestled with for years before agreeing. That in itself is an important realization. We are not in the sacred city of Jerusalem anymore. Our excavation of the creed has taken us to secular cultures in the four greatest cities of the Mediterranean world, great because of their trade, commerce, art and architecture, and cultural diversity: Athens, Rome, Antioch, and Alexandria.

To do justice to the creed or even to this one portion, we must probe its history, trace the events, debates, councils, theologians, and bishops who hammered out what ended up being accepted by the churches as the expression of their faith. Whole books have been written to tell this story. We do not have the space to retrace it here. (Some texts that go into detail will be suggested later.) We can offer a glimpse, however, of some key steps in the creed's development and see where the church's faith rests and how it has worked to arrive at that resting place.

The Nicene Creed's wording is inculturated; it comes from a particular past and looks to the present and future, striving to be faithful to the revelation of Jesus and its meaning in developing new contexts. In what has been a pattern throughout Christianity, new arguments were raised by Christians interacting with the current world and in particular with Greek culture and philosophy. At the same time, it has to be said that culture raises questions and challenges the Christian community. Not everyone was happy that such cultural influences were taken into the church. Tertullian (c. 160–220) was a native of Carthage in Africa, who received a solid pagan education, became a lawyer, lived in Rome, converted at about age 35 to Christianity, and then became a priest and theologian. He wanted to protect the faith from dangerous secular meddlers and asked a question that never quite goes away: "What does Athens have to do with Jerusalem?" Or, to put it another way, what does secular culture have to do with Christianity? Mostly the answer given by Christians in the next unfolding centuries was, "a lot." The gospel would eventually travel not just through Greek thought but also through the Roman Empire and many other cultures. In our day, it continues to travel in new encounters in Africa, China, India, Russia, Indonesia, and Brazil, just to mention the largest populations today. The church will be wherever humans are tomorrow as well, perhaps even to new places beyond the earth. Therefore, the question continues, and answers are sought.

A Question of Substance

The phrase "consubstantial with the Father" relates the meaning of a key word: *homoousios*. Passages in the NT claim Jesus to be divine. Others emphasize how human he was. Figuring out how these two claims could both be asserted and interrelated, and doing so in ways that did not lose one or the other claim, confuse them, or try to hybridize them, was difficult.

In addressing the Christological questions, authors of the Nicene documents began using a word that was not part of the scriptural accounts but that did address the questions raised about the scripture's message in their Greek philosophical climate. Jesus was described as *homoousios* with God. *Consubstantial* is the related term in Latin. A good translation is "of the same stuff" ("same substance"). Making this wording official (that is what councils do in resolving debates—they resolve to say things deliberately, officially) was the big decision with which not everyone was happy. The concern was about introducing a word not found in the NT and whether the church would be preserving the same message if it used a nonbiblical language such as philosophy.

The Nicene Creed reflects the results of debates over wording. Each Sunday, millions of Christians say that Jesus was "consubstantial with the Father." Should the phrasing matter? The church found that the central message, the *kerygma*, was at stake. The church claims that Jesus is the "same stuff" (substance) as God—that he is fully divine. He is also *homoousios* with humanity. Jesus is the "same human stuff" (substance) as us—he is fully human. This is emphasized later in the creed, where Mary is mentioned. People were arguing over whether the divine somehow outweighed the human. The Council of Ephesus brought Jesus' mother into the debates, calling Mary, *Theotokos*, "God-bearer," and in that word they identified Jesus as divine while insisting that he was a human son as well, reinforcing that he was born of Mary and is the same as us (human).

The Christological controversies within the councils of the fourth and fifth centuries illustrate that trying to understand God in human words is complex and imperfect. At the same time, by choosing words carefully, Christians can get closer to the truth of what they experience and understand about God. Words cannot say everything, but they matter tremendously.

In the messy process of clarifying the wording of the creed, the church used an old tool in a new way. Liturgical creeds, used originally at baptisms and the Eucharist, were adapted to state as clearly as possible who Jesus is. Hence, the questions raised by Greek culture could not be understood nor the truth of it conveyed by repeating phrases from scripture. The church took a significant step in introducing Greek terms, in a Christian way, that lend additional insights into its understanding of faith. At the same time, the church found that other cultures held important resources in themselves to carry the original message authentically. Hence, the paradox is that change could be part of remaining truly unchanged in the traditional understanding of Jesus.

Tradition

When the apostles were gone, the churches they left behind assumed responsibility for passing on the gospel through history. This handing down is the ongoing creating of tradition. The Latin word *tradere* means "to hand on." For example, when a young bride uses something passed down from her great-grandmother as part of her wedding gown or when we eat a Thanksgiving meal of turkey, we are continuing traditions. In a theological context, *tradition* means to remain connected and empowered by the original Christ event through history. Some examples that show how central this handing on was for the identity of the community occur in Luke 1:1–2, 1 Corinthians 11:23, and 2 Timothy 2:2.

When we study ecclesiology, history is in a sense the laboratory part of the course. We use reports issued from time to time, like the creed, to investigate the church's earlier experiences. From the early church's struggles to express itself in new and different cultures while keeping the same gospel message it received from the beginning, we gain a lesson for our own times; the church faces the same process and challenges.

History can also show us that handing on the tradition can be costly, as the following story tells us through the martyr Saint Polycarp.

The Story of Polycarp

Can you remember an elderly person in your life whom you loved and respected, who told you stories from the past about people, life, or events? Most of us have people in our lives who tell us these stories—a grandmother, an older neighbor, or a friend. After a while, we may realize that we have heard the same story quite a few times. We might even be able to tell the story or finish parts of it. Over time, we realize these repeated stories stayed with us, set our values, and helped fashion our identities. They become more precious, and we cherish them for the transmission of life they nurtured. And as we grow, we often sit around with others and retell these stories: "Do you remember the time . . . ?"

In the second century, there lived an old man named Polycarp, who for decades had been a cornerstone of the church in Smyrna. He was bishop there in a time of persecution by the Romans. Christians were given the opportunity to avoid torture and death by renouncing their faith; if they did so, they received a written certificate acknowledging that they were willing to obey the civil religion and bend their knees to the emperor. Roman officials knew that leaders like Polycarp were prime targets to change others.

When soldiers came to arrest Polycarp, they too felt a deep respect for this old, saintly man. He fed them a meal, asking them for time to pray before leaving with them, and they let him pray for two hours. The account that comes down to us from his followers, *Martyrdom of Polycarp*, describes him being led away, sitting on an ass, reminiscent of the ride taken by Jesus into the town where he was crucified. The soldiers tried to talk Polycarp into calling Caesar "Lord," so they could leave him alone to die eventually in his own bed, but he refused. At his trial, the proconsul instructed him to take the oath and gain his freedom. Polycarp replied that he could not now stop serving his Savior and Lord of eighty-six years. The proconsul warned then of the wild animals and the fire that were awaiting Polycarp. The give-and-take between this bishop, his accusers, and the crowd is a stirring story of faith (and a vivid illustration of the Greek word *martyr*, or "witness" to the faith).

The description of Polycarp's last moments tells of him surrounded by fire yet not destroyed by it, evoking the scene of Shadrach, Meshach, and Abednego from the book of Daniel (3:19–97). Eventually he was stabbed with a dagger to end his life. One of the strangest elements in the story is the description of the smell coming from the fire that surrounded Polycarp, which witnesses said was like bread baking and like incense. This account of the martyrdom of Polycarp connects him in the most direct way possible to Christ. Rather than leave this Lord for another, the old man became Christ. His body became like Eucharistic bread; his destruction was like the incense that is meant to bring prayers to God. What reasons could anyone ever have for waxing poetic in the face of an execution? In the martyrs, the early church recognized the cost of true discipleship: the whole self. After eighty-six years of prayer, Polycarp knew where his strength was. His witness would be a powerful influence on later generations; the blood of the martyrs is the seed of the church.

As we can also see in the story of Polycarp, the Christian community preserves its memory through its continuous tradition linking it back to Jesus and forward to every new challenge. Remember the ripple image with which we began this chapter? Tradition is the Christ event, as the rock entering into the water of time, sending waves outward to every new generation. The record of the ripples is tradition as it unfolds in history, which we examine next.

History Is Central

Christianity shapes and is shaped by the historical context in which we live. Indeed, at the root of the church's understanding of ecclesiology is the realization and claim that God acts in history; God deals directly with the created universe. The church asserts that people have not been abandoned but are in relationship to God.

Christianity's Jewish roots teach that this universe is, as God declares after each day's work at creation, a good place. Not everyone in the ancient world (or now) could believe this message, and it is easy to understand why. Before adequate nutrition, antibiotics, decent clothing and shelter, indoor plumbing, safe childbirth, and a wealth of other developments, life was short and hard for most people—and even today, life remains difficult and too short for many in our world. Into this difficult world, first Judaism and then Christianity brought an amazing message: The world is worth living in and caring about. As difficult as its problems are, it is worth caring for and fixing. In theological terms, it is worth redeeming. Salvation belongs to this world.

The church's worldview shares these Jewish roots. One of the most famous verses in the NT, seen sometimes on banners at sporting events, is John 3:16: "For God so loved the world that he gave his only son." The Christian's worldview is rooted in the Incarnation of Jesus Christ, the belief that Jesus is God and human in one person. Those who followed Jesus in first-century Galilee found God at work. This person who was every bit as human as they were also embodied something striking and unique. The same God whose work they found in Abraham, in Moses, in David, in the prophets, in the temple, in the Torah, and the other scriptures was at work in this Jesus from Nazareth. He came preaching the "reign of God," and they were drawn to him, enthralled, wondering, trying to understand what that reign was. Yet, frightened and disappointed, they fled and deserted him at his death. He was arrested by those who were quite sure that whatever reign this new "king" was building, it was a threat to their own power.

The church is an unlikely story. The church believes that God acted in Jesus; Jesus acts in the church. The actions of the church are in the hands of everyday human beings. God leaves incredibly important responsibilities in flimsy, fickle hands.

As Christians live in the present, they do not just look to the past. Through diverse Christian communities, even through different approaches to a common tradition, Christians can form powerful visions for the future. The journey is shared as the church also serves people of other religious traditions and all humanity as integral to its vision in Christ. Within this global service to humanity, Vatican II provides a powerful vision of Christ, present in the church, his Body, who is revealed in the actions of the church and its sacraments (Lat., *sacramentum* = "the sign"), the topic of chapter 7 (see *Lumen Gentium* 1–8). Christians' strengths and troubles are linked to Christ in the sacraments, to the sacrament of his church, just as the weaknesses and strength of the disciples were linked to Jesus. Just when his disciples were most at a loss for what he had meant, when their hopes were crushed with his death, they experienced him alive again. Because of what God did in Jesus, raising him to life, these followers who were lost were changed. They exploded with hope.

IS COMPETITION GOOD FOR THE CHURCH?

To illustrate where that hope took them, we will look at one development from the early church in some detail. First, recall the theme of Peter's Pentecost speech and the Nicene Creed. They both emphasize the paramount teaching that God is Lord and in charge in the world. We will examine how the early church forged its vision of the world in terms of creation and "the world to come" by arguing it out with their worldview competitors.

We can put the challenge this way: Is competition good for the community of the church? Should we compete over theological wording? Think of how athletes train for a contest. They prepare for a goal they want to reach. Discipline and effort help them deepen their understanding of who they are. Other types of challenges may not be competitive in the sense of creating a contest with another. Some may pit us more deeply against our selves or our previous accomplishments. Consider how a musician or a painter evolves in her craft, with new projects deepening and exploring her insights and expressions. What can competition in theology accomplish?

Gnosticism: Who Knows Best?

To illustrate how a deeper understanding of the gospel message can come through real historical struggles, it may be useful to look at how some people shook up the Christian churches with new and different beliefs. A major competitor for the early Christian church was Gnosticism. More accurately, we should refer to "Gnosticisms," in the plural, because various versions of this religion developed. Certain teachings were common to the many forms, however. *Gnosis* is a Greek word meaning "knowledge." If you say the English word *know* out loud, you will hear and be pronouncing the first syllable of the original Greek sound, because *know* comes from this Greek etymology. Gnostics claimed a special form of knowledge. It made their worldview and their groups esoteric. Some special leaders had the knowledge of God and the way to salvation. Those who wanted a share in it had to come to those who had this special knowledge. Gnostics created a select group of "insiders."

What was the different worldview of these challengers? In addition to having some Jewish influences, Gnosticism was rooted in the thought of the Greek philosopher Plato (427–347 BCE), who taught that the physical world was derived from a larger reality. The spiritual world, the world of the mind, was what was most real; the material world was an imperfect copy of what was original and true. In Gnostic thought, the spiritual and material were pushed even farther apart to form a dualism where the spirit and the gods or God were seen as good, while the body and things of the earth were definitely bad. A human being was understood as a regrettable combination of the divine and earthly; the Gnostics thought that in a human, a divine spark of the larger Godhead had been trapped in a body. The goal was to release the spark again and thereby escape this world. Consequently, most Gnostics performed austere practices like fasting and refraining from sex.

Christian Gnosticism?

A form of Christian Gnosticism developed when people within this worldview adopted and then adapted certain teachings about Jesus. It is with their understanding of the Resurrection in particular that we can see the difference between Gnostics taking on Christian terminology and the original Christians proclaiming the message about what happened to Jesus.

A Gnostic text from the late second century, called "The Treatise on Resurrection," describes how Jesus in his Resurrection made himself into "an imperishable Aeon." Jesus becomes a form of light—again. In this "spiritual resurrection," Jesus "swallows up" the psychic dimension of the person, as well as the bodily dimension. He has no use for the earth or worldly things. The Gnostic description of Jesus adapts him to their worldview. Should Christians have been concerned about new ideas and interpretations? How do Christians know whether these teachings draw them away from their central beliefs? Do these questions and distinctions matter? Right here in this discussion, we can see the significant and important role theology has: it is faith seeking understanding so as to find God. The Christian community has taken a stance that authentic understanding of God's revelation matters, judgments follow and matter, and their commitment to enter into relationship with God matters—to Christians individually and to their embrace of neighbors everywhere. The simple bottom line is that God also gave people the gift of understanding as one important way to learn from God. So we ask again from a theological perspective: Do these questions and conclusions matter to Christians?

What Should the Church Make of Competition?

Should those hearing different gospels then (and should people now) not be open to all new ideas? This is a perennial question. Certainly, a Christian response should be thoughtful. Then and now, intelligent hearers would want to listen to both sides and think about what was true in the messages. Nevertheless, it is legitimate to ask which differences matter.

The Gnostics preached the gospel of a heavenly, spiritual resurrection for Jesus. However, the Gospels of Matthew, Mark, Luke, and John describe Jesus' resurrected body as new and transformed but still very much a physical body. Jesus still eats with his friends. Could Gnostic and Christian messages both be right? At stake here is an understanding, and a claim, of how God deals with the world and the humans in it. In one view, the Gnostics saw the world as a place to be shunned. True knowledge led humans out of it to a better place beyond. Real transformation got past the merely human to make a person into a new being, a new sort of divine light, that could leave this ugly world behind. Christians, on the other hand, claim that God loves the world. The Resurrection of Jesus, and through it the possibility of human transformation, is linked to the world now. Jesus does not redeem people at the expense of their being human. He redeems them in their humanity, fulfilling it. He is the same stuff as we are. When people become one with him, they become more of who they are.

The Plot Thickens

People in the second century and people in our own time have argued about what readings can deliver the true message of the Christ event. We will spend a little more time here with a leading Gnostic to see how his competing ideas led to clarification about texts Christians were using to understand Jesus. The Gnostics' new perspective on the gospel left out something central to the original message.

A key character in the confusion created by the Gnostic challenge is a man named Marcion (d. 160), a wealthy shipowner who was excommunicated for immorality by his father, who was a bishop. Marcion then set himself up in Rome. It is not entirely clear whether Marcion was a Gnostic, but his theological agenda suggests that he either was one or was influenced by them. Marcion pushed for a reform of the Christian message, arguing that the church should move along the trajectory Saint Paul began, distinguishing Christian faith from its Jewish roots. Marcion insisted on a small core of Christianity based on love (i.e., Christian scriptures) instead of anything to do with Law (*Tanak* or Old Testament). He insisted, moreover, that the apostles and disciples misunderstood Jesus' message and that only Saint Paul truly understood it. Marcion argued that the church should leave behind what he saw as an inadequate understanding of God embedded in the Jewish scriptures. He rejected outright these Jewish writings, and he recommended selected Christian texts: certain writings of Paul and a version of Luke's Gospel that emphasized the Gentile mission. He wrote brief introductions to his selected texts, and some of those are the only writings of his that we have today.

The churches throughout Christianity reacted to what Marcion had done and rejected his narrowly selected collection of writings. They focused more carefully on texts they had been reading, works that carried a fuller presentation of the original tradition. Therefore, in reaction to Marcion, the original complete text of Luke was used. Instead of using one Gospel in isolation, the complementary perspectives of the Gospels of Matthew, Mark, and John were included as well to give the best understanding of Jesus, of his Incarnation, life, death, and Resurrection. The churches' canon of scripture emphasized that Marcion was too limiting. (The word *canon* means a "measuring stick," like a foot-long ruler by which something can be measured. The canon is a "rule" for deciding which sacred texts are authentic to the genuine faith tradition and therefore should be included in the church's reading and worship.)

In selecting the texts that would present his message, Marcion left out Christian sources that said something different from what he was preaching. At stake for the Gnostics and Christians of the second century, and at stake in this century and the future, were conflicting claims about gospel texts and their relationship to Christ. The early Christian church asserted that the Resurrection was of a certain type, expressed in the "canonical" Gospels but not in others (e.g., the *Gospel of Thomas* or the *Gospel of Peter*). An important stance went hand in hand with this choice of gospels. The church claimed not only that this message was true but also that it was what the original witnesses to Jesus' Resurrection had experienced. Whether someone chooses to believe a different gospel or not is one issue. Another one significant for historical argument is that the message claimed by the church in selecting its Gospels was the original message. The others were innovations that tried to bring in a new angle on the original gospel but in doing so changed its very identity.

This sort of plot seems to continue to thicken through history. Do we think Gnosticism is dead, buried, and forgotten? Aware or not, contemporary fans of certain gnostic ideas and texts sometimes criticize the church for dismissing or hiding other gospels. Why was the *Gospel of Thomas* left out of the canon? Fans of the popular novel *The Da Vinci Code* or the movie *Stigmata* are intrigued by several questions: Did the church hide the real gospels? Did it hide the truth? Did it not want competition? To answer these questions, we must consider that the church was identifying its roots—it was maintaining the very meaning of its message. The universal church recognized that the Gnostic's message did (and does) say something different from what the church knew to be true. The result of the confusion brought by Marcion is ironic in light of modern questions about the canon. The Christian community found that Marcion was too narrow. The Gnostics see the truest reality as ultimately "spiritual." On the other hand, an incarnational understanding of Jesus, the church, and creation sees things in a more sophisticated, holistic way.

Does this mean that new ideas cannot be heard? Should Christians avoid thinking about what others propose? Of course not. By all means, we should read the texts over which the church argued. There has not been much of a cover-up, really. The "alternate" gospels have been translated and available in libraries and bookstores for decades. The best strategy for those either in the church or outside of it who are intrigued by the debates is to do enough studying to see what all the arguing was about.

STUDYING TRADITION

When we pay attention to something as important as the wording of the creed, we are pulled directly into a concern for history and tradition. Christians believe that God started this revelation long before we were here. In our opening image, we saw the beginning of the "ripple effect" of the Christ event—the preaching of the apostles, the birth of the church, and the ongoing life of this community that moves into each era with news that God is alive in the world.

In the creed, we have found archaeological treasures where the early church met challenges. We turn now to another resource that the creed carries through history, one that shows how the church can continue to meet new challenges in every era.

As the church moved through the centuries and interacted with different ideas and cultures, it came to recognize a set of criteria for understanding when developments were legitimate or not. These criteria also are embedded in the creed. In a line that specifies what sort of church we believe in, it is described as being one, holy, catholic, and apostolic. These have traditionally been called the "marks of the church." They identify how the church continues to evolve as a living tradition.

The Marks (Signs) of the Church

One

Unity has been a concern of the church from the start. John's Gospel vividly expresses Jesus' concern for unity among his followers. In the Last Supper scene in John 17:1–26, Jesus prays that the disciples will be one, just as the Father and Jesus are one. Early on, foundational practices and structures of the church were emphasized to create unity: the Eucharist, the bishop, the creeds, arguments over doctrine, councils, and the canon of the Christian Scriptures all served the oneness of the church.

Holy

Christians are baptized into Christ himself. Each Christian is to become him. Orthodox Christianity has expressed this vividly: Christ became human so that humans could become divine. Holiness is sometimes visible, sometimes not. The most dramatic image of this mark is martyrdom.

Catholic

The Greek word *katholikos* is often translated as "universal," yet its root meaning is more accurately given as "throughout the whole." The word *catholic* expresses a dynamic image; it is like the biblical image of yeast that enlivens a whole mass of dough. It is like our ripple metaphor, where the gospel spreads outward in ever-expanding spheres of influence. In the early centuries, when new ideas about Christ's divinity and humanity were debated, the struggle was to see whether innovative expressions would spread and be accepted widely. Would churches throughout different areas and cultures find the newly developed theologies to be legitimate growths of understanding? *Homoousios* ("same nature" as God) became accepted. Marcion's canon did not. The strategy of calling all the churches (represented by their bishops) to come together in councils to argue these points came from the conviction that a "catholic" development would be proven to be from the Spirit of God, if the church moved toward a *consensus fidelium* ("consensus of the faithful")—an agreement among all believers.

Apostolic

An apostle is one who is sent. In Christian usage, it refers to those witnesses of the risen Christ who were sent to spread the gospel to the rest of the world. The role of "the Twelve" came from the fact they were witnesses to an original event (see Acts 1:15–26).

This criterion asks whether an expression or practice is connected to the original message. Has growth come from the deepest roots? Early on, apostolicity attached itself to particular cities where the seeds of the gospel were planted first: (1) Jerusalem was the birthplace of the church. (2) Antioch, a port to the north, was the launching spot for missionary journeys of Paul and others. In this city, the followers of Jesus Christ were first called "Christians" (see Acts 11:26). (3) Alexandria, long a place of scholarship and culture and the home of a large Greek-speaking Jewish community, became the home of an early thriving church, a place for theological scholarship. (4) Rome was the seat of the empire, the place from which persecutions were launched yet, ironically, the place where the blood of the martyrs became seeds for faith. From the earliest generations of the church, Rome was venerated as the place where Peter and Paul were killed, and it held a prominence among other churches. (5) A fifth city, originally Byzantium and renamed Constantinople (and now called Istanbul, in Turkey), became the "New Rome" in Christendom when the emperor Constantine moved his capital there from Rome in the fourth century. A rich mix of leadership, study, and controversy over the apostolic faith became part of its heritage.

When the church faces challenges today, when it faces difficulties from within or from outside its community, it still finds its solutions and strength most clearly by embracing unity, holiness, catholicity, and deep apostolic roots. The marks of the church have served in the past to balance and shape its growth. They are the criteria by which it can be guided today.

The image of the ripple effect continues through history, and we see it when looking back through the tradition. We can put it this way: If the apostle Peter, the preacher from the first-century Pentecost that gave birth to the church, were to return today, would he recognize what began with that first sermon? As it spread through the major cities of the Roman Empire, through Greek culture, and later through human nations and cultures on all the continents of the world, the *ekklēsia* has shown the same recognizable patterns of the original structure provided by God to the first hearers of the gospel. The ripples that flow from that event have the distinct shape and pattern of that Christ event. If Peter returned, I think he would recognize the church today in continuity with his preaching.

What Do the Marks of the Church Mean Today?

We might ask how these criteria challenge the contemporary church to embrace its full identity.

Unity

What sort of issues cause problems in a parish? In a denomination? Between different denominations? Do poor and wealthy churches often work together? Do different denominations? Practical work can unite. Hungry people do not usually quibble about who made the soup. What can be done to overcome factions in a community?

Holiness

What does holiness look like today—an act of service, an apology, a donation of time and money? Do Christians stand with someone in trouble, even if it means embarrassment? In a culture charged with materialistic values, what forms does holiness take? What does holiness say to violence? Do Christians ever let humor diffuse a situation so that they overcome the temptation to take themselves too seriously?

Catholicity

Are there areas where Christians would rather the gospel's influence not go? In what situations would they rather not be reminded of their calling? Can Christians let their own views be questioned by the humanity of others? Are they able to give a reason, explanation, or lived example for what they think and believe?

Apostolicity

Who do Christians look to as authorities? Are there elderly women and men they trust and look to for advice? Are there children who, by example, show God's presence? Why did people like Pope John Paul II, Martin Luther King Jr., Mother Teresa of Calcutta, Billy Graham, and Desmond Tutu from South Africa draw crowds from different continents that numbered in the millions or hundreds of thousands?

To address both historical and contemporary issues, we have resources in the experiences and wisdom of scripture and tradition, in the strategies and structures that have been created through human efforts and the work of the Holy Spirit. The church has drawn on the insights of church leaders and of the whole people of God. In the Vatican II document on the church called *Lumen Gentium* ("Light of all peoples"), one finds the council fathers' description of the particular role of the laity today:

> Christ is the great prophet who proclaimed the kingdom of the Father both by the testimony of his life and by the power of his word. Until the full manifestation of his glory, he fulfills this prophetic office, not only by the hierarchy who teach in his name and by his power, but also by the laity. He accordingly both establishes them as witnesses and provides them with the appreciation of the faith (*sensus fidei*) and the grace of the word (cf. Acts 2:17–18; Rev 19:10) so that the power of the Gospel may shine out in daily family and social life. (#35)

CONCLUSION: LEAVING A LOT OUT

The ripples of the Christ event are concentric, moving outward in directions we could not have known, controlled, or predicted. The variety of people and places, events and rituals, movements and eras that are connected to the Christian message over its two-thousand years of history make the task of understanding the church daunting. Anyone with any familiarity with the church will ask how we can stop our story now in the fifth century. What about the next fifteen-hundred years? What about the structures and challenges we see today? What about the many unrecognized and unsolicited contributions of women? How do we begin to explain or evaluate the messages that claim to speak for Christ and his church? Storefront churches and towering cathedrals, white-robed popes stepping off jets, polished TV preachers asking for money, arguments over how much religion should influence public life and politics—all of these images come into our living room, unless we turn them off with our remote control. The problems that hurt the church come from both outside and inside. Can common ground be found for diverse groups of Orthodox Christians, Protestants, and Roman Catholics, as well as Copts, Armenians, Syrian Christians, and others?

What we have studied here does not stop in the fifth century, or ever. It shows that the church has the resources to take up these difficult issues. The church has faced major challenges of identity and crisis, and it has not only survived but flourished. Christians believe that extraordinary charisms have been drawn out of the ordinary human members of the Body of Christ by the movement of God's own Spirit. By striving for unity and holiness, embracing catholicity that ripples even through troubled historical waters, and rooting itself in the apostolic faith that connects Christians to the movement of the Spirit in Jerusalem at the first Pentecost, the church can face the modern world too. In fact, much work lies ahead, but history has demonstrated that Christians can embrace current challenges and look through the other "ripples" of its history for the lessons still to be learned.

Vatican II, in its *Pastoral Constitution on the Church in the Modern World,* renewed the church's mandate: "The joy and hope, the grief and anguish of the people of our time, especially of those who are poor or afflicted in any way, are the joy and hope, the grief and anguish of the followers of Christ as well" (*Gaudium et Spes* 1). The church's calling here is clear: the *ekklēsia*, the gathering of the people of God in the Holy Spirit, is intended to make believers the presence of Christ in the world.

Student Activity 1: Starting at the Beginning—The Church in Acts

The oldest account of the Christian church is in the second chapter of the NT's book of Acts. In the middle of Jerusalem, Jesus' followers, who a few hours before were hiding in a closed room, spilled into the streets and started talking in different languages, called "tongues." Some people who encountered them thought they were crazy. If we examine this story carefully, we find a description not of a random collection of followers but of a communion, a distinct sort of community (*communio* in Latin, *koinōnia* in Greek). Even in the beginning, after the Resurrection, we see a group with a structure and a mission to others.

You are invited now to do a theological reading of the passage Act 2:1–47. It is not long but, as we will see, it is rich in content and has huge implications for Christianity itself. To set the stage briefly, this group preaches the good news of Jesus Christ—the gospel—right after the Pentecost event, sometimes called "the birthday of the church." In order to understand the passage and its points better, use the following questions. This is good practice in thinking "theologically."

Questions

1. Who are the principle actors in this scene? Who are all these people in the city? Who are the prophets quoted in Peter's speech?
2. How is unity described in this passage (consider verses 1, 3, 4, 32, 36, 41, 42, 44)? What is the main message? What is the reaction of the crowd? Are there different reactions?
3. When do the people ask, "What are we supposed to do with this?"
4. Where does the group meet daily? Why two places? Why both places?
5. Why are the people astounded?
6. How does the Jewish background of the apostles and their audience shape the preaching and the responses?
7. How is the involvement of God portrayed in this passage?
8. Where does the energy come from to make the gospel message public?
9. Why does the Holy Spirit allow people to hear the message in their own languages?

Writing a Theological Reflection

After thinking through this passage and talking about it with others, it is useful to collect your impressions by writing them down. Using a one-page format or a journal entry, discuss the main impact of the passage. Give some thought to the issues it presents about the nature of the church. Consider what other questions the passage raises that you did not have before.

Student Activity 2: A Classroom Exercise for Exploring Contemporary Ecclesiology

Avery Dulles's book, *Models of the Church*, has been an important influence on ecclesiological discussions since Vatican II. His original five models of the church as institutional, mystical communion, sacrament, herald, and servant can help Christians identify their own connection to the church as well as challenge individual Christians to take seriously charisms and tasks in the church to which they may not have given as much attention. In a later edition of his book, Dulles introduced a sixth model, the community of disciples, which he sees as drawing all the models into common ecclesiological reflection. The following exercise can engage classroom discussion and individual reflection.

Arrange the class into five groups. Each one should prepare and then present a basic description of one of Dulles's models of the church. The advantages and disadvantages or strengths and weaknesses of each model should be discussed. Each group should be prepared to ask the next group a question or two. Either a sixth group can be chosen at the beginning to present the communion of disciples model, or each group can be asked to respond to the sixth model, saying how it enhances its own group's understanding of the nature of the church. (If groups are chosen at random, for example, by students "counting off," students may then have to explore a model for which they are not naturally or initially supportive or knowledgeable. At the end of the exercise, students can be invited to offer a thought or two from their own point of view.)

Extended discussions of each of Dulles's models can be found in his own text and in a number of sites on the Internet.

Questions about the Text

1. What are the etymologies for the word *church*? What do they indicate to others about the church?
2. What is the definition of the word *church*?
3. Where does the word *creed* come from? What is its purpose?
4. What is meant by the Latin-derived word *consubstantial* and its Greek counterpart *homoousios?* Why is the concept important?
5. Who is Polycarp, and why is he referred to in this chapter?
6. What does the word *Gnosticism* mean, and what is it all about?
7. What are the four marks of the church? What do they mean today?

Questions for Discussion

1. What do you think of when you use the word *church*?
2. Write your own creed of what you believe. If doing this exercise with others, share your creeds with each other.
3. What role does culture play in the creeds? Can there be a creed that is not encultur-ated? How would that be done?
4. Do you know someone personally or have you read about someone who in some ways exemplifies fidelity as Polycarp did?
5. Gnostics built their belief system around special knowledge. What other special ways might people use to form religions?
6. What are some examples of the four marks of the church that witness to its understand-ing of its true identity in God?

For Further Study

Chapter Themes

Abbott, Walter M., ed. *The Documents of Vatican II.* Translated by Joseph Gallagher. New York: Herder & Herder, 1966.

Brown, Raymond E. *The Churches the Apostles Left Behind.* Mahwah, NJ: Paulist Press, 1984.

Doyle, Dennis M. *The Church Emerging from Vatican II: A Popular Approach to Contemporary Catholicism.* Revised edition. New London, CT: Twenty-Third Publications, 2002.

A wide array of contemporary topics is discussed in an engaging style. The book follows the organization and agendas of two documents from Vatican II: *Lumen Gentium* and *Gaudium et Spes.*

Dulles, Avery. *Models of the Church.* Exp. ed. New York: Image Books, 1987.

Dulles considers different ways to discuss and understand the church as institutional, mystical communion, sacrament, herald, and servant. He elaborates advantages and disadvantages of such models and ties them together with a final model, the community of disciples.

Happel, Stephen, and David Tracy. *A Catholic Vision.* Minneapolis, MN: Fortress Press, 1984.

In this look at the churches following the NT period, the author writes consciously of the need for ecumenical reflection.

McGonigle, Thomas D., and James F. Quigley. *A History of the Christian Tradition: From Its Jewish Origins to the Reformation.* Mahwah, NJ: Paulist Press, 1988.

———. *A History of the Christian Tradition: From the Reformation to the Present.* Mahwah, NJ: Paulist Press, 1996.

These two volumes are an overview of church history that presents the main events, people, and issues that continue to influence the church today.

The Creed

Johnson, Luke Timothy. *The Creed: What Christians Believe and Why It Matters.* New York: Image Books, 2004.

Marthaler, Bernard L. *The Creed: The Apostolic Faith in Contemporary Theology.* Rev. ed. New London, CT: Twenty-Third Publications, 1992.

Gnosticism

Robinson, James M., general editor. *The Nag Hammadi Library in English.* Rev. ed. New York: HarperSanFrancisco, 1990.

Reference Works

Brown, Raymond E., et al. *The New Jerome Biblical Commentary.* Rev. ed. Upper Saddle River, NJ: Prentice Hall, 1989.

Cross, F. L., et al. *The Oxford Dictionary of the Christian Church.* 3rd rev. ed. Oxford: Oxford University Press, 2005.

from the REFERENCE LIBRARIAN

Researching Using the Internet—Ecclesiology

According to Dr. Finucane, you can find on the Internet "extended discussions" of the various "models" of the church developed by Avery Dulles. Because this information comes from a professional, you know that these discussions must be worthwhile, but how do you find them?

On the day this was written, I "Googled" the following: Avery Dulles models of the church. I retrieved thousands of hits. You might also try this search with other search engines, such as Yahoo!, Dogpile, or bing.com. Note both the variety in the number of hits with each search engine and the difference in what web pages are listed on the initial page of search results. (Why do you suppose this is?)

One reason for the large number of hits is that Internet search engines only do one kind of searching: keyword. For example, many of the thousands of hits are simply from lists of used books for sale from sites such as Amazon.com. Such sites are of no use to you. Unlike using Library of Congress subject headings in your library catalog, there is no way to search the Internet with precision for what you want—in this case, a discussion of Dulles's ideas about ecclesiology.

Even if you do manage to find a web page that appears to be potentially useful, how do you know if the information provided is valid or authoritative?

TIP #1

Carefully evaluate the quality of any Internet source you intend to use for your research. Use only websites likely to be regarded as authoritative by your instructor.

The important thing is to evaluate whatever you decide to look at. An initial indication of the potential value of any web site is the "domain" shown by the site's web "address," also known colloquially as its URL (universal resource locator). For example, a web address including an ".edu" indicates that the web site is hosted on a computer owned by an institution of higher education, mostly in the United States. (Web addresses for colleges and universities outside the United States may include other abbreviations such as ".ac" or ".uni") Such a site therefore comes from an academic source; perhaps a professor has posted course materials or some of her own publications. In principle, such websites can be regarded as more trustworthy for academic purposes than other sites having a different domain such as a ".com" or a ".org," although it remains necessary to evaluate the quality of the information yourself. A ".com" in a URL has usually been seen as a sign that the site's sponsoring body is engaged in commercial activity (business) of some type. An ".org" indicates that the sponsoring body is engaged in not-for-profit activity. You might think that ".org's" are preferable to ".com's" for that reason but ".org's" can be sponsored by groups advocating particular positions, including positions on political and public policy issues, and may therefore be regarded as no less biased than a commercial organization's website which may be trying to sell something. The clear cut distinction between ".com" and ".org" is not always maintained as the Internet continues to develop.

Another website popular with students nowadays is Wikipedia. Wikipedia is an Internet encyclopedia project to which anyone can contribute. As is well known, it is not always reliable: there have been stories of individuals uploading entirely false information in biographical articles, for example. Supposedly, steps are being taken to exercise a greater degree of quality control, but Wikipedia is still a work in progress (and intends to remain so, which is both an advantage and a disadvantage). A printed encyclopedia in your library's reference collection is a more authoritative source than Wikipedia. Despite that caveat, you can find an interesting article on Avery Dulles on Wikipedia. What you learn there can be very helpful in providing suggestions, ideas, and leads for further research. Most instructors require students to cite other sources regarded as authoritative (such as those provided by your library). Note that the list of "external links" in the Wikipedia article on Dulles contains sites from all three "domains" discussed above: .com, .org, and .edu.

TIP #2

If you do cite Wikipedia or any other Internet site, a good rule of thumb for the purpose of academic research is never to accept as factual any information found on the Internet without verifying it from some other more traditional source.

The most important thing to note in evaluating the content of any website is the credentials or qualifications of the individual or group responsible. You want your professor to regard what you have to say as authoritative, which is likely only if your sources are authoritative.

Another way to try to eliminate some of the chaff you run into on the Internet is to use a more specialized search engine such as Google Scholar. This service aims to provide a "simple way to broadly search for scholarly literature." "Scholarly literature," as defined by Google, includes "peer-reviewed papers, theses, books, abstracts and articles, from academic publishers, professional societies, online repositories, universities and other web sites."

Searching Google Scholar using "Avery Dulles Models of the Church" produces (as of this writing) 1,450 "hits." Some of these are potentially useful references to books and articles. Others are less helpful, such as course syllabi simply listing Dulles's book. (Is a course syllabus an example of "scholarly literature"?) Several other factors limit the usefulness of this service, including the following:

1. Searching is by keyword only. There are no subject headings to ensure that you actually retrieve the content you want, as opposed to retrieving merely the words you type.
2. The order in which "hits" are listed is based, in part, on popularity defined as the number of times a web page has been accessed and not on relevance to your subject.
3. The "scholarly literature" indexed by Google includes all possible subjects. By contrast, most libraries offer access to subject-specific databases, including, for theology, the *ATLA Religion Database*, *Religious & Theological Abstracts*, or the *Catholic Periodical and Literature Index*. Other databases covering a broad range of subjects, such as *Academic Search Premier*, also offer far more refined search capabilities than Google Scholar (and will not retrieve any course syllabi).

(Note: As explained in the introductory chapter on library research, this textbook does not discuss the use of periodical indexes and databases. Ask your librarian what databases are available for your subject and for assistance in using them.)

In short, while Google Scholar and similar services may be good for a quick search for resources, the best way to ensure you actually get what you need and want is to use the resources provided by your library, including the journal databases, which allow direct access to authoritative article citations.

For historical research, there are reference tools available for specific periods of church history. You have already encountered the *Encyclopedia of the Early Church* in the last chapter. For the middle ages, many libraries will own the thirteen-volume *Dictionary of the Middle Ages* (1982–1989, supplemental volume published in 2004) or the more recent two-volume *Encyclopedia of the Middle Ages* (2000). Some institutions may have electronic access to this encyclopedia. For the Reformation and post-Reformation developments within Protestantism, there is the four-volume *Oxford Encyclopedia of the Reformation* (1996) or the four-volume *Encyclopedia of Protestantism* (2004).

For research focusing on the church in the United States, consult either the *Encyclopedia of American Catholic History* (1997) or the *Dictionary of Christianity in America* (1990); this latter reference work covers both Protestant and Catholic developments.

Several reference tools focus specifically on contemporary or systematic issues. Three titles mentioned in the preceding chapter—the *New Dictionary of Theology*, the *Dictionary of Fundamental Theology*, and the *Handbook of Catholic Theology*—all provide such coverage. There is even a one-volume reference work focusing entirely on ecclesiology:

> Christopher O'Donnell, OCarm. *Ecclesia: A Theological Encyclopedia of the Church.* Collegeville, MN: Liturgical Press, 1996.

As always, if your library does not own one of these titles, ask the librarian to show you an alternative.

Student Tasks

1. Choose a topic in ecclesiology and go to a web browser, type it in, and see how many hits you receive. Check a few to see what types of hits show up. Can you think of different search terms to use for your topic? What difference does it make in your results? What difference does the use of quotation marks around phrases make? Identify a website that you would be able to cite in an academic paper. On what do you base your judgment of the website's worthiness?
2. Find an encyclopedia article on a topic on the church or its history that interests you. How specific is the encyclopedia for your topic? Use the bibliography to identify subject heading(s) for that topic. Using the subject headings, identify, if possible, a book on your topic that is not listed in the encyclopedia bibliography. If you were to pursue the topic further, what would be your next step?

Protestantism, Evangelicalism, Pentecostalism: Changing Contours of Christianity in the Modern Era

Michael J. McClymond

from the EDITOR

Do you know your family tree? The people and places your family came from? Do you have relatives still living in any of those places? In fourth grade, the teacher asked us how many cousins we had. I said, "Hmm, 20?" That night my mom used this educational opportunity to teach me about this mystery, our family. With paper and pencil, we arrived at 52 cousins. As I grew, that number kept changing as more children were born, more marriages took place, and my cousins married and had children. We had picnics and gatherings where we met one another, and the family tree was a common sign of our truly being related. Most importantly, we came to know and appreciate one another through the years.

Christianity has a 2,000-year-old family tree and is still growing. (It even has 1500 years more if we bring in the Hebrew Bible.) Catholicism has more than 57 different branches alone that stem from Jesus' time, with many different languages and liturgies, yet forming one Catholic Church. Some of those branches are Byzantine, Eastern, Oriental, Orthodox, and Churches of the East (Assyrian, Chalcedon, etc.) to mention only a few. Quite a big family tree already over the world for 2000 years!

The family tree in Europe saw a western European split between Roman Catholic and other Catholics at the time, called the Protestant Reformation (1517). It is this split and its development that is examined in this chapter. This is a family story, much like a separation in the family, yet everyone wanting to remain true to God and work things through for the best. That people do some things differently over time is perhaps expected, such as prayer, worship, and ministries. This chapter examines more closely these "differences." What is of utmost importance, however, is the mutual faith, hope, and love of God.

Differences notwithstanding, cooperation and dialogue between Protestants and Catholics is actively being done. For example, these Christians share prayer and worship services, as well as outreach to the poor and marginalized. They act together, including formulating common statements, participating in action for justice, peace, and decrying racism and violations of human rights. At the momentous Second Vatican Council of the Catholic Church (1962–1965), Protestants participated as guests.

What will the Christian family tree look like 100 or 200 years from now? The next chapter has some thoughts on that. Jesus said, "Do not fear." This is a good way to approach pondering God's ways that go beyond our current horizons, and a good way to read this chapter.

INTRODUCTION

Imagine that you are standing on a beachside cliff, overlooking the ocean and watching the waves roll in. From a distance, you perceive a massive bulge in the water—a veritable tsunami—surging shoreward. When the wave hits, it resculpts the landmass. Stones long serving as place-markers wash away, leaving behind an altered landscape. As you linger at your perch, further waves wash ashore, including two large enough to again resculpt the landmass in yet more ways.

This beachside image might serve as an analogy for forces of change in modern Christianity. Three movements described in this chapter—Protestantism, Evangelicalism, and Pentecostalism—have reshaped global Christianity. These successive waves were interrelated. Evangelicalism presupposed many key ideas and practices of Protestantism, yet added new elements. Similarly, Pentecostalism assumed and developed major themes of Evangelicalism and added a new twist. To alter the wave analogy, Evangelicalism washed ashore like a wave within the Protestant surge, and Pentecostalism like a further wave within the Evangelical wave.

So the three waves might be seen as three parts of a single, unfolding movement over half a millennium. The picture is complex: many Protestant Christians would not identify as Evangelicals, and many Evangelicals would not identify as Pentecostals. Each new movement brought life, energy, novelty—and division. Over time there has been a proliferation of new groups distinct from earlier forms of Christianity and distinct from one another.

Distinctive Practices and Beliefs

Many aspects of Christianity in the modern era originated with Protestants, Evangelicals, or Pentecostals. The list includes: laypersons' Bible studies, congregational singing, written confessions and catechisms of faith, evangelical hymnody and gospel songs, elected church leaders, congregational boards of deacons and elders, climactic conversion experiences, personal testimonies, religious revivals, adult baptism (as a norm), modern missionary methods, Sunday school, mass evangelism, altar calls, voluntary societies devoted to various Christian causes, missionary-sending organizations, teachings on holiness for non-clergy, practices of divine healing, the Pentecostal "baptism in (of) the Holy Spirit," the "Social Gospel" movement, ecumenical gatherings, councils, dialogs, parachurch ministries for young people, and the impartation of charismatic gifts through the laying on of hands.

Among the key theological ideas for Protestants, Evangelicals, and Pentecostals have been justification by faith, salvation through grace, the authority of the Bible (and sometimes biblical "infallibility" and "inerrancy"), the "priesthood of all believers," the call to conversion or "new birth," and the missionary mandate to evangelize all nations (Matt 28:18-20). Among themselves, these Christians have debated the meaning and efficacy of Christian baptism and the Eucharist, pacifism versus the idea of the "just war," the proper or "biblical" form of church government (i.e., government by bishops as compared with a presbyterian or congregational structure), fundamentalism versus modernism, and charismatic gifts and their appropriate use in the church.

The analogy of the three waves oversimplifies a complicated picture. A more complete listing of interrelated movements in modern Christianity would include more than twenty distinct groups (see sidebar, "Blending of Groups").

This chapter is like a large-scale map, showing only the most prominent features. Those who wish to delve deeper into the movements

BLENDING OF GROUPS

Since a wide range of Christian groups are still with us today, and the various groups have influenced one another, the resulting picture shows many shades and nuances. There are "Fundamentalist Baptists," "Social Justice Presbyterians," and "Charismatic Lutherans." Yet one could switch these labels around and speak about "Fundamentalist Presbyterians," "Charismatic Lutherans," or "Social Justice Baptists." Generally the earlier movements—Lutheran, Anglican, Baptist, etc.—led to the emergence of enduring Protestant denominations, while later movements—Evangelical, Ecumenical, Charismatic, etc.—modified the existing denominations but did not replace or displace their structures. The Pentecostals have been an exception to this rule, since they did not merely reshape existing groups, but set off in a novel direction. Beginning in the 1950s, some observers argued that the Pentecostals represent a twentieth-century "third force" in Christianity alongside the ancient communities (i.e., Catholic, Orthodox, Eastern) and the early modern, Protestant versions of Christianity.

mentioned here should consult the bibliography at the end of the chapter.[1]

PROTESTANTISM

Roots of the Protestant Movement.

What came to be called Protestantism emerged at a time of uncertainty in Western Christendom. During the disastrous fourteenth century, the "black death" (bubonic plague) destroyed up to one third of the population of Europe between 1328 and 1351. Soon thereafter, the Avignon Schism split Roman Catholicism. Two rival claimants to the papacy occupied Rome and Avignon. The rift lasted from 1378 to 1417. The decades-long conflict was finally resolved at the Council of Constance (1414–1418). Yet the schism damaged papal prestige and intensified calls for a general council to reform the Church.

The Englishman John Wycliffe (ca. 1328–1384) anticipated many of the core beliefs later espoused in the Protestantism of the 1500s. Wycliffe (also Wyclif, Wiclef, Wickliffe, etc.) held that the Bible should be translated into the language of the people and no longer kept in Latin for the benefit of the learned. He also taught predestination to salvation, questioned the pope's authority, doubted the legitimacy of monasticism, challenged transubstantiation (i.e., the idea that the Eucharistic bread and wine become the Body and Blood of Christ), and criticized the Church of his day for its wealth and complacency. Each of these themes later emerged in the writings of Martin Luther and later Protestants. Though Wycliffe died in peace, Wycliffe's Bohemian follower, Jan Hus (1372–1415), was burned at the stake for teachings that contradicted the Church's doctrines.

During the 1400s and 1500s, the cultural and intellectual movement known as the

1. Some readers may be surprised that this chapter does not address such important modern religious groups as the Church of Jesus Christ of Latter-Day Saints (i.e., the Mormons), Christian Science, and the Jehovah's Witnesses (or Watch Tower Bible and Tract Society). These groups have sometimes been labeled as "quasi-Protestant," since they share many characteristics in common with Protestant churches and yet—in the eyes of most observers—diverge from the mainstream of Protestantism in their doctrinal positions. Thus the Jehovah's Witnesses take an Arian view of Jesus, holding that he is not co-equal or co-eternal with God the Father. The Christian Scientists also hold to an unorthodox view of Jesus and maintain the physical world is not ultimately real. The Mormons assert that God is a being of "flesh and blood," that is, with a material body, and teach that human beings may become divine. Because of the complex doctrinal issues involved, and space constraints in this chapter, it is not possible to treat such "quasi-Protestant" groups here. More than 2,300 religious groups are listed and described in J. Gordon Melton., ed., *Encyclopedia of American Religions*, 7th ed. (Detroit, MI: Gale, 2003).

Renaissance sought to recover the wisdom of the ancients, both sacred and secular. *Ad fontes* ("to the sources") was the slogan of these scholars, who devoted their lives to uncovering and studying ancient texts. While Italian humanists promoted a more human-centered and secular version of the Renaissance, Northern European humanists offered a "devout humanism" that sought to combine the best of ancient pagan wisdom (Plato, Aristotle, Virgil, Seneca, etc.) with the wisdom of the Bible and the Christian tradition. Martin Luther's compulsion to re-read and re-interpret the Bible during the 1510s should be seen against the backdrop of the Renaissance.

Luther posts his "Ninety-Five Theses."

The Eventful Life of Martin Luther

The early history of Protestantism mirrors the story of one man—Martin Luther. The origin of the Protestant movement is traced to a date and an event in Luther's life—October 31, 1517, when Luther nailed the "Ninety-Five Theses" to the door of the Wittenberg Cathedral. This act was an overture to a formal academic disputation regarding indulgences (i.e., statements of remission of penalties for sin) that the Catholic Church was then selling to raise money for St. Peter's Basilica in Rome. Neither Luther nor anyone else could have anticipated the wide-ranging theological, political, and social issues that were to emerge in the course of the indulgence dispute. At the Heidelberg Disputation (1518) and ensuing theological debates, Luther's adversaries successfully pressed him to acknowledge that he was not only questioning the Church's sale of indulgences but the pope's authority as well. This was a damaging and dangerous admission on Luther's part, since it aligned Luther with Jan Hus, who had died as a heretic.

1521 was a pivotal year, during which Luther wrote three major treatises: *The Babylonian Captivity of the Church*, *The Freedom of a Christian*, and *Appeal to the Nobility of the German Nation*. The first text argued against the Catholic system of seven sacraments, and marked Luther's final rupture with his inherited tradition. Only rituals that were directly taught in the New Testament—baptism and Eucharist (and perhaps the confession of sins)—were authentic, Luther argued. For Luther, the Church had no intrinsic power to institute new sacraments (e.g., confirmation, last rites) or other practices (e.g., monastic vows) that were not mandated in the New Testament. In the second text, Luther presented the Christian life as characterized by freedom rather than rule-keeping, a major theme for later Protestants. In the third text, Luther called on the German nobles to assist the emerging Protestant movement. In Luther's doctrine of the "two kingdoms," the church exists as an inward, spiritual kingdom, distinct from the political sphere, while the outward, physical reign of the kings and nobility exists alongside it. The church's task is the right preaching of God's word, while the Christian prince's task is to enable the church to fulfill its calling of preaching the word.

Luther debated the most famous humanist scholar in Europe: Desiderius Erasmus. The core issue was Luther's idea of human depravity. Since Adam's fall, Luther argued, all human beings were born into the world as slaves of sin and their darkened minds were unable to perceive spiritual truth. Only God's gracious initiative toward sinners could break the "bondage of the will" and bring spiritual understanding, so that faith in God and repentance from sin became possible. Erasmus asserted that, while salvation is entirely a matter of God's grace, individuals have free will and may respond to or reject God's grace. Luther told the humanist that "your thoughts of God are too human," and defended the idea that God has predestined some to be saved while leaving others in their sinful, condemned condition. It is not the part of mere mortals to question why God predestines some to one fate and some to another, argued Luther.

The term "Protestant" first arose after the Diet of Speyer in 1529, which upheld an earlier decision to condemn Luther and his teaching. The German princes who supported Luther wrote a letter of "protestation," and the term "protestant" has been with us ever since.

"Magisterial" and "Radical" Protestantism

Early Protestantism was a vast simplification of Catholicism, a kind of housecleaning wherein everything deemed unnecessary was thrown out. Four slogans—*sola scriptura*, *sola fide*, *sola gratia*, and *solus Christus*—summarized core elements of Protestant theology. While Catholicism based itself on scripture *and* tradition, Protestantism appealed to "scripture alone" (*sola scriptura*). Protestants held that the Bible was a sufficient guide to resolve all major questions of Christian faith and practice. While Catholicism taught that human beings are saved by faith *with* works, or by grace *with* merit, Protestants held to salvation by "faith alone" (*sola fide*) and by "grace alone" (*sola gratia*). While Catholicism insisted on the intercession of Mary and the saints, Protestants looked to "Christ alone" (*solus Christus*) as the mediator between God and humanity.

As the Protestant message spread to cities throughout Europe from the 1520s onward, it took different forms in different places. In Zurich (in present-day Switzerland), Ulrich Zwingli preached a more extreme form of Protestantism than Luther did. Rejecting almost all traditions that had emerged in the course of church history, Zwingli wanted to base every element of Christian faith and practice on explicit statements of the Bible. He took down statues and other forms of visual art from church buildings, calling them idolatrous. Zwingli's attitude contrasted with that of Luther, who felt that it was acceptable to retain Catholic practices and beliefs, so long as they did not directly conflict with the Bible. Compared with Zwingli, Luther was a conservative reformer. The two men clashed at the Marburg Colloquy in 1529. They divided in their understanding of the Eucharist, with Luther insisting that Christ's body and blood were truly present in the consecrated bread and wine (the view later known as "consubstantiation") and Zwingli viewing the bread and wine of the Eucharist as mere outward symbols that reminded the faithful of Christ and his atoning death. The falling out between Luther and Zwingli was a major disappointment for the early Protestants, since it meant that their movement would not remain internally unified.

Yet Zwingli's views were still not extreme enough for an emerging group during the 1520s that became known as the Anabaptists (meaning literally "re-baptizers"), and more recently as Radical Reformers. Not finding any undeniable evidence for infant baptism in New Testament times, the Anabaptists rejected the practice and insisted that, since only adults are capable of making a profession of faith, only adults may be baptized. The Anabaptists believed that the true church should have no link to governmental systems or the political order. Believers were to meet at home, in face-to-face gatherings where they might put the Bible into practice and hold one another accountable for living as true disciples. Since the Sermon on the Mount forbade Jesus' followers from retaliating against their enemies, the Anabaptists held that Christians should not bear arms—a position known as pacifism. Menno Simons—once a Roman Catholic priest—was among the Anabaptists' most influential leaders. Surprising as it seems today, the Roman Catholic authorities and most Protestant leaders during the 1500s held that Anabaptists were not only theologically mistaken but were social and political subversives who deserved to die. In the year 1527, the civil authorities of Zurich tied up Anabaptist leader Felix Manz with stones and drowned him in the frigid waters of the Limmat River—in cruel mockery of the Anabaptist practice of baptism by immersion. Fierce persecution scattered the Anabaptists throughout Europe, where many more suffered ostracism or death for their beliefs.

The Anabaptists risked martyrdom for their convictions, and were among the first Europeans to argue for freedom of religion and complete separation of church and state. In this they represented a distinct minority, as Protestant and Catholic states squared off against each other, plunging Europe into a full century of religious warfare (ca. 1550–ca. 1650). Afterward, the thinkers of the emerging Enlightenment movement began to find themselves in agreement with what Anabaptists had argued long before. True religion, the Anabaptists had said, was a voluntary matter. It could not be coerced by government regulations or by threats of persecution. Eventually the principle of religious freedom became enshrined in the First Amendment to the *Constitution of the United States* (1789) and later political documents. Yet during the 1500s this idea was not self-evident to most Europeans.

The Second Great Figure: John Calvin

Luther was immensely creative and yet also sometimes erratic. His followers, he had said, sought to make him a "fixed star" though he was a "wandering planet." His humanness was often on display, as when he declared that "he who loves not wine, women, and song, remains a fool his whole life long." Succeeding Luther, the most influential figure of the second Protestant generation was John Calvin. In fact both Luther and Calvin gave their names to divergent branches of Protestantism: the Lutheran and the Calvinist (or Reformed) traditions.

Calvin, who was trained both in law and in the best humanist traditions, showed a more systematic style than Luther. He wrote commentaries on nearly all the books of the Bible and summed up a lifetime of research in his *Institutes of the Christian Religion* (1559), to this day among the most influential Protestant works ever written. While Luther stressed God's grace to the undeserving and the good news of God's love for sinners, Calvin highlighted God's sovereign power and inscrutable will. A doctrine that aroused debate was predestination, the teaching (based on various biblical passages) that God from eternity chose some, and passed over others, for eternal salvation. Christians had been wrestling with this idea for centuries—we have already seen that Luther, too, embraced it—but predestination would come to be one of the hallmarks of Calvinist thought.

For better or for worse, "Calvinism," as it spread in England, Scotland, New England, Switzerland, and the Netherlands, was strongly associated with the doctrines of divine sovereignty and eternal predestination. A controversy among Calvinists in the Netherlands during the 1600s resulted in the decision of the Synod of Dort (1618–1619), which defined Calvinist orthodoxy in terms of "five points": humanity's *total* depravity in sin, the *unconditional* choice or election of some to salvation, the *limited* atonement of Christ (i.e., Christ died only for the "elect"), the *irresistible* grace of God that achieved its effect for those who were predestined, and the *perseverance* in grace of those who were en route to salvation. (Want to remember these five points? Note the first letter of each; combined they spell "tulip," a flower associated with Holland.) Though there was much more to Calvinism than this, the five points summarized certain distinctive features of the Calvinist teaching on salvation. Later thinkers followed the broad contours of Calvin's theology, including Theodore Beza, the Puritans of England and New England (later 1500s–later 1600s), Jonathan Edwards, the American Presbyterian Charles Hodge, and the Swiss authors Karl Barth (1886–1968) and Emil Brunner (1889–1966).

Turmoil in Europe and in Britain

The Protestant movement did not equally affect all nations and regions of Europe. The French Protestants—inspired by events in nearby Geneva under Calvin—were growing in numbers and influence in the mid-1500s. Yet a series of bloody killings around St. Bartholomew's Day in 1572 dealt a blow from which the Huguenots (French Protestants) never recovered. Thereafter, the Protestant movement was greatly diminished in France. Lutheranism found its heartland in Germany and Scandinavia: Denmark, Sweden, Norway, and Finland. The Scandinavian nations, to this day, are all at least nominally Lutheran. Lutheranism later made its way to the United States through German and Scandinavian emigration.

Calvinism migrated further than Lutheranism, taking root in Scotland, England, New England, the Netherlands, Bohemia (today's Czech Republic), and Hungary. Later there were Dutch Calvinist migrations to South Africa as well as the East Indies (Indonesia). Generally speaking, Protestantism was strongest in northern Europe, while southern and southwestern Europe (Italy, France, Spain, and Portugal) remained largely Roman Catholic, and southeastern Europe (Austria, Serbia, Croatia, and the Balkans) was divided between Roman Catholicism and Eastern Orthodoxy. Germany after 1648 was a patchwork of small principalities, some of them Protestant and some Catholic, according to the preference of the local rulers. *Cuius regio, huius religio* ("whose is the region, his is the religion")—so ran the slogan that summarized this policy of allowing local rulers in central Europe to determine the religion of their subjects.

Nowhere did the Protestant Reformation follow a more complex or circuitous route than it did in the British Isles. In 1534, King Henry VIII declared himself to be the head of the English Church. Thereafter, except for a brief return to Catholicism under Henry's daughter, ("Bloody") Mary, the national faith of England was Protestant—at least in the sense that it no longer recognized the authority of the pope. Yet for nearly a century and a half the question remained as to how much of the Catholic tradition the English Church would retain in its beliefs and practices, and how much of a moderate or radical Protestantism it would embrace. Later spokespersons for the Church of England would claim that it was a *via media* ("middle way") embracing the best of both Protestantism and Catholicism. Over time a spectrum of viewpoints emerged. *The Book of Common Prayer* (1549, with later revisions) was one of the few things that held together all the faithful in the Church of England. A few holdouts in England (especially among the nobility) remained Catholic and refused to acknowledge the English monarch as the legitimate head of the national church. Yet it was dangerous to be an English Catholic at the time. In 1605, the Catholic Guy Fawkes tried to explode the Parliament building in the so-called Gunpowder Plot. Popes in this period had sanctioned the idea that the English rulers—as religious imposters—might be killed with impunity. There were Spanish attempts to conquer England and make it Catholic again. As a result of these developments, most of the English were deeply alienated from Roman Catholicism and from the Papacy.

The Anglican Settlement in England

The majority of English Christians—or "Anglicans"—went along with the idea of a state church independent of the pope. Yet among them there were some who had gone to Geneva to escape persecution under Queen Mary in the 1550s ("the Marian exiles") and had returned more ardently Protestant and Calvinistic than ever. They were the foundation of a "Puritan" movement that sought to purify the English Church from within, embracing the Reformation more fully, and doing away with retained "Catholic" practices. The more extreme English Reformers broke with the Puritans and became "Separatists" or "Independents"; impatient with what they took to be the slow pace of reform, they thought it advisable to withdraw from the official Church of England to found separate fellowships. Their "conventicles" were declared illegal under Queen Elizabeth (reigned 1558–1603), and the persecution experienced by the stricter Protestant groups provoked some to emigrate to New England between 1620 and 1640. These emigrants laid a religious foundation for the later United States of America. Among the Puritans and Separatist there were intricate theological debates over simplicity in worship style (e.g., the wearing of church vestments by ministers) and the proper form of church government. While the Anglican Church was governed by bishops, Presbyterians favored a kind of religious parliament (or "general assembly") to make binding decisions for all local congregations, and Congregationalists wanted every congregation to be able to govern its own affairs without any interference from a bishop or general assembly. Not surprisingly, the Presbyterians and Congregationalists generally favored an imposition of strict limits on the power of the king. At the culmination of the English Civil War of the 1640s, Parliament, largely under the influence of Puritan radicals, put King Charles I on trial as the people's enemy; he was publicly put to death in 1649.

This shocking execution of the monarch—regarded by some as a sacrilegious slaying of "God's anointed"—was the first event of its kind in modern times and it foreshadowed later ideas regarding limited government. Protestant propagandists and pamphleteers challenged the idea of *Rex lex* ("the king is law") with an assertion of *Lex rex* ("the law is king"). Basing their faith on the text of the Bible, Protestants had a natural affinity for a notion of human government based on a written constitution rather than the will of the ruler. John Locke's *Two Treatises on Government* (1689) promoted limited government and popular sovereignty, arguing that all just governments ruled with the consent of the governed. These ideas were later integral to the American Revolution, as well as the *Declaration of Independence* (1776) and the *Constitution of the United States* (1789).

Scholars have argued that Protestantism was associated not only with modern representative government, but with the rise of a capitalistic economy in Europe (Max Weber), with the scientific revolution of the 1600s and 1700s (Robert Merton), and with a trans-Atlantic tradition of literacy especially strong in Protestant nations. Protestantism was thus not only a religious but a cultural phenomenon, and it inculcated such values as personal freedom, capitalistic and entrepreneurial activity, a disciplined and productive life (the so-called Protestant work ethic), the importance of reading and education, and scientific and technological inquiry. These cultural values were especially associated with Britain and the United States from the 1700s through the 1900s.

The Confessional Era

During the late 1500s and early 1600s, Protestant Christianity had entered into a "confessional" or creed-writing phase. On the Catholic side, the Council of Trent (1542–1565) brought a far-reaching reorganization and centralization to the Church. It also solidified Catholic opposition to Protestantism, condemning the idea of justification by faith, recognizing the Old Testament Apocrypha as authoritative, mandating the Latin Vulgate for reading and study (rather than the Hebrew and Greek originals), and sanctioning the reception of the Mass in one kind only (i.e., consecrated bread but not wine), indulgences, prayers to Mary and the saints, prayers for the dead, and teaching on purgatory. As the 1500s progressed, Roman Catholics and Protestants who had been hoping for agreement between the two sides found little to encourage them. Lutheranism formulated its confessional statements, including the Augsburg *Confession* (1530) and *Formula of Concord* (1577), Reformed or Calvinist Christians composed the *Heidelberg Catechism* (1563) and *Westminster Confession of Faith* (1646), and Anglicanism drew up its *Thirty-Nine Articles* (1563). These documents were widely used in instructing generations of Protestants in the distinctive tenets of their particular group.

During this era, leading Protestants engaged in extensive theological debates with Roman Catholic authors, like the redoubtable Cardinal Robert Bellarmine (1542–1621). Representative of these works is Martin Chemnitz's *Examination of the Council of Trent* (1574). Though little read today, these polemical writings occupy impressive volumes of Latin prose. The writing, reading, and study of such works occupied the lifetimes of countless pastors and professors during the era of Protestant scholasticism.

Yet the strong focus on correct doctrine and theological orthodoxy brought dangers to the Protestant churches. Some leaders, perhaps more than the laity, had come to identify true Christianity with a precise set of doctrinal beliefs, while neglecting the *experiential* and *practical* aspects of Christianity. Moreover, the Protestant-Catholic theological arguments—and intra-Protestant debates that pitted Lutherans against the Reformed—slighted the common beliefs shared by rival confessional groups. Only the differences were highlighted in the midst of argumentation. The Lutheran scholastic Abraham Calovius is said to have prayed every morning, "O Lord, fill me with hatred of heretics"! In Continental Europe, theologically technical sermons sometimes lasted for two or three hours and included long quotations in Latin—though most congregants did not even know any Latin.

New Stirrings: The Pietist Movement

A slender book, under the title *Pia Desideria* ["Pious Desires"] (1677), signaled a turn toward a more practical, experiential form of Christianity. The book's author, Philip Spener, promoted a movement known as Pietism. The Pietists offered a program for church-based renewal that centered on small groups within the larger church, termed *collegia pietatis* ("fellowships of the godly") or *ecclesiola in ecclesia* ("little churches within the larger church"). Such groups emphasized personal Bible reading and study, repentance and conversion of life, private prayer, and good works toward others. Through these groups the Pietists sought to stir the church of their day from its spiritual doldrums. When Spener died in 1705, he asked to be buried in white clothing, to signify his hope of better days ahead for the Christian church. Spener proved to be a prophetic figure. The Pietists of Germany, Scandinavia, and the Netherlands, together with Puritan and Anglican leaders in Britain in the 1600s, prepared the way for the movement known as Evangelicalism in the 1700s. With their stress on the Bible, prayer, conversion, and good works, they dug wells from which later generations drew the waters of renewal.

EVANGELICALISM

The Difficulty of Definition

Evangelicalism is harder to define than Protestantism. In German-speaking countries, *evangelisch* means "Protestant," and if one wants to find an equivalent for the English word "evangelical," then one may need to substitute the word "pietist." During the religious revivals of the 1740s, supporters of the movement were known as "friends of vital piety." It is hard to find a word today akin to "piety" in its eighteenth-century sense. It denoted an orientation of one's whole life, an aspiration to please God in all things. John Calvin defined "piety" as "that love conjoined with reverence for God which the knowledge of his benefits induces." The concept of piety was thus not new in the 1700s. Yet the church's situation called for a new emphasis within Protestantism, and this took shape in the form of Evangelicalism. Those referred to as Evangelicals from the mid-1700s onward did not set out to create new structures or church bodies within Protestantism. Instead they sought to deepen their own spiritual lives and the spiritual lives of others. The Evangelicalism of the 1700s was not a radical break with past structures, as in Luther's and Calvin's reformations. Instead it represented an *interiorization* of Christian devotion and piety.

Evangelical, as we are using the term here, refers to a discrete set of Protestant Christian movements that arose out of the spiritual awakenings that took place in Great Britain and its colonies in the mid-1700s. British historian David Bebbington has noted the presence of four basic ideas in modern Evangelicalism. The first he terms "biblicism," that is, a reliance on the Bible as the ultimate source of spiritual authority. Second is "conversionism" or a stress on the new birth. "Have you been born again?" is a question sometimes associated with this particular emphasis. Third is "activism," or an energetic and individualistic approach to living out one's spiritual duties, which are understood to include social involvement. Fourth is "crucicentrism," that is, a focus on Christ's redeeming work on the cross as the heart of essential Christianity.

It is worth noting that none of these four traits includes any reference to a particular church tradition or denomination—e.g., Catholic, Orthodox, Anglican, Presbyterian, Baptist, etc. One can be a "Catholic Evangelical" or a "Baptist Evangelical," to the extent that one belongs to a Catholic or Baptist church and embraces the four tenets just noted. Evangelicalism is not properly a denomination but a movement, and this makes it more diffuse than the historic Protestant churches and denominations that trace their roots to the time of the Reformation.

Experiential or "Heart" Religion

One mark of early Evangelicalism was its intense experientialism. Consider, for example, British soldier Sampson Staniforth, who later became a Methodist preacher and left behind an account of his conversion experience:

> As soon as I was alone, I kneeled down, and determined not to rise, but to continue crying and wrestling with God, till He had mercy on me. How long I was in that agony I cannot tell; but as I looked up to heaven I saw the clouds open exceedingly bright, and I saw Jesus hanging on the cross. At the same moment these words were applied to my heart, "Thy sins are forgiven thee." My chains fell off; my heart was free. All guilt was gone, and my soul filled with unutterable peace. I loved God and all mankind, and the fear of death and hell was vanished away. I was filled with wonder and astonishment.

John Calvin never wrote anything like this. An intensely private man, Calvin wrote many thousands of pages and yet barely mentioned any personal experiences. In contrast, Evangelicalism made a personal experience of conversion—and public testimony, recounting it to others—a distinctive theme and emphasis.

Methodist founder John Wesley, described attending a meeting at Aldersgate in London in 1738, said, "My heart was strangely warmed." Despite his upbringing as the son of an Anglican pastor and a devout mother, Wesley only became sure that Christ died "for my sins, even mine" in this moment of evangelical awakening. John's brother, Charles, also underwent conversion in 1738 and went on to become one of the finest hymn-writers of modern times. In New England, Jonathan Edwards—who emerged as Evangelicalism's leading theologian—spoke of the "new sense" of divine glory that filled his heart. Edwards led a powerful local revival in Northampton, Massachusetts in 1734–1735, resulting in the conversion of hundreds. Edwards's account of the revival, *Faithful Narrative of the Surprising Work of God* (1737), found its way to Wesley and others in England, and left a powerful impression. God was indeed doing new things—on both sides of the Atlantic. Not only were individual sinners becoming "born again" as devout, fervent Christians, but whole communities and congregations were being transformed. A revival tradition was taking shape.

Later Evangelical preachers from the 1700s through the 1900s followed a common pattern. George Whitefield, Charles Finney, Dwight L. Moody, Billy Sunday, Aimee Semple McPherson, and Billy Graham. All were awakened awakeners. Having themselves been revived in spirit, they sought to revive others. Central to the emotionalism of Evangelicalism was its worship music, the most famous of which may be "Amazing grace, how sweet the sound, that saved a wretch like me." Countless hymns, stretching from the1700s up to today's contemporary Christian music, exhibit the range and depth of evangelical experience.

The Urge to Evangelize

For Evangelicals, spiritual experience did not remain a private affair. The urge to tell others was an essential feature of Evangelicalism. Soon after Wesley's conversion, he was going into pulpits to announce the good news of salvation by grace. Within a brief time, Wesley was imitating the example of George Whitefield by preaching not only in pulpits but out of doors and in the fields to any who would listen. When Wesley was challenged regarding his right to preach beyond the bounds of any parish that had invited him, he replied, "I regard the world as my parish." Eighteenth-century ministers were supposed to respect parish boundaries. By going out to the people in the way that they did, Wesley and Whitefield were often regarded as arrogant upstarts. "Did they think there were no ministers in Boston?" asked Charles Chauncy after Whitefield came and preached to some 15,000 people at one time in the leading city of New England.

The supporters of Whitefield (known as New Lights) were opposed by traditional churchmen (known as Old Lights). The separation between them had to do with theology. Old Light ministers were generally more liberal in theology and by the early 1800s most had drifted toward Unitarianism (i.e., they denied Jesus' divinity). Yet the separation also had to do with social class. Early Evangelicalism was something of a populist upsurge, and many ministers in New England felt that the churches needed to remain under the firm, fatherly hand of educated clergymen. Whitefield's audiences appeared to them like an unruly mob. Indeed, they sometimes acted like it, throwing stones or rotten fruit at traveling preachers if they disapproved of the message.

Internal Divisions among Evangelicals

Evangelicalism sought to maintain a united front—essential if it were to fulfill its mandate to revive and renew Protestantism from within. Yet the movement suffered a lasting internal division that came, ironically enough, during the very height of the Great Awakening in the American colonies. While Whitefield was dazzling the multitudes with his powerful sermons, Wesley back in England published a sermon, called "Free Grace" (1740), declaring Calvinism to be a dangerous error and even a slander on the loving character of God. Whitefield urged Wesley not to publish this. Wesley did. Evangelicalism split into a Calvinist faction (upholding the "five points" as noted above) and a Wesleyan-Arminian faction (denying or questioning all "five points"). This theological rift has never been healed.

Another controversial aspect of Wesley's teaching was his idea of "entire sanctification." This was held to be a second work of grace—after conversion and yet during the present life—in which a believer in Christ was said to cease from conscious sin and to live in a state of "perfect love." Many Evangelicals rejected Wesley's teaching on sanctification. The idea would take on a second life among twentieth-century Pentecostals, who held that speaking in tongues was the outward mark of Spirit baptism, a second work of grace enabling one to live a more authentic and fruitful Christian life.

Revivals and Awakenings

Evangelicalism not only commenced in spiritual awakening but grew through further awakenings. Following the so-called Great Awakening (1739–1742) in New England, there was a period of relative stasis in the late 1700s, when the American colonies passed through the political crisis of the American Revolution and its aftermath. Yet beginning around 1800, a series of localized spiritual awakenings took place, lasting for some twenty to thirty years, and affecting literally thousands of local communities in the expanding American republic. Revivals were periods of intense spiritual excitement, characterized by exuberant emotion and even such unusual phenomena as people falling to the ground, losing consciousness, and undergoing strange bodily spasms. A massive revival, involving some 15,000 participants in Cane Ridge, Kentucky, in August 1801, became famous because of "jerks" among certain participants. Strange to say, some who came to jeer and mock the crowds, found themselves overcome, and fell to the ground along with the rest.

The Second Great Awakening (ca. 1795–ca. 1830) made Protestant Evangelicalism into something like an established, national religion through much of the United States during the pre-Civil War era. During its expansive phase, Evangelicalism was a populist movement that challenged the high and mighty and sided instead with the common folk. Historian Nathan Hatch calls this process "the democratization of American Christianity."

Traditional, clergy-centered denominations, such as the Congregationalists and Presbyterians, lose ground to more lay-oriented groups such as the Baptists and Methodists. To become a Congregationalist minister, one typically had to have both college and seminary training. Such education was simply not attainable for people living on the frontier. The Baptists and the Methodists responded by ordaining those who lacked seminary education. New congregations emerged in new settlements through the ministrations of Baptist farmer-preachers, who tilled the soil during the week and preached on the weekends. Methodist churches were established by "circuit riders" who shared in what one scholar called a "brotherhood of poverty," since their salaries were barely one-tenth of that paid to the Congregationalist ministers of New England. Methodist preachers were not allowed to settle long in one place, but were expected to circulate between far-flung congregations in remote, rural regions. When the weather was bad, the traditional saying was that "no one is out today but crows and Methodist preachers."

Evangelicals and Nineteenth-Century Social Reform

The early 1800s was a golden age for the founding of voluntary societies among Evangelicals. The basic concept was that any like-minded group, sharing devotion to a common cause, might bind themselves together to work as a team. Denominational identity, and one's status as cleric or layperson, mattered less than one's willingness to labor for the cause. In this way, innumerable societies took shape with various emphases: foreign missions, domestic mission (esp. in the western United States), anti-slavery, temperance (i.e., anti-alcohol), Sabbath observance, and Sunday schools. After the Civil War, the focus shifted toward mass evangelism in the cities, abolishing child labor,

Revival converts are baptized in the White River near Cotter, Arkansas, in 1943.

improving factory conditions, and female suffrage (i.e., voting rights).

The whole of the period from about 1800 to the 1920s was the era of "crusading Protestantism" in North America and to a large extent in Britain as well. In 1865, William and Catherine Booth began the Salvation Army to reach London's poor with "soap, soup, and salvation." Today the army continues as the largest Protestant social service agency in the world. During the later 1800s, Evangelicalism became increasingly preoccupied with questions concerning Jesus' second coming. While the Evangelicals of the early 1800s believed in an earthly kingdom of righteousness, established through human efforts in evangelism and social reforms, Evangelicals in the late 1800s were moving toward a new view that held that the present world had to get worse before it might get better. That is, God's kingdom would only arrive through divine intervention into this sin-sick world. In theological terms, "postmillennialism" was giving way to "premillennialism." The split vision regarding the possibility of social transformation had much to do with the eventual split between Fundamentalists and Modernists, described below.

Evangelical Missions and Global Expansion

From the standpoint of the twenty-first century, one of the most significant Evangelical endeavors of the 1800s and the early 1900s was the global missionary movement. By the end of the twentieth-century, Evangelical Christianity was widely established throughout the world in Africa, Asia, Latin America, the Caribbean, Oceania, and the Pacific Islands. Sub-Saharan Africa represented a particularly dramatic case. While in the year 1900 there may have been only about 4 million Christians in this region, by 2000 the number was close to 400 million. Through missionary efforts that began with Evangelicals—and often continued with Pentecostals—large parts of Latin America were "turning Protestant" and leaving Catholicism behind. More than 90 percent of the population of the Pacific Islands had turned from ancestral, polytheistic religions toward Christianity. Former British colonies—e.g., Canada, Nigeria, Kenya, South Africa, India, Australia, and New Zealand—were strongholds of Evangelicalism. To the surprise of many, Communist China experienced a massive growth of Evangelical Christianity in the second half of the twentieth-century. As of 2010, Christians in China today may number between 30 and 100 million.

African-American Evangelicals

During the course of the 1800s, most African Americans gravitated toward Evangelical Protestantism, with smaller numbers joining the Catholic Church. Early efforts by Anglicans to evangelize the slaves during the 1700s were mostly ineffectual. Yet when black slaves encountered a less book-centered and more experiential faith among the Methodists and Baptists, they responded. The ancestral African religions had always focused on a direct encounter or contact with God or other spiritual beings. The revivalist ethos thus matched the spiritual expectations of Africans. By the nineteenth century's end, the majority of black Americans belonged to an Evangelical Protestant group, typically a Baptist, Methodist, or independent congregation.

Because of their centuries of suffering under slavery and during the "Jim Crow" era, the black church occupied a central place in community life. It was a place where people supported one another, both spiritually and materially. It looked after its own. It gave a sense of identity. It offered hope. A stress on social justice was in the "spiritual DNA" of the black church, beginning with such figures as Sojourner Truth (ca. 1797–1883) and Frederick Douglass (ca. 1817–1895), and coming to fruition in Martin Luther King, Jr.

(1929–1968). By the early to mid-twentieth century, black Holiness and Pentecostal denominations, especially in poor urban neighborhoods, opened "storefront churches" that continued the black traditions of emotional, revivalistic worship services. Its leaders included Charles H. Mason (1866–1961) and T. D. Jakes (1957–).

Intellectual and Theological Challenges to Evangelicalism

As Evangelicalism expanded during the 1800s, it faced intellectual challenges. As a Bible-based faith, Evangelicalism was vulnerable to attacks on the accuracy and trustworthiness of the sacred scriptures. In Germany in the 1800s, biblical scholars began to challenge many traditional notions. For example, scholars taught that Moses did not write the Pentateuch (i.e., the first five books of the Bible), that the Old Testament contradicted ancient history, and that the four Gospels contained disparities—if not contradictions—when compared with one another. Others went further, insisting that the teachings of the Apostle Paul contradicted those of Jesus. Some skeptics claimed that Jesus never existed at all. Biblical scholarship became the focus of intense debates, and in several denominations a number of heresy trials took place toward the end of the 1800s. Darwinism was also much debated, since conservatives held that Darwinian evolution was opposed to the Bible's account of creation. Charles Hodge, a prominent Presbyterian theologian at that time, was blunt: "Darwinism is atheism."

By the end of the 1800s, the conditions of life in major cities—New York, Philadelphia, Chicago, St. Louis—were often appalling. Recent immigrants and other factory workers lived in filthy, crowded tenement buildings, earned substandard wages, and suffered from cholera and other contagious diseases. After years of ministry in the "Hell's Kitchen" region of New York, Walter Rauschenbusch helped to launch the so-called Social Gospel emphasis, stressing not only an individual message of salvation but also just wages, sanitary living conditions, and the need for economic reforms. The Social Gospel was, in its origins, a movement led by liberal or liberalizing Evangelicals. Yet by the early 1900s theological conservatives began to view it as tainted. Increasingly, Social Gospel concerns were associated with a rejection of traditional Christian beliefs.

Division, Decline, and Comeback

By the early 1910s and 1920s, an all-out split emerged between "Fundamentalists" and "Modernists" in a number of denominations. The former group insisted on five "fundamental" (that's where the name comes from) points of Protestant orthodoxy: the inerrancy (i.e., errorlessness) of the Bible, the full deity of Jesus Christ, Christ's Virgin birth, Jesus' atoning death on the cross, and Jesus' bodily Resurrection from the dead. (The list of points varied somewhat, with some adding Jesus' miracles or Jesus' Second Coming.) After the Fundamentalists lost control of the Presbyterian and Northern Baptist denominations, most withdrew from public life, founded separate Bible schools, and generally took a low social profile. From the 1930s onward, the defining mark of Protestant Fundamentalism has been *separatism*—i.e., a refusal to align oneself with "liberal" churches or "worldly" habits (e.g., movie-going, smoking, drinking, etc.). A Fundamentalist—according to an old adage—"didn't smoke, drink, or chew, or go out with girls that do." Bob Jones University (founded 1927) and Liberty University (founded 1971) became well-known institutions among Baptist Fundamentalists in the United States.

Following World War II, Evangelicalism made a comeback that put it once again on the American cultural map. The central figure was a young evangelist named Billy Graham. Calling themselves "Neo-Evangelicals" (later dropping the "Neo"), the new Evangelical movement

IMAGE: © BETTMANN/CORBIS

Bible in hand, American evangelist Billy Graham speaks to a crowd of intent listeners packing London's Trafalgar Square on April 4, 1954.

sought to retain a strong commitment to the Bible while becoming more socially and culturally engaged than the Fundamentalists had been. From their strongholds at institutions such as Wheaton College in Illinois, the Bible Institute of Los Angeles (BIOLA), and Dallas Theological Seminary, Evangelicals gradually made their way back into the mainstream of American life.

From the 1920s through the 1990s, they established a media empire in radio, television, cable television, and the Internet. Billy Graham remained an iconic figure—even while other television preachers rose to prominence, often only to fall again when scandals involving their personal lives became public. The international Lausanne Congress on World Evangelization (1974) marked a major turning point for Evangelical thinking on missions, since it suggested that Christians were called both to preaching the gospel message and to the work of social justice and social transformation. The unfortunate split—stemming from the Fundamentalist-Modernist controversy—between believing the Bible and caring for the poor began to be reconciled following Lausanne.

Evangelicals played a key role in the election of Ronald Reagan as president in 1980, and they have been a significant voting bloc in support of conservative candidates ever since. Through such organizations as Rev. Jerry Falwell's Moral Majority, and Ralph Reed's Christian Coalition, Evangelicals were instrumental in a variety of conservative causes, such as opposition to abortion and pornography. Popular Evangelicalism was associated with belief in "the Rapture," the *Left Behind* novels, Christian bumper stickers, "purity rings" (for youth pledging to remain virgins prior to marriage), and pro-Israel politics. Globally speaking, Evangelicalism in the late 1900s showed greatest numerical growth outside of North America, in Africa, Asia, Latin America, and Oceania.

PENTECOSTALISM

A Supernatural Kind of Christianity.

Readers of the Acts of the Apostles can hardly miss the book's supernaturalism. People there "speak in tongues," i.e., in languages they have never studied or learned (Acts 2). Peter and John heal a man lame from birth (Acts 3). Saul the persecutor of the early Christians has an overpowering vision of Jesus, becomes a Christian disciple (Acts 9), and emerges as a leading preacher and apostle. A Christian prophet named Agabus accurately predicts a famine (Acts 11). Paul has a vision that tells him where he must go next to preach, and then casts a demon out of a young female slave who is a fortuneteller (Acts 16).

Modern Pentecostals, simply put, are Christians seeking to rediscover and re-experience the supernaturalism of earliest Christianity. Such phenomena as the healing of the sick through prayer, speaking in tongues, and prophetic messages from God were not merely events of the first century, they say, but are for today as well: "Jesus Christ is the same yesterday, today, and forever" (Hebrews 13:8). That is, the Christ who healed the sick and cast out demons in the first century is doing so in the twentieth and twenty-first centuries too. Those called Charismatics are closely related to Pentecostals. The Pentecostals got started just after 1900 and soon they formed their own denominations—having been given the boot (also known as "the left foot of fellowship"!) from almost all of the existing church bodies. Like the Pentecostals, the Charismatics were Christians who spoke in tongues and experienced the "gifts of the Spirit" and yet remained within the older, established churches—Roman Catholic, Anglican/Episcopalian, Lutheran, and so on. It was not until the 1960s that the Charismatics emerged as a visible group in the churches.

Pentecostalism began in a radical Evangelical quest for greater spiritual power. The British Methodist, William Arthur, argued in *The Tongue of Fire* (1856) that the Christian church needed a "new Pentecost" or fresh infusion of spiritual power. Missionary leaders feared that the increase in the world's non-Christian population was outpacing the gains made by Christian missionaries. Only a dramatic spiritual change would enable the church to fulfill its Great Commission (Matt 28:18–20) to preach the gospel to all nations. Some missionaries gave reports of miraculous healings in various parts of the world. Such accounts stirred interest in New Testament spiritual gifts, such as healing.

Toward the end of the 1800s, a spate of new books on the Holy Spirit appeared—perhaps more than during any earlier period in church history. It is interesting to note that Pope Leo XIII commissioned a remarkable treatise on the Holy Spirit, *Divinum Illud Munus* (1897), during the same period that these Protestants were also preoccupied with the Spirit. Some authors linked the new stress on the Holy Spirit with an idea of "Spirit baptism." Methodists and Wesleyans already conceived the Christian life as containing distinct stages. So the idea of Spirit baptism as a step beyond the experience of conversion was already in place by 1900. The debate was over what outward marks or signs would indicate the Spirit was at work.

New Movement for a New Century

Against this backdrop, the Methodist-Holiness preacher Charles Parham (1873–1929) founded the Bethel Bible School in Topeka, Kansas. He asked a small cadre of students to examine the scriptures to find the "Bible evidence" of having received the Holy Spirit. Soon the students found their answer. In the Acts of the Apostles, those who received the Spirit "spoke in tongues." Parham and the students reasoned that they should expect the same "Bible evidence" today. After they prayed intensely, for days on end, the breakthrough came on the first day of the new century—January 1, 1901—when Parham laid hands on Agnes Ozman, and unknown syllables flowed fluently from her mouth. Soon Parham and others entered into the new experience. While there were earlier cases of tongues-speaking in other locations, Parham's group was the beginning of a "tongues movement." In time, the emerging Pentecostal group referred to tongues-speaking as the distinguishing mark of receiving Spirit baptism.

Parham's most important follower proved to be William Seymour, a black man from Louisiana and son of slaves, known for his humble, unassuming demeanor. With Parham's blessing, and a gift to cover a one-way rail ticket to Los Angeles in 1906, Seymour headed west. The sojourn in California began badly. Though Seymour had not himself spoken in tongues, he was fully convinced by Parham's message, and so was preaching the tongues message to others. Seymour found the church door padlocked once the minister learned that he was preaching about tongues. With nowhere to turn, Seymour was invited into a private home: there, during a ten-day period of fasting and prayer, several began to speak in tongues. After a porch collapsed—because so many people had crowded in—they moved to a former horse stable on Azusa Street, where one of the most remarkable revivals in church history began to take shape, starting on April 14, 1906.

The Azusa Street Revival, 1906–1909

Services at the Azusa Street Mission ran almost every day from 1906 to 1909. From early in the morning until the evening hours, and sometimes the wee hours, the humble building was packed with worshippers. The people sat on rough planks, stacked on top of empty nail kegs. The pulpit was an empty orange crate, turned on its side. When some wondered whether a former stable was an appropriate place for church services, it was pointed out that Jesus had been born in a stable. There was no stated order of service. There was no regular preacher. Yet the services continued unabated, with minimal guidance from Seymour and other leaders.

During these meetings, powerful inward transformations took place among worshippers. Some spoke in tongues. Others were healed of illnesses or addictions. Still others reported that God had spoken to them, and called them to preach Christ in foreign lands. The first issue (September 1906) of the *Apostolic Faith* newsletter described the scene: "Proud, well-dressed preachers come in to 'investigate.' Soon their high looks are replaced with wonder, then conviction comes, and very often you will find them in a short time wallowing on the dirty floor, asking God to forgive them and make them as little children." At Azusa Street, the powerful presence of God seemed to dissolve all social distinctions. Black men, black women, white men, and white women all served at the mission on equal terms. Many ethnic groups—Mexican, Chinese, Russian, German, Jewish, etc.—streamed to the mission and were altered by their experiences there.

The Controversial Pentecostals

From the outset, the Pentecostal movement was controversial. A reporter from the *Los Angeles Times* offered an early appraisal within days of the first services at Azusa Street. The article, entitled "Weird Babel of Tongues," revealed a strong racial bias against Seymour and characterized his followers as religious fanatics. Some suggested that tongues-speaking was a mark of insanity. Within the mainline churches, the

IMAGE: USED WITH PERMISSION OF THE APOSTOLIC FAITH CHURCH

312 Azusa Street in Los Angeles became a focal point for the spread of Pentecostalism throughout North America and the world. William Seymour ate and slept on the second floor as services ran almost continuously on the first.

image of the Pentecostal was that of an Appalachian snake-handler with missing teeth!

Throughout most of the twentieth century, Pentecostals remained religious and cultural outsiders, misunderstood if not actually despised. Early Pentecostals—like the very earliest Christians—were pacifists. They wanted to have nothing to do with human governments and their wars. Pentecostals from the 1910s until perhaps the 1950s held various cultural taboos: no smoking, no drinking, no going to the theater or watching films. Some also rejected the wearing of neckties, riding in automobiles, eating catfish, and chewing gum, activities once associated with upper-class pretentiousness. Holy Ghost people were to live simply.

Early Debates and Developments in Pentecostalism

Although Pentecostalism began as a movement within Evangelicalism, many Evangelicals had theological issues with Pentecostals, and viewed them as a distinct group. They objected to what they took to be the implied Pentecostal claim to spiritual superiority. Pentecostals sometimes called themselves "full gospel" people, suggesting that the Evangelicals, in contrast, were incomplete, for they lacked the gifts of tongues, prophecy, and healing. Evangelicals argued that people received the Holy Spirit when they were converted, and that no post-conversion experience of "Spirit baptism" was necessary, or even possible. Some held that the New Testament gifts of the Spirit disappeared within a generation or two after the time of Jesus. These "cessationists" were unwilling to admit that any of the distinctive phenomena associated with Pentecostalism were true manifestations of the Holy Spirit.

Here it is possible only briefly to sketch some of the later development in Pentecostalism. As early as the 1910s and 1920s, the early signs of racial harmony between black and white Pentecostals began to vanish. In fact, the two co-founders of the American movement—Charles Parham and William Seymour—had a falling out that had racial overtones. Parham had tried to wrest control of the Azusa Street mission away from Seymour. Embittered over Seymour's success, he tried to undermine Seymour's work. Parham became increasingly irrelevant in the Pentecostal movement that he had been instrumental in founding. For the most part, American Pentecostals split into separate white and black denominations—much as the rest of American Protestants had done. Likewise, the early prominence of women in Pentecostal leadership was soon to fade, but did not disappear entirely: during the 1920s, the Pentecostal Aimee Semple McPherson was America's best-known radio preacher.

The Pentecostals, like their Fundamentalist cousins, withdrew from the mainstream of American life during the 1920s and 1930s. Yet, for the Pentecostals, this was a crucial time for establishing new congregations, Bible colleges, and mission agencies. As with earlier nineteenth-century Evangelicalism, twentieth-century Pentecostalism found that its missionary churches outside of North America were soon much larger than the sending churches within North America.

The 1940s "Latter Rain" and Healing Revivals

In 1948, a powerful yet controversial "Latter Rain" revival broke out in a small Pentecostal Bible college in Saskatchewan, Canada. Insisting that the Pentecostals needed a new touch from God, George and Ernst Hawtin laid hands on students and spoke prophetic messages they believed were revealed by the Holy Spirit. The Latter Rain revival shifted attention away from tongues-speaking toward gifts such as personal prophecy. They practiced prolonged fasting (lasting up to forty days), experimented with new forms of worship and song, and offended Pentecostal leaders by insisting that denominational and institutional structures had never been God's intention for the church. Theirs was a more ecumenical vision, in which denominational identity mattered little. Though rejected by fellow Pentecostals, the Latter Rain people promoted spiritual gifts among mainline Protestants and Roman Catholics, and encouraged the rise of independent Charismatic congregations. From the 1950s through the 1970s, the Latter Rain existed as a spiritual diaspora in North America, Britain, Europe, Australia, East Africa, and East Asia.

The late 1940s also witnessed a revival of healing ministries among Pentecostals, led by evangelists such as William Branham and Oral Roberts. For a time, Roberts possessed the world's largest tent—bigger even than that of any circus—and seated thousands in his healing crusades. Pentecostal healing-evangelists preached the same basic message of salvation that one heard from the lips of Billy Graham. Yet they not only preached but laid on hands for healing. Female healing-evangelists, like Maria Woodworth-Etter and Kathryn Kuhlmann, took their place alongside the men. Roberts admitted that not all people benefitted from his prayers, though some case studies offered medical support for the claims of sudden healing.

Pentecostalism Goes Mainstream: Charismatic Renewal

During the 1960s, the Pentecostal message spread to mainline Protestants, attaining a new level of notoriety in 1960 when the Episcopal minister, Dennis Bennett, declared from his California pulpit that he spoke in tongues. A yet more surprising development was the emergence of "Catholic Pentecostals," later termed Catholic Charismatics. Almost simultaneously, in Pittsburgh, Pennsylvania and in Bogota, Colombia, the Charismatic Renewal took off among Catholics, and found support at the highest levels of the church, as Cardinal Leon-Joseph Suenens, the Primate of Belgium, lent it his support and endorsement. Many Catholic Charismatics reported that they had come into a deeper relationship with Christ, and had become better Catholics, since their experience of Spirit baptism.

When these members of respected, well-established churches—Episcopalians, Lutherans, Methodist, and Roman Catholics—began speaking in tongues, the old image of Pentecostals as religious and cultural outsiders began to shift. Charismatic Christians were typically better educated than the Pentecostals, and tended to be more flexible than the Pentecostals about lifestyle issues: some of them enjoyed a good movie and an occasional glass of wine. The Charismatics of the 1960s–1970s were a different breed than the Pentecostals of the 1910s–1950s, and many Pentecostals remained ambivalent about the spreading Charismatic movement.

One of the more surprising developments of the 1960s was the emergence of Evangelical and Charismatic Christianity among the hippies and street people of San Francisco and Orange County, California. Having experimented with drugs, free love, leftist politics, and Eastern spirituality, and finding none of this satisfying, the hippies turned to Jesus and soon become known as the "Jesus people." Many were permanently changed and brought new vitality to Evangelical and Pentecostal churches. What later became known as the "Third Wave" of the Holy Spirit in the 1980s, and took concrete shape in the Vineyard Church, had its roots in the Jesus People Movement of the late 1960s and early 1970s.

IMAGE: © JP LAFFONT/SYGMA/CORBIS

The joy and optimism of the early Jesus Movement was apparent at the Explo 1972, an evangelical conference and festival that took place in Dallas, Texas, from June 12 to June 17. The event was sponsored by Campus Crusade for Christ and organized by Paul Eshleman. A crowd of 80,000 mostly young people from more than 75 countries congregated to praise Jesus. An even larger crowd of 180,000 came to the nine-hour rock festival that closed the festivities.

During the 1960s, some Pentecostals began to emphasize prosperity as God's will for believers. Oral Roberts's "seed faith" teaching held that one had to give one's money away in order to reap a larger amount in return. Kenneth Hagin and Kenneth Copeland were leading "health-and-wealth" preachers, followed by the Lebanese-Canadian Benny Hinn. The prosperity message was most popular in the independent Charismatic churches. The prosperity preachers suffered a setback in 1987 when Pentecostal television preachers Jim Bakker and Jimmy Swaggert were implicated in sexual and financial improprieties and forced off the air. As of 2011, Pastor Joel Osteen was preaching to America's largest congregation—the Lakewood Church of Houston, Texas, with an average weekly attendance of more than 43,000. Despite Osteen's Pentecostal roots, his sermons and broadcasts made little or no reference to tongues-speaking, healing, and other spiritual gifts. Instead they offered a tame, inoffensive message of positive thinking and successful living. Another television preacher (and one-time candidate for the U.S. presidency), Marion Gordon "Pat" Robertson (1930-), founded the Christian Broadcasting Network (CBN) in 1960 and by the early 2000s was helping to spread Pentecostal-Charismatic television programming around the globe. Robertson's Regent University (founded 1977) represented the educational wing of his ministry.

Pentecostal-Charismatic Christianity around the World

Argentina, Korea, Nigeria, South Africa, and China have witnessed major Pentecostal revivals since the 1970s. The Argentine lay preacher, Carlos Annacondia, drew audiences of 20,000 to 60,000 people at his evangelistic, healing, exorcistic crusades. Annacondia not only healed but cast out demons from Argentines who reported involvement in witchcraft and occultism. Some pastors from the United States and Canada visited Argentina and brought the revival fire back to Toronto, Ontario, and to Pensacola, Florida, where revivals broke out in 1994–1995. Several million visitors came to the two host churches, turning each city into a Pentecostal pilgrimage site. Toronto became known as the "laughing revival" because of the exuberant spirituality seen there. As with past revivals, established churches—including some Pentecostal congregations—often looked askance. Yet attendees at Toronto reported a new experience of God's love and "the Father's blessing." The German-born Pentecostal Reinhard Bonnke conducted mass rallies in Nigeria reliably reported as having between 1.5 and 2 million present at one time, perhaps the largest Christian gatherings ever convened. Some scholars speak of a "Pentecostalization" of world Christianity, affecting Catholicism and Protestantism alike during the last generation. The most prominent fact regarding Pentecostalism during the last generation has been its phenomenal rate of growth in Latin America, Africa, and Asia. As of the year 2000, there were an estimated 524 million Pentecostal-Charismatic Christians globally, making the Pentecostal-Charismatics collectively the second largest Christian body, after the Roman Catholics. Since Pentecostal groups often include only active, adult members in their figures, the numbers are yet more impressive. Though little-known in Western nations, newly-founded Pentecostal colleges, universities, and seminaries have been mushrooming all around the world in recent decades—including Alphacrucis College and Harvest Bible College (Australia), East Africa School of Theology (Kenya), Ecclesia Bible College (Hong Kong, China), Evangelical Theological Seminary (Croatia), Hansei University (South Korea), and Regents Theological College (UK). What is more, the global Pentecostal-Charismatic movement has received increasing scholarly attention in recent years. In 2010, the Center for Religion and Civic Culture at the University of Southern California awarded a total of $3.5 million for ongoing research into global Pentecostalism. Academics debate the present direction and future of the Pentecostal-Charismatic movement. Will it continue to grow? Will the movement cool down globally, as it seems to have cooled in North America? Will it develop a more obvious political and social agenda? If the twentieth-century is any indication of what one might expect in the twenty-first, then the Pentecostal-Charismatic movement may well continue to grow and to change in the decades ahead. "The wind blows where it wills" (John 3:8).

DIVERSITY-IN-UNITY: A FINAL HYPOTHESIS

When we take a deep breath, step back from the complex developments of recent centuries, and look at what is happening in the church today, what do we see? It should be admitted that no two observers are likely to see the same thing, or to describe it the same way. The hardest time period to comprehend is generally the time period one is living through. The dust hasn't yet settled, and so it's hard to make out distinctly what is happening.

Yet there may be reason for thinking that the larger trend of the last 500 years is what we might call *convergence*. Recall that during the 1500s, Catholic authorities put Protestants to death in predominantly Catholic regions as schismatics or heretics. Likewise, Protestants persecuted and executed Catholics as well as certain fellow Protestants in regions where they had the upper hand. In the early twenty-first century it would be difficult to find any Christian in any tradition or in any part of the world that would defend such persecutions of Christians by Christians. Today it is hard for us to imagine the mindset of someone who would wish to put others to death for their theological viewpoints. Instead, there has been a growing movement to bring Christians together again, in fulfillment of the famous prayer of Jesus "that they all may be one" (John 17:21).

The most obvious expression of the tendency toward convergence is the ecumenical movement, which can be dated to the Edinburgh Missionary Conference in 1910. Yet there are other signs of convergence as well. The Catholic Church, at the Vatican II conference (1962–1965), for the very first time referred to Protestants as "separated brethren." This was a monumental first step in the direction of greater visible unity and recognition between Catholics and Protestants. From the Protestant perspective, many key themes of Vatican II—the importance of the laity in the church, the liturgy in the people's language, a new stress on the study of the Bible, and a more collegial style of decision-making—have seemed like a belated recognition of earlier Protestant teachings and emphases. In 1999, the Lutheran World Federation and the Roman Catholic Church came to substantial agreement (with a few continuing differences) on the crucial doctrine of justification.

From a Pentecostal perspective, "Spirit-filled Christians" are a global force not only for vitality but for unity as well. Indeed, in some parts of Africa, Asia, and Latin America, scholars observe a kind of "Pentecostalization" taking place, where all the older traditions—whether Catholic, Protestant, or Orthodox—are being inwardly transformed by the emphasis on experiencing the power of the Holy Spirit. The result is that it is getting harder to tell denominations apart. The Protestants and Pentecostals are also borrowing from Roman Catholics, pursuing a renewed interest in liturgy, contemplation, mysticism, social justice, and Christian unity. Christians in Catholic and Protestant contexts find that they share much in their theological and political views.

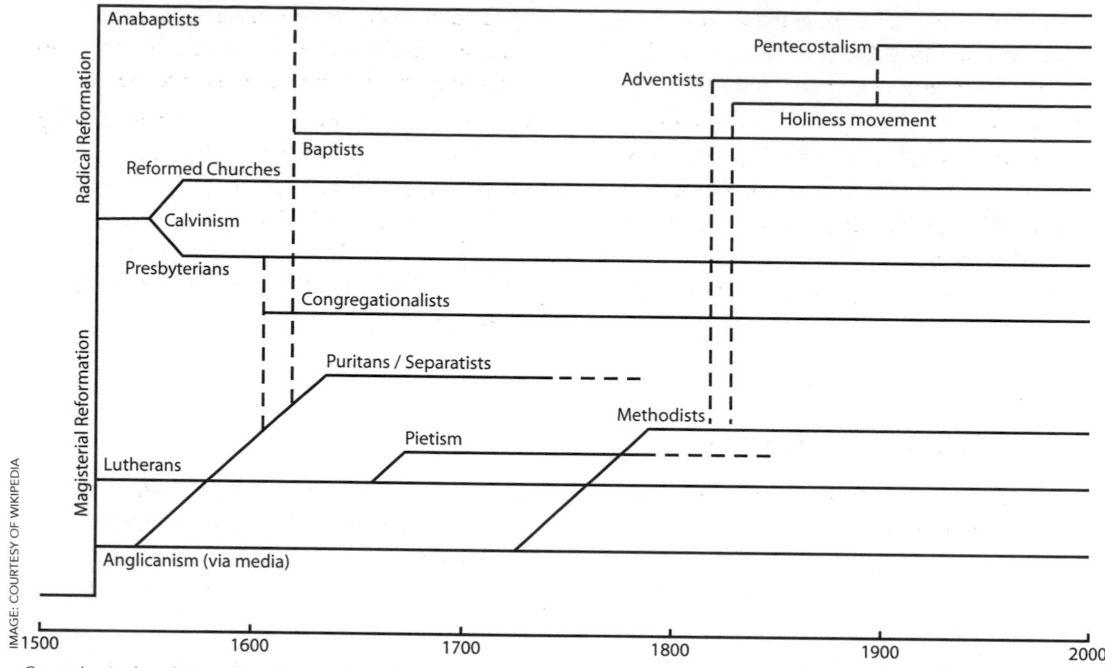

IMAGE: COURTESY OF WIKIPEDIA

Genealogical and time chart for modern Protestant movements.

An early Christian text, *The Epistle of Barnabas*, tells us that "the end is like the beginning." Could the twenty-first century become a time not of splitting apart but of coming together? Might the twenty-first-century church come to resemble the first-century church in its vitality, diversity, and unity? Is it possible to see a convergence that does not eliminate differences, yet allows for greater mutual recognition and collaboration among Christians? If the *apostolic tradition* of the Catholic Church were combined with the *apostolic teaching* of Word-oriented Protestants, and the *apostolic faith* of the Spirit-oriented Pentecostals, the outcome might be spectacular indeed.

Questions about the Text

1. Briefly define the terms Protestant, Evangelical, and Pentecostal.
2. Protestantism, Evangelicalism, and Pentecostalism arose at particular times—i.e., the sixteenth, eighteenth, and twentieth centuries—in relation to certain situations that existed at each of those times. Summarize the historical factors that contributed to the emergence of each movement.
3. The life of one man—Martin Luther—shaped Protestants' views of themselves and of their relationship with Roman Catholics. Summarize the major turning points in Luther's life and indicate how these biographical events helped to create a Protestant perspective.
4. Protestantism is not a single church but a cluster of related churches. What are the

most important branches or divisions within the Protestant world? When and why did these divisions emerge?

5. Protestant and Evangelical Christianity does not have official saints but it certainly has its role models. Make a list of six or seven men and women, named in this chapter, who could be regarded as role models. With each name, list the character trait that makes that person exemplary. (Example: George Whitefield is known for his evangelistic zeal— going out to preach to ordinary people in the fields and streets.)

6. Name at least four or five practices among today's Roman Catholics that seem to have originated, in the first instance, among Protestants, Evangelicals, and Pentecostals. (Example: One of these would be the small-group, layperson-led Bible study.)

Questions for Discussion

1. Scholars and other observers have noted the rapid growth of Evangelical and Pentecostal Christianity around the world in the last half-century. This growth has occurred in regions that were traditionally Catholic (e.g., Latin America, the Philippines), secular (Communist and post-Communist Eastern Europe), and characterized by non-Christian religions (India, China, Africa). Why do you think this growth is occurring?

2. Even in our ecumenical age, one still sometimes hears the age-old Protestant argument that Roman Catholicism is a religion of "works-righteousness," focused on external observance rather than personal experience. Is there any validity to this argument? Why or why not?

3. Protestants are known for knowing their Bibles. In your view, how important is the Bible? What role should the Bible play in spiritual life? What might be the dangers of overemphasizing—or wrongly interpreting and applying—the text of the Bible?

4. Many people lump together Evangelical and Pentecostal Christians, though this chapter drew some distinctions. How similar or different are these two groups, in your view?

5. What do you think about the Pentecostal stress on the supernatural? Is it plausible to believe that God today is giving people visions and dreams, prophetic insight into human affairs, the ability to speak unknown languages, and the power to heal the sick through prayer?

6. What, for you, are the most attractive aspects of the Protestant, Evangelical, and Pentecostal movements in Christianity? What are the most unattractive aspects?

7. This chapter ended with a stress on Christian unity. Yet the groups surveyed in this chapter are not known for showing unity. Are Protestantism, Evangelicalism, or Pentecostalism more of a help or more of a hindrance in the quest for Christian unity?

For Further Reading

Burgess, Stanley M., and Eduard M. van der Maas, eds. *The New International Dictionary of Pentecostal and Charismatic Movements*. Grand Rapids, MI: Zondervan, 2003.

Fernández-Armesto, Felipe; and Derek Wilson. *Reformations: A Radical Interpretation of Christianity and the World, 1500–2000*. New York: Scribner, 1996.

McClymond, Michael J., ed. *Encyclopedia of Religious Revivals in America*. 2 vols. Westport, CT: Greenwood Press, 2007.

McDermott, Gerald R., ed. *The Oxford Handbook to Evangelical Theology*. New York: Oxford University Press, 2010.

Melton, J. Gordon; ed. *Encyclopedia of American Religions*. 7th ed. Detroit, MI: Gale, 2003.

Noll, Mark A, David W. Bebbington, and George A. Rawlyk, eds. *Evangelicalism: Comparative Studies of Popular Protestantism in North America, the British Isles, and Beyond, 1700–1990*. New York: Oxford University Press, 1994.

Ozment, Steven. *Protestants: The Birth of a Revolution*. New York: Doubleday, 1992.

Synan, Vinson; ed. *The Century of the Holy Spirit: 100 Years of Pentecostal and Charismatic Renewal, 1901–2001*. Nashville: Thomas Nelson, 2001.

NAMED GROUPS IN PROTESTANTISM, WITH REPRESENTATIVE LEADERS OF THESE GROUPS

Group	Representative Leaders
Lutheran (1520s*)	Martin Luther (1483–1546), Philip Melanchthon (1497–1560)
Anglican (since 1534)	Thomas Cranmer (1489–1556), Richard Hooker (1554–1600)
Calvinist/ Reformed (1520s–1530s)	John Calvin (1509–1564), Ulrich Zwingli (1484–1531)
Anabaptist (1525)	Menno Simons (1496–1561)
Puritan (1560s)	Richard Baxter (1615–1691), John Owen (1616–1683)
Presbyterian (1560s)	John Knox (1510–1572), Charles Hodge (1797–1878)
Congregational (1590s)	John Winthrop (1588–1649), Jonathan Edwards (1703–1758)
Baptist (since 1609)	John Smyth (1570–1612), Roger Williams (1603–1683), Isaac Backus (1724–1806)
Arminian/ Remonstrant (1610)	Jacobus Arminius (1560–1609)
Quaker (1640s)	George Fox (1624–1691)
Pietist (1670s)	Philipp Spener (1635–1705), August Francke (1663–1727)
Evangelical (1730s–1740s)	George Whitefield (1714–1770), Jonathan Edwards (1703–1758)
Methodist (1740s)	John Wesley (1703–1791), Charles Wesley (1707–1788)
Revivalist (1800s–1810s)	Charles Finney (1792–1875), Asahel Nettleton (1783–1844)
Holiness (1830s)	Phoebe Palmer (1807–1874), Maria Woodworth-Etter (1844–1924)
Social Gospel (1870s–1880s)	Walter Rauschenbusch (1861–1918), and Reinhold Niebuhr (1892-1971)
Pentecostal (1900s–1910s)	William Seymour (1870–1922), Aimee Semple McPherson (1890–1944), David Yonggi Cho (1936–)
Ecumenical (1910s–1920s)	John R. Mott (1865–1955), Willem Vissser't Hooft (1900–1985)
Fundamentalist (1910s–1920s)	William Bell Riley (1861–1947)

continued

continued

Evangelical (1940s)	Billy Graham (1918–), John Stott (1921–), Samuel Lamb [Lin Xiangao] (1924–)	"Third Wave" (1980s)	John Wimber (1934–1997), C. Peter Wagner (1930–)
Charismatic (1960s–1970s)	Dennis Bennett (1917–1991), Kathryn Kuhlman (1907–1976)	Emergent Movement (1990s)	Brian McLaren (1956–)

** Dates indicate time of emergence for each group.*

from the REFERENCE LIBRARIAN

Getting the Most out of Encyclopedias

One of the main purposes of the "From the Reference Librarian" sections in this book is to convince you of the value of using reference tools such as encyclopedias. By this stage, you have already seen how encyclopedias help you "get your feet wet" on a subject by providing basic information about or an overview of a subject and also by giving you a simple way into the labyrinth of the library catalog by using encyclopedia bibliographies to discover subject headings. Encyclopedias, especially those published more recently, frequently offer other helpful features, and the wealth of reference titles available for this chapter's subject matter provides the opportunity to point out some of these features. Some of these features will be covered in more detail in subsequent "From the Reference Librarian" sections but they will be mentioned here by way of preview.

First, before we explore these features, let's note some of the encyclopedias useful for researching "Christianity in the Modern Era." The following two encyclopedias focus on Protestantism during the period of the Reformation itself or throughout the entire historical sweep of Protestantism.

> Hans J. Hillerbrand, ed. *The Oxford Encyclopedia of the Reformation.* 4 vols. New York; Oxford, UK: Oxford University Press, 1996.

> Hans J. Hillerbrand, ed. *The Encyclopedia of Protestantism.* 4 vols. New York; London: Routledge, 2004.

Other reference sources focus specifically on the development of Christianity in the United States. Note the presence of the word *religion* in the title of some of these, indicating that religions other than Christianity (e.g. Judaism, Islam, etc.) are covered as well.

> Charles H. Lippy and Peter W. Williams, eds. *Encyclopedia of Religion in America.* 4. vols. Washington, D.C.: CQ Press, 2010.

> Edward L. Queen II, Stephen R. Prothero, and Gardiner H. Shattuck, Jr., eds. *Encyclopedia of American Religious History.* Rev. ed. 2 vols. New York: Facts On File, Inc., 2001.

> Daniel G. Reid, ed. *Dictionary of Christianity in America.* Downers Grove, IL: InterVarsity Press, 1990.

A number of reference titles cover specific aspects of the development of Christianity in the United States. For example, the following title concentrates on women and American religion (including Christianity).

> June Melby Benowitz. *Encyclopedia of American Women and Religion.* Santa

Barbara, CA; Denver, CO; Oxford, UK: ABC-CLIO, 1998.

The next two titles focus on the African American religious experience.

Larry G. Murphy, J. Gordon Melton, and Gary L. Ward, eds. *Encyclopedia of African American Religions.* New York; London: Garland Publishing, Inc., 1993.

Marvin A. McMickle. *An Encyclopedia of African American Christian Heritage.* Valley Forge, PA: Judson Press, 2002.

The interaction between Christianity and American politics is covered by the following titles:

Paul A. Djupe and Laura R. Olson, eds. *Encyclopedia of American Religion and Politics.* New York: Facts On File, Inc., 2003.

Jeffrey D. Schultz, John G. West, Jr., and Iain Maclean, eds. *Encyclopedia of Religion in American Politics.* Phoenix, AZ: Oryx Press, 1999.

Other encyclopedias cover particular manifestations of Christianity in the American or global context.

Michael McClymond, ed. *Encyclopedia of Religious Revivals in America.* 2 vols. Westport, CT; London: Greenwood Press, 2007

Samuel S. Hill and Charles H. Lippy, eds. *Encyclopedia of Religion in the South.* 2nd ed. Macon, GA: Mercer University Press, 2005.

Stanley M. Burgess and Eduard M. Van Der Maas, eds. *The New International Dictionary of Pentecostal and Charismatic Movements.* Rev. and exp. ed. Grand Rapids, MI: Zondervan, 2002.

Randall Balmer. *Encyclopedia of Evangelicalism.* Rev. and exp. ed. Waco, TX: Baylor University Press, 2004.

Finally, there are a number of relevant biographical reference sources for research on individual persons.

Henry Warner Bowdon, ed. *Dictionary of American Religious Biography.* 2nd ed. Westport, CT; London: Greenwood Press, 1993.

Timothy L. Hall. *American Religious Leaders.* New York: Facts On File, Inc., 2003.

Timothy Larsen, ed. *Biographical Dictionary of Evangelicals.* Leicester, UK: Inter-Varsity Press; Downers Grove, IL: InterVarsity Press, 2003.

J. Gordon Melton, ed. *Religious Leaders of America.* 2nd ed. Detroit; San Francisco; London; Boston; Woodbridge, CT: Gale, 1999.

Most academic libraries will have several of these titles. As always, ask your reference librarian for help if you are unable to identify readily an encyclopedia for a topic you want to study.

Now let's explore some of the features these encyclopedias offer. One important feature of encyclopedias we have not mentioned concerns the persons who actually write the individual encyclopedia articles. An encyclopedia often has a list, designated as a "List of Contributors" (or something similar), of all those who have contributed articles. This list usually contains at least some of the following information for each contributor: institutional affiliation (usually, but not always, an academic institution), academic degrees, title (e.g. professor, etc.), and a list of the articles contributed by that individual. Note that, when such a list is included, the articles are usually "signed," that is, the name of the author appears at the conclusion of the article. By contrast, some encyclopedias are the work of one (or perhaps only a handful) of individuals. Three of the encyclopedias listed above—the *Encyclopedia of American Women and Religion*,

An Encyclopedia of African American Christian Heritage, and the *Encyclopedia of Evangelicalism*—were each produced by an individual. The articles are not individually "signed" because only one author wrote all of them. Other things being equal, signed encyclopedia articles are regarded as more authoritative than unsigned articles but this is not a hard and fast rule and should not be regarded as grounds for avoiding single-author encyclopedias. Randall Balmer, for example, is well known as a scholar of evangelicalism, and so can write with authority on the subject (you wouldn't be expected to know that but the librarian should). But no individual can give the same kind of coverage to a topic that a team of qualified writers can, each one writing in his or her own field of expertise. Such individually authored reference works run the danger of being more an expression of a particular author's "take" on the subject than representing either a scholarly consensus or the specialized knowledge of someone who has studied a particular topic in depth. This is not a reason to avoid using such works but something to keep in mind when you consider the quality of the information you gather from such works.

Encyclopedias covering more specialized subjects often include helpful introductory articles (sometimes quite extensive) presenting a survey or overview of the subject. For example, the *Dictionary of Christianity in America* starts with an essay on "Division and Unity: The Paradox of Christianity in America," which gives a historical overview. The *Encyclopedia of Religion in the South* has four introductory essays offering historical surveys of religion in the southern United States during four distinct historical eras, the colonial, antebellum, postbellum, and recent periods. The *Encyclopedia of Religion in American Politics* begins with a twenty-one page essay on "Religion in American Politics." Finally, the *Encyclopedia of African American Religions* includes three introductory essays covering the African American religious experience, Martin Luther King, and black womanist theology respectively. Sometimes, these essays can be as much or more helpful than the subsequent articles.

For subjects that have a historical dimension, encyclopedias will sometimes include a chronology or timeline highlighting events of particular significance in relation to the subject. The *Encyclopedia of American Women and Religion* includes a chronology covering the years 1697 to 1997 (the encyclopedia was published in 1998). *The New International Dictionary of Pentecostal and Charismatic Movements* has a "Pentecostal and Charismatic Timeline." Both the *Encyclopedia of African American Religions* and *An Encyclopedia of African American Christian Heritage* include timelines but note that the first covers 1618-1991 while the second covers 1701–2001.

Another feature sometimes found in encyclopedias with a historical dimension is the inclusion of the texts of primary source documents. "Primary" sources are sources that bring you into direct contact with the events with which they are concerned, unlike "secondary" sources (such as encyclopedias) which act as intermediaries between you and the events they describe. The *Encyclopedia of Religious Revivals in America* (published in two volumes) devotes the entire second volume to the texts of 153 documents, many of which contain first-hand accounts by participants in the distinctive religious phenomenon of a "revival." The *Encyclopedia of Religion in American Politics* includes twenty-five "significant speeches and documents" pertaining to the interaction between religion and politics.

The features of encyclopedias remaining to be considered all try to fulfill the same purpose—making it easier for you to find exactly what it is you're looking for. There are several types of such "finding aids." The first of these is the simplest, an alphabetical list of all the articles appearing in the encyclopedia. In effect, this is a table of contents— but one that is significantly longer than a table of contents you are accustomed to using, since an encyclopedia can have hundreds of articles. In spite of this length, such a list is helpful because it allows you to see at a glance what is included in the encyclopedia (and what is not included) instead of flipping through pages trying to find an article on your subject. Most of the encyclopedias listed above contain such a list (note that in the case of biographical reference sources, this will be a list of names).

A second type of finding aid, indexes, are important and will be explored in more detail in "From the Reference Librarian" following chapter 10. At this point we will note two things regarding indexes. Some encyclopedias have only a single index while others distribute the content of the encyclopedia across two or more indexes. For example, *The New International Dictionary of Pentecostal and Charismatic Movements* has indexes for "Personal Names," "Countries and Regions" (note the potential relevance of this to the subject of global Christianity discussed in chapter 12), "Groups and Associations," "Publications," as well as a general index of subjects.

Unfortunately, some encyclopedias are published without any index at all. However, one way by which the producers of these encyclopedias (at least the conscientious ones) try to compensate for the lack of an index is by extensive cross-referencing throughout the encyclopedia. Cross references to other relevant articles in the encyclopedia can appear either at the conclusion of an article or within the text of the article itself (the cross reference being indicated in some way such as marking a word with an asterisk or printing a word entirely in capital letters). Two encyclopedias from the list above, the *Dictionary of Christianity in America* and the *Encyclopedia of Evangelicalism*, both of which lack an index, contain such in-text cross-references.

The final type of finding aid to be mentioned is a relatively recent innovation in encyclopedias. This feature also provides a list of articles appearing in the encyclopedia but arranges them into separate categories that pertain to the overall subject matter of the encyclopedia, so that, for example, any one article may appear more than once in the "synoptic outline of contents" ("synoptic" means to "view together" so you can see at a glance all of the articles relevant to a particular category). Such lists are designated in various ways; besides "synoptic outline," you may also encounter "synoptic index," "thematic outline," "thematic table of contents," etc. The "Synoptic Outline of Contents," in volume 4 of the *Oxford Encyclopedia of the Reformation* arranges the entries into such categories as "Sites, Region, Politics," "Historical Events," "Religious Groups and Movements," "Creeds, Confessions, Texts," "Theology," "Popular Religion," and "Biographies," among others. A variant of this kind of finding aid can often be found in the biographical reference sources listed above: the names of those with an entry in the encyclopedia are arranged by denominational affiliation or perhaps geographical area. (For fuller discussion of the synoptic outline, see the "From the Reference Librarian" sections following chapters 8 and 11.)

We could describe other encyclopedia features such as maps, charts, illustrations, and photographs, but those described above should be sufficient to demonstrate that many encyclopedias try to make it as easy as possible for you to tap into the wealth of information and knowledge they contain, in other words, to get the most out of using an encyclopedia.

Grace and Sacraments: The Mystery of the Divine-Human Encounter

Jay M. Hammond

from the EDITOR

The previous chapter on ecclesiologies examined the structure of the community, what it means to belong, its macro-structures, identity concerns, and purpose in the world. This chapter considers the interior, or micro, theological understanding of sacraments and grace—the way one celebrates, communicates, initiates, solemnizes, and lives in God's love. In a theological nutshell, it is all about communication between God and humanity, and humanity together.

We all know what it is to communicate to another person what is deepest in our hearts, to be heard, to be ourselves, to be understood, and to be loved as we are. It is no less with the Christian community, where God is the source, support, and end. While communicating privately with God in individual prayer is necessary, the community also must engage God. This communication comes in many forms, but this chapter theologically explores the role of signs belonging to the heart of Christianity. Christians of different traditions do not agree on the subject of sacraments. Since this chapter is primarily concerned with the Roman Catholic understanding of grace and sacraments, much of the discussion refers to the way that God is believed to interact with "the [Catholic] Church" through the sacraments. This is not meant to imply that God works only through the Catholic Church, but that the theology of sacraments set out in this chapter specifically reflects the understanding of the Catholic Church, and may or may not apply as well to other denominations.

This chapter should be read in conjunction with chapter 5, "The People of God: The Church." This chapter investigates theology's understanding of grace (God's self communicated) by investigating the role of communication and symbol. Grace is foundational to Christian theology because it describes the interaction of God with humanity. Grace describes the binding of the community called "church" and its communal symbols—such as baptism and Eucharist—called "sacraments." Both mediate God to humanity in symbols (invisible and visible together) that are grace-filled and that teach one how to live one's daily life. Sacramental Christianity is at the heart of Christian spirituality as a paradigm of how to live a life of love in discipleship. This chapter explores a Catholic understanding of the meaning and purpose of life itself, in symbol, in communication, in holy encounter with God.

OVERVIEW

The two preceding chapters on Christology and ecclesiology provide the framework for understanding the sacramental theology that emerged from Vatican Council II. On the one hand, Jesus is the primordial sacrament of God's presence and action, which means that Jesus' life, death, and Resurrection reveal the mystery of God's love for creation because, for Christians, the Incarnation is the mystery of the divine-human encounter. On the other hand, the Church is the fundamental sacrament of Jesus' presence and action, which means that the Church is a sacrament because it makes Christ present in the world. Thus, the Church, symbolically called Christ's Body (Rom 12:4–6), vicariously participates in the divine-human encounter because when two or more are gathered in Jesus' name, he is among them (Matt 18:20).

To understand how Jesus Christ (Christology) and the Church (ecclesiology) inform Catholic sacramental theology, this chapter will (1) explain the importance of signs and symbols, (2) describe and define at greater length the word *sacrament*, (3) consider the two basic sacraments of Jesus and the Church in more detail, (4) survey the symbolic rituals of the seven formal sacraments celebrated by Roman Catholics, and (5) end by considering how active Christians themselves are living sacraments that point to and manifest God's presence and actions in the world.

SIGNS AND SYMBOLS: CREATING MEANING IN HUMAN COMMUNICATION

Humans are awash in symbols. They are ubiquitous in all our activities, thoughts, and dreams. We can neither construct meaning nor communicate with each other without them. However, we often take signs and symbols for granted. For example, you could not even read this text, or any text for that matter, if you had not learned the complex sign system of the English language. Likewise, discussion of this book, or any conversation, would be impossible without the symbols that both contain and communicate the meanings expressed by the sign system. The very act of your reflection about these meanings involves several levels of complex symbolic thinking through, in, and by which you just had a thought, whatever it was.

Accordingly, all communication and the meaning created therein assumes a common use of signs and symbols. On the other hand, communication breaks down when we interpret signs and symbols inaccurately, use them incorrectly, or are dishonest about them, that is, when we intentionally misconstrue our signs and symbols to others. In effect, signs and symbols are the basic building blocks of all human language, according to which we create meaning from our experiences and communicate it with others. They are the retainers, transmitters, and translators of all we know and love. Thus, we do not know or love reality immediately but can only experience reality mediated through the various symbolic systems that we call language. This principle of mediation is foundational to the meaning of sacramentality.

A sign and symbol are not the same. A sign is something that points to another reality and means what it signifies; the meaning is mostly fixed. In contrast, a symbol is a multidimensional sign that points to another reality and manifests the reality to which it points. For example, most readers would interpret and understand a stop sign in the same way: the sign signals them to stop at the intersection, but the sign is not the intersection. Likewise, they would know that a sign reading "St. Louis 10 miles" will lead them to the city but is not itself the destination. But the same cannot be said of a symbol as simple as a kiss, which can manifest many things to different people: love and affection (e.g., parent to child, between spouses, or between acquaintances), romance and seduction (e.g., husband to wife, boyfriend to girlfriend, or those on a date), greeting and farewell (e.g., a kiss hello, a kiss goodbye), respect and reverence (e.g., to kiss a ring, flag, or cross), forbidden and forced (e.g., used in incest, adultery, pedophilia, rape), betrayal and death (Judas kissing Jesus, and Michael Corleone kissing his brother Fredo in the movie *The Godfather, Part II*), and anger or frustration (e.g., "kiss my butt," "kiss off"). Other examples further illustrate the point. The sculptor Rodin was disappointed with people's reactions to his statue *The Kiss* (1886) because he thought most misunderstood his intention. And we would be remiss if we excluded the 1970s glam-rock music phenomenon KISS. While many other examples could be given, the point is this: Is a kiss ever really just a kiss?

Likewise, a symbol manifests the reality to which it points. For many, the activity of kissing manifests love, yet love is more than kissing. Saying, "I love you," also expresses love, but love is more than words. Love is a mom or dad hugging a child tight, but love is more than a hug. Paul says that love is both patient and kind (1 Cor 13:4), yet love is still more. Jesus taught that one should love God above all and one's neighbor as oneself (Matt 22:37–39; Mark 12:29–31; Luke 10:27), but even the golden rule does not exhaust the depths of love because there are many more dimensions to the mystery of love. Thus, while symbols manifest the reality to which they point, they always allude to more:

> A symbol is charged with many meanings, and once it has caused an interpreter to take account of its many meanings, its work still continues. There is always more depth of meaning to be uncovered in it, more questions to be asked of it, because the abundance and richness of its meaning are inexhaustible. The human mind can never get to the bottom of a symbol and be done with it. (Lawler, 1995, 21)

The inexhaustibility is the tricky thing about symbols because it moves away from "objective" knowledge that is quantifiable and observable to more "subjective" knowledge that is qualitative and personal. For some, this causes a problem because they prefer "objective" knowledge to symbolic ways of understanding. The empirical prejudice echoed in dismissive comments like "it's only a symbol" restricts human knowing to a narrow category of experience. While symbols may struggle to describe the human phenomenon of love, few doubt the reality of love. Experience dictates the existence of love, and humans use symbols to understand love's meanings and to communicate them with others. Thus a better way to understand symbols is to interpret them as being fully real because they concretely and effectively communicate personal meanings that escape easy description. Otherwise, to say a symbol is not real prevents the communication of meaning, which is so integral to our human experience.

Of course, there are many variations in between a sign and symbol. Smoke can be interpreted as a sign—"where there is smoke there is fire"—but also as a symbol; for example, we say a person who is performing at a high level is "smoking," which does not mean that person is physically aflame. Nevertheless, while all symbols are signs, not all signs are symbols. The difference between the two often depends on the function of the sign according to the context within which it is used. A simple sign normally points to a physical activity or object, but a symbol opens to the human activity of creating meaning that moves beyond the physical world into the "spiritual" dimensions of human experience. The key is the activity of interpretation, because signs and symbols require a personal response before their meanings can be understood. How we interpret a sign or symbol greatly influences what that sign or symbol means, but our interpretations are significantly shaped by the communities to which we belong, because while all of us were born naked into the world, none of us was born into a naked world. Accordingly, signs and symbols have socialized all of us, and we must personally interpret them if we want to participate in the human process of communicating meaning. In short, sacraments depend on signs and symbols.

DESCRIBING AND DEFINING THE SACRAMENTS

Describing a Sacrament

Like signs and symbols, the sacraments are about the mystery of a threefold communication: from God to humans, from humans to God, and among humans in community. The very idea of communication implies relationship and interpretation. Thus, when one reads or hears the word *sacrament*, for example, at the liturgy of the Eucharist during the mass when the bread and wine are elevated, broken, distributed, and so on, one should ask: "To what do the signs/symbols point? What do the signs/symbols communicate? How do the signs/symbols cultivate relationships?" These may seem like simple questions, but if they are overlooked and left unanswered, then the meaning of the sacraments will remain individually and communally obscure, confusing, and boring.

Moreover, signs and symbols provide the "content" for sacramental rituals, and those ritual actions, communally celebrated, supply the "context" for interpreting and understanding the significance of the sacraments. Such an understanding of the sacraments parallels the idea that the signs and symbols we use involve both our individual interpretations and the communal contexts that shape our perceptions. Thus fuller participation in the sacraments requires that we understand both because to miss either the "content" of the sacraments' symbolism or the "context" of their communal celebration is to decrease their ability to convey meaningful communication.

Roman Catholics call their symbolic rituals "rites" (content), which they celebrate during the liturgy (context). While a rite describes the prescribed actions and words needed for administering a sacrament, the liturgy is the actual celebration of a sacrament by the community. Since all relationships require the work of the participating members, the liturgy, communicated through and in its symbolic rituals, is a special and significant locus for the reciprocal "work" that unveils the mystery of the divine-human encounter. In this relationship, the work is primarily God's action, but it also involves the participatory work of the community to love and serve God and neighbor. A better understanding of how "sacramental language" describes and expresses these relationships can open up a greater appreciation of and participation in the sacramentality of all created reality.

Defining Sacraments

All world religions have sacraments, but only Christians call them sacraments (Martos, 2001, 3–16). Most Christian churches celebrate sacraments, but there is a wide spectrum of understandings on the number and meaning of the sacraments. Historically, while the term *sacrament* comes from the Latin word *sacramentum*, the concept has much to do with its Greek equivalent, *mystērion*. *Mystērion* means "something hidden or secret," which has been retained today with the word *mystery*. Thus, even before Christianity began, the term *mystērion* described an experience of the divine or God's activity in human affairs. Thus *mystērion* was also closely linked with the idea of revelation; that is, God's revelation is a mystery. These two concepts of mystery and revelation are common in both the Hebrew and Christian Scriptures, especially Ephesians and Colossians. However, it was not until the third century that theologians Clement and Origin explicitly applied the meaning of *mystērion* to Christian ritual practices. Today *mystērion* points to the fact that the core meaning of the symbolic rituals we now call sacraments involves mystery and revelation of God's self-communication.

Tertullian (d. 230) was a native of Carthage in North Africa. He had a pagan education, became a lawyer, lived in Rome, converted to Christianity about 195 CE, and then became a priest. He was one of the first Christian theologians to write in Latin and became one of the great early theologians, especially in Christology and the Trinity.

An important development in this discussion happened in the third century when the theologian Tertullian sought to translate *mystērion* into Latin. He chose the word *sacramentum*, which meant a "sacred oath" taken by a recruit joining the Roman army. In the same way the soldier uttered a *sacramentum* to the emperor, who was considered a deity, the Christian pledges a sacred oath to Christ. Thus Tertullian used *sacramentum* to mean a religious initiation into the Christian community via baptism and Eucharist, which were both a sign of initiation and the means of sanctification. Today, *sacramentum* points to the fact that the core meaning of the symbolic rituals we now call sacraments involves an initiation into a community of believers that seek experience of God's mystery.

Following Tertullian was the fifth-century Augustine of Hippo. He developed the notion that a *sacramentum* is a sign that sanctifies because it is efficacious, meaning that the sign produces an intended effect or that it is effective. For example,

Augustine (d. 430) was also from Carthage. He studied philosophy and rhetoric and became professor of rhetoric for the imperial court at Milan. After his conversion to Christianity in 386, he became bishop of Hippo (North Africa) in 396. He is one of the most influential Christian theologians, and the Catholic Church recognizes him as a "Doctor (teacher) of the Church."

Christ and the Spirit make effective, through grace, the cleansing that water signifies. Thus, for those with faith, baptism purifies by grace. Augustine did not only consider religious rituals to be *sacramenta* but he listed over three hundred sacraments. The church would gradually pare back the number of sacraments by distinguishing between those celebrated as symbolic rituals by the community, which were retained as sacraments, and those that came to be identified as sacramentals, that is, signs and practices that assist persons in their devotion and prayer (e.g., genuflection, crossing oneself, and a rosary). Nevertheless, Augustine's towering influence on Western Christianity framed the understanding of the sacraments as sacred signs. Thus, when the twelfth-century theologian Peter Lombard (France, d. 1160) devised the technical definition that states, "A sacrament is a sign of a sacred thing that is capable of conveying the grace of which it is the sign" (*Liber Sententiarum* IV, d. 1, c. 4), he was largely following in the footsteps of Augustine. Today, the medieval technical definition of a sacrament points to the fact that only those symbolic rituals that confer the grace they signify are called sacraments.

The history of the terms *mystērion* and *sacramentum* demonstrate that sacraments involve (1) the mystery of the divine-human encounter wherein God reveals the divine presence, (2) the initiation of a believer into a communal participation of that divine-human encounter, and (3) the faith community's active celebration of those symbolic rituals that confer the grace they signify.

With these three points in mind, a sacrament can be theologically defined as a symbolic ritual comprised of words, gestures, and material signs (bread, wine, water, oil, etc.) that points to and manifests Jesus' own actions, for the purpose of communicating God's grace to those who, by faith, perform and participate in their action. These three aspects are traditionally defined as (1) a sign (2) instituted by Christ (3) to give grace. Let us look at each aspect more closely.

A Sign

Previously we made an important distinction between a sign and a symbol. While a sacrament is definitely a sign in that it points to another reality, it is also properly understood as a symbol because it manifests the reality to which it points. A good example is the Eucharist, which points both to the multifaceted mystery of Jesus' paschal meal, and to the manifestation of Christ's real presence in the Eucharist and among believing communities. Sacramental theology translates the symbol's two notions of pointing and manifesting into the understanding that the sacraments "effect what they signify" or "cause by signifying" (Lawler, 1995, 34). Thus sacraments, like symbols, both point to or signify God's action and manifest, effect, or cause the grace of Christ that sanctifies the recipient.

The key is the signification because sacraments cause by signifying, so if they do not signify, then they do not cause. Simply stated, a sacrament is that which effects something by its significance, but sacraments do not always effectively signify for every person because the signification or meaning of the sacramental signs and symbols may be misunderstood or the participant may lack faith. For example, if my wife and I have been in an argument and she offers reconciliation with a kiss, if I do not understand the significance of the kiss or I do not trust her intentions, then the kiss will fail to effect or manifest what it signifies: forgiveness and reconciliation.

The point is that we need sacraments to communicate in the same way that we need symbols. Sacraments provide a language for relationship with God.

> In human life, signs and symbols occupy an important place. As a being at once body and spirit, man expresses and perceives spiritual realities through physical signs and symbols. As a social being, man needs signs and symbols to communicate with others, through language, gestures, and actions. The same holds true for his relationship with God. (*Catechism of the Catholic Church* [*Catechism*], n. 1146)

Sacraments, like symbols, strive to accomplish the difficult task of communicating spiritual reality. Just as symbols are necessary for human communication, sacraments are necessary for the communication of the divine-human encounter. However, we should not assume that the sacraments restrict God's activity; God does not need the sacraments to communicate with those he loves, but they are principle instruments that ritually manifest God's presence and actions to the community that celebrates their mystery.

Instituted by Christ

The Fourth Lateran Council (1215) held at Rome was the first council that officially numbered the sacraments at seven. The Church later confirmed this number at the Councils of Lyon II (1274), Florence (1439), and Trent (1547). During the Reformation (beginning in 1517),

Pascha is Greek for "Passover." Thus *Paschal Meal* is a term that refers to the Jewish Passover meal that Jesus shared with the Apostles the night before he died. By participating in the Paschal Meal, Christians share in the "paschal mystery," the redemption effected by Christ in his life, death, and Resurrection.

a thorny debate arose concerning the number of sacraments explicitly instituted by Christ. Many Protestants argued for the two dominical (*dominus*—"lord") sacraments of baptism and Eucharist because scripture records Jesus as directly instituting them. In contrast, the Council of Trent argued that Christ instituted all seven sacraments, and the council was left with the rather difficult task of demonstrating how Jesus historically instituted the specific rituals or general formula for each of the seven sacraments.

So who was right? As with most things, it depends on how one frame's the question. If one looks for specific scriptural instances where Jesus directly institutes the sacraments via word and action, then one will likely arrive at the two sacraments of baptism and Eucharist. However, if one looks at Jesus as explicitly instituting the Church in a sacramental way, that is, the Church is Christ's body that locates Christ in the world, then Christ's explicit institution of the Church is the implicit institution of the Church's seven sacramental actions that reenact Jesus' own actions. In this view, Christ instituted the sacraments in a derivative sense because by "instituting the Church, Christ instituted the sacraments" (Rahner, 1963, 62).

Accordingly, the question of Christ's direct institution of the sacraments becomes subordinate to the question of Christ's direct institution of the Church as a sacrament of himself. Such an understanding of Christ's institution of the sacraments hinges on two notions: (1) Jesus as sacrament of God and (2) the Church as sacrament of Jesus. We will investigate these two important ideas in the third section of this chapter, but here it is important to mention that "the Christian sacraments are an attempt on the part of the Church to extend into the world the actions of Jesus in his humanity" (Noll, 1999, 30). Christ's institution of the sacraments requires nothing less than an imitation of Christ's own actions by Christians who celebrate the sacraments: (1) Jesus was baptized and commissioned the apostles to baptize (Matt 28:19), so the Church celebrates baptism as the initiation into discipleship with Christ; (2) Jesus' actions and teachings confirmed his Father's reign, so the Church celebrates Christians' confirmation to do the same; (3) Jesus shared many meals with others and, at the Last Supper with his disciples, said, "Do this in remembrance of me," so the Church today celebrates a communal meal called Eucharist, where Christ continues to give himself, Body and Blood, to those he loves; (4 and 5) Jesus healed sickness and forgave sins, so the Church continues Christ's healing and forgiving actions in the anointing of the sick and reconciliation; (6) Jesus chose disciples and sent them as apostles into the world to serve others (John 20:21), so the Church continues the activity of Jesus' ministry in ordination; and (7) as Jesus lived in intimate friendship with the Father, thereby fulfilling the covenant relationship, so the Church today celebrates the covenant of marriage as a relationship centered in intimacy with God in Christ. In sum, Jesus did not institute the specific rituals of the sacraments; rather, he instituted the Church as a sacrament of himself to extend, in a tangible manner, his actions into the world.

To Give Grace

To understand the third aspect of a sacrament's traditional definition, we need to understand what "grace" means and how the sacraments "give grace."

First, the Church understands grace (*charis* in Greek, *gratia* in Latin) as the free, unmerited assistance that God gives to humans for their salvation, which is nothing less than participation in God's life and love. In effect, grace makes a person a friend of God. Grace is both the cause and the effect of this friendship. Grace is the cause because grace is God's self-gift to humans that transforms, heals, and nurtures human existence. In theological terms, this is called either "uncreated grace" or "supernatural grace" because God's own presence personally dwells within those whom God draws into friendship, just as a lover experiences the personal presence of the beloved. Grace is also the effect because grace is the transformation of human nature, which brings forth depths of human growth that would otherwise remain dormant. In theological terms, this is called either "created grace" or "actual grace" because all the gifts God gives to humans, including their very existence, potentially deepen their friendship with God. In short, uncreated and created grace are two sides of the Creator-creature relationship that necessarily leads to the transformation of human experience. Thus the mystery of grace lies at the heart of the mystery of the divine-human encounter.

In practical terms, *grace* means "gift." Thus all good things are gifts from God, and can rightfully be called grace. For example, my wife, children, and friends are all grace because they are gifts that manifest the gift of God's presence. A deeper examination of grace leads to the insight that "grace touches everything in our lives; it pervades everything we are and do" (Cooke, 1994, 79). What we should remember is that grace is a gift from God offered through the Son and in the Spirit. Thus grace is not a thing; rather, it is always relational and comes to build authentic relationships between the divine and human communities. Grace is always the root of this relationship, and friendship is its intended fruit.

Second, sacraments are not magic, nor are they grace machines. Rather, the grace that the sacraments "give" involves a relationship that emerges from, affirms, and returns to the mystery of the divine-human encounter. On one side of the relationship, God always offers the grace communicated by a sacrament. Thus a sacrament is a means of grace simply because God offers it. The terminology of the Council of Trent (1545–1563) called this "from the work worked" (Lat., *ex opere operato*), that is, properly performed sacraments, because they involve the agency of the risen Christ and the Spirit, contain and confer the grace they signify. This claim stresses that God, in Christ, is the primary agent of the grace offered in a sacrament. On the other side of the relationship, the participant must also accept the gift of grace that God offers for the sacrament to be an effective sign. Thus the actual mediation of grace requires the recipient's participation. This dimension of the sacrament is called "from the work working" (*ex opere operantis*), that is, a freely participating subject who, through the Spirit, celebrates the sacraments by placing no obstacle to receiving them faithfully.

Simply stated, sacraments presuppose a personal faith where God offers and humans receive the grace of Christ. Such personal encounter rejects any passive, mechanistic, or magical understanding of the sacraments. Rather, sacraments are gifts of personal encounter between Christ and the Church.

THE TWO BASIC SACRAMENTS OF CHRIST AND CHURCH

The years before Vatican Council II (1962–1965) saw a renewal of sacramental theology as theologians sought to return to the historical roots of the sacraments by recovering their original and primary meaning. In particular, the ideas of two theologians spearheaded the renewal: the German Jesuit Karl Rahner (1904–1984) and the Belgian Dominican Edward Schillebeeckx (1914; pronounced Skĭl-ah-bākes).

These two theologians explained the sacraments in ways that were both new and traditional because the same basic sacramental principles of Jesus and Church were operative at the inception of Christianity and are still operative today. Both of their groundbreaking works appeared in 1960. On the one hand, Rahner's *The Church and the Sacraments* envisions the Church itself as the basic or "fundamental" sacrament. The seven sacraments are sacraments because they are the ritual actions of that sacrament that is the Church. On the other hand, Schillebeeckx considers Jesus Christ the basic or "primordial" sacrament of God. As such, Jesus is the preeminent outward sign of God's love and favor, so the Church and the seven sacraments are themselves sacraments because of God's self-communication in Jesus Christ.

Karl Rahner was one of the most influential Roman Catholic theologians of the twentieth century. He was born in Freiburg, Germany, and died in Innsbruck, Austria. His theology influenced Vatican Council II. Central to all his theology is the belief that God is self-gift. Thus the fulfillment of human existence occurs in receiving God's gift of himself, which is only fully experienced at the end of time but is present now as grace.

Edward Schillebeeckx is a Belgian theologian born in Antwerp. His books on Christology have made him one of the most well-known modern Roman Catholic theologians. Moreover, the influence of his thought at Vatican Council II contributed greatly to the reformist theology that emerged after the council.

Jesus, the Primordial Sacrament of God's Presence

The person of Jesus Christ pinpoints the mystery of the divine-human encounter. Specifically, Jesus' actions, as the Gospels record, provide the primordial meaning of the sacraments: "If you want to know what a sacrament is and what a sacrament does you can do no better than look at Jesus as we find him in the New Testament" (Noll, 1999, 20). In effect, the sacraments are the acts of Jesus Christ, and all other sacraments derive from him. But what does this mean? How is this possible? Schillebeeckx provides an answer for the first question: "Even in his humanity Christ is the Son of God. The second person of the most holy Trinity is personally man; and this man is personally God. Therefore Christ is God in a human way, and [human] in a divine way" (Schillebeeckx, 1963, 13–14). The foundation for such thinking goes back to Jesus' words: "Whoever has seen me has seen the Father" (John 14:9; see also 1:18). Christ reveals the personal encounter with God, and celebration of the sacraments draws the Christian believer into personal relationship with Christ in his human actions that point to and manifest God's presence. Thus, to answer the second question (How is this possible?), we need to understand how the sacraments participate in Jesus' own ministry as performed and enacted in his life, death, and Resurrection. Otherwise, the sacraments may become passive observation instead of active participation, service to rituals rather than service to neighbor, impersonal obligations instead of personal encounters, and abstract theory rather than embodied praxis.

Jesus' actions point out that sacraments are not things but religious actions that express particular relationships that manifest presence. On one level, Jesus is God's mystery personified by revealing the relationships that both form and transform human experience. On another level, Jesus is God's meaning personified by revealing who God is and who people are and should become through and in their human relationships. Together, the mystery and meaning of Jesus' life, death, and Resurrection transform human reality because the significance of Christ's actions forms the Christian understanding of human experience and existence. Jesus embodies a new way of human existing, and he gives ultimate meaning to everything that was and is human. To perceive this significance is to open the door to a fresh understanding of the sacraments and sacramentality. For example, baptism celebrates the mystery of birth and transforms its meaning by recognizing that Christ himself invites the believer to participate in the mystery of his death and Resurrection. Thus the relationship expressed in baptism gives new meaning to the archetypical mystery of birth/death/rebirth because the significance of Jesus' past and present actions transforms how Christians experience God's presence in their lives.

Church, the Fundamental Sacrament of Jesus' Presence

With the birth of the church in the gift of the Holy Spirit, Jesus gave the world a sacrament of himself: "Rising from the dead, [Christ] sent his life-giving Spirit upon his disciples and through this Spirit has established his body, the Church, as the universal sacrament of salvation" (*Lumen Gentium* 48). Through and in the activity of the Holy Spirit, the Church prepares for the reception of Christ by recalling the mystery of Christ and by working to make that mystery present in the world today. Thus the Church is authentic to the degree it manifests Christ's humanity, actions, and ministry in the world. Just as Jesus only taught the words of the Father (John 8:28, 14:24), the Church should only teach the example of Christ, but because sinful humans comprise the Church, it often falls short of this realization. This fact should demonstrate that the Church is a sign of salvation but that it is Christ through the Spirit's activity that makes the sign effective.

Specifically, in this understanding, it is the Spirit that animates Christ's Body, the Church. This imagery teaches that the "Spirit is the very soul of the Church" (Noll, 1999, 36) because the Spirit brings the human community into relationship with the divine community: "The universal Church is seen to be 'a people brought into unity from the unity of the Father, the Son and the Holy Spirit'" (*Lumen Gentium* 4). Thus, just as the Father sent Jesus, Jesus sends forth the apostles by sending forth the gift of the Spirit (John 20:21–22). In short, the actions of Christ become the actions of his Church through and in the Spirit's power.

As a fundamental sacrament of Christ's presence and actions, the Church's vitality springs from the Spirit-filled celebration of the seven formal sacraments in a twofold sense.

> They are "by the Church," for she is the sacrament of Christ's action at work in her through the mission of the Holy Spirit. They are "for the Church" in the sense that *the sacraments make the Church*, since they manifest and communicate to [humans], above all in the Eucharist, the mystery of communion with the God who is love, One in three persons. (*Catechism*, n. 1118, emphasis added)

These two dimensions of Christ and Church express the divine-human encounter. On one level, the sacraments are understood as the acts of Christ in the Church, which means that the Church can only be a sacrament because it is in proper relationship with Christ. On another level, as sacrament, the acts of the Church are understood as sacramentally "incarnating" Christ's presence and actions in the world today through the communal concelebration of the sacraments by the human and divine communities.

Diagram: The Sacramental Economy of Salvation

The following diagram illustrates the Catholic understanding of the sacramental economy of salvation. The diagram operates on three levels: First, letters A–F point to the persons (Father–Son–Spirit, Christians) and personal actions (sacraments) involved in the mystery of the divine-human encounter. Letters A–C indicate that the sacramental economy of salvation parallels the Trinitarian economy of the Father sending the Son and Spirit into the world, and letters D–F depict how the seven Sacraments respond to God's activity by drawing active Christians into the mystery of the divine-human encounter.

Second, numbers I–VI call to mind the relationships that comprise the reality of the sacramental mystery. The Father sends Jesus Christ as the personal sacrament of God's love for all humankind. After his death and Resurrection, Christ sends the Spirit to guide his Church, which is a personal sacrament of Christ. The Spirit animates the Church as it reenacts Jesus' own actions in the celebration of the seven sacraments. The graces of the seven sacraments transform active Christians into living sacraments who live in the basic attitudes and values of Jesus Christ. Finally, active Christians participate in the mystery of God's ongoing revelation by existing as living sacraments that point to and manifest God's love, forgiveness, healing,

THE SACRAMENTAL ECONOMY OF SALVATION

→ A. — I → B. — II → C. — III

A. God the Father

1. Transcendent mystery who desires relationship with creation through and in the Son and Spirit
2. The giver of all gifts or graces
3. The mystery of the Trinity reveals distinction of persons (individual) and unity of nature (community)

B. God the Son

1. Jesus Christ:
   Primordial sacrament of God the Father's presence and actions
2. Jesus is the gift or grace of the Father
3. Jesus Christ is the individual and personal revelation of the Father

C. God the Spirit

1. Church:
   Fundamental Sacrament of Jesus Christ's presence and actions
2. The gift or grace of the Father and Christ
3. The Church is a personal community that continues Christ's actions in the world

VI — F. ← V — E. ← IV — D. ←

D. Seven Sacraments

1. Initiation
   Baptism: acceptance
   Confirmation: commitment
   Eucharist: thanksgiving
   Healing
   Reconciliation: forgiveness
   Anointing: strengthening
   Vocation
   Marriage: service
   Orders: service
2. Sacraments confer the grace they signify, i.e., they reenact Christ's actions by the power of the Spirit
3. Communal and personal celebration of Jesus' presence and actions by a Spirit-filled community of faith

E. Christians

1. Active Christians are Living Sacraments who manifest Christ's presence and activity in the world. Since they live their lives in Christ, Christian individuality is always an imitation
2. Grace enables Christians to live into becoming more fully Christian
3. Individual and personal imitation of Jesus' actions by active Christians

F. Divine-Human Encounter

1. The mystery of the divine-human encounter analogously manifests itself throughout I-V, whereby all relationships begin from and return to the Father (A, F)
2. The self-giving that is grace configures the mystery of interpersonal relationships, both divine and human
3. Human relationships are individual and communal simply because they are personal

and acceptance in their everyday encounters with others. Thus all authentic human relationships and activities sacramentalize the divine-human encounter.

Third, the six sets of numbers 1–3 point out that grace is not a thing but a personal gift with individual and communal dimensions. Jesus Christ is the individual and personal gift of the Father. The Church is the communal gift of the Son and Spirit personally shared within the human community. The gifts of the sacraments enable the Church to celebrate communally Jesus' presence and actions. The gift of community enables individual Christians to imitate Jesus' attitude and actions in everyday life. Finally, the gift of self-giving itself indicates that the mystery of interpersonal relationships requires a communal and individual sharing, which the divine life reveals (one God = community; three persons = individuality) and human experience confirms (humans are psycho/individual social/communal beings). In short, Jesus as the primordial sacrament of God's presence and action shows that an authentic celebration of the sacraments should be a personal and individual encounter, while the Church as the fundamental sacrament of Jesus' presence and actions shows that an authentic celebration of the sacraments should also be a personal and communal encounter. Such individual and communal encounters transform active Christians into living sacraments that are always personal.

THE SEVEN SACRAMENTS

The Roman Catholic Church recognizes seven formal sacraments: baptism, confirmation, Eucharist, reconciliation, anointing, holy orders, and marriage. These seven sacraments can be classified in three groups: sacraments of initiation (baptism, confirmation, Eucharist), sacraments of healing (reconciliation and anointing), and sacraments of vocation (holy orders and marriage).

Sacraments of Initiation: Baptism, Confirmation, Eucharist

Baptism

The first sacrament of initiation, baptism, is a symbolic plunging/washing of a person in water that incorporates the person into the mystery of Jesus Christ and his Church and signifies the forgiveness of sin. These two effects are linked. The initiation into the Christian community is the forgiveness of sins because by forgiveness, Christ and his Church accept a person through a ritual whereby sin loses its power. The focus is on acceptance via forgiveness, not on the sin that causes alienation. This is pointedly expressed by the fact that Jesus, who was without sin, still desired to be baptized so as to be accepted by his Father, "You are my Son, the Beloved; with you I am well pleased" (Mark 1:11; also see Matt 3:17, Luke 3:22). In short, the example of Jesus teaches that "baptism is the basis of the whole Christian life, the gateway to life in the Spirit, and the door which gives access to the other sacraments" (*Catechism*, n. 1212). Thus baptism is the first of the three sacraments of initiation.

Water is the main sacramental sign and accomplishes what it signifies—new birth, new life, and new creation—by incorporating the initiate into Jesus' life, death, and Resurrection. Baptism's womb–tomb symbolism conveys this mystery. Immersion in the water symbolizes dying with Christ, while the extraction from the water symbolizes being reborn with Christ (Rom 6:3–4; Col 2:12, 3:3). Both the pouring of water over an infant's head and the plunging of an adult under the water symbolize the passing from the death of the community of sin into the life of the Christian community (granted, adult baptism conveys this meaning more explicitly).

Likewise, the symbolic act of the laying on of hands by the priest, parents, and godparents during the anointing of the initiate with chrism emphasizes the sacrament's communal character. It stresses that the sacrament is an initiation into a community (1 Cor 12:13; Gal 3:27) and sets in motion a lifelong process. The laying on of hands signifies that the initiate will not have to undergo this journey alone because she will have the support of the Christian community. Other symbols include the baptismal candle, which signifies that Christ will light the person's journey; and the white baptismal gown, which symbolizes that the initiate has "put on Christ." Thus, while on the journey of this life, the initiate should be recognized as following Christ by her attitude and actions toward God, self, and neighbor.

The central mystery of baptism's symbolic ritual communicates a rebirth into new life in Christ, whereby the initiate becomes a child of God in joining the Church as a member of Christ's body through receiving the gift of the Spirit. In short, baptism is an initiation into the divine-human encounter between the divine community of persons, Father, Son, Spirit, and the human community of the Church that celebrates the Trinitarian mystery. This mystery echoes in the Rite of Baptism:

> Father, look now with love upon your Church and unseal for her the fountain of baptism. By the power of the Spirit give to this water the grace of your Son, so that in the sacrament of baptism all those whom you have created in your likeness may be cleansed from sin and rise to a new birth to innocence by water and the Holy Spirit. We ask you, Father, with your Son to send the Holy Spirit upon the waters of this font. May all who are buried with Christ in the death of baptism rise also with him in newness of life. We ask this through Christ our Lord. (*The Rites of the Catholic Church I* [*The Rites I*], n. 91, p. 400)

Confirmation

Confirmation, the second sacrament of initiation, is a symbolic anointing with oil on the forehead that signifies (1) the public renewal of baptismal promises that (2) strengthens participation in the Church by (3) sealing the initiate with the gifts of the Spirit. These three aspects are interconnected. Due to the fact that confirmation complements, that is, completes, baptism, it should not be separated from baptism. So, if baptism is when Christ offers the Spirit's gifts to the initiate (either infant or adult), confirmation is when the person publicly accepts those same gifts of the Spirit. However, the confirmation of the gifts is twofold. On the one hand, the initiate confirms his or her baptismal promises, and on the other, the bishop confirms the person's desire to become an adult member of the ecclesial community by bearing and sharing the Spirit's gifts with the Church and wider community. In short, "the reception of the sacrament of Confirmation is necessary for the completion of baptismal grace" (*Catechism*, n. 1285) because the person must accept what has been given. This is true whether the initiate was baptized as an infant or adult.

Originally, confirmation was the third, postbaptismal anointing, administered by the bishop, which finalized the person's initiation into the church. However, during the legalization of Christianity in the fourth century, there was a massive influx of people wanting to become Christian. The influx meant that the bishop could not be present at all the baptisms, which were therefore delegated to priests and deacons. Yet the bishop retained the third anointing by later "confirming" the initiates' baptism, which reminded the local church of their unity with the universal church. Thus, over time and for practical reasons, confirmation became separate from baptism, and two distinct rites developed. The French councils of Riez (439) and Orange (441) identified confirmation as an independent sacrament. Although the separation of confirmation from baptism has led to some confusion regarding its theology, confirmation is best understood as the conclusion to baptism, which invites the initiate to share in the community's Eucharistic celebration.

Oil is the main sacramental sign that accomplishes what it signifies, a spiritual seal that identifies the initiate as belonging to Christ: "It is God who establishes us with you in Christ and has anointed us, by putting his seal on us and giving us his Spirit in our hearts as a first installment" (2 Cor 1:21–22). Anointing symbolizes that the initiate confirms Jesus' call to join him as both disciple and apostle. As disciple, one who follows Christ, the anointing signifies that the initiate personally decides to follow the example and teachings of Jesus Christ, that is, to be personally named Christian. As apostle, literally "one who is sent out," the anointing signifies that a Christian is sent to serve the wider communities of church and world. The symbolic act of laying on of hands by the sponsor and bishop during the anointing highlights the sacrament's communal character. On the one hand, the bishop, as a symbol of the universal church, confers the sacrament by anointing the initiate's forehead with the sign of the cross while saying the words, "Be sealed with the Gift of the Holy Spirit." On the other, the sponsor, as a symbol of the local church, presents the initiate to the bishop and supports him or her as they together say "Amen" or "Yes" to the decision to accept the Spirit's gift of faith in Christ. The dual symbolic act of laying on of hands stresses that the sacrament is an initiation into relationships of mutual support; the community supports the initiate, who in turn builds the community.

The central mystery of confirmation's symbolic ritual communicates acceptance or confirmation of the gift of the Spirit, whereby initiates pledge their lives to God by accepting a share in the mission of Jesus Christ according to the Spirit's fullness of life. Again, confirmation invites the initiates into the mystery of the divine-human encounter, where the Trinitarian community draws the church community into relationship. This mystery echoes in the Rite of Confirmation:

> My dear friends, in baptism God our Father gave the new birth of eternal life to his chosen sons and daughters. Let us pray to our Father that he will pour out the Holy Spirit to strengthen his sons and daughters with his gifts and anoint them to be more like Christ the Son of God. (*The Rites I*, n. 24, p. 490)

Eucharist

The name of the third initiation sacrament, *Eucharist*, comes from the Greek word for "thanksgiving." This sacrament signifies the new covenant of Jesus' body and blood, which (1) is "the source and summit of the Christian life" (*Lumen Gentium* 11; *Catechism*, n. 1324) that (2) completes the initiation sacraments, unites the seven sacraments, and sustains all ministerial activity by (3) drawing the Christian most fully into Christ's paschal (Easter) mystery. These three aspects build upon one another. Since Eucharist completes baptism and confirmation, it signifies that God's offer of friendship in baptism, and the initiate's acceptance of that friendship in confirmation, fully becomes an enduring friendship through and in the activity of sharing a sacred meal together. During the last supper, Jesus said to his disciples:

> This is my commandment, that you love one another as have I loved you. No one has greater love than this, to lay down one's life for one's friends. You are my friends if you do what I command you. I do not call you servants any longer, because the servant does not know what the master is doing; but I have called you friends, because I have made known to you everything that I have heard from my Father. You did not choose me but I chose you. And

> I appointed you to go and bear fruit, fruit that will last, so the Father will give you whatever you ask him in my name. I am giving you these commands so that you may love one another. (John 15:12–15)

Jesus' table fellowship is marked by love and friendship, a friendship enacted by following Jesus' invitation that "as I have loved you, you also should love one another" (John 13:34). One way Christians love as Jesus loves is by celebrating the sacraments. Specifically, just as all of Jesus' own actions led to and were fulfilled in the loving act of his passion, the six other sacraments either involve the celebration of the Eucharist or lead the participant to the Eucharist. Thus all Christian ministries should extend the paschal mystery, which Jesus was offering to his disciples at the Last Supper.

Bread and wine are the main sacramental signs of the Eucharist, and the Church believes that they accomplish what they signify: Christ's real presence, which "by the words of Christ and the invocation of the Holy Spirit, become Christ's Body and Blood" (*Catechism*, n. 1333). Since the thirteenth century, transubstantiation has been the technical term for describing Christ's real presence in the Eucharist. Later in the sixteenth century, when the meaning of real presence was theologically argued by many of the new Reformation groups, the Council of Trent declared: "By the consecration of the bread and wine there takes place a change of the whole substance of the bread into the substance of the body of Christ our Lord and of the whole substance of the wine into the substance of his blood. This change the holy Catholic Church has fittingly and properly called *transubstantiation*" (*Catechism*, n. 1376). Although transubstantiation attempts to explain how Christ is essentially or ontologically (the nature of being; ontology is the branch of metaphysics concerned with the nature or essence of being or existence) present in the Eucharist as a result of a metaphysical change in the bread and wine, today this often leads to serious misunderstandings. Whereas medieval peoples understood substance as a metaphysical reality, we today understand substance as a physical reality. Michael Lawler explains this point well:

> In contemporary mentality substance no longer means what the medievals meant by it. Worse, it means something quite contrary. By taking substance in an essentially physical sense, moderns are tempted to understand transubstantiation in an essentially physical sense, which is not only contradicted by the unmistakable evidence of their senses, but is also the very interpretation that Scholastic theology wished, in the first instance, to exclude by the use of the term. By the use of the term *transubstantiation* the Scholastics, and the Church, wished to assert, on the one hand, the reality of Christ's presence in the eucharist and, on the other, the metaphysical nature of the wondrous change which takes place, leaving unchanged the physical properties of bread and wine. (Lawler, 1995, 124)

Scholastic theology refers to a method of learning taught by academic theologians at the first European universities, ca. 1100–1500. The primary purpose of scholasticism was to use the method of dialectical analysis to find answers to particular questions or to resolve a contradiction.

Transubstantiation tries to explain how the bread and wine are physical signs that point to and manifest the metaphysical reality of Christ's real presence. However, without proper understanding of medieval philosophy (substance/accident, form/matter), the "how" of transubstantiation will largely remain misunderstood by modern interpreters who mistake substance to mean a physical or "accidental" change rather than a metaphysical or "substantial" change of the sacramental elements. The Council of Trent was clear on this point when it declared that "the species of bread and wine alone remain" while their substance converts into Christ's body and blood (Session 13, Canon 2). In other words, while the substance (the metaphysical inner reality of a thing) changes, the accidents (the external, physical qualities of a thing, e.g., color, weight, taste) of the bread and wine, which are known by our senses, remain unchanged. Unfortunately, the new *Catechism of the Catholic Church* does not explain this important point nor does it explain the philosophy upon which transubstantiation depends. Thus, in today's scientific framework, many are confused by transubstantiation because if they do not understand and accept the philosophical framework transubstantiation presupposes, then it is likely that they will misunderstand, or even deny, the explanation of the real presence.

Instead of having to accept medieval philosophy to explain the real presence, the three words *consecration*, *conversion*, and *communion* can help explain the mystery of the real presence in a way more suitable to our modern thinking.

First, the *consecration* is when the priest extends his hands over the bread and wine and says, "Lord you are holy indeed, the fountain of all holiness. Let your Spirit come upon these gifts to make them holy, so that they may become for us the body and blood of our Lord, Jesus Christ" (*Sacramentary*, Eucharistic Prayer II, p. 549). The symbolic act of laying on of hands that transforms the eucharistic elements into Christ's real presence again signifies the communal character of the sacraments. The Church believes that God's Spirit makes Christ present in the Eucharist so that it can be shared. Just as Jesus shared himself with his disciples at the Last Supper, the laying on of hands today points to and manifests the mystery of Christ's self-gift to his friends so that the Church can become the Body of Christ by sharing the Body of Christ.

Next, the consecration signifies a real *conversion* of the elements. The *Catechism* employs the term in this way: "It is by the conversion of the bread and wine into Christ's body and blood that Christ becomes present in this sacrament" (n. 1375). The effect of this conversion is the new reality of Christ under the visible signs of the bread and wine. In what sense, moreover, does the "inner or deepest reality" of Jesus become present in the transformed elements? An example from popular anthropology, which has its own limitations, may help explain the conversion. Like the medieval peoples, most today imagine a person to be comprised of body and soul, and most would consider the conversion of a person's "deepest reality" to involve the soul and only secondarily the body. In a similar way, the conversion of the elements means that the "deepest reality" of Christ is personally present in the Eucharist while the physicality of the species remains unchanged. In this sense, Christ's presence is not a thing but a personal presence that the signs of bread and wine point to and manifest. The symbolism realizes Christ's presence in his act of breaking and sharing the bread and wine because in that act, Christ reveals his "deepest reality" of sacrificially existing for others so as to fulfill his Father's will through the forgiveness of sins. This interpretation squares with the Jewish mentality of Jesus' time that focused on what a person did, rather than a person's abstract essence or being. In short, Christ is present in the Eucharist because it is Christ who acts in the Eucharist.

Finally, the conversion effects what it signifies in *communion*, which is the communal sharing of the body of Christ. On one level, communion signifies that Christ offers his very self to the Eucharistic community. Here Christ acts by offering his body and blood to his friends. On another level, communion signifies the social dimension of Christians communing with each other through and in the presence of their Lord. Christians act by accepting Christ, whereby they become his body, the Church. The fact that the Eucharist is an initiation sacrament should point out that the Eucharist calls Christians into deeper relationship with Christ and neighbor, and this is why it is called the source and summit of the ecclesial life (*Catechism*, nn. 1324–1327).

The Eucharist is understood as the primary act by which Christ offers his sacramental presence to the Church and the primary act by which the Church worships God. Yet such lofty language about the Eucharist should not lead Christians from the startling mystery that the grandeur of divine-human encounter transpires with the down-to-earth act of sharing a meal in which the divine community celebrates with the human community. This mystery echoes in the Eucharistic Rite:

> Before he was given up to death, a death he freely accepted, he took bread and gave you thanks. He broke the bread, gave it to his disciples, and said: Take this, all of you, and eat it: this is my body which will be given up for you. When the supper was ended, he took the cup. Again he gave you thanks and praise, gave the cup to his disciples, and said: Take this, all of you, and drink from it: this is the cup of my blood, the blood of the new and everlasting covenant. It will be shed for you and for all so that sins may be forgiven. Do this in memory of me. (*Sacramentary*, Eucharistic Prayer II, p. 549)

The Eucharist concludes the three initiation sacraments. Their ancient order was baptism, confirmation, Eucharist, but for historical reasons, they were separated, and more recently, Pius X inverted their order to baptism, Eucharist, confirmation by declaring in 1910 that the proper age for first communion is 7 (Martos, 2001, 254), while confirmation was delayed until a later date. However, their original and proper order, retrieved by the 1972 *Rite of Christian Initiation of Adults*, allows for a better understanding of the process of initiation. In baptism, God offers the gift of relationship; in confirmation, the initiate, sponsor, and bishop communally accept God's gift of relationship; and in Eucharist, God shares relationship with the Church community via a ritual meal. Gift offered, gift received, gift shared—these are the simple yet profound dimensions to the process of Christian initiation.

Building on this process, we can also look at the mystery of Christian initiation through the ancient tradition of hospitality. The story of Luke records the essentials of hospitality: washing, anointing, and the sharing of food with someone invited into your house:

> One of the Pharisees asked Jesus to eat with him, and he went into the Pharisee's house and took his place at the table. And a woman in the city, who was a sinner, having learned that he was eating in the Pharisee's house, brought an alabaster jar of ointment. She stood behind him at his feet, weeping, and began to bathe his feet with her tears and to dry them with her hair. Then she continued kissing his feet and anointing them with the ointment. (Luke 7:36–38)

The Pharisee did not fully offer hospitality to Jesus because he only offered food without offering the usual washing and anointing. Luke 7:44–46 makes this point clear: lapses in hospitality imply a lack of love. In contrast, the earliest origins of Christian initiation were synonymous with the gracious offer of hospitality. The initiate was washed (baptism), anointed (confirmation), and fed (Eucharist), which signifies loving acceptance. By recovering the richness of the symbolic acts of hospitality, we can envision God as offering hospitality in the initiation rites. When initiates come into God's house, that is, a church,

God washes, anoints, and feeds his guests. When taken together, the symbolism of baptism, confirmation, and Eucharist are understood as signifying that God offers hospitality to the wayfarers in this world. Thus God's hospitality is the foundation for the interpersonal relationships that the initiation sacraments symbolize and is why "the sacraments of Christian initiation—Baptism, Confirmation, and the Eucharist—lay the foundations of every Christian life" (*Catechism*, n. 1212), simply because God's hospitable love is that foundation.

Sacraments of Healing: Reconciliation and Anointing

Reconciliation

Reconciliation is heard in the words of forgiveness by the Church through the priest. The priest's words of absolution and gesture of extending the right hand over the penitent's head signify both (1) forgiveness of sins and (2) reacceptance into the ecclesial community. These two aspects are always connected because sin alienates people from God and damages the relationships within the Church community. If Jesus teaches his followers to love God, neighbor, and self, then sin is a rupture of those same three relationships that must be reconciled in the act of forgiveness. The Gospels clearly record that Jesus' ministry was one of reconciliation. His announcement of the coming of his Father's reign was practically synonymous with the forgiveness of sins (Matt 1:21; Mark 2:5; Luke 1:77; John 1:29). Thus, just as the forgiveness of sin lies at the very heart of Jesus' public ministry and passion, reconciliation should comprise the very heart of Christianity. Because forgiveness is *for giving*, the Christian community, in imitation of Jesus' own actions, must reconcile with its members who become alienated by either personal or social wrongdoings. In short, God's forgiveness always works toward communal reconciliation: "And forgive us our debts, as we also have forgiven our debtors" (Matt 6:12; also see John 20:22–23).

Although the modern ritual of **penance** only calls for the priest to extend his right hand above the head of the penitent while giving absolution, it is important to realize that the gesture of "extending the right hand" echoes back to an earlier tradition where there was an actual laying on of the priest's hands upon the penitent's head. Such a symbolic act fitly signifies the forgiveness and healing offered in the sacrament.

The words of forgiveness and the laying on of hands express the main sacramental sign of penance, which confers what it signifies on two levels. On one level, it sacramentally manifests God's healing forgiveness, for "only God forgives sins" (*Catechism*, n. 1441). On another level, because private confession makes the role of the community less obvious, the priest simultaneously represents the community's reconciliation with the penitent. Since sin is relational, forgiveness too must be relational, and this requires real reconciliation that points to the mystery of the divine-human encounter by manifesting the actual reconciliation within the human community. Such a relational understanding counters the common sentiment that "God has already forgiven me, so I don't have to go to confession" for two reasons. By speaking their sins, those who confess stop denying the reality of their sinfulness and its destructive power, which in turn actually signals their acceptance of forgiveness because they no longer feel compelled to hide their sins from others. Thus the power of forgiveness transforms the dynamics of human relationships because without forgiveness, no interpersonal relationships would survive.

The 1973 revised *Rite of Penance* offers four different liturgical rites: (1) the rite for reconciliation of individual penitents, which transpires between the person and the priest in a private setting; (2) the rite for communal liturgy and examination of conscience followed by individual confession/absolution in a private setting; (3) the rite for communal examination of conscience, silent confession, and general absolution, which canon law restricts to the discretion of the local bishop; and (4) the abbreviated rite for emergency situations where death is imminent. While there are four forms, the guidelines for the revised rites stress that the liturgical celebration of the sacrament, in normal circumstances, should emphasize God's offer of forgiveness by the reading of appropriate scripture and highlight the role of ecclesial reconciliation by preferring public forms of penance to private forms.

Reconciliation ritually extends Christ's forgiving actions, which the Church believes reconcile humans with God and one another. Just like all relationships, the mystery of divine-human encounter would be impossible without the transformative and uniting grace of forgiveness. This mystery reverberates in the words of absolution during the Rite of Reconciliation:

> God, the Father of mercies, through the death and resurrection of his Son has reconciled the world to himself and sent the Holy Spirit among us for the forgiveness of sins; through the ministry of the Church may God give you pardon and peace, and I absolve you from your sins in the name of the Father, and of the Son, and of the Holy Spirit. (*The Rites I*, n. 46, pp. 546–547)

Anointing

Anointing is a symbolic laying on of hands with oil upon the forehead and hands of the sick person that (1) signals Jesus' compassion toward the sick and suffering by (2) his healing and forgiveness of sins, which (3) involves the faith of the one being healed. Suffering and sickness are universal aspects of human life and poignantly speak of human powerlessness and finitude unto death. While not necessarily causally linked (i.e., sin does not necessarily cause illness, nor does illness necessarily cause sin), the threat of death, whether physical or spiritual, is one of the gravest problems of life, and both sin and illness can have the same effect: the destruction of human dignity, life, and spirit. Thus Jesus himself makes the link between healing and forgiveness (Mark 2:5–12) because illness can be a symptom of sin and sin a symptom of illness. So, as the good physician, Jesus came to cure both: "Those who are well have no need of a physician, but those who are sick; I have come to call not the righteous but sinners" (Mark 2:17).

Oil is the primary sign of anointing, and the Church believes that it accomplishes what it signifies: a person's participation in Christ's redemptive suffering and death, and faith in the promise of the Resurrection, which grants the gift of peace. Just as in baptism and confirmation, where the community applies oil to signify their support of the initiate's new life, the oil in anointing signifies the community's solidarity with the suffering person who draws into deeper participation in Christ's paschal mystery. The communal laying on of hands and prayer support the person as he or she undergoes the trials of sickness and suffering, which not only harm the body but also can ruthlessly ravage the human spirit. The communal support can help a person approach sickness and death as an opportunity to deepen his or her faith relationship with God. For example, the Gospels repeatedly link Jesus' acts of healing with the recipients' faith (Matt 9:22; 15:28; Mark 5:34; 10:52; Luke 8:48; 18:42; cf. Matt 13:58). Thus sickness can occasion faith if a person is open to the Spirit's power. Nevertheless, psychological and physical illness still glimpse the darkness of death and can destroy a person by overcoming faith with fear, hope with despair, and love with depression and bitterness. Anyone who has had much experience with illness and death knows just how horrible and powerful these realities can be. Yet, from this darkness, "Christ continues to 'touch' us in order to heal us" (*Catechism*, n. 1504).

The anointing of the sick is meant to ritually extend Christ's healing ministry to those who suffer physical or mental illness. Anointing transforms sickness and suffering into an occasion that manifests the mystery of the divine-human encounter where the Trinitarian God of life overcomes the human fear of suffering and threat of death. This mystery echoes in the Rite of Anointing of the Sick:

> God of all consolation, you chose and sent your Son to heal the world. Graciously listen to our prayer of faith: send the power of your Holy Spirit, the Consoler, into this precious oil, this soothing ointment, this rich gift, this fruit of the earth. Bless this oil and sanctify it for our use. Make this oil a remedy for all who are anointed with it; heal them in body, in soul, and in spirit, and deliver them from every affliction. (*The Rites I*, n. 123, p. 824)

The sacraments of penance and anointing point to and manifest Jesus' acts of forgiveness and healing, which the Church now extends and celebrates as it continues to reconcile and restore the human community. On the one hand, the grace of God's forgiveness and the penitent's repentance and conversion are the basic ingredients of reconciliation, which build healthy relationships by transforming the alienating power of sin. On the other hand, the grace of God's healing and the sick person's faith in God's providential care are the basic ingredients of anointing, which alleviate the mental and physical sufferings of illness or old age by transforming the alienating power of death. In short, the Church believes that these two sacraments "continue, in the power of the Holy Spirit, [Jesus'] work of healing and salvation" (*Catechism*, n. 1421).

Sacraments of Vocation: Holy Orders and Marriage

Holy Orders

The holy orders is a symbolic laying on of hands upon an ordination candidate by a bishop, which signifies that (1) bishops, priests, and deacons continue the apostolic ministry enacted by Christ to (2) "nourish the Church with the word and grace of God" (*Lumen Gentium* 11) by (3) serving the local and global ecclesial community in the name and person of Jesus Christ. Although we can distinguish these three aspects, they all derive from Christ's own commission to his apostles: "Peace be with you. As the Father has sent me, so I send you. . . . Receive the Holy Spirit" (John 20:21–22). By the gift and power of the Spirit, Jesus sent his apostles (recall that *apostle* means "one who is sent out") to extend his mission of serving the people of God. In the understanding of the Church, ordained ministers continue that service.

While the New Testament evidences that Jesus called the apostles to continue his ministry, it also demonstrates that the organization of ministerial order was a process in development. The earliest evidence comes from Paul, who teaches the tripartite division of apostles, prophets, and teachers (1 Cor 12:28; ca. 54–55 CE). The Acts of the Apostles make it clear that such ministerial order emerged because the apostles needed pastoral assistance (Acts 6:2–7; ca. 80–85 CE), and so the twelve appoint, by prayer and laying on of hands, seven candidates whom the church community elected. Still later, the Pastoral Epistles of Titus and 1–2 Timothy (ca. 100–110 CE) mention a new tripartite division of overseers (*episkopoi*), elders (*presbyteroi*), and servants (*diakonoi*), which seems to be normative by the early second century. Thus, within a century of Paul's initial and rather loose tripartite structure of apostles, prophets, and teachers, the church adopted the new hierarchy ("sacred order," *hieros* + *archē*; hence, the term *holy order*) of episcopate (bishops), presbyterate (who were increasingly functioning as priests, which parallels the rising understanding of the Eucharist as sacrifice), and diaconate (deacons).

One explanation for this development could be the synthesis of Jewish Christian and Gentile Christian structures of leadership. On the one hand, the Jewish Christian leadership consisted of a council of elders or presbyters, while the Gentile Christian leadership consisted of a single overseer or bishop who was assisted by several assistants/servants or deacons, which followed the Roman model of governance. During this earliest development (50–100 CE), women may have served as deacons (Rom 16:1; 1 Tim 3:8–11), but scholars argue over whether the term *deacon* in the relevant passages technically refers to ordained deacons or is being used in the generic sense of "servant."

The laying on of hands upon the ordination candidate's head and solemn prayer of consecration (distinct prayers and ritual actions for each order) by the bishop is the main sacramental sign of holy order, and the Church believes that it confers what it signifies on three levels. First, episcopal ordination is the fullness of the sacrament of holy order (*Catechism*, nn. 1555–1561) whereby the bishop, as a successor of the apostles, serves, by the Spirit's power, as "teacher, shepherd, and priest" in the name and place of Christ. Accordingly, the bishop simultaneously governs the local church entrusted to him and shares in the apostolic leadership of the universal church. As signs of his responsibility to teach and govern, at least three bishops usually lay their hands upon the bishop's head; his head is anointed with oil; the book of the Gospels is presented; and the new bishop is vested with a miter, ring, and crosier (pastoral staff) and is seated on the bishop's chair.

Second, the Church understands priestly ordination to be the calling of priests, by the Spirit's power, to be the bishop's coworkers within the ecclesial community by preaching the gospel and administering the sacraments, especially the Eucharist, which exercises "in a supreme degree their sacred office" (*Catechism*, n. 1566). As signs of his responsibility as "coworker of the episcopal order," the bishop lays his hands upon the priest's head; then, the priest is anointed on the hands with chrism, is vested in his proper vestments by fellow priests, and is given the bread on a paten and the wine and water in a chalice for the celebration of Mass. Third, deacons are ministers ordained for service in the Church by assisting "the bishop and priests in the celebration of the divine mysteries, above all the Eucharist" (*Catechism*, n. 1570). As signs of his responsibility as "servant" in liturgy, word, and charity, a bishop lays hands upon the deacon's head, and then the deacon is vested in appropriate vestments by fellow deacons and is given the book of the Gospels.

Although the ordained hierarchy is threefold, the laying on of the hands during the three ordination rites contains a uniform symbolism in three ways. On one level, it signifies that bishops, priests, and deacons, each in their own way, have accepted the Spirit's power to fulfill the apostolic task of preaching the gospel, teaching the faithful, and caring for those with physical and spiritual needs. In return, while in the Catholic tradition the laity no longer exercise the early church practice of electing their ecclesial leaders, each of the ordination rites calls for the people's consent for those who will lead, teach, and serve them. Here, the laying on of hands emphasizes the Church's sacramental character, which the Church believes exists by the Spirit's power. The laying on of the hands also signifies that the local bishop is part of the universal Church and that the ecclesial ministries of priests and deacons participate in this apostolic service, which originates from Christ himself, the "High Priest" (Heb 4:14–15), who "came not to be served but to serve, and to give his life [as] a ransom for many" (Mark 10:45). Here, the laying on of hands emphasizes ordination as manifesting the sacramental character of Christ's own ministry.

The central mystery of holy orders involves Jesus sending his apostles forth to love and serve God and neighbor. Apostolic ministry continues Christ's own mission that manifests the mystery of the divine-human encounter in obedience to the Father's will and through service to neighbor by the Spirit's power. This Trinitarian mystery echoes in the Rite of Priestly Ordination:

> Almighty Father, grant to this servant of yours the dignity of the priesthood. Renew within him the Spirit of holiness. As a co-worker with the order of bishops may he be faithful to the ministry that he receives from you, Lord God, and be to others a model of right conduct. May he be faithful in working with the order of bishops, so that the words of the Gospel may reach the ends of the earth, and the family of nations, made one in Christ, may become God's one, holy people. (*The Rites II*, n. 22, pp. 44–45)

The sacrament of **marriage** (an English word) is sometimes referred to through its Latin language root as "matrimony" (*matrimonium*), which means "the union of man and woman as husband and wife." Hence, we often see the phrasing "the sacrament of matrimony" as well.

Marriage

The final sacrament, marriage, is a covenantal union between spouses that signifies (1) "the mystery of that unity and fruitful love which exists between Christ and his Church" (*Lumen Gentium* 11) manifested in (2) "an intimate community of conjugal love" (*Gaudium et Spes*, n. 48) where (3) husband and wife freely and totally commit themselves to each other in Christ as a celebration of God's love. These three aspects are closely linked. Ephesians 5:21–33 portrays marriage as a symbol of Christ's union with his Church, which signifies that marriage is directly rooted in the two basic sacraments of Christ and Church. In one way, marriage challenges spouses to selflessly love as Christ loved (John 13:34, 15:12). In another way, the community of love fostered by the Spirit creates "the domestic Church" (*Lumen Gentium* 11), which bears witness to and builds up the wider ecclesial community.

In this understanding, the spouses themselves are the main sacramental sign of marriage who cause what they signify: Christ's free and self-giving love to another. The couple's holding of hands during their exchange of vows acts as a laying on of hands whereby the two confer the sacrament on each other, which is a communal event on two levels. First, the couple forms a community in Christ by the gift and power of the Spirit, and second, the ecclesial community that witnesses the vows supports the spouses in their decision. The exchange of vows while holding hands manifests human love as a symbol of and participation in God's covenantal love. While the post-Vatican II Church still defines marriage as a contract, it also expands its understanding by explicitly naming it a covenant:

> The matrimonial covenant, by which a man and a woman establish between themselves a partnership of the whole of life, is by its nature ordered toward the good of the spouses and the procreation and education of offspring; this covenant between baptized persons has been raised by Christ the Lord to the dignity of a sacrament. For this reason a matrimonial

> contract cannot validly exist between baptized persons unless it is also a sacrament by that fact. (Canon 1055, nn. 1–2)

Notice that the "the good of the spouses" precedes procreation and care of children. Thus the Church recognizes that mental, emotional, spiritual, and sexual intimacy are necessary for a mature sacramental marriage. All these aspects coalesce into the mystery of intimate friendship: "Perhaps the most basic sacrament of God's saving presence to human life is the sacrament of human love and friendship" (Cooke, 1994, 80). Understood as sacrament, marriage invites couples into Jesus' friendship (John 15:14–16), where they learn daily how to love their spouses as themselves.

The central mystery of the self-giving and self-communication of marriage is understood as a sign, symbol, and sacrament of God's own loving self-giving and self-communication. In short, the joys and sorrows of marriage act as a special locus of the divine-human encounter because "authentic married love is caught up into divine love" (*Gaudium et Spes* 48). The Rite of Marriage conveys this mystery:

> Father, you have made the union of man and wife so holy a mystery that it symbolizes the marriage of Christ and his Church. . . . Father, keep them always true to your commandments. Keep them faithful in marriage and let them be living examples of Christian life. Give them the strength which comes from the gospel so that they may be witnesses of Christ to others. Bless them with children and help them to be good parents. May they live to see their children's children. And, after a happy old age, grant them fullness of life with the saints in the kingdom of heaven. (*The Rites I*, n. 33, pp. 730–31)

The Church understands the sacraments of holy orders and marriage as pointing to and manifesting Jesus' ministry of loving service, which brings communion with God and peace through justice to the human community. On the one hand, the grace of holy orders expresses the Church's sacramental reality, and through it, Jesus Christ continues his ministry of salvation by the Spirit's power. On the other hand, the grace of marriage reveals God's love for his people in Christ, which is a community of love animated by the Spirit's power. In short, both sacraments "are directed towards the salvation of others; if they contribute as well to personal salvation, it is through service to others that they do so. They confer a particular mission in the Church and serve to build up the People of God" (*Catechism*, n. 1535).

CONCLUSION: CHRISTIANS AS LIVING SACRAMENTS

In the understanding of the Church, Christians do not celebrate the sacraments simply because they are Christian; rather, they celebrate the sacraments because they are human, and humans communicate through and in symbolic ritual. Christians call these symbolic rituals "sacraments," which help them identify, interpret, enact, and manifest the mystery of the divine-human encounter. Thus sacraments are "masterpieces of God" (*Catechism*, n. 1116) that call humans into relationship. There is an ancient truism, "sacraments are for people," and they are for people so that they can become living sacraments. In a very real sense, when Christians choose to imitate Jesus, to act as he acted and to love as he loved, they become living sacraments that point to, participate in, and manifest for the world Jesus' own teachings and actions. When Christians love, serve, and honor others, they become a sacrament of Jesus' own love, service, and honor, which sacramentally realizes, reveals, and enacts his Father's parental care for creation. The sacraments are the Father's gifts offered through Christ's actions in the Spirit's power, which each of the sacraments confers by the laying on of hands. Repeatedly, the simple gesture of the laying on of hands points to and manifests the mystery of the divine-human encounter, where the divine community of persons communes with the human community of persons and vice versa. The symbolic "language" of sacramentality mediates such interpersonal communication.

Questions about the Text

1. What is the difference between a sign and a symbol? Give your own example.
2. What is the meaning of *mystērion*, the Greek word for sacrament?
3. What is the meaning of *sacramentum*, the Latin word for sacrament?
4. What is the theological definition of sacrament?
5. What is the etymology of grace, and what does grace mean?
6. Why does Schillebeeckx call Jesus the "primordial" sacrament?
7. Who or what is the fundamental sacrament of Jesus' presence?
8. What are the sacraments of initiation? Identify their main signs. Why are they called this?
9. What are the sacraments of healing? What are their signs?
10. What are the sacraments of vocation? What are their signs?

Questions for Discussion

1. In your interactions with others, can you give any examples of differences among a sign, symbol, and sacrament?
2. Why might the physical signs of each sacrament be important? What communicative role might they play, and how would they function?
3. The Church has defined only seven sacraments. Do you think other experiences described in the chapter might share in some ways with a sacrament?
4. In what ways do the seven sacraments as a whole reflect what the Church is about?
5. What do the sacraments indicate about believers' lives in God?
6. How might a Christian explain to a person from a non-Christian religious tradition, such as Hinduism or Islam, what the Eucharist is all about?
7. The conclusion speaks about Christians as living sacraments. What might this mean and imply for being Christian?

For Further Study

Catechism of the Catholic Church (Part II, Sections 1–2). Liguori, MO: Liguori/Triumph, 1994.

Cooke, Bernard. *Sacraments and Sacramentality*. Mystic, CT: Twenty-Third Publications, 1994.

Lawler, Michael. *Symbol and Sacrament: A Contemporary Sacramental Theology*. Omaha, NE: Creighton University Press, 1995.

Martos, Joseph. *Doors to the Sacred: A Historical Introduction to Sacraments in the Catholic Church*. Revised and updated ed. Liguori, MO: Liguori/Triumph, 2001.

New Dictionary of Sacramental Worship. Edited by Peter Fink. Collegeville, MN: Liturgical Press, 1990.

Noll, Ray. *Sacraments: A New Understanding for a New Generation*. Mystic, CT: Twenty-Third Publications, 1999.

Rahner, Karl. *The Church and the Sacraments*. New York: Herder & Herder, 1963.

The Rites of the Catholic Church. Vols. I II. Collegeville, MN: Liturgical Press, 1990.

The Sacramentary. New York: Catholic Book Publishing Co., 1985.

Schillebeeckx, Edward. *Christ the Sacrament of the Encounter with God*. New York: Sheed & Ward, 1963.

Smolarski, Dennis. *Sacred Mysteries: Sacramental Principles and Liturgical Practice*. New York: Paulist Press, 1994.

Vatican Council II. Edited by Austin Flannery. New York: Costello Publishing, 1998.

from the REFERENCE LIBRARIAN

Combining Subject Headings—Sacraments

SKILL KEY #1

Use the library's reference collection to begin your research.

a) Use a subject-specific encyclopedia to acquire specialized knowledge about a subject.
b) Use a subject-specific encyclopedia whose scope is appropriate for both your topic and the approach you want to take to that topic.

Once again, the kinds of topics available for researching the sacraments fall into the basic categories of history, on the one hand, and systematics (concepts, issues), on the other. If you are researching a historical topic, make sure the reference tool you use includes historical coverage. If you are researching a systematic topic, you will want a tool that includes this type of topic. The first three titles listed focus specifically on the sacraments and vary in their historical and systematic emphases.

Paul Bradshaw, ed. *The New Westminster Dictionary of Liturgy and Worship*. Louisville, KY: Westminster John Knox Press, 2002.

This text incorporates ecumenical scholarship from both Protestants and Catholics, so the views of both Catholic and non-Catholic Christians are included. For example, the article on marriage includes sections for "Baptist," "Lutheran," "Methodist," and so on, as well as for Catholics. The focus is on systematic topics with some historical coverage.

Peter E. Fink, SJ, ed. *The New Dictionary of Sacramental Worship*. Collegeville, MN: Liturgical Press, 1990.

This title was written by and for Catholics as indicated, for example, by the fact that several articles on marriage would be of interest mainly to a Catholic audience ("Marriage, Canonical Issues Concerning," "Marriage, Liturgy of," "Marriage, Sacrament of"). The focus is on systematic topics.

Michael O'Carroll, CSSp. *Corpus Christi: An Encyclopedia of the Eucharist*. Wilmington, DE: Michael Glazier, Inc., 1988.

As the title indicates, this encyclopedia focuses entirely on the sacrament of the Lord's Supper and offers a somewhat haphazard mix of systematic and historical coverage.

Titles mentioned in previous chapters, such as *The Oxford Dictionary of the Christian Church* or the *Dictionary of Historical Theology*, will primarily be of use for historically focused research (see also other titles among those mentioned in the chapters on Christology and ecclesiology whose scope includes historical coverage).

For coverage of systematic topics, the *Handbook of Catholic Theology*, which includes both historical and systematic coverage but with emphasis on the latter, is a good resource and even has an article entitled "Sacraments: Contemporary Issues."

Two additional titles that, like the *Handbook of Catholic Theology*, place the emphasis on coverage of systematic issues while including historical elements are the following:

Karl Rahner, ed. *Sacramentum Mundi: An Encyclopedia of Theology*. 6 vols. New York: Herder & Herder, 1968–1970.

Karl Rahner, ed. *Encyclopedia of Theology: The Concise Sacramentum Mundi*. New York: Seabury Press, 1975.
(This is an abridgement and partial updating of *Sacramentum Mundi*.)

Don't let the word *sacramentum* throw you off; both of these works are comprehensive in covering the field of theology, not just sacraments.

Expanding Skill Key #2: Combining Subject Headings

In the introductory chapter on research, we explained how to use the bibliographic information from encyclopedia articles to determine subject headings to use to find books on a topic.

Unfortunately, no subject classification scheme is perfect, including Library of Congress subject headings. The main reason is that authors can choose to write a book about any subject or range of subject matter they please. Authors do not write a book thinking that it has to correspond to a particular subject heading, so there may not be a single subject heading that applies to the subject (and therefore the book) you want to find. In a case like this, you will need to combine two or more subject headings in a single search to find a book on your subject. We can now add another refinement of the technique for searching the library catalog.

SKILL KEY #2

Use the library's catalog to locate sources of information.

a) Use subject headings to locate precisely books on your topic.
b) Use subject headings whose scope fits your topic as closely as possible, then adjust your search with a broader or narrower subject heading as necessary.
c) As an alternative to using encyclopedia bibliographies, use keyword searching to identify subject headings for your topic.
d) **Combine one or more subject headings in a search to retrieve books on a topic for which no single subject heading exists.**

There are two basic ways of using subject headings. The first applies if there is a single subject heading (sometimes including a subdivision) that covers your topic. Taking up the subject matter of this chapter, let's say you are interested in the views of Saint Augustine on the Eucharist. We have already seen that one subdivision often found with theologians' names in library catalogs begins with the words "Contributions in. . . ." To search for books on Augustine and the Eucharist in the library catalog, you could use the following subject heading.

Search format:

Last name	*Descriptive phrase(s)*	*Subdivision*
Augustine	Saint, Bishop of Hippo	Contributions in Doctrine of the Lord's Supper

Such specific subject headings are more likely to be found in large research libraries, especially those with large theology collections; smaller library collections (or even large libraries with nothing under this subject heading) may require the use of a broader subject heading, such as the following (see Skill Key #2b):

Search format:

Last name	*Descriptive phrase(s)*	*Subdivision*
Augustine	Saint, Bishop of Hippo	Contributions in theology

"Theology" is a broader subject than the "Lord's Supper," so books with this subject heading may (or may not) include material specifically on the Lord's Supper. The only way to tell if a book does include such material is by looking at book titles, tables of contents, or indexes to see whether and where the subject is covered.

The second way of using subject headings applies when there is no single appropriate subject heading (as would be the case, for example, in libraries following the Library of Congress practice of doing away with the "Contributions in . . ." subdivision; see the previous discussion on this in chapter 4). For example, if I were interested in the views of Saint Thomas Aquinas on the sacraments, as it happens, there is no "Contributions in . . ." subdivision with the heading "Thomas Aquinas Saint" that relates specifically to sacraments (although there is a subdivision "Contributions in Theology"). In this case, I can combine the subject heading "Thomas Aquinas Saint" with the subject heading for sacraments, which is "sacraments" (not all subject headings are difficult). The important thing is that instead of entering a single subject-heading "string," as you have been doing so far, you are combining two separate subject headings. The precise way you combine subject headings varies from one library catalog to another. Some library catalogs allow the use of "Boolean operators" (AND, OR, NOT) to combine subject headings. The use of "AND" in a search statement means that all of the terms must be present in any record retrieved. The use of "OR" means that any of the terms (always at least one) may be present in any record retrieved. The use of "NOT" with a search term means that none of the records retrieved will include that term.

Different library catalogs will provide different ways of accomplishing this. For example, some library catalogs may not allow you to combine subject headings but will allow you to combine keywords. In that case, you can simply treat your subject headings as if they were keywords. What you should understand now is that you can do this; you can always ask the reference librarian to show you how.

Search format:

Subject heading #1	*Boolean operator*	*Subject heading #2*
Thomas Aquinas Saint	AND	Sacraments

Combining these two subject headings produced the following catalog record, which is exactly what we are looking for. Note that you do not have to know the subdivisions after "sacraments" to be able to combine it with another subject heading in a search.

Author	Garland, Peter B.
Title	*The definition of sacrament according to Saint Thomas.*
Published	Ottawa : University of Ottawa Press, 1959.
Subjects	*Thomas, Aquinas, Saint, 1225?–1274.* *Sacraments—History of doctrines—Middle Ages, 600–1500.*

In my library, there are currently 1167 titles listed with the subject heading "Thomas Aquinas, Saint, 1225?–1274." Combining that search with a search on "Sacraments" is much faster than plowing through 1167 titles to find what you want.

Student Tasks

1. Using a dictionary, encyclopedia, or handbook, find one resource that treats the topic of sacraments from a historical approach and one that takes a systematic approach (concepts, issues).
2. Choose the name of a theologian. Search for books about that person in your library catalog, using the person's name as the subject heading. Do any "Contributions in . . ." subdivisions appear with the name?
3. Combine subject headings in a search using the name of a theologian as one subject heading and the subject heading for one of the sacraments as the other. If you feel adventurous, expand your skills and try this kind of search on one of the topics from the earlier chapters on the Old or New Testament, Christology, or ecclesiology. You will need to use a valid subject heading you have come across in the earlier chapters to do this.

THE CHURCH'S MISSION IN THE WORLD

Christian Morality: Choosing God in This World

Barbara W. Blackburn

from the EDITOR

In Christian circles there is a provocative question that goes like this: "If you were arrested for being a Christian, would there be enough evidence to convict you?" The evidence presented would need to include events or actions witnessed by others, not simply one's privately held beliefs. If I say, "I love you," then I must mean it and prove it in action; if I say, "I trust you," then I must mean it and prove it in action; if I say, "I will be there when you need me—I am your friend," then I must mean it and actually do it. It is a matter of religious integrity, of actions matching beliefs and intentions. In assessing the avowed Christian's faith, the criteria evaluated are not the individual's disposable commitments; we are talking cherished beliefs and hopes. For this, Christians rely on the grace of God for sustenance.

Theology reflects on these daily experiences of trust and mistrust, fidelity and infidelity, truth and lies. This theological discipline is called "Christian morality," or sometimes "Christian ethics." It is Christian because it flows from a religious belief in God's encounter with the individual, a love relationship; consequences result where one's "actions speak louder than words." Theology evaluates an action as moral or ethical based on the response to two interrelated questions: (1) Is the action truly human, or not? and (2) Does it express love of God and neighbor, or not?

The following examination of Christian morality will address these various areas of decisions and the formation of conscience toward what is good. It takes on the question of one's freedom and limitations, the twin wisdom sources of tradition and authority, and how to think morally. An important condition for moral decisions is the changing situations and circumstances of life. The challenge of living a moral life requires Christians to reflect on, examine, and clarify their motives; consult others; and pray to God for guidance to respond as loving followers of Jesus. If the Christian is living a moral life, then there will be abundant evidence to convict.

DECISIONS, DECISIONS, DECISIONS

Life is full of decisions—which school to attend, which course of studies to pursue, which organizations to join, careers, friends, parties. Every morning, we face a decision to get up or hit the snooze button, eat breakfast or just grab some juice, dress in jeans or shorts. Should I go to my first class or study for my second class? Sometimes our decisions involve choosing between good things (tacos or pizza), and other times they involve choosing between things that are difficult but unavoidable (8:00 a.m. chemistry lab or Spanish lab). Even when we are not totally aware, we are making choices of what to look at, what direction to walk or drive, what to say to people we meet.

While these types of choices and decisions are a part of our daily life, other types of choices can be a greater challenge. What would you do if you found a $20 bill on the floor in the cafeteria? Would you ask if someone dropped it? Hand it to the cashier in case the one who lost it asks about it? Would you pocket it on the principle of "finders, keepers"? How would you decide? Would it make a difference if it were a $100 bill? In another scenario, what would you do if your best friend asked you to help her find an abortion provider? Would you help her find counseling and support? Would you get out the Yellow Pages and call the first abortion clinic listed? Would you dump her as a friend? How would you decide? What would be the basis for your decision? Would you seek advice? Where? From whom? These kinds of decisions are called "moral decisions" because they involve choices between what is right and wrong, between good and evil.

This chapter examines the nature, sources, and methods of moral theology—that is, what moral theology is, what are the sources and the tools for forming one's conscience and making moral decisions, and how does one use the sources and tools to make decisions in a morally appropriate way.

What Moral Theology Is

Christianity, like other major religious traditions of the world, is a way of life expressed in creed, cult, and code.

Creed

A *creed* is a profession of common beliefs that a community maintains as the essential truths forming the identity of the community. To be a member of a faith community means to believe, as a community and as an individual, those certain basic tenets of truth that unite individuals into a believing community. In the moral life, this means one lives out what one claims to believe.

Cult

In a *cult*, believers come together to express those beliefs in rituals and customs of worship. The ancient Latin saying "*Lex credendi sequetor lex orandi*" suggests that the "church praying gives rise to the church believing." Ritual is, therefore, both normative and formative to a religious tradition. In the moral life, this means that as one prays, one lives.

Code

There are implications of faith for the way people live. Professing a set of common beliefs and publicly ritualizing those beliefs leads to an all-encompassing way of life. What we believe and how we express it becomes who we are, how we act, and what choices we make. Christianity is, therefore, situated within the context of a faith tradition. It is a response to what people believe God has done for them in and through Jesus Christ.

Moral Theology

How do we define *moral theology*? During the age of Scholasticism, Saint Anselm of Canterbury (d. 1109) defined the entire discipline of theology as "faith seeking understanding." His theological successor, Peter Abelard (d. 1142), added: "I believe in order that I might understand." Pope John Paul II also examined the relationship of faith and reason for our time in his document titled *Faith and Reason* (1998). As a formal theological discipline, moral theology is the study of how persons live in response to what God has done for them.

Moral Theology	Morality
Study of the implications of faith for the way we live.	From the Latin *mores*; group customs or rules

As we continue to explore the definition of moral theology, we consider another term often used in the study of human conduct: ethics. What is the relationship between the terms *morality* and *ethics*?

MORALITY/ETHICS?		
It feels right (?)	Obedience (?)	Happiness (?)
What is legal (?)	What everyone is doing (?)	

Ethics can be defined as a discussion of the formation of human conduct—how responsible human beings capable of critical judgment should live using reflection on fundamental issues and description of concrete cases.

Morality is all that and more. Morality is concerned with human conduct but goes to a deeper level of personhood, such that our conduct is a reflection of who we are, a reflection of our character.

Any discussion of morality involves a discussion of character and how it is formed, because being a Christian carries a particular commitment to becoming a certain sort of person, living a way of life that entails certain reasons for being moral, and making certain choices that follow from Christian beliefs. Human conduct is integral to morality, but since the Second Vatican Council, there has been a shift in focus from the act to the person. Faced with a moral dilemma, we often ask, "What should I do?" A more basic question would be "Who am I?" or "What sort of person acts this way?" So, for example, what sort of person does not turn in a $20 bill or a $100 bill? Why would I or would I not turn it in? Character counts; it will influence how we act and the decisions we make. In turn, the choices we make shape the sort of person we become.

It might go something like this: the first time you tell a lie, it might be difficult. You might feel as if you are acting out of character. The fifth time you tell a lie, it is easier. By the time lying becomes a habit, you are a "liar." The first time you are challenged to tell the truth, it might be difficult. The fifth time, it becomes easier as you become a "truthful person." Aristotle taught that people do not naturally become morally excellent or practically wise. They become so only as a result of lifelong effort to build character.

Character	Values
A settled disposition to behave in a morally good way.	Basic truths that undergird human excellence; include attitudes and affections chosen as pivotal realities and source of meaning

Character is developed by monitoring behavior along with motivations, intentions, relationships, and values, which have often been referred to as "pillars of character." Employers know that character tells them how and why a person will act in a big decision. Voters know that character tells how and why a political candidate will most likely act in a big decision or crisis. Appreciation of human values forms a person's character.

DECISIONS DECISIONS DECISIONS

AIDS

Stem Cell Research

Poverty

Global Economics

Human Cloning

War and Peace

We need not wander aimlessly in a life full of moral dilemmas without guidelines. As humans, we have been gifted with sources of conscience formation that serve to direct us through a lifetime of choices. Moral theology provides us with sources and systems to examine fundamental issues and concrete cases.

Christianity teaches that in order to become persons of reason informed by faith, one must seek information and wisdom from a variety of sources that will be defined and explained in this chapter:

Scripture
Natural law philosophy
Magisterium
Theology
Sensus fidelium
Empirical sciences

For Roman Catholics, both faith and human resources are dimensions of discovering the moral demands of being human. Some of these sources come as revelation (the Bible), and some are based on the faith tradition (*magisterium* and theology). Some are based on human reason (empirical sciences), and give the facts, data, figures, and definitions of the moral issue. Some sources are based on what it means to be a human being (natural law) of reason informed by faith (*sensus fidelium*). These sources, which will each be explained, are seen as the basic tools needed to form one's conscience and help one make good moral decisions.

It is important to avoid thinking of morality as an exclusively "rational morality" or as an exclusively "revealed faith morality." The former yields humanism and the latter sectarianism, such that only Christians can be truly moral. What is needed is a creative tension of faith in divine revelation and human reason. This understanding of human conscience formation understands that (1) divine grace builds on human nature and is not opposed to it, (2) human beings bear the image of the Creator, and (3) God has gifted humanity with God's self-revelation through the scriptures and the tradition of the church.

Before we begin a study of the basic sources, we must examine how conscience enters into its important role in morality. Let me propose it in a slightly different and more pointed way: Without conscience, would there be any morality?

What is conscience? Does everyone have a conscience? What if a conscience is misinformed? Is conscience individual or communal?

Conscience is a difficult term to pin down because it involves several aspects of human reasoning. The Second Vatican Council explained that conscience is the voice of God written in our hearts: "On his part, man perceives and acknowledges the imperatives of the divine law through the mediation of conscience. In all his activity a man is bound to follow his conscience faithfully, in order that he may come to God for whom he was created" (*Declaration on Religious Freedom* 3).

Look also at the following and notice what it says is characteristic of conscience:

> In the depths of his conscience man detects a law which he does not impose upon himself, but which holds him to obedience. Always summoning him to love the good and avoid evil, the voice of conscience can when necessary speak to his heart more specifically; do this, shun that. For man has in his heart a law written by God. To obey it is the very dignity of man; according to it he will be judged. Conscience is the most secret core and sanctuary of a man. There he is alone with God whose voice echoes in his depths. (*Pastoral Constitution on the Church in the Modern World* 16)

We can say, then, the following about conscience:

1. Conscience is the fundamental characteristic of being human that makes it possible to know and do good. It involves an awareness of personal responsibility, a general sense of value, and an inner vision of reality.
2. The aim of conscience formation is not simply to increase facts and skills for solving moral dilemmas but, rather, to help determine what sort of person I ought to become. An act of conscience is expressive of who I am. Conscience is an exercise of moral reasoning involving discussion and analysis of sources or moral wisdom. It is the ability to make up one's mind *for* oneself but not *by* oneself.
3. Conscience is a judgment, a determination of good versus evil in a specific case. Conscience is, therefore, a human characteristic, a human process, and a concrete judgment of good versus evil.
4. Conscience is also both individual and communal. Human persons with conscience construct and maintain many societies, both in numbers and in types. Society does not have a conscience; people do. Hence, society needs a critical conscience formed by the reciprocity of many consciences. The morality into which we are socialized is not so much a set of rules but rather a collection of stories and images of what makes life worth living. Being a part of a community—its history, its language, its rituals and celebrations—forms our "moral imagination."

At times, society is challenged by people who have the vision and courage to shake us up and unmask our errors. This "prophetic voice" is as ancient as the prophets of the Hebrew scriptures—Isaiah, Jeremiah, Ezekiel, Hosea, Amos, and so on—and as contemporary as social justice advocates of our own times—Martin Luther King Jr., Mother Teresa, Ghandi, Oscar Romero, and Dorothy Day—who remind us that "the way things are" might not be "what should be."

The development of conscience is a lifelong task. The decisions we make today might need to be revised as we gain additional wisdom and insight. Moral certitude seldom equals absolute certainty. We make the best decision we can given the information we have at our disposal, knowing that, if new information emerges, we might need to rethink our decision. Christians understand it as a lifelong process of loving God and neighbor.

If we later change our mind about an ethical decision we have made, does that mean our original decision was immoral? The *Catechism of the Catholic Church* explains, "A human being must always obey the certain judgment of his conscience. If he were deliberately to act against it, he would condemn himself. Yet it can happen that moral conscience remains in ignorance and makes erroneous judgments" (*Catechism*, 1797).

The *Catechism* goes on to explain that ignorance can sometimes be imputed to personal responsibility. We are responsible for informing our decision making. If, however, we have truly consulted the moral sources and then later discover that our choice or decision needs to be changed because it is now considered wrong or evil, then we are not responsible for the evil that resulted from our original decision.

Conscience is not an imaginary friend on our shoulder or an occasional pang of guilt, fear, or anxiety located in some part of our body. These feelings, however, are powerful and, in many cases, monitor our behavior. People might say, "My conscience is bothering me." They might lose sleep, lose their appetite, experience nightmares, or become physically or emotionally ill because of a decision they question or regret. While guilt is a powerful tool that can regulate our conduct, it cannot always be trusted as a completely objective indicator of what is a good or bad decision. That is because people have varying degrees of the capacity for guilt. Some people feel guilty about almost everything—mistakes, minor faults, or imperfections. These people are called "scrupulous." Other people might not feel guilt at all, even when they are aware that they have made an evil decision.

We also make a careful distinction between conscience and superego, which is the conscience of another person superimposed on our own to serve as an internal sensor to regulate our conduct by using guilt as its powerful weapon. Superego is related to our need to be loved and maintain approval of authority figures. It can be a step in the early development of conscience as we store advice from authority figures in the process of growing up: "Brush your teeth." "Walk in from recess in a straight line." "Keep your room neat." "Do your homework." "Respect authority." As we mature, however, superego cannot be a substitute for using our own conscience.

What is missing in superego is the personal involvement of two critical aspects of moral decision making: freedom and knowledge.

Freedom

The *Catechism* states:

> Freedom is so central to the moral life that without it we cannot properly speak of being moral persons at all. Responsibility for an action can be diminished or even nullified by ignorance, duress, fear, habit, inordinate attachments, and other psychological or social factors. . . . If we are beyond freedom, we are beyond morality. Freedom properly defined is not unbridled liberty. Theologically speaking, freedom is the ability to choose the good. The choice to do what is evil is an abuse of freedom and leads to the slavery of sin. (*Catechism*, 1735, 1739)

Knowledge

Knowledge is critical for all decision making. We must be aware that what we have chosen is good or evil. Two types of knowledge are necessary for moral decisions: cognitive knowledge and evaluative knowledge. *Cognitive knowledge* is gained through information and facts ("head" knowledge). For example, I can memorize the Ten Commandments and be aware that the Third Commandment states, "Keep holy the Lord's Day." *Evaluative knowledge* is gained through relationships and experience and involves a personal, heartfelt grasp of value (heartfelt knowledge). With evaluative knowledge, I view the Third Commandment as not so much an obligation as an opportunity to celebrate my relationship with the risen Savior along with a community of believers. Cognitive knowledge and evaluative knowledge represent acceptance of both the "letter of the law" and "the spirit of the law." Both are

SIN

Relational | Personal | Social | An Evil Choice

An Action | Scandal | Crime

critical in moral choices. If, therefore, we freely choose to do what we know is wrong, we "sin."

The book *What Ever Became of Sin?* by Karl Menninger asserts that while fewer sermons are given on sin these days and the lines for making confession are shorter, sin looms as large as ever. There are several reasons why we do not hear much about sin. One of the reasons is that the definitions of sin and our understanding of sin have changed in some ways. For Catholics, a number of changes have occurred since the Second Vatican Council. Moral theology prior to Vatican II (the Council of 1962–1965) emphasized sin as an action or an omission in violation of God's law. Since Vatican II, there has been more of an emphasis on the person who acts. The emphasis switched to the person as a disciple, a person of virtue, a person of character and moral maturity on a journey of faith. Morality became equated with a person's spirituality in a much more holistic manner.

The Church understands sin as a human reality involving the whole person, including his or her intellect and will. Sin is never an accident. No one makes us sin or become sinful people. The human condition is, however, prone to sin. This human inclination to sin, theologically referred to as "concupiscence," is described by Saint Paul in his Letter to the Romans: "For I know that nothing good dwells within me, that is, in my flesh. I can will what is right, but I cannot do it. For I do not do the good I want, but the evil I do not want is what I do. . . . Wretched man that I am!" (Rom 7:18–19, 24).

Why is it sometimes difficult to know and choose what is good?

Where did this human condition originate?

Didn't God make us good?

The creation accounts in Genesis 1 and 2 describe the goodness of God's creation in which humanity is the epitome of God's creative work. Genesis 1:27 describes man and woman as the "*imago Dei*": "So God created humankind in his image, in the image of God he created them; male and female he created them." Unique in all creation, Adam and Eve were gifted with intellect and will, so they would be able to know and choose what was good. Instead, they chose to go against the goodness for which they were created. Genesis 3 describes humanity's fall from a perfect relationship with the Creator. When the relationship was broken through pride and disobedience, all relationships suffered. Adam and Eve experienced guilt and shame for the first time and covered their nakedness with fig leaves (Gen 3:7). The peace and harmony these humans experienced in paradise was shattered as they felt new and horrible feelings of regret. Adam and Eve's relationship with themselves was damaged. The word *sin* in Hebrew, *hatta'*, means "to miss the mark, the target" and, in this case, to miss being human, which is to be related to God and act accordingly.

Whatever the transgression, it had the effect of destroying the intimate trust and friendship between God and humanity. After the sin, Adam and Eve hid from God (Gen 3:8). The relationship between husband and wife was damaged as they blamed each other for what they had done—the first family argument. Harmony within creation was broken, and death made its entrance into human history. This story teaches that the disharmony and alienation of sin affects all relationships.

1. Relationship with self is one of shame and regret.
2. Relationship with others is damaged with blame and argument.
3. Relationship with God is changed from intimacy to alienation.

The Church teaches that, in spite of this dismal situation experienced by all persons since the fall of humanity, the human condition, while wounded, flawed, and weakened, is not totally corrupted or destroyed. Grace, the capacity to overcome this state of affairs, comes to us as the gift of an inner elevating and transforming power. Grace restores relationship and kinship with God, self, and others. As Saint Paul explained to the Romans: "Where sin increased, grace abounded all the more . . . through Jesus Christ our Lord" (Rom 5:20–21). As horrible as sin is, Christians believe that the grace of God is even more powerful, if they are open to radical transformation.

While original sin marked humanity as a whole, the Church teaches that people, as individuals or as a society, are also capable of choosing to go against the goodness for which they were created. This is called "actual sin." In describing and understanding actual sin, three aspects must be considered:

1. The intention—the purpose, the end in view. This formal element gives meaning to the action.
2. The means used—the kind of action this is. This is the external, observable material element of the action.
3. The circumstances—Who? What? Where? When? How much? How little? What if? What else? These are all reality-revealing questions.

We do not have a true moral evaluation until the intention, act, and circumstances are considered together. The act in itself cannot be accurately evaluated as moral or immoral apart from considering the intention, means, and circumstances as one reality. While we examine each of the three elements, each is dependent on the others. For example, we must consider the intention of the person acting. A good intention, however, cannot justify simply any means used. Only an action congruent with the intention adequately and morally expresses the intention. For example, a person who is passionately against abortion kills an abortion provider in order to save hundreds of babies' lives. The means used, murder, is incongruent or inconsistent with the intent of saving lives. Another example illustrates the role of circumstances in moral evaluation. Suppose you are walking alone when you see a stranger walking toward you. You take a gun from your pocket and shoot the person approaching you. Is this self-defense or murder? Is this a moral or an immoral act? We cannot evaluate this situation without asking questions about the circumstances, as well as about your intention. What circumstances would render you guilty of murder? Of self-defense? The intention, means, and circumstances comprise one act. If any one aspect is incongruous with the others, the act or decision is immoral. If any one aspect (the intent, means, or circumstances) is evil in itself, intrinsically evil, then the entire action or decision is morally evil. Let's take a controversial example today:

Intent:	Discover a cure for Parkinson's disease
Means:	Destroy human embryos to extract stem cells for research
Circumstances:	Carefully monitored, legal lab procedures

If respect for human life is a primary value, and if human embryos are understood as human life as the Church teaches they are, their destruction is immoral because intentional destruction of human life, even at its earliest stage, is an intrinsic evil. Even if the research results in the discovery of a cure, the entire process is immoral because the end cannot justify the means used. If, on the other hand, stem cells were obtained from adult donors or from donated umbilical cord blood, the entire research effort could be considered moral. The intent, the means used, and the circumstances would be proportionate or congruous with each other.

This method of moral evaluation is called "casuistry" or "case study." It is based on logic and the human ability to use reason informed by faith.

QUESTIONS FOR DISCUSSION

1. How would you define sin?
2. Could a sin ever be considered a "mistake"? Why or why not?
3. What are some psychological factors that could diminish a person's ability to make a moral decision?
4. Give examples of how duress or fear could keep a person from making a moral decision.
5. What are some social factors that could diminish a person's ability to make a moral decision?
6. What is the difference between killing in self-defense, manslaughter, or murder, considering that in each case a person is dead?

Natural Law

Natural law is considered one of the major sources of moral theology and answers the question: How do I know what is good or evil?

Throughout the history of humanity, natural law has been a factor in our decisions of what is morally right and wrong, good and evil. Christians believe that God fashioned the world such that the laws guiding all activities of created beings are somehow built into the nature of these beings. For humans, this means moral knowledge is accessible to anyone willing to reflect on human experience. Natural law is not dependent, therefore, on a particular religion or belief system but on insight into human experiences.

In the Christian Scriptures, Saint Paul's Letter to the Romans says that those who have not heard of the Law of Moses, the Ten Commandments, still know what is right and wrong because "what the law requires is written on their hearts" (Rom 2:15).

This knowledge of what is right and wrong, somehow written on people's hearts, has traditionally been referred to as the natural moral law. We discover these basic laws by observing human behavior and by using common sense. No government, bishop, or ruler made up the natural law. Rather, the Church understands natural law as an objective moral order imprinted on humanity that directs humanity to God, the Creator whose image we bear. The *Catechism* tells us that "natural law is a participation in God's wisdom and goodness . . . expressing the dignity of the human person and forming the basis of his fundamental rights and duties" (*Catechism*, 1978). To violate the norms of natural law, therefore, is to violate one's own humanity. Since the natural law is universal, it is very general: do good and avoid evil.

Its prescriptions are basic: be respectful, honest, keep promises, play fair, care for children, and so on. The natural law is not a written code of conduct. It is not static because it changes as people continue to discover what it means to be human and what the moral community discovers in its experiences to contribute to human wholeness. We are always discovering more about nature and the natural law. New moral issues surface as we continue to reflect on human experiences: child labor, organ transplants, endangered species. Certain positions regarding some of these issues might previously have been considered immoral according to natural law but are now considered the moral norm. The idea of organ donations was once considered abhorrent and immoral. Now it is considered to be a heroic act to donate organs and morally commendable to transplant them. Other issues might have previously been considered moral but are now considered "inhumane" or immoral—for example, sweatshops, slavery, and child labor. Issues emerge as society and technology continue to develop. The natural law will always compel humanity to seek the good and avoid evil. Christians understand this as God's eternal law written upon the human heart.

QUESTIONS FOR DISCUSSION

1. Give some examples of how we expect people to act in a "humane" manner.
2. Give further examples of situations that had previously been considered natural to humanity but are now considered inhumane.

Scripture

Examining the sacred scripture of the Christian faith tradition helps answer such questions as whether the Bible can help people make moral decisions, how it can do so, and whether it can be misused. In this regard, the Second Vatican Council made some important statements about the relationship of sacred scripture and moral theology. The bishops of the council affirmed scripture as the "soul of theology" (*Constitution on Divine Revelation* 24), stating, "Special attention needs to be given to the development of moral theology. Its scientific exposition should be thoroughly nourished by scriptural teaching" (*Decree on Priestly Formation* 16). In addressing the challenge of how to use scripture in moral theology, the bishops wrote:

> The Church guards the heritage of God's Word and draws from it religious and moral principles, without always having at hand the solutions to particular problems. She desires thereby to add the light of revealed truth to mankind's store of experience, so that the path which humanity has taken in recent times will not be a dark one. (*Pastoral Constitution on the Church in the Modern World* 33)

What the council confirmed was that, even though the Bible nowhere mentions such contemporary issues as genetic engineering, cloning, nuclear weapons, AIDS, or global economics, the Church can use the principles found in the Bible to help make moral decisions on specific issues, for it is the Bible that grounds Christians' basic convictions. The Bible is both the normative and the formative articulation of the Judeo-Christian belief system. It is the place where God's intentions for humanity are revealed. The question of how to use the Bible has sometimes resulted in two extremes:

Irrelevance
The Bible is literature Concerned with specific cultural interests Deals with ancient history Not relevant to contemporary moral issues
Biblicism
Literal interpretation Prooftexting or quoting out of context to prove a pre-established point

In order to use the Bible effectively in moral theology, both extremes must be avoided. Historical criticism recognizes that the biblical text is a result of human expressions of faith and that this book, which Christians regard as the truly inspired word of God, cannot come to us apart from time-bound cultural categories. Christianity asserts that God has spoken through history, events, people, and experiences that are only interpreted after the fact. Finding the original meaning of the original text using the tools of historical criticism allows one to apply the meaning of that message today. This interpretation, called "hermeneutical criticism," is the application of the message of the ancient text to a contemporary audience. For example, the story of exodus relates the events of the Israelite's escape from slavery in Egypt through Yahweh's saving intervention. Moses, who serves as a messenger and a mouthpiece of Yahweh to the pharaoh and to the people, is the human instrument of God's plan to deliver the Israelites into a new land and a new way of life. Hermeneutical criticism of the text would require that one apply the lessons of this story to issues faced today. Use the following questions to interpret the meaning (the hermeneutic) of the exodus for today.

QUESTIONS FOR DISCUSSION

1. Can you think of situations today in which certain groups of people are intimidated, persecuted, or held captive, because of their ethnic or religious beliefs?
2. Give examples where people in different parts of the world are denied the opportunity to own the land on which they work.
3. How might one apply the lessons of the story of the exodus to these people?
4. What are some situations, habits, or human circumstances that "tie you down" or keep you from being who you really want to be?

Thus the Church asserts that the Bible can and must be used as a tool for making moral decisions but never as a weapon to prove a pre-established point by choosing and lifting an isolated quotation, which is prooftexting, or by referring only to an isolated book of the Bible to the exclusion of others, which is genre reductionism. To use the Bible correctly, the entire collection of its books must serve as reference, even as each book has its individual contribution within the context of the whole. For example, while referring to the story of the exodus, one must keep its story in the context of what the other books of the Bible reveal about the themes of covenant, freedom, promise, and so on.

The Bible was not written as a detailed rulebook for morality. In fact, the Bible nowhere establishes a singular or systematic method for moral decision making. Instead, it serves as a context for the attitudes and dispositions of the human heart. Christians understand the Bible as the drama of a relationship between God and humanity. In the Bible, this relationship, called "covenant," was initiated by God with the great patriarchs and matriarchs of the Hebrew Scriptures: Noah, Abraham and Sarah, Moses, and all of Israel. The covenant is based on a promise made by God to establish a relationship with a specific group of people, the Israelites. The relationship is simply stated, "I will be your God and you will be my people." The history of this promise spans the Hebrew and the Christian Scriptures as humans continue to discover what it means to respond to God's call to relationship.

Moral theology continues to study how Christians, as a people who have been called to covenant, should appropriately respond to that call. Moral theology continues to ask the questions: What does it mean to be a people of God? How do God's people behave? How do they live? What do they stand for? Christians find the answers to these questions guided by the principles and themes found in the stories, poetry, parables, letters, and events in the Bible. Many major themes thread through the Bible, holding its message in a tapestry depicting the history of the relationship between God and humanity. Three of the most important moral themes are covenant law, the voice of the prophet, and discipleship.

Covenant Law

What is the place or the purpose of "law" in making moral decisions? No society can survive without some organization; laws identify certain basic values. Laws safeguard public order. Laws protect rights and freedoms. Laws serve as a basic roadmap through conflicting situations in life. Laws free us to go about the business of living. Laws interconnect and rank more- or less-important values. They establish a hierarchy of values, ranking the significance of values from most important to least important.

QUESTIONS FOR DISCUSSION

1. What is your opinion of law?
2. Do you see law as keeping you from what you want to do? Explain.
3. How is law beneficial at your school or in your society?
4. How can law be a source of pride?
5. Who has authority to give laws? Why?
6. How do you decide if you will obey a law?

The ancient Israelites considered the Ten Commandments to be the basis of all the laws that united them in covenant to God and each other. The Decalogue, the Ten Words of God, was a gift from Yahweh providing the people of Israel with the means, the know-how, to live in covenant relationship. The Law given to Moses on Mount Sinai provided the Israelites with an identity. They became known as "the People of the Law." The Law bound them together in fidelity to Yahweh and each other, safeguarded the public order, and provided a basic guide by which to live the covenant relationship. The Law became a point of pride, a symbol of the divine gift of election. Obedience to the Law was considered a privilege. Happiness was impossible apart from obedience to the Law. Psalm 119 is an example of Israel's praise of and sentiment for God's Law:

> Happy are those whose way is blameless, who walk in the law of the Lord. (Ps 119:1)

Eventually, the 613 dietary and disciplinary laws of the Torah ordered every aspect of life, but the first and the greatest law was always the *Shema*, the creed every Jew knew by heart: "Hear, O Israel: The Lord is our God, the Lord alone. You shall love the Lord your God with all your heart, and with all your soul, and with all your might" (Deut 6:4–5).

In the New Testament (NT), the Gospels of Matthew, Mark, and Luke recount that Jesus referred to this passage when questioned by the Pharisees as to what was the greatest law or commandment. Jesus' answer was the *Shema*, the command to love God and neighbor. Christians believe that Jesus brought the law of love to its ultimate climax on the cross, when he died as a total gift of self. This is the kind of love his followers are challenged to have for God and each other in imitation of Jesus. For Christians, therefore, the "New Testament" is the "new covenant" established by Jesus Christ, bringing humanity into an intimate and eternal relationship with God. To be a Christian is to be a person of the new covenant, this new relationship with God and each other based on the example of Jesus.

The Voice of the Prophet

The second major theme of scripture that we will examine is referred to as "the voice of the prophet." A prophet is a messenger and a mouthpiece for God. The prophets' job was to remind Israel of the covenant commitment and its implications for the way people should live. The message of the prophet was often a challenge against the complacency toward oppression of the poor, corruption in courts and in the marketplace, infidelity to relationships, or abandonment of the marginalized in society. For the prophet, the greatest sin is the ability to stand dry-eyed in the face of injustice. Prophets unmask prejudices and challenge set ways of looking at realities. They remind us that the way things are might not be the way things should be. We become so used to the status quo that we are sometimes unaware of a better and more just way of behaving. The prophet opens people's eyes to reality and challenges them to do better in a world often marked with racism, materialism, sexism, homophobia, militarism, genocide, economic colonialism, consumerism, and greed.

One of the major messages of the prophets is that God wants the hearts of his people to be pure, full of compassion and mercy. The opposite of this is to be "hard hearted." Repeatedly, the prophets challenged Israel to change her heart, considered the very core of her being. Rituals, sacrifices, and holocausts (burnt offerings) are all important in observance of the Law. The prophets reminded the people, however, that sincerity was pivotal to all of these undertakings. The prophet Amos, as a mouthpiece for God, insisted: "Even though you offer me your burnt offerings and grain offerings, I will not accept them. . . . But let justice roll down like waters, and righteousness like an ever-flowing stream" (Amos 5:23–24).

The prophets also reminded Israel of her covenant relationship with Yahweh and her duty to fidelity. Israel was not to chase after false gods. The prophet Hosea compared his own marriage to the spiritual marriage of Yahweh and Israel. Hosea's wife, Gomer, was unfaithful to him just as Israel had been to Yahweh. Through his passionate story of betrayal, Hosea calls Israel to return to the way of life prescribed by the covenant relationship.

The prophet Micah offered a simple message of what God really expects of his people: "Do justice, and . . . love kindness, and . . . walk humbly with your God" (Mic 6:8). Though simple, it is also a challenging message.

QUESTIONS FOR DISCUSSION

1. What would be the difficulties or challenges of being a prophet?
2. Who might be some prophets of our own time? What is their message?
3. What prejudices or "old notions" do they unmask?
4. What might the term "hard-heartedness" mean today?
5. What injustices remain part of our reality today?
6. How can art, media, poetry, or movies awaken our sensitivities?

Discipleship

As the covenant provided Israel with the motive for observing the Law, so Jesus' example of ultimate love became the motive for all his disciples to imitate him in all aspects of their lives. Jesus' disciples became known as "the people of the way" because their way of life was centered on him. Imitation of the lifestyle of Jesus became normative for the Christian moral life. Christians hold that the center of discipleship is a relationship with the risen Christ, and this relationship influences how disciples live, the decisions they make, their attitude toward life, and their very character. It is as if Christ supports them from their past and draws them to a new future in God.

Conversion to discipleship can be sudden and abrupt, such as Saint

Paul's conversion in chapter 9 of the Acts of the Apostles, or a slow and lifelong journey of faith. However and whenever this conversion happens, it involves the transformation of the whole person, affectively, intellectually, morally, and religiously. The biblical term for conversion (*metanoia*) means "change of mind or regret," an about-face after discovering one is traveling in the wrong direction, and it is often used to describe this graced transformation with God.

The *Didache* ("teaching" or "instruction"), a short, first-century instructional manual on morals and church practice, describes this total conversion as a choice between two ways: the way of life and the way of death. The way of life is described: "First love the God who made you; secondly, your neighbor as yourself. Do not do to another what you do not wish to be done to yourself" (*Didache* 1). This beautiful summation of Jesus' words to love God above all things and your neighbor as yourself puts it in the context of a choice to be made and a community of faith where it is lived out. Twenty centuries later, Christians still make this choice through which every aspect of life is changed and directed toward relating with Jesus Christ in the community of believers.

QUESTIONS FOR DISCUSSION

1. Describe a time when you totally changed your mind about a decision or lifestyle with which you had been involved. Was it sudden or gradual?
2. What changes have you experienced in your personality or spiritual outlook on life since you started grade school? High school? College?
3. Who has had an important influence on your decisions or inspired you to do something special?

WHAT RESOURCES ARE AVAILABLE?

Magisterium, Sensus Fidelium, and Theology

This section will describe the teaching authority of the Roman Catholic Church, known as the *magisterium*; the source of moral theology, known as the *sensus fidelium*; and the discipline of theology in order to answer the questions: What or who is the Church? How can the Church help Catholics to make moral decisions? How does the Holy Spirit guide the Church today?

The Catholic Church teaches that scripture and tradition form one source of revelation. The two are considered one source because tradition is understood as scripture in the ways it is lived, prayed, and proclaimed in the life of the faithful community. The followers of Jesus Christ, the early church, wrote the Bible, and Catholics believe that the Church today continues to keep the word of scripture vital in the contemporary Catholic community.

There are many models, or ways of describing what the church is and how it functions. Through the centuries of church history, the church has been known as the following:

1. Institution with a hierarchical authority and administration
2. Prophet to the world
3. Servant of all God's people
4. Missionary
5. Mother
6. Body of Christ
7. Teacher
8. Community of disciples
9. Temple of the Holy Spirit

The Second Vatican Council described the Church as "The People of God who share in Christ's priestly, prophetic, and kingly offices" (*Dogmatic Constitution on the Church* 9). In each of these models, the Church serves as a source and a guide for moral decisions and for developing moral character. It is in the role of teacher that the Church exercises its authority as a source for the formation of Christian conscience. In the Catholic Church, this teaching authority is called the *magisterium* (Lat., *magister*—"teacher").

The Catholic Church is responsible for proclaiming and living the "good news" of Jesus, the final command or sending forth: "Go therefore and makes disciples of all nations, baptizing them in the name of the Father and of the Son and of the Holy Spirit, and teaching them to obey everything that I have commanded you" (Matt 28:19–20; cf. Mark 16:15). The Catholic Church maintains that the pope, and the bishops in union with the pope, are responsible to teach authoritatively on faith and morals with unique prerogatives. The *magisterium*, which the Church believes is aided by the Holy Spirit, helps protect the Church from errors. Either a worldwide gathering of bishops, called an ecumenical council, or the pope, as head of the bishops, can exercise ultimate doctrinal or moral authority in rendering a definitive judgment on a particular question. When the pope defines a dogma of faith, he is said to speak *ex cathedra*—"from the chair," meaning he is speaking in his authority as successor to Saint Peter, the first pope. The most recent pronouncement of such an extraordinary statement is the teaching about the Assumption of the Blessed Virgin Mary, defined by Pope Pius XII in 1950. Other examples of ordinary teaching authority include the sixteen documents generated by the Second Vatican Council, pastoral letters of bishops' conferences, encyclical letters of the pope, or bishops' pastoral letters to their own dioceses.

The presumption of truth in the Church's teachings is based on faith that it is the Holy Spirit who guides the Church and will not allow the Church to turn away from God or to self-destruct. Since the Second Vatican Council described the Church as "the People of God," we understand that the Holy Spirit guides popes, bishops, and lay people. The Church believes that the people of God have been gifted with an instinct or "sense" about moral truth called the *sensus fidelium*. Vatican II taught:

> The body of the faithful as a whole, anointed as they are by the Holy One, cannot err in matters of belief. Thanks to a supernatural sense of the faith which characterized the People as a whole, it manifests this unerring quality when from the bishops to the last member of the laity, it shows universal agreement in matters of faith and morals. (*Dogmatic Constitution on the Church* 12)

Because the Church believes that the Holy Spirit is present in the entire people of God, the *sensus fidelium* is a source for moral decision-making that complements and includes the magisterial authority of the Church. The *sensus fidelium* is understood not as a majority vote or a public opinion poll but as a charism of the Holy Spirit moving the Church toward truth. The authority of the Church, therefore, is found in scripture and tradition expressed in the *magisterium* and the *sensus fidelium*.

The question remains as to how to use these sources to make a moral decision. With regard to obedience to authority, one must avoid two extremes:

1. Unquestioning obedience where people are more comfortable under the guardianship of others; the motto here would be "Just tell me what to do." While assent of faith and respect for the wisdom of authority are true virtues, blind obedience is not the same as making a moral decision. Moral choice always involves a personal decision.

2. Rejection of authority—the opposite of unquestioning obedience. This is not a sign of maturity but rather a sign of adolescent behavior. For people of reason informed by faith, the acceptance of authority does not mean the abandonment of reason. As people of faith, there are situations when we assent to a mystery, even when understanding is not possible.

The Church teaches that the balanced and mature way of using authority as a guide for making moral decisions is to respect the wisdom of the Church and combine Church teachings with the other sources: scripture, natural law, the *sensus fidelium*, empirical sciences, and theology. Church teachings are available to the public and can be found in such sources as the sixteen documents of Vatican II or the *Catechism of the Catholic Church* (1994). These magisterial sources form a foundation for making decisions on many issues.

The process of applying the universal values included in these sources to specific decisions that challenge us today is the work of moral theology. Theology is the science that studies and speaks the good news to each new generation in terms and ways that are meaningful. A theologian is a degreed professional who writes or teaches about the faith, describing the foundations of faith for diverse audiences and investigating implications of the faith for the way we live. New moral situations and challenges emerge as medicine, technology, and global societies continue to develop. Issues not yet even dreamed of will confront us tomorrow. Today, we can clone animals; tomorrow, humans? Today we can map human genes; tomorrow, re-engineer them? What we will be able to do might not be what we should do. Moral theology will offer help in making those decisions.

Even though most people are not official "moral theologians," one can use the same method to make moral choices. To do moral theology, even in everyday life, is to consult all the sources of reason and faith. For the Catholic, these include scripture, natural law, *magisterium*, *sensus fidelium*, empirical sciences, and theology. One can then ask the questions: What if? What else? How? When? Students of moral theology can gift others with their understanding, so they too can come to the necessary freedom in God to make their decisions well. The study of moral theology at the college level is not only for the student but also for others, a gift to the Church and to society.

RECOGNIZING MORAL ISSUES

Recognizing moral issues can be a challenge. We are surrounded with realities that often numb us into complacency. In society, issues such as war, poverty, immigration, or child abuse seem so overwhelming that we might feel any individual effort we attempt would be insignificant and futile. In scientific and medical advances, many issues are morally controversial—stem cell research, fertility and reproductive technologies, and so on—and most of us lack the professional expertise to decide for ourselves the value and the goodness of such progress. Living in a fast-paced world of ever-changing politics, economics, social values, and scientific and medical breakthroughs can dizzy us. Ignoring the issues or even insulating ourselves from them may seem easier. Students often explain that they consider reading or watching the news to be a depressing waste of time. They feel that because they cannot solve the issues, they would rather not be confronted with them. Ignorance of contemporary issues seems to create a more manageable personal life. After all, why should we invest personal concern, time, or emotions in problems we cannot solve?

Remember what was said previously: insulating myself from moral challenges that surround me is, in fact, a decision. It is actually a decision to live a life where the other person's problems are not my problems. We are all in it for ourselves. The attitude of "You work on your problem, I'll work on mine" is a characteristic of individualism so woven into the fabric of our contemporary society that it can be a stumbling block to true moral living.

A primary challenge to moral living, then, is to live with eyes and hearts wide open to the realities of the world of yesterday and today and to the possibilities of tomorrow.

Faith traditions, including Christianity, have rich histories of leading people to holiness in and through the challenges of daily life. Christians call this "incarnational living." Christians believe that this means that the ordinary and the extraordinary events of our life can be made holy because Jesus Christ became part of our human reality, embraced it, and transformed it into God's reality. To become fully human, therefore, requires a moral decision by each believer to be aware of the needs, hopes, dreams, possibilities, fears, and pain of other humans and the world we share. Christians call this decision "Christian intentionality." However, it goes beyond all faith traditions. Natural law theory, at the same time, would argue that it is a universal imperative placed on all humanity. This universal imperative—to be human—is integral to incarnational living and to Christian intentionality. Admitting the interdependence of all humanity is a first step in moral living.

When I admit that I am a part of a living, breathing, human community, I have awakened my "moral imagination." The next step is to inform myself with what is happening in the world, for better or worse. Moral issues can be found as close as my classroom, dorm, family, sorority, fraternity, or campus, or as far away as the Middle East, Africa, Latin America, Asia, and now, outer space, beyond the planet Earth. For example, "Star Wars" missile defense systems; satellites of all kinds (where would television and cell phones be without them?); space junk; and proposed colonies on the moon are some of the everyday issues in the news that will not be going away. In fact, they will only increase.

Moral issues, moreover, go further. Moral issues are also political, economic, medical, or sexual. Moral issues are present in the bedroom and the boardroom, the media and advertising, banks and food pantries, universities and preschools. What might I do? The daily newspaper might be a good place to begin a personal confrontation with the real world, but even here, some critics of journalism would remind us that the reporting of news involves moral decisions about what information to include or exclude, which nuances to add, and so on. Therefore, no news is pure information. With that caution in mind, I can continue with the news as a starting place: What are the headlines? What stories have been deemed by the editorial staff to be worthy of our intellectual and emotional energies? The wars in Afghanistan, Iraq, and the Middle East; conflict in Africa; acts of terrorism; child abductions; airplane crashes; wildfires; global warming; political disputes; economic trends; scientific breakthroughs; acts of heroism.

Turn then to the sports section. What stories have been included along with the statistics of winners and losers? Allegations of misconduct by players, coaches, officials; bribery or betting scandals; performance-enhancing drugs. Who is deemed worthy of admission into a hall of fame? Who are our true sports heroes?

Now turn to the entertainment section. Check the movies that are playing. What do they say about society's appetite for violence, sex, deceit, or decadence? Are there some movies that challenge us to explore new ways of viewing reality or that open our eyes to the needs and tragedies of people? What entertains us or makes us laugh? Slapstick has amused us for many generations, but is it at the expense of respect for a particular race, gender, or creed?

Turn to the business section. Money is never morally neutral because it involves the human being who needs it, earns it, spends it, shares it, invests it, saves it, and so on. Businesses are deemed moral or immoral depending on how they affect the lives of workers, stockholders, CEOs, managers, and consumers. Dishonesty, greed, or corruption can topple the smallest or the mightiest corporation, affecting the lives of countless people. Mergers, takeovers, and acquisitions might seem objective and carefully calculated but can involve the often-hidden human expense of loss of jobs; diminishment of income; destruction of pensions and insurance coverage; uprooting of families; and changed lives, sometimes for the better and sometimes for the worse. Economic and business decisions can improve the quality of life for many people or line the pockets of the exclusive few.

Turn to the comics section. Some of the wisest philosophers of our day share their profound insights in the form of a comic strip. Many have taken on the issues of honesty, fidelity, and friendship and the consequences of deceit, selfishness, laziness, pride, and so on. Their pithy wisdom and often-humorous look into our own humanity make this the first section of the paper many people open each day. Here, we see our own moral dilemmas unmasked. We can relate to Garfield's sloth and gluttony or Lola's disregard for speed limits and traffic lights. A successful comic strip is one that helps us see ourselves. Comics are valuable moral material as we humorously examine what makes us "tick" and how we choose to become a certain sort of person.

The local or university newspaper is a valuable, but not exclusive, tool for broadening our moral imagination. Internet, television, radio, magazines, and periodicals add to our sources of moral issues. While we might not have the energy to address a study of every issue confronting humanity, there are times when we are personally challenged to deal with a specific moral dilemma. For example, honesty is a moral issue in politics, economics, business, entertainment, sports, and so on. There are ramifications of honesty or dishonesty at the international, national, or local levels of all human endeavors. Sometimes, honesty can be a personal issue in the classroom, in research, or in personal relationships.

What would I do if . . . ?

This incomplete question can frame the scenario for many decisions a student might encounter. Try these examples. What would I do if someone offered me a copy of an exam I was scheduled to take tomorrow? What would I do if I needed an "A" to get into graduate school, and the only way I could be sure to get it was to take answers into the exam room by writing them on my hand or on hidden notes? What would I do if I saw someone else doing this? What if I could save money on cable access or Internet access by splicing wires and "sharing" with my next-door neighbors? Most of these scenarios involve personal integrity and might be guided by conscience, but what if the issue seemed more complex and required information and guidelines from sources other than a personal sense of right or wrong?

Let's take a high-visibility example on campus that affects the school and its reputation. What if I am an athlete on scholarship? There are many demands on my time and energy. My grades were good enough to get into college, but keeping up my GPA has been a challenge. I feel a sense of responsibility to my team and my school to stay eligible to play. Traveling to "away games" creates academic challenges. I miss Thursday and Friday classes almost every time we travel. I get notes and the instructor cooperates, but it is tough to grasp the information and the concepts. If I do not do well on midterms, my career on the team and my scholarship are in jeopardy. Teachers have accommodated my absence from midterms by sending the exam with a proctor who will let me take the test on the bus or in a hotel room. They all trust me to be honest, but the pressure is on. I have a responsibility to my team, my school, and my family. It would be so easy to use notes of some kind to help me get the grade I need. So much is riding on this that I am confused as to the right thing to do.

Certain questions and sources should inform my decision. What are the facts here? What is my GPA? What have I needed to do in order to maintain it? What are the team and school rules for administration of exams off campus? What is the likelihood of being discovered using unauthorized assistance? What would be the consequences of being discovered? How prevalent is such activity? What are the consequences if I do poorly on this exam? What are the consequences if I lose my scholarship? What would be the consequences for the team if I were discovered? Will the whole team be held suspect? These are all real questions and concerns for such a decision. When asking so many questions, I feel like a detective and a lawyer, but decisions have ramifications for myself and society. Detectives and lawyers try to raise questions that are important and significant, but how do they find answers?

The Bible offers stories about people who needed to make difficult decisions. The Bible also puts forth both honesty and responsibility as important virtues. Warriors and great leaders are praised for their cunning in securing favorable outcomes in difficult situations. The point seems to be that God helps those who help themselves. At the same time, other stories praise those who put their trust in the Lord during times of insecurity and self-doubt. Some stories seem to say that honesty is its own reward, even if the results are undesirable. Is the Bible saying it is okay to do whatever it takes to meet one's responsibilities, or is it saying that one's greatest responsibility is to be honest at all costs? These values may seem to be in conflict in life. How can one choose both when these values seem mutually exclusive? Even the Ten Commandments include a prohibition against deceit but also a command to honor one's mother and father. The moral dilemma seems to be whether living up to so many expectations justifies cheating on an exam.

Seeking wisdom in this difficult decision, I could turn to the natural law, believing it to be inherent to human behavior. What is the essential human obligation in this situation? What do reason and my conscience tell me? My conscience would bother me if I referred to unauthorized notes in order to do well on my exam. Maybe I could rationalize my way out of guilt feelings. Maybe those feelings of guilt would haunt me even though I would be glad to stay on the team and keep my scholarship. Would I be able to live with myself?

Does my faith tradition, my church, offer any advice that might help me here? I remember my pastor once noting how difficult it is to maintain integrity in today's complex world. I remember a religion teacher who once said that how we reach our intended goal does matter. From what I remember, it seems that the decision is either moral or immoral depending on the integrity of the intention, the means, and the circumstances. The result might be desirable but wrong because of the means used. This all seemed so useless and academic when we discussed it, but it makes sense now. If I use notes on a closed-book exam, even if I intend to accomplish something important to me and other people, I will go against my integrity. I cannot use dishonest means to meet my responsibilities in this situation. Cheating is not the answer to my moral dilemma. The situation worries and frightens me, but I know this is my decision for now—to try my honest best and face the consequences with whatever courage and hope I can muster.

Some decisions are difficult and complicated. We might even question a decision and wonder if we made the right choice, the "good" choice. How do we know if we have made the best decision? That is difficult. Sometimes, only time will tell. Sometimes, if new information becomes available, we might need to change our mind about a decision. If a person has truly sought the sources of moral wisdom, has reflected and (if the person is a believer) prayed about a decision, chooses what to do, and then discovers it was the wrong choice, he is free to change his mind and make a new choice, but he need not be troubled with guilt for his original decision. As people of reason, we can only stand where we are and make decisions with the resources available to us. In addition, people of faith believe in a God who understands human limitations and forgives people's failings. Integrity before God is a matter of people living life as best they can. Morality is a lifelong journey of discovering and choosing the good.

Suggested Activities

1. Research Rosa Parks and her courageous refusal to cooperate with racial segregation on public transportation in the 1950s.
2. Watch the movie *Romero*, the story of Bishop Oscar Romero of San Salvador, who was martyred for his refusal to cooperate with military oppression of the poor and landless natives.
3. Volunteer at a soup kitchen or shelter. Take time to listen to the stories of the people there.
4. Read the Acts of the Apostles, chapter 9, to discover what it means to be "knocked off your high horse." What does that expression mean today? Describe a time when you might have been "knocked off your high horse."

Questions about the Text

1. Explain how Christianity is a way of life.
2. What does it mean to be a person of reason informed by faith?
3. Describe the role of character development in making moral decisions.
4. What is natural law, and how does it inform one's conscience?
5. What are the two extremes to be avoided in using scripture as a source for moral theology?
6. Explain the role of the "voice of the prophet" in forming individual and communal conscience.
7. Distinguish between "conscience" and "superego."
8. Explain two kinds of knowledge necessary for moral decisions.
9. What are the three aspects of any act or decision that must be considered as one is evaluating the act as moral or immoral?
10. What is the *magisterium*, and how does it serve Roman Catholics as a source for moral theology?

Questions for Discussion

1. How do you know when you have made a good decision?
2. Whose opinion do you seek when you make an important decision?
3. What role do you think obedience to authority serves in making moral decisions?

For Further Study

Ashley, Benedict M., and Kevin D. O'Rourke. *Ethics of Health Care: An Introductory Textbook.* 2nd ed. Washington, DC: Georgetown University Press, 1994.

This text on medical ethics from a Christian perspective includes case studies and reflection on the meaning of health care.

Bohr, David. *In Christ a New Creation: Revised Catholic Moral Tradition.* Huntington, IN: Our Sunday Visitor, Inc., 1999.

This introductory summary of contemporary Catholic moral teaching offers good sections on the history of moral theology and good use of encyclicals and the *Catechism of the Catholic Church.*

Callahan, Sidney. *In Good Conscience: Reason and Emotion in Moral Decision Making.* San Francisco: Harper Collins, 1991.

This text deals with aspects of conscience, including the place of personal emotions in making moral decisions.

Catechism of the Catholic Church. Part III, *Life in Christ.* Washington, DC: U.S. Catholic Conference, 1994.

This section of the official Catholic catechism summarizes Catholic ethics, from its foundations to its many specific teachings.

Crossin, John W. *What Are They Saying about Virtue?* Mahwah, NJ: Paulist Press, 1985.

This text is a good summary of the meaning, interpretation, and place of virtue in ethics.

Gomes, Peter. *The Good Book: Reading the Bible with Mind and Heart.* New York: William Morrow & Co., 1996.

Gomes's book provides an overview of historical critical methodology for biblical interpretation on issues of race, women, homosexuality, and anti-Semitism and deals with the use and abuse of scripture in these and other moral issues.

Gula, Richard M. *What Are They Saying about Moral Norms?* Ramsey, NJ: Paulist Press, 1982.

This is a comprehensive introduction to fundamental aspects of moral theology.

Hamel, Ronald P., and Kenneth R. Himes, eds. *An Introduction to Christian Ethics: A Reader.* Mahwah, NJ: Paulist Press, 1989.

This is a collection of articles on many aspects of moral reasoning from a Christian perspective with good contributions on the use of scripture as a source of conscience formation.

O'Connell, Timothy E. *Principles for a Catholic Morality.* Rev. ed. San Francisco: Harper & Row, 1990.

This thorough examination of a systematic moral theology includes conscience, natural law, scripture, sin, and virtue, with good attention to pastoral and spiritual implications.

O'Keefe, Mark. *What Are They Saying about Social Sin?* Mahwah, NJ: Paulist Press, 1990.

This text is a discussion of what is meant by social sin and a discussion of the challenges it poses for ethics.

Spohn, William C. *What Are They Saying about Scripture and Ethics?* New York: Paulist Press, 1984.

This short, easy-to-read summary of contemporary theologians' views of scripture serves not as a rulebook for Christian morality but rather as a context for attitudes and dispositions of the Christian heart such as, for example, response and discipleship.

from the REFERENCE LIBRARIAN

The Synoptic Outline—Moral Issues

The vast array of possible research topics on moral issues includes specific ethical issues (e.g., abortion, employer hiring practices, plagiarism), individuals or groups who are of historical or contemporary significance in the area of ethical thought (Mahatma Gandhi, Martin Luther King Jr., Greenpeace), or specific ethical concepts or various approaches to ethics (virtue, deontological ethics, feminist ethics).

We could give many other examples of possible topics in moral theology, but the goal of this textbook is to help you become an independent learner, to seek out and find what interests you as you learn, and to give you the skills to learn how to continue to learn all your life.

An encyclopedia might help you in your quest for a topic. Encyclopedias often provide a feature that, at a glance, will give you an idea of the specific subjects covered (within the subject scope of the encyclopedia) while at the same time providing a list of possible topics for research. This feature goes by various names, such as "synoptic outline of contents," "list of entries by category," "topical list of entries," and so on. Whatever the name, this feature always provides a list of broad subject categories under which the various individual articles relating to that broad subject are listed. Such a simple step lets you begin to dialogue with the entire tradition in this field.

Let's see how a synoptic outline can be used. To demonstrate, I will use a portion of the "List of Entries by Category" in volume three of *Ethics* (ed. John Roth, listed in the reference bibliography). This list organizes the encyclopedia's 1007 entries into 31 categories.

LIST OF ENTRIES BY CATEGORY

Society for the Prevention of Cruelty to Animals, 1393

Vegetarianism, 1543

Vivisection, 1564

World Society for the Protection of Animals, 1607

(From *Ethics*, ed. John Roth, Rev. ed., vol. 3, Pasadena, CA: Salem Press, 2005.)

Let's take the very first category listed—"Animal Rights." Note that all of the types of topics mentioned earlier are included among the fourteen articles listed, for example, specific ethical issues ("cruelty to animals," "vivisection"), individuals and groups ("Peter Singer," "People for the Ethical Treatment of Animals"), and ethical concepts and approaches ("Animal rights," "Moral status of animals"). You can observe not only what topics might be available but also cases where you might want to examine more than one article for the same topic (e.g., animal rights, moral status of animals).

If the encyclopedia you are using does not have a synoptic outline of contents, try using the encyclopedia's index to explore possible research topics; this works best if you have some idea of what interests you, unless you want to browse through the entire index. It would be helpful to know already that you are interested in, for example, animal rights. In this case, the index of *Ethics* has not only several entries under "Animal rights" but also several other entries containing the word *animal* that might suggest an idea for a topic ("Animal research," "World Society for the Protection of Animals").

TIP

If the encyclopedia you are using has neither a synoptic outline nor an index, try a different encyclopedia.

Another feature of encyclopedias that is often ignored is the cross-references to other relevant articles that appear in addition to the bibliography at the end of the article. Notice the cross-references appearing at the end of the article on the "Moral Status of Animals" in *Ethics*:

SEE ALSO: Animal consciousness; Animal research; Animal rights; Endangered species; Environmental ethics; Nature, rights of.

(From *Ethics*, ed. John Roth, rev. ed., vol. 2, Pasadena, CA: Salem Press, 2005.)

Note that some of the cross-references to other articles in the encyclopedia may not have appeared anywhere we have looked previously (e.g., "Endangered species" is not listed under "ANIMAL RIGHTS" in the "List of Entries by Category," although it does appear in the index under "ANIMAL RIGHTS").

TIP

Use cross-references to identify additional encyclopedia articles relevant to your topic.

Expanding Skill Key #1 by Using Skill Key #2

So far in each chapter of this textbook, in accordance with Skill Key #1, you have been given the titles of encyclopedias whose scope is appropriate for the subject of each chapter. At this point, you are ready to start identifying relevant encyclopedias on your own (if you choose to do so; remember, you can always ask the librarian to help you identify relevant encyclopedias). The way to identify encyclopedias exploits what we have learned about subject headings and keyword searching. If you look at the catalog record of any of the encyclopedias mentioned thus far, you will notice that "Encyclopedias" usually appears as a subheading following the main subject heading. For example, the *Encyclopedia of Early Christianity* has the subject heading "Church history, Primitive and early church, ca. 30–600 Encyclopedias." (Sometimes, "Dictionaries" is also used, especially in the case of reference works more like what we have been describing as "concise dictionaries.") Knowing this, we can do a keyword search with some broad term related to a topic we are interested in (unless you just happen to know the correct subject heading) combined with "Encyclopedias," which we now know is used in subject headings as a designation for this kind of reference work. For example, to see what encyclopedias that include coverage of ethical issues your library owns, try entering the phrase "ethics AND encyclopedias" as a keyword search in your library's catalog. (Remember that the use of "AND" in a search statement means that all of the search terms must be present in items retrieved.)

The following titles might be among those retrieved.

Title	Encyclopedia of science, technology, and ethics / edited by Carl Mitcham.
Published	Detroit, MI : Macmillan Reference USA, c2005.
Description	4 v. (cxiv, 2378 p.) : ill., maps ; 29 cm.
Bibliography	Includes bibliographical references and index.
Subjects	Science—Moral and ethical aspects—Encyclopedias. Technology—Moral and ethical aspects—Encyclopedias.

Author	Roberts, Robert North.
Title	Ethics in U.S. Government: an encyclopedia of investigations, scandals, reforms, and legislation / Robert North Roberts.
Published	Westport, CT: Greenwood
Description	xix, 367 p. : ill. ; 25 cm.
Bibliography	Includes bibliographical references and index.
Subjects	Political ethics—United States—Encyclopedias. Political corruption—United States—Encyclopedias.

Title	An encyclopedia of war and ethics / edited by Donald A. Wells.
Published	Westport, CT: Greenwood Press, 1996.
Description	ix, 539 p. ; 25 cm.
Bibliography	Includes bibliographical references and index.
Subjects	War—Moral and ethical aspects—Encyclopedias. Just war doctrine—Encyclopedias.

Notice that while "ethics" may appear anywhere—in these examples, either in the title or the subject heading—"Encyclopedias" consistently appears in the subject heading and indicates an encyclopedic reference work.

One kind of question that often comes up when students research ethical issues is how to find material presenting both pro and con arguments. Unfortunately, there is no way of searching by subject, and no efficient way of keyword searching, to find specifically "pro" or "con" books in the library catalog. Let's see why that is.

If you look at records for the titles in the bibliography from the article on "Moral status of animals" referred to above, you will discover a number of useful subject headings, including the following:

Subject heading	Subdivision ("moral and ethical aspects")
Animal experimentation	Moral and ethical aspects
Animal rights	Moral and ethical aspects
Animal welfare	Moral and ethical aspects
Vivisection	Moral and ethical aspects

The subdivision "Moral and ethical aspects" also appears in the catalog records for both the *Encyclopedia of Science Technology and Ethics* and *An Encyclopedia of War and Ethics*. Librarians call this type of subdivision a "floating" subdivision; that is, it can be used with various subject headings. This means that you can often find this phrase used in a subject heading for a book on the moral or ethical aspect of many topics: politics, public policy, economics, science, business. In short, it can be found in any subject with a moral and ethical component. Are you interested in the moral aspects of abortion? Try "Abortion—Moral and ethical aspects." Genetic engineering? Try "Genetic engineering—Moral and ethical aspects." What about the ethics of writing books? Try "Authorship—Moral and ethical aspects."

[Note: "Religious aspects" is another floating subdivision that may be useful when researching the ethical aspects of an issue. When the "religious aspects" covered in the book are those of a specific religion, there will be an additional subdivision for that religion, for example, "Abortion—Religious aspects—Christianity," "War—Religious aspects—Judaism," and so on.]

Now look at the following library—catalog records, both of which share the same subject heading: Animal welfare—Moral and ethical aspects.

Author	Rodd, Rosemary.
Title	Biology, ethics, and animals / Rosemary Rodd.
Published	Oxford [England]: Clarendon Press; New York: Oxford University Press, 1990.
Bibliography	Includes bibliographical references and index.
Subjects	Animal welfare—Moral and ethical aspects. Animal rights. Bioethics.

Author	Scully, Matthew.
Title	Dominion : the power of man, the suffering of animals, and the call to mercy / Matthew Scully.
Published	New York, NY: St. Martin's Press, 2002.
Bibliography	Includes bibliographical references (p. [399]–421) and index.
Subjects	Animal rights—Moral and ethical aspects. Animal welfare—Moral and ethical aspects.

What do you think Matthew Scully's position might be on the question of animal rights? Rosemary Rodd's? How do you know? The only hints come from the words used in the respective titles, words like *suffering* and *mercy*.

Author	Leahy, Michael P. T., 1934–
Title	Against liberation: putting animals in perspective / Michael P.T. Leahy.
Published	London; New York: Routledge, 1991.
Bibliography	Includes bibliographical references (p. 260–265) and index.

Subjects Animal rights.
Animal welfare—Moral and ethical aspects.

The same subject heading appears—"Animal welfare Moral and ethical aspects"—but this time, the title seems to express a point of view opposed to that of Matthew Scully's book. If you had used a keyword search combining the terms *animals* and *liberation* to retrieve this record, thinking that *liberation* might be a good word to use to find a "pro" animal rights perspective, you would be disappointed in this case because "liberation" appears after "against"; the entire phrase thus denotes precisely the opposite of what you are looking for. This is one reason why keyword searching is often inexact. This is a problem we have already encountered in the discussion of searching the Internet in chapter 5. You would still have identified a "con" author, but that's not what you were looking for by combining keywords such as *animals* and *liberation*.

TIP

The important thing to remember is that the subject heading will be the same regardless of an author's point of view. Nevertheless, the advantage of using the subject heading is that you know exactly what the book is about (i.e., pro or con, it is about animal welfare as an ethical issue). You must examine the information about the book in the library catalog or the book itself to determine whether the author is "pro" or "con."

As you continue to read and explore the further sources that you find using the research techniques we have described, you will begin to learn who is "pro" and who is "con." More importantly, you will begin to absorb the overall contours of the debate, develop an understanding of what the debate is about, and learn what the substantive issues are, not just who is on which side of an issue. In a word, you will start to become an educated person.

To sum up, subject headings are helpful, but they do not do everything. The use of subject headings helps to ensure that a book is actually about the topic you are researching, but subject headings cannot inform you in advance of an author's point of view.

In this chapter, we have expanded our library skills in a number of ways:

SKILL KEY #1

Use the library's catalog to locate sources of information.

a) Use a subject-specific encyclopedia to acquire specialized knowledge about a subject.
b) Use a subject-specific encyclopedia whose scope is appropriate for both your topic and the approach you want to take to that topic.
c) Use encyclopedia bibliographies to identify subject headings for your topic.
d) Use a concise subject-specific dictionary to look up the specialized vocabulary of a particular field.
e) Use an encyclopedia's index to locate information on subjects (including persons) for which there is no separate article.
f) Examine the synoptic outline of contents (or however it is designated) in an encyclopedia (1) to get a quick overview of the contents and (2) to get topic ideas for research.
g) Use an encyclopedia's index to get ideas for research topics.
h) Use cross-references to locate additional relevant material in an encyclopedia.

SKILL KEY #2

Use the library's catalog to locate sources of information.

a) Use subject headings to locate precisely books on your topic.
b) Use subject headings whose scope fits your topic as closely as possible, then adjust your search with a broader or narrower subject heading as necessary.
c) As an alternative to using encyclopedia bibliographies, use keyword searching to identify subject headings for your topic.
d) Combine one or more subject headings in a search to retrieve books on a topic for which no single subject heading exists.
e) Use the floating subdivision "encyclopedias" in combination with a keyword to identify encyclopedias on a subject.
f) Use the floating subdivision "moral and ethical aspects" to identify material, whether "pro" or "con," related to the ethical aspects of an issue.

Student Tasks

1. To see what encyclopedias that include coverage of ethical issues your library owns, try entering the phrase "ethics AND encyclopedias" as a keyword search in your library's catalog. How many encyclopedias relevant to ethics can you locate in your library catalog?
2. Try the same technique to find encyclopedias on subjects we have already encountered ("Bible AND encyclopedias," "theology AND encyclopedias"; how would you search for an encyclopedia where you might find material on Christology? Ecclesiology?).
3. Locate a synoptic outline of contents in any encyclopedia. Look up the article on a topic suggested to you by the outline.
4. Find an encyclopedia article on a topic in moral theology. After you have identified subject heading(s) for that topic, use those subject headings in combination with the subheading "Moral and ethical aspects" and see what results you get.
5. Use the same subject heading with the subdivision "Religious aspects." Are there further subdivisions indicating particular religions? Judging by the titles, how do the books you retrieve with the "moral and ethical aspects" subdivision seem to compare with the books retrieved with the "religious aspects" subdivision? Do any titles appear with both subdivisions in the catalog record?

Social Justice: Gospel Witness and Mission of the Church

J. A. Wayne Hellmann

from the EDITOR

Christian theology teaches that Jesus revealed God's love for us in a tiny area of the world about seventy miles long, stretching from the Sea of Galilee to the Dead Sea. It is a trip most bicyclists can make in one day, yet Jesus preached in word and deed the reign of God that encompassed all of human experience. In Jesus' time, when "neighbor" meant someone from one's own religious, tribal, or ethnic group, Jesus told the simple and astonishing parable of the Good Samaritan, a shunned outsider who stopped and cared for the beaten man lying on the lonely, winding road and even paid for the man's lodging and medical bills. With that parable, Jesus exploded all borders, limits, and excuses, proclaiming that our neighbor is everyone we encounter.

Nowadays, those who are our neighbors can be far removed from the house next door. We encounter people not only by physical presence but also through information resources, such as television, cell phone, digital news, the Internet, and newspapers. Followers of Jesus are challenged to expand their hearts to include all the neighbors whom they encounter: the rich and poor; those who work seven days a week (including children) and still cannot feed their family; those who take jobs in hazardous conditions, exposed to toxic materials or subject to working conditions without safety features; those ravaged by slave trade, war, famine, tsunamis, hurricanes, the AIDS pandemic, environmental degradation—the list goes on and will only increase in our lifetime.

For Jesus, the call to love as God does means all humans are inextricably involved in every life. Our hearts, according to Jesus, can expand to encompass all. Furthermore, if people love so that they can even include the unthinkable—their "enemies"—then love has no limits. That is what Jesus did and demonstrated to his followers.

We will not find the phrase "social justice" in the Gospels, but Jesus preached it in the terms of his times. For Christians, social justice relates to Christian spirituality, the way in which Christians live out their particular relationship with God. Christians are called to take responsibility to direct resources in a Christ-like way while also being aware of and responsible for their global connectedness to others. This is love in action and is what the community called "church" is all about. As church, and as individuals who comprise the church, Christians are called to probe this concept of social justice. The stakes have never been higher or more involved. By his example, Jesus gave hope that all people can love the world, regardless of arbitrary borders and boundaries.

OVERVIEW

Let's look at a historical snapshot of why social justice is so important to Christians today. Since the advent of the nineteenth-century industrial revolution in Europe, there has emerged within the Church an increasing consciousness of the plight of the poor, initially of the workers who were deliberately abused by an economic system that did not provide them with an adequate salary. The twentieth century witnessed the masses of poor in new and underdeveloped nations who had suffered the tragic consequences of recent colonialism. Foreigners had come into their land, stolen their natural resources, and crushed their culture and way of life. Two world wars in the twentieth century caused the most massive destruction of human life ever known. Also, in the latter part of the twentieth century in the United States, evils of racism that deprived black people of civil rights became even more apparent. At the beginning of the twenty-first century, simply in order to survive, masses of humanity, especially from the southern hemisphere, are forced to migrate to strange and cold places in the North where they are often not welcome.

The majority of these millions suffer not because of natural disasters of floods and earthquakes but because of economic, political, and military decisions made by their fellow human beings. The decisions of a minority in positions of power and excessive influence exclude a great majority of human beings from the economic and social benefits of life in the human family. As a consequence, they have no recourse to meet their basic human needs. Tragically, this reality separates human beings from each other more and more.

In response to the gospel in these new situations, the popes, bishops, teachers of social sciences, and theologians have attempted to move the Catholic community and all men and women of good will to acknowledge and then to address these appalling social evils. They have provided the necessary leadership to step back and reflect on these new social realities in the light of the gospel teachings of Jesus. Their purpose was to draw attention to the needs of our next-door neighbors and the millions who suffer through no fault of their own, and to articulate gospel principles as a basis for responding to their agonizing cry. The result is that a new body of Catholic social teaching has grown and developed over the last 125 years.

This new and ever-developing teaching of the Catholic Church has shifted from emphasis on charity for those in need to an intentional focus on ways to correct unjust social situations. As a result, the Church has moved away from its traditional support for the established social order and has become an active agent for social change. It no longer simply makes moral appeals to the rich and powerful to be more generous, but it encourages all members of society, including the poor themselves, to work for the reform of social and economic structures that oppress and deprive people of their basic human dignity. Catholic social teaching is a new development in the 2000-year tradition of Catholic teaching, and it forms the basis for social action now known as social justice.

The foundation for this new social teaching remains rooted in the ancient biblical teaching of the Jewish and Christian Scriptures, especially in the teaching and example of Jesus as found in the four Gospels, for example, the Beatitudes (so named because of the first word, "blessed"), in Matthew 5:3–12 and Luke 6:20–26. Catholic social teaching interprets and applies the teaching of Jesus to today's complex world, including encouragement for needed actions and decisions for change. Unless the followers of Jesus take responsibility for the structures of society that oppress others, how do they love their neighbor? The great commandment Jesus gave to his followers remains unfulfilled. Catholic social teaching simply attempts to help followers of Jesus implement that great commandment. The Church's mission to serve the human family now explicitly and consciously includes commitment to overcome unjust social and economic structures that cause the suffering of so many.

The following discussion is theological and concerned primarily with the Catholic social justice tradition. However, the discussion presupposes that doing justice is always in cooperation with other religious communities, groups, and organizations.

The essay has two parts and a theological reflection. The first part asks and examines what it means in today's world to be a witness of the gospels and a follower of Jesus. Pursuit of this question moves toward a reflection on the Beatitudes as found in the Gospel of Matthew, as well as a review of how Christians throughout the centuries have responded to Jesus' teaching in the Beatitudes. The second part of this essay reflects on the new consciousness of the mission of the Church, which is to search for new and effective approaches to social justice and to confront directly the reality of social sin. The essay then moves toward an overview of contemporary Catholic social teaching and to an enumeration of eight principles for social justice that emerge from this overview. Finally, the essay concludes with a short theological reflection on what all of this might mean for the spiritual life of a follower of Jesus.

GOSPEL WITNESS

Following Jesus

What does it mean to follow Jesus in the world today?

The Christian vocation is simple: it is to follow the example and the teaching of Jesus. Following him leads to the way of his cross, where his followers are invited to share in the pouring out of his life for others, that is, in his suffering, death, and ultimately his Resurrection. A life of gospel witness proclaims the "good news" that all are loved. A disciple or follower of Jesus is first called to know him, to follow him, and to experience a profound mystery of God's love. Christian discipleship is based on the new law of love that embraces the whole human family and knows no limits. Why? Because in the Gospels, Jesus proclaims a salvation that extends "to the ends of the earth" (Acts 1:8).

In the acceptance of the new law of love, every Christian is called in the name of Jesus to witness to the dignity of every human person, to foster the vocation of every human person, and to live in respectful relationship to and within the whole human community. To follow Jesus as a disciple demands a faith that trusts totally in God's plan for the salvation of all, a hope that empowers difficult practical decisions and sustains a perseverance that moves society toward a more just world, and ultimately a love that makes all members of humankind truly brothers and sisters (see the *Compendium of the Social Doctrine of the Church* 3).

In 1971, the College of Catholic Bishops articulated a strong statement that the pursuit of social justice on earth is at the heart of the gospel message and the mission of the Church: "Action on behalf of justice and participation in the transformation of the world fully appears to us as a constitutive dimension of preaching of the Gospel, or, in other words, of the Church's mission for the redemption of the human race and its liberation from every oppressive situation" (*Justice in the World* 6). The key word in their statement is *constitutive*. In their bold statement, the bishops argue that there can be no living or preaching of the gospel message that does not follow through with "action on behalf of justice." This clearly means we are not following the example and teaching of Jesus if we have no care or concern to liberate others "from every oppressive situation."

John Paul II not only reaffirmed this position of the 1971 Synod of Bishops but he also developed it. He emphasized that "action on behalf of justice" is essential to the mission of the Church. He proclaimed "concern for human beings, for their humanity, for the future of the human race on earth and therefore also for the direction of the totality of development and progress—to be inextricably linked to the Church's own mission and an essential element of it" (*Redemptor Hominis* 15). Both of these statements are important in the more recent development of Catholic social teaching, for they offer a new manner of interpreting the gospel and explain in a more profound way what it means to be a disciple of Jesus. In today's world, the gospel is not about preserving the current social order. Rather, for the sake of and out of love for one's neighbor, the gospel demands that the followers of Jesus work together for social change.

In the twenty-first century, the power of the gospel message and the mission of the Church marvelously merge in wholehearted commitment to the struggle for human dignity, that is, for greater human freedom and for liberation of those oppressed by poverty, exploitation, and abuse of any kind. This means those who follow Jesus must take responsibility for all aspects of human development and progress. Any scientific, economic, military, or social progress that oppresses human persons rather than liberates them must be critiqued, challenged, and changed. This implies, of course, that those who do so must be competent to address the ever more complicated and technical issues that shape our world.

An important step toward further understanding of what it means to follow Jesus in today's world is the emergence of a new concept: the preferential option for the poor. This phrase was first used by the Latin American bishops in 1979, and the U.S. bishops identified it as a central feature of their 1986 pastoral letter, *Economic Justice for All.* And again, in his 1987 encyclical *On Social Concerns*, Pope John Paul II developed this same concept of "a preferential option for the poor." This means the "rightness" of social structures, of economic policy, and of ever-increasing military investment must all be examined from the perspective of the poor, the marginalized, and the powerless. As members of society, people must always ask questions about the decisions made by those in positions of responsibility for society. How do specific policies or administrative structures affect children, the aged, the sick, single mothers, immigrants, refugees, minorities, the homeless, victims of natural disasters, victims of war, and the peoples of underdeveloped poor nations of the world, for example?

In order to answer this question, Pope John Paul II teaches it is first necessary to "stand with the poor"; that is, explicitly and experientially, he invites the followers of Jesus to cross the bridge that separates the wealthy few from the massive majority on suffering and forgotten margins. One must always listen to them and in some way share in their experience. John Paul II suggests that only in this way can one learn how the poor are affected by the decisions of political or economic powers. He boldly proclaims that the follower of Jesus must experience the suffering of the poor in order to know how "to organize socio-economic life . . . in such a way that it will tend to bring about equality between people, rather than putting a yawing gap between them" ("Address to Bishops of Brazil," 1980, 135).

For those in the United States, this first means the widespread cultural bias toward the rich must be overcome. In the United States, economic policy, politics, media, and ambition are built on worship of the "rich and famous." Action for social justice must be countercultural, giving priority and attention to the poor. This priority runs counter to the so-called "American dream" that emphasizes wealth, power, and individualism, but it moves toward the heart of the gospel message of simplicity, humility, and solidarity.

It is not that poor people are better than rich people; it is rather that the world's poor live in misery, and their basic human needs are not met. John Paul II connects "preferential option for the poor" and "action for social justice" when he speaks of the "duty of solidarity." Solidarity is "the shared and multilateral commitment toward effective action" that will change the economic, social, cultural, and political "ways of doing things" that perpetuate the structures that oppress the poor and marginalize the weak. According to John Paul II, new inclusive structures and new forms of cooperation are necessary so that the poor may participate in decisions that affect them.

Solidarity with the poor, the pope writes, is not a "vague feeling of compassion or shallow distress at the misfortunes of so many people, both near and far. On the contrary," he writes, "it is a firm and persevering determination to commit oneself to the common good; that is to say, to the good of all and of each individual because we are all really responsible for all." This demands that the followers of Jesus oppose unrestrained "desire for profit" and "thirst for power." They are called for "commitment to the good of one's neighbor with the readiness, in the Gospel sense, to 'lose oneself' for the sake of the other instead of exploiting him, and to 'serve him' instead of oppressing him for one's own advantage." Only in fidelity to the gospel way of love for and service of one's neighbor can evil mechanisms and structures of sin that oppress and marginalize the poor at home and in the developing nations of the world be overcome (*Sollicitudo Rei Socialis*, 1987, #38).

The Beatitudes: "Blessed Are They . . ."

Why are the Beatitudes important?

In the previous citations on solidarity from *On Social Concern* (pp. 38–40), John Paul II draws from the Gospel of Mark 10:43–44: "Whoever wishes to become great among you must be your servant, and whoever wishes to be first among you must be slave of all." Solidarity with the poor brings us back to the Gospels. In the Gospels, Jesus teaches his disciples how they are to live and work so that the kingdom of God might be realized in this world. Many would agree that the Beatitudes are among the most important passages of the Gospels. The Beatitudes capture the vision of Jesus and the new way he interprets and applies the earlier Jewish biblical tradition.

There are two accounts of the Beatitudes. One is in the Gospel of Matthew, and the other is in the Gospel of Luke (Matt 5:3–12; Luke 6:20–26). In Matthew's Gospel, Jesus is the new lawgiver, and he ascends the mountain just as Moses ascended Mount Sinai. There he begins to teach. Matthew's account further emphasizes the solemnity of Jesus' instruction by the sitting posture he adopts, the same posture taken by the great teachers in the Torah schools. In Luke's Gospel, the Beatitudes are situated in the context of prayer and the call of the twelve apostles. The Beatitudes are announced on the plain, a level playing field for all.

Both evangelists present the oldest summary of Jesus' teaching: Jesus fulfills Old Testament (OT) promises and inaugurates a new age. Notice Matthew's version:

> When Jesus saw the crowds, he went up the mountain; and after he sat down, his disciples came to him. Then he began to speak, and taught them, saying:
>
> "Blessed are the poor in spirit, for theirs is the kingdom of heaven.
>
> "Blessed are those who mourn, for they will be comforted.
>
> "Blessed are the meek, for they will inherit the earth.

"Blessed are those who hunger and thirst for righteousness, for they will be filled.

"Blessed are the merciful, for they will receive mercy.

"Blessed are the pure in heart, for they will see God.

"Blessed are the peacemakers, for they will be called children of God.

"Blessed are those who are persecuted for righteousness' sake, for theirs is the kingdom of heaven.

"Blessed are you when people revile you and persecute you and utter all kinds of evil against you falsely on my account. Rejoice and be glad, for your reward is great in heaven, for in the same way they persecuted the prophets who were before you." (Matt 5:1–12)

Luke's version follows:

> Then he looked up at his disciples and said:
>
> "Blessed are you who are poor, for yours is the kingdom of God.
>
> "Blessed are you who are hungry now, for you will be filled.
>
> "Blessed are you who weep now, for you will laugh.
>
> "Blessed are you when people hate you, and when they exclude you, revile you, and defame you on account of the Son of Man. Rejoice in that day and leap for joy, for surely your reward is great in heaven; for that is what their ancestors did to the prophets.
>
> "But woe to you who are rich, for you have received your consolation.
>
> "Woe to you who are full now, for you will be hungry.
>
> "Woe to you who are laughing now, for you will mourn and weep.
>
> "Woe to you when all speak well of you, for that is what their ancestors did to the false prophets." (Luke 6:20–26)

Matthew's version is longer than Luke's; Luke's version has four beatitudes and Matthew's has nine. Some scripture scholars would argue that the first three beatitudes found in both Luke and Matthew are the earliest and most authentic. Matthew's additional beatitudes are a further development to situate this material in the prophetic biblical tradition of the OT. His expansion of the first three beatitudes into an additional five reflects the spirit of many of the psalms and prophets, especially the prophet Isaiah:

> The spirit of the Lord God is upon me, because the Lord has anointed me;
> he has sent me to bring good news to the oppressed,
> to bind up the brokenhearted,
> to proclaim liberty to the captives,
> and release to the prisoners;
> to proclaim the year of the Lord's favor,
> and the day of vengeance of our God;
> to comfort all who mourn;
> to provide for those who mourn in Zion—
> to give them a garland instead of ashes,
> the oil of gladness instead of mourning,
> the mantle of praise instead of a faint spirit.
> They will be called oaks of righteousness, the planting of the Lord, to display his glory.
> They shall build up the ancient ruins,
> they shall raise up the former devastations;
> they shall repair the ruined cities,
> the devastations of many generations. (Isa 61:1–4)

Matthew's version of the Beatitudes can then best be read and understood in light of the prophet Isaiah. Both versions, however, draw explicit attention to the lowly, the wailing, the captives, and all who live in "the ruined cities, for the devastations of many generations." In both versions, we find the fundamental teaching Jesus gives his disciples. His mission is to those who are needy, both in the socioeconomic and in the personal and moral dimensions of life. This obviously makes demands on those who follow Jesus. To share in his mission to the poor and lowly, his disciples must be hungry for holiness. They are called to be merciful, single-hearted peacemakers and to be willing to suffer persecution. His disciples are the "oaks of righteousness" that "shall repair the ruined cities." They will be blessed because they have connected with the poor by crossing the social and economic divide to embrace them and all the alienated of society. This is discipleship. Disciples are those who share in the revolutionary stance of Jesus, who throughout his public ministry aligned himself with the poor and outcasts, and he calls his followers to do the same.

The Beatitudes through the Centuries: How Have the Beatitudes Been Lived?

In the early centuries of the Christian experience, Matthew's version of the Beatitudes was used to instruct believers in basic requirements of the Christian life. Saint Augustine (d. 430) may have been the first one to name the Beatitudes in Matthew's "Sermon on the Mount" (Matt 5). He believed these passages applied to all Christians, and he taught that the Beatitudes are "the perfect measure of the Christian life." Saint Gregory the Great (d. 604), in his *Pastoral Care*, turned to the same Sermon on the Mount to explain it was the duty of all Christians to reach out to the poor. Martin Luther (d. 1546) moved this same perspective into the Reformation. These words of Jesus are ordered to challenge every aspect of one's life, that is, one's professional or official duties and one's personal or spiritual relationship to God and others.

Concern for the poor has marked the centuries of Christianity; the many lives of the saints idealized care of the poor as God's deliberate plan of salvation. Monasteries of the early Middle Ages not only were centers of prayer and study but also contributed to the economic development of the areas around them. Monastic hospitality, however, was specifically directed to the poor. The monk voluntarily chose to become poor, and through this voluntary asceticism, he opened his heart to those who were involuntarily poor. With the arrival of Saint Francis of Assisi (d. 1223), the poor were honored as the bearers of salvation. Saint Francis recognized that Christ was not only the Son of the living God but also "a poor man and a transient who lived on alms." Therefore Saint Francis taught his brothers they "must rejoice when they live among people of little worth and who are looked down upon, among the poor and the powerless, the sick and the lepers, and the beggars by the wayside" (Armstrong and Brady, 1982). The disciple of Christ is to share the lot and the life of the poor. The poor are all brothers and sisters of Christ, and it is to them that Christ leads all his disciples.

Later in the seventeenth and eighteenth centuries, religious congregations provided hospitals, orphanages, shelters, and schools. Saint Vincent de Paul articulates this social aspect of discipleship. In his *Talks to the Daughters of Charity*, he encourages the sisters to interrupt their schedule of prayer when the poor call upon them: "If you hear the poor calling you, mortify yourselves and leave God for God. It is not leaving God to leave God for God, that is, one work of God for another." In other words, no facet of personal life or spiritual exercise can be a reason for separation from the poor.

In the twentieth-century United States, Dorothy Day (d. 1980) is an outstanding example of one who dramatically brought to life the gospel message. She saw it as imperative that the followers of Jesus participate in socioeconomic action on behalf of the deprived and the oppressed. Her life of advocacy for the poor was articulated in her newspaper, *The Catholic Worker*. Her Houses of Hospitality were open to all, and these became centers of conscious involvement in social politics on behalf of workers who were exploited as cheap labor. In her autobiography, *The Long Loneliness* (1981), she wrote that "to give what you have for relief . . . is not enough. One must live with them; share with them their suffering too" (214). Far ahead of her time, she understood what was meant by "the preferential option for the poor" and "solidarity." She was a living example of the Beatitudes. Throughout her life, therefore, she was puzzled how Catholics in the United States could in conscience tolerate the death-dealing social structures of a "filthy rotten system" that marginalizes and oppresses the poor.

SURA 30:38–39 QUR'AN

38. So give what is due to kindred, the needy and the wayfarer. That is best for those who seek the Countenance of God, and it is they who will prosper.
39. That which ye lay out for increase through the property of (other) people, will have no increase with God: but that which ye lay out for charity, seeking the Countenance of God, (will increase): it is these who will get a recompense multiplied.

Mission of the Church

Why Is Social Justice Inseparable from the Mission of the Church?

The previous section noted that "action on behalf of justice" is a "constitutive dimension" of preaching the gospel. It also stated that action on behalf of justice is the mission of the Church. John Paul II was very clear when, as cited previously, he stated, "Concern for human beings . . . the future of the human race . . . is linked to the Church's own mission and an essential element of it." *The Pastoral Constitution on the Church in the Modern World* (*Gaudium et Spes* ["Joy and Hope"]) from the Second Vatican Council also emphasized this same point. The Church's mission is to participate in defense of human rights, promote human dignity, and build up the unity of the human family. Just as gospel preaching is identified with action on behalf of justice, must not the mission of the Church, whose mission it is to preach the gospel, also be identified with that same "action for justice"? The mission of the Church is not just about salvation of souls or the holiness of its individual members. It is rather more about the salvation of the world. Jesus is not just a personal savior, but more importantly, his life, death, and Resurrection are for the salvation of the whole world. He poured out his blood for all. Thus, following Jesus and sharing in the mission of the Church must include concern about the formation of public and social order. This now includes how members of the Church relate to the earth and its resources and how they care for the heavens of outer space. It is a commitment to construct a world more genuinely human. Catholics are called to do this not by political power or ideology but by constant reflection on the signs of the times, that is, on the actual realities of the world in which they live and on the teaching of Jesus in the Gospels. This ongoing reflection gives birth to Catholic social teaching intended to help Catholics, other Christians, and all believers and nonbelievers work toward solutions for the many problems that tear apart human social relationships. It is out of this understanding of its mission to foster human solidarity that the Church's modern concept of social justice has emerged.

Social Justice

What Is Social Justice?

The first use of the term "social justice" in the Catholic Church is credited to Pius XI in 1931, though as a general concept social justice had already begun to emerge earlier in the late nineteenth century with the 1891 publication of Pope Leo XIII's encyclical, *Rerum Novarum*. Official papal letters are usually identified by the opening words of the official Latin text. In this case, the title literally means "on new things." The "new things" to which Pope Leo referred were the new social problems resulting from industrialization. After examining the situation of poor people and the workers in recently industrialized countries, he condemned employers who abused workers as "mere instruments for making money." He called for a "just wage." While upholding the right to private property, he insisted the worker receive sufficient means for meeting basic human needs, thereby rejecting radical socialism. He challenged laissez-faire capitalism, believing the economy should not function only according to the laws of the market, without oversight of the state. However, what was truly new about Pope Leo's encyclical is that he applied both the biblical tradition of works of mercy, such as feeding the hungry and clothing the poor, and traditional moral principles, beyond the simple duty of doing charitable works to the daunting task of constructing a just social order.

With this encyclical, according to theologian Richard McBrien and others, Leo XIII laid the foundation for a theology of social justice. The pope made it clear that social justice is not about rejection of wealthy people, but it is about bringing the spirit of the Gospels and the Beatitudes to the manner in which all social structures operate. Fundamentally, the social task is to develop a society in which no human being is deprived of human dignity or of basic human needs that impede the necessary freedom to develop his or her full human potential. Concern for the poor is not about feelings of compassion. It is about concrete and persevering decisions to change the social, economic, and political structures that marginalize and oppress any human person.

Why "Social"?

The Catechism of the Catholic Church defines social justice in the following manner: "The respect for the human person and the rights which flow from human dignity and guarantee it. Society must provide the conditions that allow people to obtain what is their due, according to their nature and vocation" (1930). In this definition, the emphasis is on the responsibility of all members of society to provide positive conditions in society that foster "respect for the human person." Especially after Pius XI's 1931 *Quadragesimo Anno* ("Forty Years Later," i.e., after *Rerum Novarum* [1891]), it became clearer that social justice is about the "common good" of all human persons who make up society, especially in the distribution of benefits and burdens.

All people are bound together as members of one human family and share one planet. Social life is therefore not something "added on" to human life, but it goes to the heart of what it means to live as a human being. Family and community provide the context for human growth, identity, and fulfillment. The family is "the first vital cell of society" and the place where the generations come together, and family has a social role in building up the broader human community. According to the Second Vatican Council, other "reciprocal ties and mutual dependencies increase day by day and give rise to a variety of associations and organizations, both public and private," and "this human interdependence grows more tightly drawn and spreads by degrees over the whole world" (*Gaudium et Spes* 25, 26). Multiple relationships are essential to the human experience, but they must be ordered in a way that fosters the growth and dignity of all persons.

Human life is thus embedded in a world of multiform relationships. A human life is a social life. The idea of a totally autonomous person misses the reality of what is human. The Bible asserts that, from the beginning, God created all members of humanity to be with and for each other. God created human persons "in his image, in the image of God" (Gen 1:27). Just as the revelation of three divine persons, Father, Son, and Holy Spirit, are bound in a community of love, so human persons are called to mirror that community of divine persons bound in relationship to each other by love. This was the prayer of Jesus: "That they may all be one. As you, Father, are in me and I am in you" (John 17:21).

However, social relationships do not develop automatically, out of their own doing. Social relationships require intentional choices and decisions. Actualization of mutual values and goals requires organization structured in such a way to support human interaction, foster collaboration, and provide a stable framework for humans who live and work together. A guiding principle for a just society is not simply the good of the majority. This can disenfranchise the minority of their rights and dignity. Rather, for a just society, it is the common good that must be the guiding light for all structural and organizational decisions. The Second Vatican Council addressed this principle of the common good and its complexity. One of the final documents of that council, *Gaudium et Spes*, proposed a comprehensive description of the common good:

> The common good, that is the sum of those conditions of social life which allow social groups and their individual members relatively thorough and ready access to their own fulfillment, today takes on an increasingly universal complexion and consequently involves rights and duties with respect to the whole human race. Every social group must take account of the needs and legitimate aspirations of other groups, and even of the general welfare of the entire human family. (*Gaudium et Spes* 26)

It is precisely in these multiform dimensions of social life that justice becomes vital in order to protect and foster the welfare of all members, communities, and groups within broader human society.

What Does *Justice* Mean?

Justice (Hebrew: *tsedaqah*) in the OT is identified with the nature of God and with the activity of God. The Ten Commandments establish justice in the lives of God's people. To be "just" is depicted as knowing Yahweh and imitating the divine activity of Yahweh. Ultimately, justice will prevail in the messianic reign. In the New Testament (NT), *justice* (Gk., *dikaiosynē*) is used only once in Luke and not at all in Mark, but in Matthew it is found seven times. One of these uses is in the Beatitudes, and the other six uses concern respectful relationships with the poor. In addition, John the Baptist sees Jesus as the fulfillment of all justice. The proclamation of the gospel is about justice. All in all, this means that in the Old and New Testaments, the experience of God's justice is meant to overflow into a harvest of justice in the world.

Later, in the Middle Ages, moving to the writings of Thomas Aquinas, which were based on Aristotle's *Nichomachean Ethics*, the general virtue of justice was defined as "the strong and firm will to give to each his due." According to Aquinas, justice subordinates individual human behavior to the common good. This means the good of the individual cannot be separated from the common good of the community. Three more distinctions traditionally characterize different aspects of the virtue of justice: commutative, distributive, and legal.

Commutative justice is about the relationships of society's members with one another, that is, about how they give and take with one another.

Distributive justice governs the fair distribution of benefits and burdens between a government and its people. The community is to assure the basic rights of all members of the community, especially the needy. *Legal* justice governs the responsibilities of citizens toward the state. Social justice includes all of the aforementioned characteristics, but it goes beyond these three dimensions. Social justice moves beyond the individual person or the manner in which a social group operates. It looks deeper and more comprehensively into the multiple structures that shape human relationships, including the environment and all living creatures.

So then, what is justice? The U.S. bishops refer to it as doing "what is right." Martin Luther King Jr. went to the heart of the matter when he commented upon the difference between "just" and "unjust" laws. He said, "Any law that uplifts the human personality is just. Any law that degrades human personality is unjust" ("Letter from the Birmingham Jail," 1963). Finally, the Irish bishops were plainspoken about the matter:

> Justice is about my work, my business, my commercial dealings, my style of life. Justice is about paying a fare wage for a job, and doing a just and honest job for the wage. Justice is about buying and selling. It is about employing men and women or making them redundant. Justice is about meeting my contracts, promising and delivering what I promise at the promised time. Justice is about fair prices and just profits. It is about honesty and truthfulness and straight dealing in business, in public service, in political life.

How Is Sin Social?

We have seen that since the time of Pope Leo XIII at the end of the nineteenth century, greater awareness of the need for justice in all social structures has developed. It is now more clearly understood that the reality of sin is therefore not only personal and private but it is also somehow much broader. Theologians have reflected on the injustices facing the millions of poor people in the developing world and in modern industrialized urban areas, and they realized that the common traditional notion of sin is too narrow and individualistic. Sin, they insist, is more than personal acts of disobedience, dishonesty, laziness, lust, greed, or envy. Evil caused by social interactions or by social factors rooted in human institutions is also sinful, for example, sweatshops, child labor, toxic dumping, and unsafe working conditions, to mention only a few. This implicates sincere and good persons who, by their uncritical acceptance and support of such institutions, indirectly cause the suffering of others. Thus people who may personally and individually be moral and good people and have no intention of inflicting harm on others often share in a collective guilt called "social sin."

Some theologians have linked this insight to the doctrine of original sin because social sin attests to solidarity in sin. In some sense, social sin is an inherited reality. All of us inherit the unjust social structures into which we are born. Sin goes beyond the acts of a simple individual to permeate the collective action of all the members of community. Saint Paul addresses this issue in the NT books of Corinthians and Romans. He speaks of the world and the reign of sin. He writes that sin enslaves humanity because the rulers and spirit of the age oppose God. Although

MARTIN LUTHER KING JR., 1962 SERMON

"Any religion that professed to be concerned about the souls of men and not concerned about the city government that damns the soul, the economic conditions that corrupt the soul, and the slum conditions, the social evils that cripple the soul, is a dry, dead do-nothing religion in need of new blood."

Saint Paul does not use the specific term "social sin," he understood that some kind of collective sin is found in groups and in communities.

Why? Some of us find advantages in social structures that at the same time cause disadvantage to others, for example, tax structures, salary structures, and access to health care. This biblical appreciation of social sin was revived shortly before and again after the Second Vatican Council. The Council itself alluded to sinful structures that make a society unjust. John Paul II again went even further. He said that social sins are the "collective behavior of certain social groups, big or small, or even of whole nations or blocks of nations" (*On Social Concern*, n. 65). However, he maintained that unjust collective behavior of social groups ultimately remains the responsibility of persons. Social sin becomes personal sin of individuals through complicity, indifference, or reluctance of those in a position to exert influence for change who do not do so. John Paul admonished those who "take refuge in the supposed impossibility of changing the world" and who "sidestep the effort and sacrifice," and thus make "social sin" their "personal sin" (*On Social Concern*, n. 65).

The development of even further understanding of social justice in society has led to greater awareness of the social sin that stands behind sinful structures. This calls for social conversion. The first step, and often most painful step, toward social conversion is the need to unmask unjust realities that hide behind legitimized structures or institutions. The followers of Jesus are to oppose sin in all forms and manifestations. To bring into light of day the dark and hidden unjust realities of commonly respected social institutions goes to the heart of what it means to work for social justice. This is why social justice is about both personal and social conversion. This demands a high price, but the followers of Jesus remember his teaching: "Blessed are those who are persecuted for righteousness' sake" (Matt 5:10). To be effective, however, drawing public awareness to hidden social sins of respectable institutions must be done in a manner that does not condemn but invites conversion and embrace of the gospel.

A clear example of social sin in the United States is the racism that has permeated the social fabric of U.S. life from its origin. Racism predated the founding of the United States. When initial social structures in the new republic were formed, racism in the form of slavery was accepted by the founding fathers as a given social reality. This social sin was already present in those who settled the United States, and they sealed this sin into the structure of U.S. life. The social structure of slavery provided profit for the economy and furthered the development of the nation. Many people enjoyed the economic benefits that flowed from a social system based on the oppression of those who had been abducted from their African homeland. So it is easy to understand why the U.S. court system, in the Dred Scott decision of the court of St. Louis, declared that black people were property that could be bought and sold. Even after the abolition of slavery, the social sin of racism continued to marginalize black persons and deny them access to work, education, and housing.

In this horrible social sin, most generations of Americans have been uncritical active accomplices (*What Are They Saying about Social Sin?* 58–75). It took Rosa Parks (d. 2005), a seamstress who in 1955 refused to give up her seat to a white person on a public bus, to unmask the sin of the accepted social and legal structure that relegated her to the back of the bus. When she sat down where it was not permitted for black persons to sit, she stood up to an unjust system. At that moment began a social conversion known as the civil rights movement, which can rightly be called work for social justice. Confession of this social sin of racism was an important step forward for Americans to begin to make their society more just and more accepting of others. When we begin to see in new ways, we also begin to see more. When we see the injustice of such an example, we often see more than we thought. For example, a follow up question must be asked: Will Americans ever acknowledge and come to terms with that other social sin prevalent in the founding of their country—yet untold crimes against Native Americans? The list may go on and into other circumstances of social sin in our history.

Social Teaching

What Is Meant by "Catholic Social Teaching"?

Pope Leo XIII stands out as a giant. He is the one who provided the starting point for what is now more than a century of Catholic social teaching. He was the first to emphasize the radical primacy of human dignity and human solidarity and use these as basic moral criteria for evaluating the validity of political, social, or economic policies and structures. The pope proclaimed a firm "no" to those who attempted to privatize religion and to those who espoused an excessive individualism at the expense of the broader community. This was his "yes" to the gospel message and to the example of Jesus. His Magna Carta for justice was his encyclical letter *Rerum Novarum*, already mentioned. Over more than one hundred years, subsequent popes up to and including John Paul II have continued to develop and apply the principles of human dignity and human solidarity to criticism of emerging social, political, and economic situations. There has thus developed within the Catholic tradition of the last hundred years a body of literature known collectively as "social teaching." The *Catechism of the Catholic Church* defines social teaching: "The teaching of the Church on the truth of revelation about human dignity, human solidarity, and the principles of justice and peace; the moral judgments about economic and social matters required by such truth and about the demands of justice and peace" (2419–2422). John Paul II reflected on this further when he described Catholic social teaching:

CALL TO JUSTICE IN WORLD FAITHS

Christianity "In everything do to others as you would have them do to you; for this is the law and the prophets." (Matt 7:12)

Islam "None of you shall be true believers unless you wish for your brother the same that you wish for yourself." (Sunnatt)

Judaism "That which you do not wish for yourself you shall not wish for your neighbor. This is the whole law: the rest is only commentary." (Talmud, *Shabbat* 31)

Taoism "The successes of your neighbor and their losses will be to you as if they were your own." (T'ai-Shang Kan-Ying P'ien)

Buddhism "Do not offend others as you would not want to be offended." (Udanavarga 5:18)

Hinduism "Everything you should do you will find in this: Do nothing to others that would hurt you if it were done to you." (Mahabharata 5:1517)

Confucianism "Is there any rule that one should follow all of one's life? Yes! The rule of the gentle goodness: That which we do not wish to be done to us, we do not do to others." (Analectas 15:23)

> Nor is it an ideology, but rather the accurate formulation of the results of a careful reflection on the complex realities of human existence, in society and in the international order, in the light of faith and of the Church's tradition. Its main aim is to interpret these realities, determining their conformity with or divergence from the lines of the Gospel teaching on man [sic] and his vocation, a vocation which

> is at once earthly and transcendent; its aim is thus to guide Christian behavior. It therefore belongs to the field, not of ideology, but of theology and particularly of moral theology. (*On Social Concern*, 44)

Thus Catholic social teaching looks to gospel teaching to form the moral foundation for the Catholic approach to questions of social justice. It assists the disciple in the ongoing task of reflecting on the challenge of Jesus in the Sermon on the Mount and in discerning what it means in a consumer, technological, and globalized society to be poor in spirit and to embrace the sorrowing and the lowly. The whole body of social teaching moves forward from the conviction that every aspect of human endeavor, although having distinct and unique operative principles, is accountable to moral scrutiny. The call of the gospel is constant, and it demands continuous rethinking and reassessment of what the dignity of the human person means in the complex and ever-changing organizational structures of our society.

Although texts of papal encyclicals and of the Second Vatican Council are important for the development of the body of literature now known as the social teaching of the Church, there are many other contributions to this broad and diverse body of literature. There are documents from bishops. In this regard, the Latin American bishops (called CELAM for *Conferencia del Episcopado Latinoamericano*) took the lead, beginning with their conferences at Medellin (1960) and Puebla (1979). There are two important documents from the North American National Conference of Catholic Bishops (NCCB, now called the United States Catholic Conference or USCC): *The Challenge of Peace* (1983) and *Economic Justice for All* (1986). These documents manifest an ongoing learning process. They are largely the result of a broad dialogue among bishops and specialists in social ethics and the social sciences, as well as other well-informed observers from among the people of God. There has been broad participation. This is in the spirit of the Second Vatican Council that all Christians are called to "the duty of scrutinizing the signs of the times and of interpreting them in the light of the Gospel" (*Gaudium et Spes* 4).

Broad participation in the social mission of the Church is imperative. Pope Paul VI (d. 1978) made concrete this directive to observe and examine the signs of the times:

> It is up to the Christian communities to analyze with objectivity the situation which is proper to their own country, to shed on it the light of the gospel's unalterable words . . . and in dialogue with other Christian brethren and all men of good will, to discern options and commitments which are called for in order to bring about the social, political and economic changes seen in many cases to be urgently needed. (*Octogesimo Adveniens* 4)

Thus the body of social teaching develops within broad Catholic experience in order to present an organic and ongoing discernment of gospel teaching. This discernment has given rise to three basic steps: observe the situation, reflect on the gospel, and act out of love on behalf of the oppressed.

Eight Principles for Social Justice

In a 1998 document, *Sharing Catholic Social Teaching*, the U.S. Catholic bishops highlighted a number of principles that flow out of their understanding of Catholic social teaching. What follows is based on their insights but has been developed further to accentuate several current issues important in the Church's mission of concern for the human person and the future of the human race. These can be helpful for the discernment of today's follower of Jesus.

1. **Life and dignity of the human person.** Human dignity means that all persons have worth and value. Why? The Church believes that God's likeness bears on every dimension of the human being. Created in the image of God, the human person has characteristics of God and is therefore a being intimately and essentially related to God. The human person is at the center and the summit of the created order. The origin of social life is the human person, and every expression of the social order must be directed toward the dignity and the welfare of the human person. Humans ultimately share in God's freedom, a freedom that enables recognition of what is good and the will to choose it. Human dignity is not something that humans decide. Its origin is the wisdom of God, whose love created and continues to sustain every person. Disrespect of a fellow human being is blasphemy or an attack against God. As the bishops stated, "Every human being is created in the image of God and redeemed by Jesus Christ, and therefore is invaluable and worthy of respect as a member of the human family" (Sharing Catholic Social Teaching, 1998).

Furthermore, because the dignity of the human person is rooted in the actual creation of the human person, dignity applies to every moment of human life, from beginning to end. Thus the bishops are consistent when they point out that the human person enjoys an inherent dignity from the moment of conception to natural death. John Paul II, in his encyclical *On Human Life* (n. 101), likewise taught that "unconditional respect for the right to life of every innocent person . . . is one of the pillars on which every civil society stands." Any society or civil government that fails to do this thus fails in its duty. As a result, its decrees in this regard are wholly lacking in binding force. Human dignity comes before any social structure or political power. More and more, John Paul applied this principle to questions about the death penalty and about war. With regard to the death penalty, John Paul, in his 1999 St. Louis visit, stated, "The dignity of human life must never be taken away, even in the case of someone who has done great evil." According to John Paul II, capital punishment is no longer necessary to protect society, and thus, it should rarely, if ever, be used. Concerning war, saddened by the failure of his attempt to dissuade the United States from going to war against Iraq, he simply cried out, "War is always a failure for humanity" ("Address to the Diplomatic Corps," Vatican City, January 13, 2003).

2. **Call to family, community, and participation.** Children are conceived in a relationship and have a natural right to be nurtured in the enduring and loving relationship of their parents. This helps children become capable of loving relationships. The human person is not only a "being intimately and essentially related to God" but also a being ordered to relationships with fellow human beings that extend beyond the immediate family. From the sphere of the family, one moves into participation with the broader society of the human race. Thus the U.S. bishops teach that "the family is the central social institution that must be supported and strengthened, not undermined. Furthermore, people have a right to and duty to participate in society, seeking the common good and well being of all" (*Sharing Catholic Social Teaching*, 1998).

3. **Rights and responsibilities.** The most fundamental rights are the right to life and the right to the means necessary and suitable for a full human life. This includes the right to a standard of living in keeping with human dignity. Everyone has a right to active participation in society, to share in the benefits of society, and to move between countries. The right to religious liberty and what flows from it (i.e., freedom of conscience, public exercise of faith, and the promotion of cultural tradition) is intimately connected to the right of a full human life. Religious freedom, according to John Paul II, is basic to understanding the dignity

of the human person. As the human person exists prior to the state, any state that restricts religious freedom deforms itself because it restricts human persons from expressing concretely what is deepest within them and attempts to deny that dimension of the human person that transcends the state. This is why denial of religious liberty often leads to a totalitarian state.

Rights, however, have corresponding responsibilities and duties. With the right to life comes the responsibility to foster the lives of others, especially those associations that support the family and foster human growth and economic development. This includes active support for national and international bodies that work for justice among nations and safeguard the natural environment. This duty extends far beyond the responsibility to vote; it means taking responsibility for the political landscape and for the shape of specific policies. The right to participate in society is the obligation to participate, not ideologically but critically. The right to freedom of religion is also a responsibility to respect and foster all faiths and religious traditions.

4. **The common good.** As indicated, the common good involves creating social conditions that permit all people to participate and realize their human dignity. Today, in an increasingly interdependent and globalized world, the common good involves a universal common good that creates international structures to coordinate resources and projects for the good of the human race and the care of the planet.

5. **The preferential option for the poor.** This principle has already been treated; however, it is worth noting how Peruvian theologian Gustavo Gutierrez underscored the reason for the option for the poor: "We must be committed to the poor because we believe in the God of the Kingdom. The preferential option for the poor is a theocentric option. We must be committed to the poor, not necessarily because they are good, but because God is good" (*Theology of Liberation*, 266). Thus, according to this principle, the important question to ask about policies and decisions of government and the manner of constructing society is this: How will this affect the poor? To answer this question properly, however, one must know the poor and have experienced in some way their misery and powerlessness. Today this principle urgently forces the question about the "rightness" of developed consumer societies based on surplus of goods while the remaining underdeveloped societies suffer from hunger.

6. **Dignity of work and rights of workers.** The economy must serve people, not the other way around. John Paul II said work is the key to the whole social question. Labor is not to serve capital as a tool in the productive process, but rather, capital is to serve labor. This implies not only a more equitable redistribution of income and wealth but also a more equitable redistribution of work itself in order to provide employment for all. John Paul II insisted on a just wage and other social allowances that "suffice for establishing and properly maintaining a family and for providing security for its future" (*Laborem Exercens* 3, 19). This right to work applies to the handicapped and to those forced to migrate from their homeland in order to find work elsewhere. In the eyes of the Church, all work has dignity because all work is done by human persons created by God, and as workers, they participate in the creative activity of God. Respecting the right of all persons to work "promotes an economy that protects human life, defends human rights, and advances the well being of all" (*Sharing Catholic Social Teaching*, 1998).

7. **Principle of solidarity.** The principle of solidarity became a key component of John Paul's approach to social issues. He wrote that we are all responsible for all. In *On Social Concern* (76–78), he emphasized that solidarity is the Christian virtue that "helps us to see the other—whether a person, a people, or a nation— . . . as our

'neighbor,' a 'helper' [cf. Gen 2:18–20], to be made a sharer, on a par with ourselves, in the banquet of life to which all are equally invited by God." He reflected on this principle in the light of reason and in the light of faith. In the light of reason, he taught that solidarity is the path to peace and to global human development. On the global scale, solidarity is interdependence "that in itself demands the abandonment of the politics of blocs, the sacrifice of all forms of economic, military or political imperialism, and the transformation of mutual distrust into collaboration" (*On Social Concern*, 1987, 39). This advocates solidarity among individuals and nations. On the level of faith, the pope goes further. Solidarity takes seriously the gospel command of forgiveness and reconciliation. One's neighbor must be loved, even if an enemy, even to the ultimate sacrifice: "to lay down one's life for one's friends" (John 15:13; cf. 3:16). This solidarity is the solidarity of the follower of Jesus that will bring him or her to share in the suffering of his cross.

8. **Principle of stewardship.** The principle of stewardship, that is, the careful and responsible management of something entrusted to you, is related to the principle of solidarity. Followers of Christ are called to relate respectfully not only to people as their neighbors and to the interdependent world of peoples and nations but also to the shared space of the earth, the air above, and the resources below. Interdependence applies also to the entire ecosystem. Each creature, every being of the planet, is profoundly implicated in the life and existence of every other being. This is because Christians believe that each creature and creation itself taken together as a harmonious whole was spoken by God. Human persons are created in the image of God, but every created being is a manifestation of the glory of God. The beauty of the earth invites awe, reverence, and wonder.

Saint Francis of Assisi expressed this understanding when he called all creatures his "brothers and sisters." Saint Francis realized he shared life with the earth and all that is of the earth. He believed that he, along with all creatures, whether worms, birds, or stones, came forth from the same origin, the same Father, who created heaven and earth. As the common inheritance of the human race, the earth provides for human needs. It nurtures the body with its nutrients and the soul with its awesome beauty. Thus the earth and its environment must be honored, preserved, and shared. It is not to be dominated or exploited by one group against another, including the current generations now living against the future generations not yet born. Stewardship cares and protects the earth's resources. Stewardship contains, therefore, within it the principle of sustainability. On this point, Gandhi's observation about the sustainability of the resources of the earth bears repeating: "The earth is sufficient for everyone's needs but not for everyone's greed."

SEVEN DEADLY SOCIAL SINS (M. K. GANDHI)

Wealth without work

Pleasure without conscience

Science without humanity

Knowledge without character

Politics without principle

Commerce without morality

Worship without sacrifice

CONCLUSION: SOCIAL JUSTICE AND CHRISTIAN SPIRITUALITY?

Faith That Acts to Promote Justice

"Follow me" (John 21:19) is the invitation Jesus extends to all. Those who respond to his call embrace the vision and program Jesus outlines for his followers in the Beatitudes. They take seriously the command to love God and to love neighbor and enter into dynamic relationship with Jesus. That is, they share his experience of obedience and worship of God, the Father, which is so beautifully expressed in the prayer he taught, the Lord's Prayer. In this manner, his followers receive the gift of the Spirit that transforms hearts of stone into hearts of flesh, connecting them with the human family. In this, the followers of Jesus manifest the heart of the Church's mission. They learn to share in the joy and hope, the suffering and anguish of the human family. This is what conversion and the baptismal promise of "renouncing sin" are all about: liberation from egoism, from self-seeking, and from focus only on one's own advantage. Conversion is a new and graced freedom that enables one humbly and courageously to challenge the spirit of the world that glorifies the minority of rich and powerful while dismissing the great masses of poor, suffering, and hungry. Commitment to social justice requires a faith that is not a simple conviction about a truth, the revelation of God in the Incarnation of Jesus, but rather a faith that is a personal act in which the follower of Jesus turns his or her whole life totally over to God. To do so is to respond to Jesus' invitation: "If any want to become my followers, let them deny themselves and take up their cross daily and follow me" (Luke 9:23). That is not a wooden cross but the cross of reality that Christians are called to bear each day; that is the world in which they live and in which they encounter God.

Faith trusts in the mystery of the unlimited love that God has for all. Faith justifies, heals, and makes whole in God's love. This requires great openness of mind and heart and makes possible works of justice. Faith affirms that the mystery of God's love is for all. It proclaims a love that is readiness to give from the very substance of one's life so that others too may experience and live in that love. This is the social justice that is, at the same time, response to the gospel call of Jesus and powerful experience of the communion of saints. This is the kind of faith Christians experience in the mystery of the Church, which is ever called to be a sign of God's presence in the world and an instrument of unity among all.

Works of social justice that correct the economic and social structures that divide and oppress peoples are more than doing good and avoiding evil. They look evil directly in the eye and attempt to overcome it, or at least to lessen its effects that destroy human community, depriving our neighbors of their food, their health, their families, their education, and their cultural development. Social justice challenges ravenous market systems of economics and excessive militarization of nations. It negotiates with decision makers to protect workers, environments, local cultures, and the vulnerable. Social justice is not then just charitable aid, although that too is necessary, but it is also about policies and structures that make charitable aid necessary. However, although social justice is not just charity, it begins and ends in charity. Thus, for Christians, action for justice begins with exclusion of any kind of violence because it begins with the conviction that love of God and of neighbor is undivided and excludes no one. Working for justice then ends with a profound and even mystical experience of being loved by God, a love that empowers all to love and be loved.

In fact, from a theological perspective, injustice is a denial of God. It denies the image of God in one's brothers and sisters and in the rest of creation. Social justice always rests on the fundamental and opening lines of the Nicene Creed, accepted by all Christians: "We believe in God, the Father Almighty, Creator of heaven and earth." It follows, then, that every creature and every human person shares in the power, beauty, and awesome dignity of the Creator. Social justice based on the teaching of Jesus acknowledges, and thereby worships and honors, the Creator of all. The whole body of Catholic social teaching ultimately points toward the great mystery of a God who, in the divine Being itself, is an immense dynamic communion of interpersonal love and equality among persons. Working for social justice thereby allows the followers of Jesus to be instruments of that triune love of Father, Son, and Holy Spirit overflowing into human interpersonal love and equality.

For Catholics, social justice teaching is a profound insight into two realities: into the mystery of God and into the basic unity of the human race. Both of these speak of harmony, forgiveness, and reconciliation. Both are about relationship—relationship to God, to each other, and to the gifts of the earth. Both are shaped by the Word of God and graced with a message of hope for the future.

Social justice then sends the followers of Jesus on the road of a long pilgrimage to build the kingdom of God here on earth. To remain faithful to the insight and vision taught by Jesus in the Beatitudes, the followers of Jesus must repeatedly reconstitute themselves in his own Body and Blood and renew themselves in the memory of his command to love God and neighbor. Thus, in the liturgy of the Eucharist or in the celebration of the Mass, by breaking bread and pouring wine, followers of Jesus rejoice in marvelous gifts of the earth shared by all; in the Eucharistic blessing, they believe that they themselves share in the Body and Blood of Christ, broken and poured out for all. In this radical openness, the followers of Jesus are made holy. They then bless all the elements of the earth and all their brothers and sisters, wherever they may be. In the celebration of the Eucharist, Christians extend themselves beyond their own secure worlds to the vastness and vulnerability of the human race. In 1981, Father Robert Hovda, in writing about the social experience of the Eucharist, expressed it this way:

> Where else in society are all of us called to be social critics, called to extricate ourselves from the powers and principalities that claim rule over our daily lives in order to submit ourselves to the sole dominion of God before whom all of us are equal? . . . Where else are food and drink blessed in a common prayer of thanksgiving, broken and poured out, so that everybody, everybody shares and shares alike? (Henderson, Quinn, and Larson, 1989, 79)

Questions about the Text

1. How did the industrial revolution impact the concept of social justice?
2. What does the word "solidarity" mean in this document?
3. What does "preferential option for the poor" mean and imply?
4. What does the "theocentric option" mean and imply?
5. Why are the Beatitudes important?
6. What is the meaning of commutative, distributive, and legal justice?
7. List the eight principles for social justice offered by the U.S. Catholic bishops.
8. What does the sentence "Injustice, in fact, is a denial of God" mean in the conclusion?

Questions for Discussion

1. Describe a firsthand experience of social injustice, done either to you or to someone else.
2. What are some new areas of social justice today?
3. What strategies might be considered for making one's voice for social justice heard in our world?
4. Who are the voiceless, invisible, and powerless in our world? In our city? In our households?
5. On what grounds should the Christian community be involved in public questions? How should they do this?
6. Does the separation of church and state in the United States mean that religion and religious people have nothing to say to the state? How should religion relate to the state? The state to religion?
7. What does one's spirituality have to do with social justice?

For Further Study

Introductions to the Topic

Armstrong, Regis J., and Ignatius C. Brady. *Francis and Clare: The Complete Works*. Mahwah, NJ: Paulist Press, 1982.

Burkhart, Walter, SJ. *Justice: A Global Adventure*. Maryknoll, NY: Orbis Books, 2004.

This prophetic book draws heavily from the biblical tradition of the Old and New Testaments to illustrate that biblical justice is about relationships based on covenant. The author then applies this biblical vision as the basic social ethic, especially for the critical stance necessary for evaluation of ever-increasing globalization.

Day, Dorothy. *The Long Loneliness*. San Francisco: Harper & Row, 1981.

Henderson, J. Frank, Kathleen Quinn, and Stephen Larson. *Liturgy, Justice and the Reign of God: Integrating Vision and Practice*. New York: Paulist Press, 1989.

Krammer, Fred, SJ. *Doing Faith Justice: An Introduction to Catholic Social Thought*. New York: Paulist Press, 1991.

In this manageable book, the student will find a clear, engaging, and dynamic theological reflection on basic elements of Catholic social teaching.

Church Documents

Compendium of the Social Doctrine of the Church. Pontifical Council for Justice and Peace: Liberia Editrice Vaticana, 2005.

This compendium is a resource that presents in a systematic manner one hundred years of official Catholic social teaching, mostly in the form of official texts, arranged according to various themes: principles, family, human work, economics, political life, international community, peace, and environment.

Calvez, Juan-Yves. *Faith and Justice: The Social Dimension of Evangelization*. Translated by John E. Blewett. St. Louis, MO: Institute of Jesuit Resources, 1991.

This book offers a summary of the discussion and resolution of the Jesuit General Congregation in 1975. At that time, the Jesuits rearticulated their common mission to be "in the service of faith of which the promotion of justice is an absolute requirement."

Sharing Catholic Social Teaching: Challenges and Directions. Washington, DC: USCCB, 1998.

Encyclicals

John Paul II. "Address to Bishops of Brazil," *Origins* 10, no. 9 (July 31, 1980): 135.

On Social Concern (*Sollicitudo rei socialis*). Washington, DC: United States Catholic Conference, 1988.

In this encyclical letter, Pope John Paul II develops further the earlier encyclical letter of Paul VI, *On the Development of Peoples* (1967). John Paul applies principles of economic and human development to address the widening gap between rich nations and the poor nations where the majority of human beings live.

from the REFERENCE LIBRARIAN

"Floating" Subdivisions and Social Justice Issues

We'll branch out now to research a different topic: social justice issues. You might begin by using some of the topics mentioned in Fr. Hellmann's chapter using the sources and techniques you have learned in the previous chapters. For example, you could explore the social significance of the Beatitudes by using the sources and techniques learned in chapter 3, or you could study important individuals, such as Augustine, Gregory the Great, and so on, with regard to their importance for Catholic social thought using the sources mentioned in chapter 4.

However, as Fr. Hellmann makes clear, the deliberate focus on the social aspect of Catholic theology is a fairly recent development in the broad sweep of church history. For that reason, the sources described in the previous chapter on moral theology, whose scope encompasses contemporary ethical/moral issues, many of which have a social component, may also be useful.

However, what you really need for the subject matter of this chapter is a reference tool that focuses specifically on the social aspect of ethical issues, that is, on social justice. You could, therefore, try your luck with another keyword search (Skill Key #2d), using the phrase "social justice AND encyclopedias" to see what relevant reference sources your library might have. (What keywords other than "social justice" might you use?) Your search might turn up an item such as the following:

Title	Encyclopedia of American social movements / Immanuel Ness, editor.
Published	Armonk, N.Y.: M.E. Sharpe, 2004.
Bibliography	Includes bibliographical references and indexes.
Subjects	Social movements—United States—History—Encyclopedias. Social change—United States—History—Encyclopedias. Social justice—United States—History—Encyclopedias.

(Notice the other subject headings "Social movements" and "Social change" that might give you additional points of access in the library catalog.)

None of the subject headings included in the catalog record for the *Encyclopedia of American Social Movements* (*EASM*) appears to focus specifically on the religious or theological aspects of these topics, though they could encompass coverage of such aspects along with other aspects; check the index, synoptic outline, and so on of the *EASM* to find out.

You might have noticed that none of the subject headings assigned to the *EASM* is specifically theological or religious. Remember what you learned about "floating" subdivisions in the previous chapter. You can always try to focus on the religious/theological aspect of a subject by using either "Moral and ethical aspects" or "Religious aspects" as subdivisions with any subject, including nonreligious/theological ones. Another useful subdivision for social justice issues is the subdivision "Social aspects." (Remember that a "floating" subdivision can be used with various subject headings for various topics. This does not mean that such subject headings will always be valid, but you will not know until you try them out, and neither will most librarians.) Using all the possible combinations of the three subject headings in the previous record with the three "floating" subdivisions, I was able to find the following two subject headings in my own catalog (what you find in your own library's catalog will vary depending on what your library actually owns).

Search format:

Subject heading	*"Floating" subdivision*
Social conflicts	—Religious aspects
Social justice	—Religious aspects

Even if what you find under such headings does not look promising, don't give up. Remember, you are doing research. Time and effort are often required to find what you want. The computer makes things a lot easier, but you still have work to do. What at first appears to be an unprofitable search may, in fact, prove very profitable indeed. For example, the heading "Social justice—Religious aspects" produced the following record of a book in a language most of us probably cannot read. You may recognize the author's name as one mentioned by Fr. Hellmann.

Author	Gutiérrez, Gustavo, 1928–
Uniform title	Dios o el oro en las Indias. French.
Title	Dieu ou l'or des Indes occidentales, 1492–1992 / Gustavo Gutiérrez; traduit de l'espagnol (Pérou) par Lucile et Martial Lesay.
Published	Paris : Cerf, c1992.
Note	Translation of: Dios o el oro en las Indias.
Bibliography	Includes bibliographical references.
Subjects	Casas, Bartolomé de las, 1474–1566. Indians, Treatment of—Latin America. Indians—Missions. Social justice—Religious aspects.

Even if I cannot read this book (a French translation of a book originally in Spanish), I can use the other subject headings assigned to it to continue searching. Note the subject heading "Indians, Treatment of—Latin America." If I choose to pursue that topic, I find my library catalog lists a large number of titles under that heading. In this way, you can discover both subject headings (and possible topics for papers) that might not otherwise have occurred to you and what books your library owns on the particular topic.

What do you think the subject heading would be for the treatment of Indians in the United States? We will learn more about the use of geographical descriptors as both subdivisions and as subject headings in their own right in a later chapter.

What if you need a reference tool specifically on social justice issues from a theological perspective? As always, you can consult the *New*

Catholic Encyclopedia on various social justice issues; look at the column of entries under "Social justice" in the index, for example. The two reference tools listed below, however, are dedicated entirely to social issues from a Catholic theological perspective:

Michael L. Coulter *et al*, eds. *Encyclopedia of Catholic Social Thought, Social Science, and Social Policy.* 2 vols. Lanham, MD: Scarecrow Press, 2007.

Judith A. Dwyer, ed. *The New Dictionary of Catholic Social Thought*. Collegeville, MN: Liturgical Press, 1994.

These two works will treat many of the same issues covered by the reference sources mentioned in the previous chapter but will do so from the perspective of social justice; for example, the article on abortion in *The New Dictionary of Catholic Social Thought (NDCST)* appears under the rubric "Abortion, Social Implications of."

The *NDCST* contains most of the helpful features of encyclopedic reference works we have been emphasizing, such as article bibliographies, cross-references, and an index. There is also an alphabetical "List of Entries" you can scan to identify relevant articles. The *Encyclopedia of Catholic Social Thought, Social Science, and Social Policy* contains a detailed subject index.

Let's say you want to research social justice as it pertains to economic life. Scanning through the list of entries in the *NDCST*, your eye will fall upon a number of possible research topics, ranging from such specific items as "Association of Catholic Trade Unionists" to broader areas such as "Banks and Banking," "Capitalism," "Corporations," "Economic Order," and so on.

Once you have found an article that interests you, you can proceed to use it to acquaint yourself with the topic and to collect further possible sources of information in your library catalog, as we have been describing.

One important matter to keep in mind is that social justice issues touch just about all areas of human life and endeavor, including many complex issues of science, technology, economics, business, political and military activity, and so on. As Fr. Hellmann states, many of these areas involve complex technical issues that require Christians to be "well prepared, educated, and competent to address [them]."

Thus, with respect to economics, it may not be enough just to consult an article on "Economic Order" in the *NDCST*, for example, but, to make sure that you have an adequate understanding of the economic issues involved, you may have to consult reference and other sources whose focus is from the perspective of economics. I hope by now that you have a good idea of how to get started doing research on a topic that may be unfamiliar to you (hint: start by locating relevant reference sources; enter "economics AND encyclopedias" in your library's catalog to see what your library has). The library skills you have been learning in the context of studying theology work the same way in any other subject.

Two organizations mentioned by Fr. Hellmann, CELAM and the United States Conference of Catholic Bishops (USCCB), have websites where you can find much information, including the full text of some (not all) official pronouncements or documents. (Note the .org extension on the URL, indicating the nonprofit nature of these organizations.)

http://www.celam.org

http://www.usccb.org (see especially the link to "Social Justice Issues" on this page)

However, you will discover at least one major problem with each of these websites. First, the CELAM website is entirely in Spanish (not surprising for an organization based in Latin America). The use of Google Translate (or a similar online translation service) may help somewhat.

Second, although the USCCB website does have the full text of many pronouncements, news releases, and so on, the official documents such as those mentioned by Fr. Hellmann are offered for sale only.

However, your library may own publications of both groups in its collection. Some CELAM documents have been translated into English. You can do an author search in your library's catalog using CELAM as a corporate author to see if your library owns any of them (you do not have to spell out the full name because your library's catalog should automatically refer you to the full form of the name). If your library does not own any document, remember that you can still get CELAM publications through your library's interlibrary loan service, assuming you already know the title of the CELAM document you want.

You can find publications of the USCCB using the name of that organization for your corporate author search in the library catalog. Unfortunately, the name the U.S. bishops have chosen for themselves has changed several times throughout the twentieth and the beginning of the twenty-first centuries. So, it may be possible to find listings in your library catalog under each of the following corporate author entries. The dates refer to the years when each name was used:

National Catholic Welfare Council (1919–1922)

National Catholic Welfare Conference (1922–1966)

National Conference of Catholic Bishops (1966–2001)

United States Catholic Conference (1966–2001)

United States Conference of Catholic Bishops (2001–)

Library catalogers prefer to maintain consistency in the names of both persons and organizations, so only one form of the name is used at any one time. Do you know how many ways William Shakespeare's name can be spelled? To ensure that users of library catalogs can always find his books in the catalog, only one form of "Shakespeare" is actually used, and anyone who enters an alternate spelling ("Shakspeare," "Shakspere," etc.) will automatically be directed to the form of the name actually used in the catalog.

Names of organizations can change over time—more readily than names of persons—so when searching for publications produced by a particular organization, it is necessary to know the name of the group at that particular time. You need to keep this in mind when searching for publications of the Catholic bishops in the United States.

The actual forms of names used by libraries for two of these are as follows (your library catalog should automatically direct you to these without your having to type "Catholic Church" at the beginning):

(Corporate) author
Catholic Church National Conference of Catholic Bishops
Catholic Church United States Conference of Catholic Bishops

You can also use the following forms of the names (your library catalog should automatically redirect you to the form just given):

(Corporate) author
National Conference of Catholic Bishops
United States Conference of Catholic Bishops

You may wonder why the bishops had two names for themselves from 1966 to 2001. The reason was to distinguish the bishops' actions and statements regarding internal Church matters—liturgy, priestly life, ministry, and so on—from their actions and statements regarding external matters, or relations with the secular world, such as social concerns, education, public policy, and so on. The name "National Conference of Catholic Bishops" was used for the former, while the name "United States Catholic Conference" was used for the latter. Which corporate author entry do you think is likely to be most useful in finding official publications about social justice issues for the years 1966–2001?

Fortunately, the bishops decided to do away with the dual nomenclature; the single organization name "United States Conference of Catholic Bishops" will make searching for bishops' statements in the twenty-first century a little easier. Just remember to use the correct corporate author name, depending on when the document was published.

We can now add the following to our Library Skill Keys:

SKILL KEY #1

Use the library's reference collection to begin your research.

a) Use a subject-specific encyclopedia to acquire specialized knowledge about a subject.
b) Use a subject-specific encyclopedia whose scope is appropriate for both your topic and the approach you want to take to that topic.
c) Use encyclopedia bibliographies to identify subject headings for your topic.
d) Use a concise subject-specific dictionary to look up the specialized vocabulary of a particular field.
e) Use an encyclopedia's index to locate information on subjects (including persons) for which there is no separate article.

continued

continued

f) Examine the synoptic outline of contents (or however it is designated) in an encyclopedia (1) to get a quick overview of the contents and (2) to get topic ideas for research.
g) Use an encyclopedia's index to get ideas for research topics.
h) Use cross-references to locate additional relevant material in an encyclopedia.

SKILL KEY #2

Use the library's catalog to locate sources of information.

a) Use subject headings to locate precisely books on your topic.
b) Use subject headings whose scope fits your topic as closely as possible, then adjust your search with a broader or narrower subject heading as necessary.
c) As an alternative to using encyclopedia bibliographies, use keyword searching to identify subject headings for your topic.
d) Combine one or more subject headings in a search to retrieve books on a topic for which no single subject heading exists.
e) Use the floating subdivision "encyclopedias" in combination with a keyword to identify encyclopedias on a subject.
f) Use the floating subdivision "moral and ethical aspects" to identify material, whether "pro" or "con," related to the ethical aspects of a subject.
g) Use the floating subdivision "religious aspects" to search for religious/theological aspects of nonreligious/nontheological subjects.
h) If necessary, use all the subject headings assigned to a book to identify material on a particular subject.
i) Use the name of an organization or group as an author to search for documents produced under the aegis of that group. Be aware of the possibility of changes in the group's name over time.

Student Tasks

1. Using *The New Dictionary of Catholic Social Thought* or some other encyclopedia, find an article on a social justice issue of interest to you.
2. Use the bibliography of the article you found in #1 to identify relevant Library of Congress subject headings for your topic of interest.
3. Add the following "floating" subdivisions to the subject headings identified in #2 to see what you can find in your library's catalog.

   Moral and ethical aspects

   Religious aspects

   Social aspects

   [Note: Write down the complete subject headings (with subdivisions) that resulted in finding relevant titles.]
4. Search your library's catalog to see if you can find any documents from the United States Catholic Conference. Find a document the U.S. Catholic bishops published in the 1980s.
5. See if you can find anything relevant to your topic at the website for the United States Conference of Catholic Bishops.

PART IV

THE ABRAHAMIC FAITHS: CATHOLICISM AND RELATIONSHIPS WITH JUDAISM, ISLAM

Judaism, the Jewish People, and the Church

Ronald Modras

from the EDITOR

Christianity, Judaism, and Islam share a common origin that goes back to Abraham. Theology often refers to the three "Abrahamic traditions" because all three trace their roots to Abraham in their sacred scriptures. Theologically, many questions arise about Christianity's relationship to Judaism and Islam—more questions than answers. To go further, many questions abound about all the major religious traditions. As an introductory theology text, it is beyond the scope of this book to examine the complex relations between Christianity and every major world religious tradition, but chapters 10 and 11 will examine relations with Judaism and Islam because of their Abrahamic connection and affiliation with Christianity. Doing so also provides a method for examining and understanding any other religious tradition. Additionally, the Reference Librarian skills presented in these chapters will equip readers with the research capability to delve deeper into other religious traditions.

Chapter 2 on the Old Testament (OT) provides a solid introduction to Judaism; this chapter will build on that foundation and go more deeply into some of the historical relations between Christianity and Judaism.

These two chapters demonstrate the significant role of theology in answering questions and seeking understanding about the relationship of the Abrahamic faiths. Sometimes this means agreeing to disagree until more is known. Sometimes this means inching forward by listening and learning from the faith experience of others and how they understand their experience of God with them. Why are there other religions? Probably for a million reasons. In the end, we do not have an answer to that question—we have one another, and I, for one, think that God is inviting everyone into the mystery and that one must listen carefully and in new ways. Christianity calls its members to love everyone, no matter their religion, as everyone is a neighbor and all are God's family.

This chapter examines the situation of Judaism at the time of Jesus, the developments within Judaism, events that shaped Rabbinic Judaism, traditional Jewish prayer and ritual (spirituality), modern Judaism confronting a changing world, and finally, ongoing Jewish–Christian relations. While it would be best, of course, to walk with someone from Judaism for days or weeks or even a full faith year and attend synagogue with that person, here one can at least take a step along the path to understanding the why, what, when, where, and how of Judaism. Theology is an important part of that understanding because it has a broader perspective than a single person's understanding of his or her faith.

OVERVIEW

Necessarily, as an introduction to Catholic theology and not an encyclopedia, this book cannot be exhaustive. So why is an entire chapter devoted to Judaism? Because we cannot fully understand Christianity without understanding Judaism.

With good reason, Pope John Paul II described the Jewish people as the Church's "elder brothers" during his 1986 historic visit to the synagogue in Rome. Both Judaism and Christianity, as practiced today, grew out of Second Temple Judaism, the religion practiced by Jesus and the first Christians. The Hebrew Scriptures constitute the first and longest part of the Christian Bible. The roots of the Catholic Mass are found in the prayers of the synagogue and Jewish feast of Passover. Even the most familiar words *amen* ("so be it") and *halleluia* ("praise Ya[weh]") are Hebrew words taken from Judaism. Moreover, as the latter word indicates, Yahweh, the God of Israel, is the God of Christianity. Out of reverence for that name, observant Jews do not even speak it but instead say *Adonai*, the Hebrew word for Lord. So when Christians or Jews pray, "The Lord is my shepherd," or when the priest at Mass says, "The Lord be with you," standing behind that English word *Lord* is the Hebrew name for God, *Yahweh*.

Just as Hinduism refers to the religious beliefs and practices of the people of India, Judaism refers to the religious beliefs and practices of the Jewish people. As one should expect with any people, there is a wide diversity among Jews, ranging from the devout to those who are completely nonreligious. Judaism refers to the religion of the Jewish people, but the Jewish people are also an ethnic group and, since 1948 and the modern state of Israel, once again a nation. Given their wide-ranging diversity, which will be demonstrated in greater detail, one should be wary of ever referring to the Jewish people as if they were some homogeneous entity. Their differences make it difficult to ever simply say "the Jews"—just as there is great diversity among the beliefs and practices of Christians, which makes it difficult to lump all of them together under this one term.

With a religious history that goes back more than three-thousand years, the beliefs and practices of the Jewish people have undergone significant evolution. One can see this in the pages of the Hebrew Bible itself. Dramatic changes took place after Roman armies destroyed the Second Temple in 70 CE. Jews became a diaspora people without a country, living wherever they went as a religious minority. Surviving centuries of hostility and periodic persecution, Judaism continues to evolve today as Jews address the challenges of modernity as once their ancestors addressed the challenges of worshipping without a temple.

A Christian consideration of Judaism must necessarily look at the thorny, often painful history of Christian-Jewish relations. In the two-thousand years that Jews and Christians have been relating, it was in 1965, less than fifty years ago at the Second Vatican Council, that a sea change took place. One of the beneficial consequences of that change is a more unbiased perspective of how, in the first century CE, Jews and Christians first came to see one another as alien to each other's interests. Christians, in particular, forged their identities both with regard to and in contradistinction to the Jewish people.

FIRST-CENTURY JUDAISM

Jesus was born, lived, and died a Jew, an obvious fact from the Gospels but one often overlooked. One cannot understand who Jesus was and what he was about without first understanding the Judaism of his day. Much like Judaism in our own day, it was marked by widespread diversity.

Divisions in Jewish Society

Judea in Jesus' day was an occupied nation. Under the domination of the Romans, the Jews were compelled to pay taxes to the empire or else suffer the consequences. Those unable to pay had their property confiscated and, when that was gone, they lost their freedom. Slavery was at the heart of the empire's political-economic system, enforced by state-sponsored terror. Any slave who attempted to run away, as well as anyone tempted to rebel against Roman rule, faced the likelihood of capture and condemnation to a slow, agonizing death by crucifixion. Crosses were a regular feature of the landscape in Roman-occupied Judea.

For the sake of peace and order, the Romans did not interfere with the religious practices of the peoples they subjugated, so they allowed Jews to continue offering sacrifices at the Temple in Jerusalem (rebuilt after the return from exile in Babylon in the sixth century BCE and splendidly ornamented by Herod the Great in the first century BCE). They also permitted Jews to manage their own internal and religious affairs by way of a Supreme Council or *Sanhedrin*, with the high priest of the Temple at its head. Controlling the Sanhedrin were the Sadducees, a small group of leading priests and wealthy aristocrats. It was from their numbers that the Roman governor selected the high priest, recognizing that the Sadducees were committed to the status quo, which is to say the survival of the Temple, the Sanhedrin, and their own favored position.

Jews in Jesus' day worshipped not only at the Temple in Jerusalem but also in synagogues, gathering places for the reading and study of the Torah, the first five books of the Hebrew Bible. Attributed to Moses, the Torah was often referred to simply as "the Law" because of the hundreds of commandments it contains. The Pharisees were a movement focused on understanding and interpreting the Torah to achieve holiness through exact observance of God's commandments. Emerging about a century before the time of Jesus, the Pharisees viewed it as the vocation of every male Jew to live as if he were a priest, presiding at the most everyday, ordinary meal as if it were a sacrifice. The Pharisees developed these ideas in an oral tradition of Torah interpretation (the so-called "oral Torah"); this included belief in an afterlife, which, remarkably enough, receives no mention in the written Torah. The more conservative Sadducees rejected the oral Torah and the Pharisees' belief in an afterlife as innovations. As one can imagine, there was no love lost between the two groups.

Also prominent in the first century were a number of groups that engaged in armed resistance against the Romans. The most prominent of these were the Zealots, who formed about 67–68 CE (during the Jewish War) and quickly became the dominant group. Originating in Galilee shortly before the time of Jesus, armed resistance groups were consumed with a sense of religious outrage that God's chosen people were being compelled to take from the fruits of their holy land and pay taxes to the heathen Romans. They considered this no less than a blasphemy that called for violent resistance; to lead them in that struggle, they looked for a military leader like their great king David, eleventh century BCE, as the promised messiah. These armed resistance groups abhorred the Roman occupation and just as much, if not more, the Sadducees and Jewish tax collectors, whom they saw as collaborators. Though in the view of the Romans they were dangerous revolutionaries and terrorists, these groups considered themselves freedom fighters for the cause of God.

A fourth faction was a group of radically pious Jews called the Essenes, not mentioned in the Gospels but better known today because of scrolls discovered near the ruins of a monastery at Qumran on the shore of the Dead Sea. From these Dead Sea Scrolls, we learn that the

Qumran community also detested the Sadducees for their collaboration with the Romans. They regarded the Temple leadership, and in some instances Jewish society altogether, as corrupted. They were sure that the time was coming soon for a cosmic confrontation between good and evil, more specifically, between righteous Jews and idolatrous pagans.

Yeshua ha Notzri

All of these various groupings within first-century Jewish society were sure that theirs was the right way of doing God's will in response to the Roman occupation of Israel. Amid this welter of diverse Jewish opinion came Jesus of Nazareth (*Yeshua ha Notzri* in Hebrew) and his movement out of Galilee. Nonviolent but in essence more revolutionary than the Zealots, Jesus preached a countercultural way of life that he described in terms of an impending "reign" (which can also be translated as "empire") of God. He drew the contours of this way of life from the Hebrew Scriptures and its faith in a God who cares about widows and orphans, a Jewish way of describing the most marginal and defenseless persons in a patriarchal culture. He called for trusting in a God who provides "daily bread" and for imitating God's compassion by forgiving debts and even enemies.

Like his fellow Jews, Jesus focused on life here and now ("on earth as it is in heaven"). When he and his followers came to Jerusalem for Passover (a freedom festival), Pilate, the Roman governor, and the Sadducees had reason to be apprehensive. Jesus was from Galilee (a hotbed of armed resistance movements), preached about an "empire of God" (an alternative to the Roman Empire), and was popular with the Jewish masses. If not a revolutionary, he was perceived as close enough to being one and, in any case, clearly a potential troublemaker. Nonviolent resistance is still resistance. With the collaboration of the Sadducees, Pilate had him executed.

Jesus was but one among countless Jews who died as victims of Roman terror. He would have been forgotten, not even a footnote in history, had it not been for the fact that his disciples began experiencing him as raised up, exalted at "God's right hand." The Jesus movement did not die out with Jesus' death but instead exploded as his former disciples experienced what they understood to be the power and presence of God (described as God's "Holy Spirit," another symbol drawn from the Hebrew Scriptures—e.g., it is God's Spirit who "inspired" the prophets).

JEWISH CHRISTIANITY

Under the influence of this power and presence, the Jesus movement saw itself as gifted with prophets who spoke in the name of the risen Jesus. But how should they describe him? By what titles? During his lifetime, Jesus appears to have been called *rabbi* ("teacher") and "a prophet," but now, in a community filled with teachers and prophets, those titles were not enough. The Jesus movement began referring to him as "Messiah" ("Anointed One" in Hebrew, a metaphor for "King"), *Christos* in Greek. A word that in Jesus' lifetime would have denoted a sword-wielding king like David was now used to describe the Risen One "enthroned" at God's right hand. Jesus had become "the Christ," and his followers came to be called Christians.

Not surprisingly, this new community drew regularly from the rich symbolism of its Jewish heritage. They baptized new members into their community and partook of a common meal they called the Lord's Supper, but they were all still Jews, observant of the Mosaic laws, circumcising their male children, and worshipping at the Temple. Their fellow Jews accepted them as Jews, despite their peculiar belief that Jesus of Nazareth had been exalted after his death and was God's Messiah. For Jews then, as in our own day, religious beliefs mattered but not so much as practice.

So long as they maintained observance of the Mosaic laws, their fellow Jews tolerated the Jewish Christians as just one more sect or faction within Judaism. However, when Gentiles began professing faith in Jesus and asking to become Christian, the inevitable question of whether these Gentiles had to be circumcised before they were baptized arose within the nascent church. In other words, did they have to become Jewish before becoming Christian? No, answered Paul of Tarsus, himself a former Pharisee. The question was a crucial one for the early church, and contentious. Nevertheless, Paul's thinking eventually prevailed, and he became the "apostle to the Gentiles."

Because of Paul's answer to the question of Christian observance of the Mosaic laws, the church went on to become increasingly Gentile and less Jewish. Only because of that answer could Christianity become the world religion it is today. However, Paul agonized over the fact that, while Gentiles were accepting Jesus as the Messiah, his fellow Jews were not (Rom 9:2–3). Why that was the case, he ultimately left to the inscrutable and mysterious will of God (11:33). Nevertheless, of one thing he was sure: though his fellow Jews rejected Jesus as God's Messiah, God had not rejected them. Jews were still heirs of God's promise, "for the gifts and the calling of God are irrevocable" (11:29).

The Christian church originated within a first-century Judaism that was fractured into diverse, competing, and mutually antagonistic groups. The Pharisees were further divided into two major schools of Torah interpretation: the followers of Rabbi Shammai contending with those of Rabbi Hillel. The resistance fighters were also divided among themselves, as became clear when their long and eagerly awaited rebellion against Rome finally broke out in the Great War (66–70 CE).

At the beginning of the war (66 CE), the Jewish Christians fled Jerusalem, an act viewed by other Jews as disloyalty to Jewish national aspirations. By the year 69, the Roman legions had retaken the countryside and laid siege to Jerusalem. Internal fighting among the revolutionaries weakened the resistance, and in the summer of the year 70, the Romans finally breached the walls. Jerusalem and the Temple were demolished, and perhaps as many as a million Jews perished. In Rome today, one can still see the Arch of Titus depicting Roman legions carrying the Temple's massive seven-branched candlestick in triumph as the spoils of war. Neither Judaism nor Christianity would ever be the same.

RABBINICAL JUDAISM

The destruction of Jerusalem and the Second Temple saw the demise of the Sadducees, Zealots, and Essenes. The priestly class no longer had an altar on which to sacrifice. Among the competing factions within first-century Judaism, only two groups survived: Christians and Pharisees.

Judaism without a Temple

The story is told of Rabbi Yohanan ben Zakkai, leader of the Hillel school of Pharisees. Shortly before the fall of Jerusalem, he had himself smuggled out of the city and went to Vespasian, the general of the Roman legions. Yohanan knew Vespasian would soon become emperor, and Vespasian knew that the Hillel school of Pharisees was opposed to the rebellion. At Yohanan's request and for the sake of restoring order in Judea, Vespasian allowed the Hillel Pharisees to gather in the village of Jamnia (Yavneh), west of Jerusalem. There the Pharisees set about recreating Judaism without a Temple.

The task was daunting but not impossible because the Pharisees had already developed a way of life centered on the Torah and synagogue. Observance of the Torah and its commandments would serve to substitute for Temple sacrifices. As to the challenge of interpreting the Torah and its many commandments, the Pharisees already had an oral tradition of interpretation that went back for centuries (the oral Torah). Now that they dominated Judean religious life, the Pharisees were in a position to make those interpretations official. They came to be called *rabbis*.

Judaism after 70 CE was much more defensive than it was before. The rabbis at Jamnia felt compelled to impose uniformity upon Jewish thought and practice. Perhaps as early as the year 80, they inserted a prayer into the synagogue service (into the *Shemone Esreh*) that called upon God to punish the *minim* ("heretics"). There is no doubt that this was meant to include Jewish Christians and was tantamount to excommunicating them from the synagogue. Jews and Christians began viewing each other with animosity as hostile outsiders.

It is at about this time that the Gospel according to Matthew was written, its description of Pharisees marked by a bias more commensurate with the church's situation in 80 CE than of the Jesus movement in the year 30. In the same Gospel, we find the Christian interpretation of the destruction of Jerusalem. Under the influence of the Torah's teaching that God punishes misdeeds with calamity (Deut 28:15–68), the rabbis themselves agonized over what terrible sin Israel could have possibly committed to warrant the destruction of its Temple a second time. Influenced by the same assumptions, Christians concluded that the calamities of the year 70 must have been divine punishment for the death of Jesus: "His blood be on us and on our children!" (Matt 27:25). Jesus had been the victim of Pontius Pilate and the Roman occupation of Judea with the collaboration of the much-despised Sadducees. Based on the destruction of Jerusalem and the Temple, however, Christians came to place the blame for Jesus' death almost exclusively upon Jews, primarily the Jewish leadership but by extension all Jews who refused to accept Jesus as the Messiah.

In 135 CE, the Romans put down another Jewish rebellion. Thousands more Jews lost their lives by believing Simon bar Kochba to be the messiah who would restore Israel to independence. The rabbis responded to the loss of Jewish life by insisting that any restoration of Israel and its temple would be at the end of the world, at a time when justice and peace would reign universal. That day could be hastened only by perfect observance of the commandments, indeed, by one perfect Sabbath. The rabbis' new interpretation of "messiah" served both to quell further use of arms to gain Jewish independence and to answer claims being made by the Christian church. If Jesus is the messiah, why are violence and bloodshed still rampant? Why is the lion not yet lying down with the lamb (Isa 65:25)?

From Oral Torah to the Talmud

The rabbis continued to adapt to new situations and answer questions about Jewish observance by resorting not only to the written Torah but also to their oral tradition. According to that tradition, there were hundreds more commandments beyond the usual ten, commandments about prayer, diet, property, marriage—in fact, 613 commandments in all. In the early years of their movement, including during Jesus' lifetime, the Pharisees had resisted writing down their legal opinions, but by the year 200, rabbinical leadership decided that the Oral Torah would be lost if it were not recorded. The result of that decision was the Mishnah, a compilation of rabbinical legal opinions up to that time.

In the Mishnah, one finds the basic ethical principles of rabbinical Judaism, particularly in a tractate called the "Ethics of the Fathers" (*Pirke Aboth*). There we read, for example, of the centrality of Torah, prayer, and the practice of charity. The very word for commandment in rabbinical tradition, *mitzvah* (*mitzvoth* in the plural), also means good deed or favor. How altruism or compassion relates to self-interest is expressed in a famous saying: "If I do not care for myself, who will? But if I care only for myself, what kind of person am I? And if now is not the time to do good, when is?" (Here, evidently, simplistic claims identifying Christianity with charity and Judaism with justice do not survive scrutiny.)

The Mishnah emphasizes the importance of Torah study; ignorance of the law is no excuse for transgressions. (Rooted in the commandment requiring Torah study is the high regard Jewish tradition has for scholarship altogether.) However, just as important as study is making "a fence around the Torah," by which the Mishnah means drawing up regulations that act against even those transgressions that are not deliberate. Thus, to protect against breaking the commandment that prohibits using Yahweh's name in vain, Jewish legal tradition forbade using Yahweh's name at all, even in prayer. As mentioned previously, when coming upon the name Yahweh in reading the Torah, the word *Adonai* ("Lord") would be spoken instead.

Jewish legal tradition continued to develop and evolve, as rabbis focused now not on the written Torah but on the Mishnah. They argued questions such as how was the Sabbath day to be kept "holy," that is, "separate" from the other days of the week? Clearly, by resting, not working, but what kinds of activity constitute work? The rabbis decided that, among other activities, cooking, carpentry, and even writing were prohibited as being labor. (Note that writing was the professional work of a scribe.) And how was one to "make a fence" around those activities to avoid coming even close to transgressing the commandment? By not lighting a spark; by not even picking up a hammer, pen, or pencil. But what if some sort of work was a matter of life or death, for example, lifting up a weapon in self-defense? The rabbis had long held that the Sabbath rest could be broken to save life. Jews were to live by the law, not die by it.

Arguing all sides of questions like these, the rabbis continued to develop a legal tradition around the commandments of the written and oral Torah. According to the Mishnah, both were given by God to Moses at Mount Sinai and had equal weight and validity. Finally, around the year 500, the amount of rabbinic commentary (called *gemarra*) grew so massive that it too came to be compiled together with the Mishnah. Rabbis in present-day Iraq created the Babylonian Talmud, a virtual encyclopedia of rabbinic legal discussion, its many volumes comprising some six thousand pages and capable of filling three feet of space on a bookshelf.

One often sees depictions of rabbis with long, white beards dressed in prayer shawls and pondering heavy books. The books being portrayed are those of the Talmud. To be regarded as a scholar in rabbinic Judaism requires mastery of the Talmud and the ability to make judgments based on its ethical and legal principles. Some parts of the Talmud (called *haggadah*) consist of inspirational stories, ethical sermons, and illustrations. Most of it by far (called *halaka*, from the Hebrew word "to walk") consists of rabbinic legal discussion on how Jews are to live a Torah-centered life.

Although a small fraction of Jews rejected the Talmud and rabbinic tradition (so-called Karaites, quite possibly descendants of the Sadducees), for the vast majority of Jews, the Talmud became the foundational document for Jewish thinking, attitudes, and behavior. Whether in North Africa, Europe, or the Middle East, in Christian or eventually Muslim lands, Jews were everywhere a minority, tempted to assimilate to the religion and culture of the majority population. The fact that they did not, the fact that they survived as a distinct people, can be directly attributed to the influence of the Talmud and the distinctively Jewish way of life it created.

TRADITIONAL JEWISH FAITH AND PRACTICE

Though Judaism is often described as "ethical monotheism," the more accurate descriptive would be "monotheistic ethics," with the emphasis on ethics. Judaism is more a way of living than of thinking. (With its roots in Judaism, Christianity also began as a way of life, but under the influence of intellectual Greek culture, it came to emphasize correct thinking or orthodoxy in expressing its faith.) Talmudic Judaism does have doctrines and a theology too, however; they simply were not formalized until rabbis in medieval Spain felt themselves challenged by Christian and Muslim cultures. There the great twelfth-century Talmudic scholar and philosopher, Rabbi Moses ben Maimon (Maimonides), formulated the most widely recognized list of Jewish doctrines in his so-called Thirteen Principles.

God

In Jewish theology, as formulated by Maimonides, God exists and is uniquely one. Judaism had always held Yahweh to be *ehad*, a Hebrew word that can mean "alone" or "one." In opposition to the gods of other nations, biblical Judaism originally emphasized that Yahweh alone was their God. Eventually, Judaism came to emphasize the oneness of God. In either case, central to Jewish worship is the classic statement of Jewish faith taken from the Torah (Deut 6:4), the *Shema*: "Hear (*Shema*), O Israel: the Lord (*Adonai*) is our God, the Lord alone (*ehad*)."

God has no body, Maimonides continues, no material parts. Biblical references to the face or hand of God are to be taken not literally but as metaphors. Moreover, God is eternal, existing before all else, and alone is to be worshipped. The rabbis took literally the prohibition against idolatry and disallowed any physical images of God, but they developed a rich literature that abounds in verbal images of God. Not surprisingly, given the patriarchal cultures in which both biblical and rabbinic Judaism originated, virtually all those images are male. The one major exception is Shekinah, a feminine image for God's indwelling. Originally the cloud and pillar of fire that traveled with Israel in the exodus out of Egypt,

IMAGE: © JOHN RENARD

Shown here is a statue of the great medieval Iberian rabbi Moses Maimonides (1135–1204), which sits in the old Jewish quarter of his hometown, Cordoba, Spain.

the symbol of the Shekinah functions within Judaism in a way analogous to the Holy Spirit within Christianity, as a way of speaking of God not as transcendent in some seventh heaven but mysteriously close and present.

Torah, Covenant, and Israel

Central to Maimonides' account of Jewish faith are doctrines relating to God's actions with respect to Israel: God's word has been communicated to Israel by way of prophets. The greatest of these prophets was Moses. To him, God communicated the entire Torah (written and oral). The Torah is immutable; nothing may ever be added to or subtracted from it.

The focal point in any synagogue is the "holy ark," the receptacle that contains the central symbol of rabbinical Judaism, the Torah scroll. Specially trained scribes can spend as long as a year painstakingly making a single copy of the Torah, scrupulously following rabbinical regulations as to how and where to place the Hebrew words on specially prepared sewn-together pieces of parchment. Revered in Jewish tradition as the very word of God, Torah scrolls are regularly dressed with decorated cloth covers and elaborate crowns.

The word *Torah* in Hebrew means "teaching" or "instruction" but came to be translated into Greek (the Septuagint) as *nomos*, which means "law." This was because, besides the creation stories, patriarchal narratives, and chapters on the life of Moses, the rest of Torah consists of laws and regulations. As noted earlier, the Torah is only one part of the entire Hebrew Bible (the Tanak, an acronym for Torah, Prophets [Nebi'im], and Writings [Ketubim]). Whereas Christians read the entire Hebrew Bible as equally inspired, rabbinic Judaism gives pride of place to the Torah (written and oral); the rest of the Tanak is commentary.

For Judaism, the Torah and its commandments are Israel's part of the covenant (*berit*) or "sacred contract" that God made with Moses and the Jewish people at Mount Sinai. Variously compared by the prophets to a marriage or an adoption, the covenant was the agreement whereby Israel became Yahweh's chosen people. By this covenant, Yahweh would provide Israel with protection, freedom, and a land. Israel, in return, was to worship Yahweh alone and obey the commandments.

The idea of a chosen people was not unique in the ancient world, in which various gods were seen as adopting various peoples, but when monotheism came to replace polytheism, the idea of Jews seeing themselves as the chosen people of the only God, the question arises of whether Jews saw themselves as superior to everyone else.

Rabbinical Judaism explains the covenant in terms of Israel being chosen to receive and observe all 613 commandments of the Torah. This does not make Jews more favored. Even less does it mean that only Jews can be saved, that is, have a place in "the world-to-come." In rabbinic tradition, Gentiles come under the covenant God made with Noah. Under the Noahide covenant, non-Jews are required to observe only seven (not all 613) commandments. To have a place in the world to come, Gentiles need only to keep the commandments prohibiting actions like idolatry, blasphemy, murder, and adultery and requiring establishment of a just society, that is, courts of law.

The Messiah and the World to Come

Maimonides' final doctrines have to do with the future: After death, God, who is aware of all human deeds, will reward the good and punish the wicked. God will send the messiah, and there will be a bodily resurrection of the dead.

The concept of the messiah originated in Judaism with the promise to David of an eternal dynasty (2 Sam 7:16). When David's descendants fell short of the ideals that should have guided them as monarchs of God's chosen people, Israel's prophets began to look forward to a better future under a better son of David, when swords would be beaten into plowshares (Isa 2:4). The concept of a messianic age has had tremendous impact, first on Jewish and then Christian thinking and ultimately on Western civilization and culture.

With its implied criticism of the status quo, messianism has sparked revolutions (the first-century Zealots), the idea of a New World (the Pilgrims and Puritans of New England), and, in a secular form (messianism without God), a faith in the future, in scientific and technological progress (modern Western culture after the Enlightenment). The main point here is that the concept of a messiah was never unambiguous. After the fall of Jerusalem in 70 CE, rabbinical Judaism maintained faith in a future personal messiah but insisted that all attempts to calculate or speed up the coming of the messianic age be resisted. Today many Jews see the messiah not as a person but as a symbol for the Jewish people.

Belief in an afterlife is not mentioned in the written Torah. The Oral Torah recorded in the Mishnah of the Talmud professes faith in what it calls "the world to come," when God will reward good deeds and punish evil, but Jewish tradition never dwells on it. Instead, it provocatively maintains that even a few minutes in the here and now are better than the entire afterlife. In those few minutes, one can perform good deeds (*mitzvoth*). The world to come is in God's hands, not ours, the rabbis reasoned, so there is no need to think much or speculate about it. Emphasis is always on life here and now. Hence the traditional Jewish toast when raising a glass of wine is *l'chaim*, "to life."

Daily Prayer and Life-Cycle Rituals

Rabbinic Judaism does not leave prayer to happenstance. Following a minutely detailed order, Jewish men put on a prayer shawl (*tallit*) and pray three times a day: morning, afternoon, and evening. In the morning, they also strap on to their right arm and forehead leather boxes (*tefilin*) holding small pieces of parchment containing verses from the Torah. Blessings or prayers of gratitude to God are to be said throughout the day, most of them beginning with the same formula: "Blessed be thou, Lord our God, Ruler of the Universe. . . ." The positive regulations ("thou shalt") determining prayer are directed only to Jewish men; women and men alike are bound to observe the negative commandments ("thou shalt not").

In addition to the daily prayers incumbent upon Jewish men as individuals, rabbinical Judaism surrounds life-cycle rituals with communal prayer. Eight days after the birth of a baby boy, the ceremony of circumcision (*bris milah*) is performed, marking the child as a son of Abraham. At the age of 13, the boy assumes the rights and responsibilities of adult Jewish males as a "son of the commandment" (*bar mitzvah*). The rite of passage is marked by the young man ascending to the pulpit in a synagogue sanctuary and reading a portion of the Torah in Hebrew. He now counts in any *minyan*, a quorum of ten or more Jewish males required for certain forms of Jewish worship. Women in rabbinic tradition do not count for a *minyan*.

Marriage is also surrounded with distinctive Jewish ceremonies: the signing of a marriage contract (*ketubah*) and standing under a canopy (*huppa*) where the bride and groom share a cup of wine, symbolic of the life they will share under a common roof. The most striking part of a traditional Jewish marriage ceremony is the breaking of a glass immediately followed by the assembled family and friends shouting "*Mazel tov*" (literally "good luck" but meaning one has *had* good luck; hence, congratulations). Though it is commonly claimed that breaking the glass is meant to remind the assembly of the destruction of the Temple and the trials Jews have had to suffer over the centuries, the more likely explanation for the custom is that the noise (like honking horns, tin cans, or rice at a non-Jewish wedding) is meant to distract evil spirits.

Traditional ceremonies surrounding death are also distinctively Jewish. Rabbinical Judaism calls for burial within a day if possible, without public viewing or embalming of the body. After that, the immediate family remains at home, refraining from customary activity for seven days (sits *shiva*), as mourners bring food and gather to pray and express their sympathy. Central to the rituals surrounding death is the recitation of the *Kaddish*, a mourner's prayer that blesses God's name and does not even mention death. At the death of a parent, a son is expected to gather with a *minyan* (usually at a synagogue) and recite the *Kaddish* prayer every day for a year.

Dietary Laws and Holy Days

The Torah lays emphasis on Israel's responsibility to be "holy" in the Hebrew sense of that word, to be "set apart." Certainly the life-cycle rituals set Jews apart from other religious traditions, but Jewish dietary laws and holy days separate Jews from their Gentile neighbors even more so.

Among the kosher dietary laws, the prohibition against eating pork is certainly the most well known. Also forbidden, however, is shellfish, indeed any fish without fins and scales (not only shrimp, crab, and lobster but also catfish and shark). To be kosher (which means "fit" for eating), meat has to be ritually slaughtered, that is, with a prayer, the animal's throat is slit quickly with a very sharp knife, and its blood poured out completely. Blood is also not kosher, making a rare steak forbidden, as is the mixing of meat and dairy products, meaning there is no such thing as a kosher cheeseburger. Moreover, to make a fence around the law that prohibits mixing meat and dairy, Jewish law calls for separate dishes and cooking utensils for each.

Judaism also has its own calendar of holy days, each beginning with sundown of the day before. Thus the Sabbath begins with sundown on Friday evening and ends with sundown on Saturday. Jewish tradition calls for the lighting and blessing of candles before sundown, followed by a festive meal prepared that afternoon. No lights or fires can be made (no lighting of a spark) on the Sabbath, although modern technology has eliminated much of the inconvenience with central heating, automatic timers, and thermostats. Prayer at the synagogue, study, and rest are the order of the day (though tradition allows and even encourages married couples to make love on the Sabbath).

The cycle of Jewish holy days is determined by a lunar calendar, beginning in early autumn with the New Year (*Rosh Hashanah*), the onset of the High Holy Days that culminate ten days later with the Day of Atonement (*Yom Kippur*). The New Year is marked by a festive meal that customarily includes apples dipped in honey. The synagogue service includes the blowing of a ram's horn (*shofar*) and an attitude of serious reflection on how one is living one's life. *Yom Kippur* is marked by a complete fast (food, drink, sexual relations) accompanied by prayers of repentance (*teshuva*).

Following the High Holy Days is the autumn Feast of Tabernacles (*Sukkot*), a harvest thanksgiving festival at which traditional Jews are required to eat at least one meal a day in a kind of shed or booth (*sukka*) decorated with harvest symbols. In December, Jews celebrate Hanukkah, commemorating the rededication of the Second Temple after it was defiled by enemy forces. In memory of the relighting of the menorah, the seven-branched candlestick that stood in the temple, Jews light a nine-branched Hanukkah menorah, eat food prepared with oil (tradi-

IMAGE: © JOHN RENARD

This monumental menorah is engraved with low-relief biblical scenes and sits near the Israeli Parliament (Kenesset); twentieth century.

tionally *latkes*, potato pancakes), and exchange small gifts. Although originally a minor feast in the Jewish calendar, Hanukkah has grown in importance under the influence of Christmas, with both holidays in the December darkness constituting a "season of lights."

Passover (*Pesach*) is the spring festival when Jewish families and friends gather for a ritual meal (*seder*) and recall the exodus from Egypt. (As one wry observation about Jewish life puts it: They tried to kill us, they didn't succeed, let's eat.)

The ritual part of the meal consists of eating certain foods, most notably *matzo* (unleavened bread), and connecting them with Israel's escape from bondage. Ordinary leaven (yeast or baking powder) is strictly not kosher during the weeklong celebration, just as forbidden as pork. Hence, to put a "fence" around the law, rabbinic tradition calls for a Jewish household to have separate dishes and cooking utensils for Passover.

There are other holidays and observances in Jewish life beyond the limitations of an introduction. Suffice it here only to point out once again that everywhere in the world, for almost two thousand years, Jews were ethnic minorities with a distinct religious subculture. Whether in Spain, North Africa, or Turkey, where Sephardic Jews (from *Sepharad*, the Jewish name for Spain) spoke Ladino; or in Europe, where Ashkenazic Jews (from the Jewish name for northern France and Germany) spoke Yiddish (a mixture of Hebrew, medieval German, and Polish), Talmudic observance enabled Jews to resist the temptation to assimilate to Christian or Muslim cultures. The challenge to assimilate intensified, however, with the onset of modernity and secular culture.

MODERN JUDAISM

Among the tenets of modern culture is the separation of church and state, making religious faith and practice a matter of conscience and personal choice. This was the freedom of conscience written from the beginning into the U.S. Constitution and Bill of Rights. When the French Revolution (1789) made church-state separation a matter of civil law, it led to the emancipation of France's small Jewish community. French Jews became French citizens with rights equal to French Catholics and Protestants. Napoleon and his armies carried this secular form of government to other nations in Europe, including Germany. There, German Jews, who for centuries had only read and written Yiddish, began to learn to speak modern German, read German script, and assimilate into German culture. The result was the break-up of the hegemony enjoyed for centuries by Talmudic tradition and the origin of Reform Judaism.

Reform Judaism

The rabbis responsible for the rise of Reform Judaism saw themselves as equal in authority to those who determined Jewish practice at the demise of Second Temple Judaism. Originating in Germany and the United States, the Reform movement declared that Jews were citizens of their homelands, belonging to a separate religion but not a separate nation. Reform Judaism embraced the Enlightenment principle of individual rights, which included the right of Jews as individuals to decide how they would live and practice their Judaism. In practice, this amounted to the disavowal of Talmudic tradition, particularly those laws that separated Jews from Gentiles, like strict observance of the Sabbath or complete adherence to the kosher dietary laws.

Today, if Reform Jews keep any dietary prescription, it is the prohibition from eating pork. If they attend a synagogue service on Friday night or Saturday morning, they will drive to a temple for what looks very much like a Lutheran service, about an hour in length with organ, choral singing, and a sermon by the rabbi, much of it in the vernacular. (This is obviously quite different from traditional Judaism's three-hour service, to which the congregants walked, all of it in Hebrew.)

One of the most noticeable innovations of Reform Judaism is mixed or family seating at the temple. Rabbinic tradition calls for women to sit separately from men, in some synagogues behind a wall, up in a balcony, or separated by a screen going down the middle of the aisles. The Talmud calls for celebrating the birth of a Jewish boy with a *bris* and his coming of age with a *bar mitzvah*; for girls, there was nothing. Reform Judaism has embraced women's equality and rights as part of its very self-definition. It celebrates the birth of baby girls and boys with naming ceremonies and has created the *bat mitzvah* (daughter of the commandment) ceremony. When Reform Judaism began to allow women to stand at the pulpit and read publicly from the Torah, it was only a small step to allow women to become rabbis.

What is being described here is Reform Judaism (not reformed, as if the reform was something in the past, now over). Under the influence of women rabbis, the reform of Judaism is continuing today, particularly in the area of language. Although the Hebrew terms are maintained as they are, new English translations of the prayers and sacred texts are being rendered in more inclusive, gender-neutral language, with terms like *Lord* and *King* being translated as "Eternal One" and "Sovereign."

Conservative Judaism

Many Jewish immigrants to the United States, especially those from Eastern Europe, found some of the Reform movement's changes from rabbinic tradition (like family seating at worship) attractive but other changes too extreme. Thus there arose Conservative Judaism, which is really a middle-of-the-road form of Jewish practice; not the individual but the community decides what to change in the tradition. Conservative Jews are more likely than Reform Jews to adhere strictly to the kosher dietary laws but will drive on the Sabbath to a three-hour service in Hebrew. In the last several years, Conservative Judaism has come under Reform influence and allowed both the *bat mitzvah* and women rabbis.

Orthodox Judaism

About 90 percent of religious Jews in the United States today are either Conservative or Reform. Only a small minority adhere completely to the tenets of Talmudic tradition. Although usually referred to as Orthodox Jews, the term is something of a misnomer because, as pointed out, it is not correct thinking (orthodoxy) that is most at issue but correct Jewish practice (halaka). Yet orthodoxy is not altogether a nonissue, because Reform Jews accept modern scientific scholarship about the compilation of the Torah centuries after the time of Moses. For Orthodox Jews, that is a heresy running contrary to the rabbinic dogma that God communicated the entire Torah to Moses.

Although they all adhere to classical rabbinic tradition, Orthodox Jews are no more monolithic than their Conservative or Reform counterparts are. So-called "Modern Orthodox" Jews strive to observe all 613 commandments while living in the modern world. They work alongside and socialize with Gentiles, attend movies and concerts, and send their children to public schools. At most, the men and boys stand out by wearing a *yarmulka* or skullcap (*kippa* in Hebrew).

Quite different from the Modern Orthodox are so-called ultraorthodox Jews who avoid socializing not only with Gentiles but with nonorthodox Jews, thus creating their own self-imposed ghettoes. Most conspicuous among the ultraorthodox are the Hassidic Jews (*Hassidim*), a movement going back to villages of eighteenth-century southern Poland and Ukraine. The Hassidim early on treated their rabbis (called *rebbes*) more like spiritual masters or gurus than as mere scholars, and the movement fractured into splinter groups. The largest ultraorthodox group is the Lubavitch Hassidim, conspicuous for the men wearing long sideburns, black coats, and black hats (or fur hats on occasion). Centered mostly in the Williamsburg area of Brooklyn and in Israel, the Lubavitch Hassidim educate their children in completely separate schools, prohibit them from watching movies or television, and are intent on converting the rest of American Jews to their separatist way of thinking and practice.

On the Sabbath, however, even Modern Orthodox Jews drop out of the modern world with its wide assortment of high-tech gadgetry. When Thomas Edison first closed an electrical circuit, the rabbis had to decide if doing so constituted lighting a spark, this being forbidden on the Sabbath. Demonstrating the extraordinary influence of religious authority, the Orthodox rabbinate decided that yes, it did. Ever since that time, the Sabbath for Orthodox Jews has become a day for escaping from the world of automobile ignitions and elevator buttons, computers, iPods, and e-mail. Some of them get around the prohibition of using electricity by having their lights on timers on the Sabbath so they do not need to do the work of switching on lamps.

CHRISTIAN-JEWISH RELATIONS

No introduction to Judaism would be complete without at least some consideration of Christian anti-Judaism that eventually led to anti-Semitism. Many, perhaps most, Christians are blissfully unaware of the malice and violence that Jews have suffered over the centuries and that those hostile attitudes have often been excused by appeals to the New Testament (NT). There is no discounting the fact that for two-thousand years, Christians and Jews have largely looked upon one another with antagonism, nor is there any denying that, because of that longstanding alienation, Nazi Germany was more easily able to perpetrate the genocide of European Jews that we know as the Holocaust.

Bitter Beginnings

The mutual animosity that has marked Christian-Jewish relations goes back to the first century. As we learned, Pharisees and the infant church presented rival views of the kind of life God wanted Jews to live. Pharisees stressed the Torah and obedience to its commandments; Jewish Christians emphasized the prophets, whose words they interpreted as fulfilled in Jesus. An intrafamily quarrel became increasingly bitter as Jewish Christians began accepting and eating with Gentiles. Shortly after the destruction of Jerusalem and the Second Temple, the rabbis excommunicated as heretics nonconformist Jews, including Jewish Christians.

The church interpreted the destruction of the Temple as historical proof of God's displeasure with the Jewish people. Israel must have committed some terrible crime, and Christians were quite sure they knew what it was. Jews were being punished for the death of Jesus; God had come to reject the Jewish people because of their rejection of Jesus. Despite the Gospel evidence that Jesus was popular with the Jewish masses, Christians began viewing not just a handful of Sadducees but all Jews as Christ-killers. The church began seeing itself and its covenant as the new Israel, replacing the old Israel with its "old" covenant. (The technical name for this replacement theory is *supercessionism.*)

It did not help matters that John's Gospel (20:19) describes Jesus' Galilean Jewish disciples as locking doors for fear of the *Iudaioi*, a word that makes sense as "Judeans" but has traditionally been translated as "the Jews." The infant church was in fact a persecuted minority, and there is no lack of historical evidence that in its early years, Christians suffered at the hands of Jews, most notably during the Bar Kochba revolt (135 CE). Christians would harbor those memories for nearly two thousand years as proof of unwavering Jewish hostility.

Christian Ambivalence

Christian fortunes changed markedly, however, in the fourth century. First, the Emperor Constantine conceded toleration to the Christian church (313 CE). Then the Emperor Theodosius the Great declared Christianity to be the sole official religion of the Roman Empire, decreeing both paganism and heresy to be crimes against the state (380 CE). As happens so often in history, the formerly oppressed became themselves oppressors. A series of repressive measures legally forbade Jews to make converts, to own Christian slaves, or to hold public office. In a series of sermons notorious today for their inflammatory rhetoric, Saint John Chrysostom (d. 407) preached against Christians visiting synagogues or having anything to do with Jews.

Yet both in imperial and later medieval church law, the basic Christian posture toward Jews was one of toleration. Why Jews were tolerated, while pagans and Christian heretics were not, can be credited largely to the influence of Saint Augustine (d. 430), who interpreted the Jewish people as marked with the "sign of Cain" (Gen 4:15). Jews, like Cain, had blood on their hands for the death of Jesus, but their punishment was to wander the earth; they were not to be killed.

Offensive as it appears to us today, the metaphor of Cain lay at the root of traditional Christian ambivalence toward Jews. On the one hand, it allowed Jews to survive in medieval Europe. On the other hand, it explains why Catholic monarchs could drive Jews out of England, France, and then, most painfully, Spain, without any qualms of conscience. In their eyes, they were simply demonstrating the superiority of Christianity and God's righteous judgment upon a people now rejected and accursed.

The situation of Jews in the Middle Ages was not one of uninterrupted abuse. There were good times as well as bad. (No people, Jews included, want to see themselves as the objects of unrelenting hostility.) They constituted a kind of middle class in the feudal system, serving as merchants and tradesmen. Though subordinate to the land-owning gentry, Jews were permitted by law to travel. That made them analogous to the knights and superior to the great masses of peasants who were tied to the land. Jews were also permitted, unlike Christians in the Middle Ages, to engage in moneylending, an occupation that easily prompted resentment and more than once led to anti-Jewish riots for the purpose of destroying debt records.

In Norwich, England, shortly before Easter in 1141, the discovery of a dead boy's body led to the accusation that Jews had killed him in a ritual murder meant to mock Christ's crucifixion. This was the origin of the so-called "blood libel," which in various forms spread throughout Europe, stereotyping Jews as murderers who use Christian blood to make Passover matzos or wine. Knowing the strict rabbinical prohibition against consuming blood, popes, kings, and emperors denounced the blood libel repeatedly. That it persisted well into the twentieth century is testimony to the fact that a lie, no matter how outrageous, if told often enough, will be believed.

The popular identification of Jews as murderers made them likely scapegoats during the fourteenth-century epidemic known as the Black Death. Two centuries later, having been driven out of England and France, Jews then found themselves caught between warring Catholics and Protestants in German-speaking lands. Martin Luther maintained the traditional medieval stereotype of Jews. He wrote a particularly venomous tract or pamphlet, "Against the Jews," which came to be widely quoted by the Nazis. Increasingly, Jews moved eastward into Poland and eventually Ukraine, where the Polish aristocracy used them as agents and tax collectors among the much more numerous peasantry. Jews enjoyed more self-governance in Poland than in anywhere else in Europe. It became their land of refuge. For that reason, many Jews were concentrated there when Nazi Germany invaded Poland in September 1939.

THE HOLOCAUST AND VATICAN II ON JEWS AND JUDAISM

Understandably, the Holocaust has made an indelible mark on the consciousness of Jews today. Christians too have reason never to forget it. Nearly six-million Jews, including a million and a half children, were murdered in the heart of what once was called Christendom. Moreover, virtually all the perpetrators had been baptized Catholic or Protestant. To be sure, there were tens of thousands of Christians among the so-called "Righteous Gentiles" who made attempts to save Jews, risking their own lives and those of their families, but most Christians were unwilling to take such risks and stood by passively, sometimes even complacently, influenced by a tradition that for centuries had characterized Jews as hostile to Christian interests.

One Christian who did not stand by passively was Archbishop Angelo Roncalli, later elected Pope John XXIII. As a papal diplomat to Turkey and Greece during World War II, he was personally responsible for saving tens of thousands of Jews through the issuance of false baptismal certificates. That experience obviously stayed with him, as when he convened the Second Vatican Council (1962–1965), he expressed the hope that the Council would make a statement about the Catholic Church and Judaism. That hope was realized on October 28, 1965, when his successor, Pope Paul VI, promulgated *Nostra Aetate*, the Council's Declaration on the Relation of the Church to Non-Christian Religions.

Nostra Aetate was a watershed document that not only impacted Catholics but also challenged other Christian churches to look at their thinking and attitudes toward Judaism and the Jewish

The term **anti-Semitism** was first coined by Wilhem Marr, a nineteenth-century German atheist who hated Jews and Christians equally—too vast a topic to be treated here. Suffice it to be said that it was rampant in nineteenth-century Eastern Orthodox Russia and widespread in the United States up to and during World War II.

people. In its wake, the Vatican has issued documents on how to preach about Jews and Judaism, how to interpret the Jewish Scriptures, and how important it is to remember the Holocaust. In December 1993, Pope John Paul II approved the establishment of diplomatic relations between the Vatican and the state of Israel, pressing for Israelis and Palestinians alike to acknowledge one another's rights to live in peace and security in their own homelands. This constituted official recognition by the Vatican that attachment to the land of Israel is one of the defining hallmarks of Judaism.

Today, Christians and Jews collaborate on any number of peace and justice issues, socialize as friends, celebrate at one another's weddings, and attend one another's funerals. Today, Christian theologians give greater attention to the Jewish roots of Christianity. Indeed, hardly a chapter or a topic in this book has not been affected by the rethinking initiated by *Nostra Aetate*.

Jewish leaders have likewise begun a reconsideration of Christianity. In a statement entitled *Dabru Emet* (Hebrew for "Speak the Truth"), prominent rabbis and Jewish scholars have acknowledged, for example, that Jews and Christians worship the same God, that Christians accept the moral principles of the Torah, and that Nazism was not a Christian phenomenon. Not all Jews have endorsed that statement, but neither have all Christian churches endorsed *Nostra Aetate* or the dialogue between Christians and Jews that it initiated. Jews and Christians are not monolithic faith communities; they never have been.

The important question for individual Christians is whether they, personally, endorse *Nostra Aetate*, and what does that imply for them? Moreover, what does it imply for their attitude toward members of other faith communities? Jews and Christians once lived side by side and yet remained strangers to one another. It was not until they began sharing conversations with one another that walls began breaking down. Christians need to ask themselves, "Who are the strangers in our midst? When is the last time I had a conversation with someone outside my 'comfort zone'?"

With *Nostra Aetate*, Christians began a long-overdue conversation in 1965. It is still going on, and all Jews and Christians are invited to join in.

This document needs to be read with the heart because it is from and to the hearts of two religions seeking to be faithful to the same God. The following is an excerpt:

> As the sacred synod searches into the mystery of the Church, it remembers the bond that spiritually ties the people of the New Covenant to Abraham's stock.
>
> Thus the Church of Christ acknowledges that, according to God's saving design, the beginnings of her faith and her election are found already among the Patriarchs, Moses and the prophets. She professes that all who believe in Christ—Abraham's sons according to faith—are included in the same Patriarch's call, and likewise that the salvation of the Church is mysteriously foreshadowed by the chosen people's Exodus from the land of bondage. The Church, therefore, cannot forget that she received the revelation of the Old Testament through the people with whom God in His inexpressible mercy concluded the Ancient Covenant. Nor can she forget that she draws sustenance from the root of that well-cultivated olive tree onto which have been grafted the wild shoots, the Gentiles. Indeed, the Church believes that by His cross Christ, Our Peace, reconciled Jews and Gentiles making both one in Himself.
>
> The Church keeps ever in mind the words of the Apostle about his kinsmen: "theirs is the sonship and the glory and the covenants and the law and the worship and the promises; theirs are the fathers and from them is the

Christ according to the flesh" (Rom 9:4–5), the Son of the Virgin Mary. She also recalls that the Apostles, the Church's main-stay and pillars, as well as most of the early disciples who proclaimed Christ's Gospel to the world, sprang from the Jewish people.

As Holy Scripture testifies, Jerusalem did not recognize the time of her visitation, nor did the Jews in large number, accept the Gospel; indeed not a few opposed its spreading. Nevertheless, God holds the Jews most dear for the sake of their Fathers; He does not repent of the gifts He makes or of the calls He issues—such is the witness of the Apostle. In company with the Prophets and the same Apostle, the Church awaits that day, known to God alone, on which all peoples will address the Lord in a single voice and "serve him shoulder to shoulder."

Since the spiritual patrimony common to Christians and Jews is thus so great, this sacred synod wants to foster and recommend that mutual understanding and respect which is the fruit, above all, of biblical and theological studies as well as of fraternal dialogues.

True, the Jewish authorities and those who followed their lead pressed for the death of Christ; still, what happened in His passion cannot be charged against all the Jews, without distinction, then alive, nor against the Jews of today. Although the Church is the new people of God, the Jews should not be presented as rejected or accursed by God, as if this followed from the Holy Scriptures. All should see to it, then, that in catechetical work or in the preaching of the word of God they do not teach anything that does not conform to the truth of the Gospel and the spirit of Christ.

Furthermore, in her rejection of every persecution against any man, the Church, mindful of the patrimony she shares with the Jews and moved not by political reasons but by the Gospel's spiritual love, decries hatred, persecutions, displays of anti-Semitism, directed against Jews at any time and by anyone.

Besides, as the Church has always held and holds now, Christ underwent His passion and death freely, because of the sins of men and out of infinite love, in order that all may reach salvation. It is, therefore, the burden of the Church's preaching to proclaim the cross of Christ as the sign of God's all-embracing love and as the fountain from which every grace flows.

Questions about the Text

1. Draw a timeline of events and people in this article from Alexander the Great (333 BCE) to Bar Kochba (135 CE).
2. Explain what you think are the three most important relationships between Judaism and Christianity in the first century.
3. How did the destruction of the second Temple in 70 CE change Judaism, and how did rabbinic Judaism help form that response?
4. Explain one topic by the twelfth-century talmudic scholar Maimonides that most interested you, and explain why you chose it.
5. How do rabbinic Jews pray daily, and how do they celebrate weddings in their religious ritual?
6. On what calendar are the Jewish holy days set? Make a list of five holy days and the events they celebrate.
7. What three major groups make up Modern Judaism? How do they differ?
8. What are the three major points of *Nostra Aetate?*

Questions for Discussion

1. What kind of relationship exists between Christians and Jews, according to this chapter?
2. What does this chapter say about responsibility for the death of Jesus?
3. Without using the term, what does this chapter say about supercessionism, that is, the theory that the Christian church has replaced the Jewish people as God's chosen?
4. What does this chapter say about anti-Semitism?
5. What are the implications of this chapter and this statement for contemporary Christians?

For Further Study

An easily accessible insight into Hassidic life and thinking can be found in the novels of Chaim Potok, especially his first, *The Chosen*.

Bishops Committee for Ecumenical and Inter-Religious Affairs, ed. *The Bible, the Jews, and the Death of Jesus: A Collection of Catholic Documents*. Washington, DC: U.S. Conference of Catholic Bishops, 2004.

This text is a collection of Catholic statements on responsibility for the death of Jesus.

———. *Catholics Remember the Holocaust*. Washington, DC: U.S. Conference of Catholic Bishops, 2004.

This collection of Catholic statements on the Holocaust implements the Vatican document, *We Remember*.

Boys, Mary, ed. *Seeing Judaism Anew: Christianity's Sacred Obligation*. Lanham, MD: Sheed & Ward/ Rowman & Littlefield, 2005.

This is a survey of Jewish–Christian relations and a Christian theology of Judaism.

Fisher, Eugene. *Faith without Prejudice: Rebuilding Christian Attitudes toward Judaism*. New York: Crossroad, 1993.

A leader in Christian–Jewish dialogue looks at such issues as Jesus' Jewishness, alleged anti-Semitism in the Gospels, and who is responsible for the death of Jesus. The text contains key Vatican and U.S. bishops' statements up to 1993.

Wylen, Stephen M. *Settings of Silver: An Introduction to Judaism*. New York: Paulist Press, 1989.

This text was popularly written by a rabbi on Jewish faith, practice, and history.

from the REFERENCE LIBRARIAN

The Encyclopedia Index in Research—Judaism

The library skills you have been learning apply equally well for researching religions other than Christianity. For example, try the keyword search "Judaism AND encyclopedias" to see what encyclopedias on Judaism are in your library's reference collection. Remember that the library skills you are learning in this book are transferable to *any* subject, theological or not.

Where you start researching a topic in Judaism depends, in part, on which one of the three broad divisions of Judaism described by Dr. Modras is your main area of interest; that is, you want to match your topic with an encyclopedia of appropriate scope. For example, there are encyclopedias focusing on Biblical Judaism, and others that focus on Modern Judaism.

Pride of place for researching *any* topic in Judaism goes to the second edition of the *Encyclopaedia Judaica* (22 vols.), published in 2007. Not only is the coverage of all aspects of Judaism exhaustive but also those responsible for the encyclopedia made this vast amount of material even more accessible by the care they gave to the index. The index is an indispensable tool for using the encyclopedia. "Only by consulting the Index will [the user] grasp the full treatment of any subject" (Preface). This is so because the editors planned the overall structure of the encyclopedia to avoid articles overlapping with one another; different aspects of a particular subject are treated in different articles. Therefore, it is essential that users of this encyclopedia consult the index to see where various aspects of the subject are dealt with in the text. Let's illustrate the use of the index with a biographical example mentioned by Dr. Modras: Maimonides. You will find an article on Maimonides in volume 13 of the *Encyclopaedia Judaica*. However, if you look in the index under "Maimonides," you will see dozens of subentries referring you to articles throughout the entire encyclopedia.

For an example of a conceptual topic, look at the index entry for "Reform Judaism." Following the reference to the main article on Reform Judaism, you will find, among other things, subentries for various countries, significant individuals, and important concepts referring you to almost every other volume in the encyclopedia.

Doing research on the Talmud can be a daunting exercise for the uninitiated, but using the index can help to bring order to a complex subject. The subentries in the index under "Talmud" extend across five printed pages. At a glance, you can locate several articles related to such Talmudic topics as "civil law," "*halakhah*," or "punishments."

The example of the *Encyclopaedia Judaica* (*EJ*) underscores the importance of making use of indexes in all encyclopedias. Not all encyclopedia indexes are prepared with as much care or desire for comprehensiveness as the one in the *EJ*; nevertheless, an encyclopedia index will almost always help you to find things you would have missed otherwise, and the more experience you have with encyclopedias and indexes, the more you will appreciate a high-quality index.

The *EJ* is a standard reference tool and should be in most libraries either in print or in its electronic version. Other standard reference sources for Judaism, none of which are as comprehensive as the *EJ*, include the titles listed below.

Jacob Neusner, Alan J. Avery-Peck, and William Scott Green, eds. *The Encyclopedia of Judaism*. 2nd ed. 5 vols. Boston, MA: Brill, 2005.

Louis Jacobs, *The Jewish Religion: A Companion*. Oxford, UK: Oxford University Press, 1995.

R. J. Zwi Werblowsky and Geoffrey Wigoder, eds. *The Oxford Dictionary of the Jewish Religion*. Oxford, UK: Oxford University Press, 1997.

Geoffrey Wigoder, ed. *The New Encyclopedia of Judaism*. New York: New York University Press, 2002.

Specialized reference works focusing on particular aspects of Jewish religion and history include the following:

Dan Cohn-Sherbok. *A Dictionary of Judaism and Christianity*. Philadelphia, PA: Trinity Press International, 1991.

This reference work explores "in direct and simple language" the "important connections" between Judaism and Christianity.

Israel Gutman, ed. *Encyclopedia of the Holocaust*. 4 vols. New York: Macmillan, 1990.

Edward Kessler and Neil Wenborn, eds. *Dictionary of Jewish-Christian Relations*. Oxford, UK: Cambridge University Press, 2005.

Schmuel Spector, ed. *The Encyclopedia of Jewish Life Before and During the Holocaust*. 3 vols. Jerusalem: Yad Vashem; New York: New York University Press, 2001.

Here is the latest addition to our set of Library Skills:

SKILL KEY #1

Use the library's reference collection to begin your research.

a) Use a subject-specific encyclopedia to acquire specialized knowledge about a subject.
b) Use a subject-specific encyclopedia whose scope is appropriate for both your topic and the approach you want to take to that topic.
c) Use encyclopedia bibliographies to identify subject headings for your topic.
d) Use a concise subject-specific dictionary to look up the specialized vocabulary of a particular field.
e) Use an encyclopedia's index to locate information on subjects (including persons) for which there is no separate article.
f) Examine the synoptic outline of contents (or however it is designated) in an encyclopedia (1) to get a quick overview of the contents and (2) to get topic ideas for research.
g) Use an encyclopedia's index to get ideas for research topics.
h) Use cross-references to locate additional relevant material in an encyclopedia.
i) **Use an encyclopedia's index to locate all (or as much as you want) relevant material on your topic. Note especially how detailed the index is and whether the editors of the encyclopedia make any special comments about it.**

SKILL KEY #2

Use the library's catalog to locate sources of information.

a) Use subject headings to locate precisely books on your topic.
b) Use subject headings whose scope fits your topic as closely as possible, then adjust your search with a broader or narrower subject heading as necessary.

continued

continued

c) As an alternative to using encyclopedia bibliographies, use keyword searching to identify subject headings for your topic.
d) Combine one or more subject headings in a search to retrieve books on a topic for which no single subject heading exists.
e) Use the floating subdivision "encyclopedias" in combination with a keyword to identify encyclopedias on a subject.
f) Use the floating subdivision "moral and ethical aspects" to identify material, whether "pro" or "con," related to the ethical aspects of a subject.
g) Use the floating subdivision "religious aspects" to search for religious/theological aspects of nonreligious/nontheological subjects.
h) If necessary, use all the subject headings assigned to a book to identify material on a particular subject.
i) Use the name of an organization or group as an author to search for documents produced under the aegis of that group. Be aware of the possibility of changes in the group's name over time.

Student Tasks

1. Go to your library and use the keyword search "Judaism AND encyclopedias" to see what encyclopedias your library has on this subject (are there other terms besides Judaism you could use?). Check the indexes in at least two of the encyclopedias. How do they compare? Is one index more detailed than the other? Pick a particular topic in Judaism and compare the index entries. Does one of the indexes prove to be more useful?
2. Choose one of the persons mentioned in this chapter, and find an encyclopedia article on that person. Now look at the index entry for that person. Is there more information in the encyclopedia or in the article you looked up?
3. Choose a conceptual topic from the chapter, and use an encyclopedia index to locate information on that topic throughout the encyclopedia.
4. Search the Internet for information on the same person you looked up in #2. Do the same for the conceptual topic you looked up in #3. How easy is it to find authoritative information? How many different ways can you search for this kind of information on the Internet?

Islamic Religious Experience: Foundations, Scripture, and Spirituality

John Renard

from the EDITOR

From the other chapters in this book, one can see that the wellsprings of religion are deep and orient the direction of people's lives, individually and communally. Even the word *religion* means "to tie or bind again" (Lat.: *ligare*, meaning "to tie or bind"; and *re*, meaning "again"). Religions bind themselves to God by their commitment and actions. Islam is a religious tradition that ties believers continuously in their particular relationship with the one God, Allah (Arabic for "the Deity"). Muslims understand this invitation as offered by Allah through divine revelation to his prophet Muhammad.

As Islam is the most recent of the three Abrahamic religions, some commonalities might be expected. Islam and Christianity share with Judaism the religious tradition that goes back to Abraham ("The Father of Faith"), as well as the prophets sent by God. Islam shares with Christianity a high regard for Jesus as a prophet, with deep respect for his mother Mary. Theologically, it seems clear that the three religious traditions pray to the same God.

We shall read more on this shortly, but for now, theology has to start somewhere deeper than superficial observations, impressions, or general ideas. It must move to understanding tied to respect and desire to know the other's religious experience. The appreciative understanding of listening and learning is the same method used in the previous chapter on Judaism and is applicable for understanding any religious tradition.

This chapter is not a typical explanation with facts and dates about Islam. It challenges the reader to step beyond merely knowing intellectually about Islam to appreciating its religious experience—the why beneath the what. It prompts one to ask what the Islamic experience is and why that experience forms Muslim's lives. The goal is to develop in readers an appreciation of and an insight into the Islamic believer's world.

The chapter discusses Islam in four parts. (1) Our journey toward the soul of Islam begins with God, not in an abstract way but in the concrete images of God that people pray with every day. (2) The chapter then examines what Islam teaches God has revealed to humanity in the sacred scripture of the Qur'an (or "Book"), which binds Muslims to God in their daily lives. (3) Next, we will look to God's human collaborators and the sacred role that Muslims believe they have played. (4) Finally, in exploring scriptural themes in Islamic spirituality, the soul itself is discussed, that inner center where the different ways in which one worships, prays, and lives in the world come alive. To provide a better appreciation of concepts, terms, and the sacred Qur'an, the chapter includes key Arabic words and their translations.

OVERVIEW

Islam as a religious tradition developed in the rich religious and cultural matrix of the Middle East. With its three foundational theological elements, Islam stands firmly in the line of the Abrahamic monotheistic faiths. Belief in an omnipotent creative deity, in the centrality of a revealed sacred scripture, and in the necessity of prophets to communicate the mind of the deity to humankind links Islam explicitly to Judaism and Christianity. We will investigate how images of God as creator and guide, of the Qur'an as light and guidance, and of Muhammad as prophet inform an Islamic spirituality—or approach to life.

Non-Muslims are often surprised, even shocked, to hear that Islam's central spiritual and ethical presuppositions are virtually identical to those of Judaism and Christianity. Why then, many people ask, do Jews, Christians, and Muslims not get along better, especially in the Middle East? Perhaps the best response to that and similar queries is that strife is simply endemic to the human race. Why do the Catholics and Protestants of Northern Ireland hold so tenaciously to their ancient rivalries and hatred? They are, of course, all Christians. Most Christians and Jews will find it simple enough to distinguish between what individuals or groups do and the ideals and values for which a faith tradition stands—at least when it comes to their own. However, non-Muslims too often and too readily equate the behavior of a minority of Muslims, generally identified as extremist, fundamentalist, revolutionary, or right-wing fanatics, with the whole of a tradition and the generality of its adherents.

A sad fact of human history has been that communities of persons—ethnic, political, economic, or religious—tend to become closed systems bent on defending themselves against the threat posed by other such communities. That their religious affiliations are more often blamed for factionalism and intolerance than are other equally liable forces is really only a testimony to the intensity of the emotional responses that religious language and imagery can elicit.

What if one could approach the study of Islam (or any religious or cultural tradition, for that matter) free of the prejudices and suspicions that so easily cloud one's vision and skew one's judgment of other persons? Though none of us can claim true objectivity, we can at least begin with the assumption that the qualities we have the greatest difficulty accepting in another reflect in large measure what we cannot accept in ourselves.

Much of the allegedly objective journalism that has fed American curiosity about the Middle East in recent years reeks of condescension and thinly veiled bigotry. One television correspondent, reporting on the aftermath of the Persian Gulf conflict of 1991 (also known as "Desert Storm") but not limited to that war, characterized Saudi Arabia's policy as "Pray and pay: pray to Allah, and pay anyone who can provide" necessary services and protection. The tone of his remark was inherently demeaning, but beyond that, it seemed to suggest that Christian America and Jewish Israel would of course never rely on such a strategy.

One could cite numerous examples of that peculiar attitude. Just after the cease-fire in the first Persian Gulf hostilities, another reporter interviewed a young soldier who had secured as souvenirs an AK-47 rifle and a Qur'an. Asked what he intended to do with the book, the soldier replied that he would spend some time reading about what sort of being "this Allah" was. He clearly expected the worst, but he did not find it strange to be fighting shoulder to shoulder with coalition troops who read the same scripture as the enemy.

ISLAMIC IMAGES OF GOD

But who is "this Allah" of whom Muslims speak? Many non-Muslims have the impression that the term *Allah* refers to some despotic deity with a taste for violence and infidel blood. Perhaps that is because so many television and movie images of Muslim soldiers depict them screaming, "Allahu Akbar!" ("God is supreme") as they attack or celebrate victory. How is it, some may wonder, that Muslims seem so readily to associate Allah with violence? In Arabic, the word *Allah* is simply a compound of *al-* (the definite article, "the") and *ilah* ("god," "deity"). Joined together, they signify "God." You may find this a bit shocking, but it is very significant that nearly all Arabic speakers, including Iraqi Jews and Syrian Christians, refer to their Supreme Being as Allah.

Images of God are central to virtually every religious tradition and crucial to one's understanding of how religious motivation works. For example, most people tend to believe that God is on their side—even people who do not believe in God except when it suits their purposes. Hence, proprietary ideas of who God is, what God likes and dislikes, and how God deals with human problems make it challenging indeed to open one's mind to the images of God that other people hold dear—never mind that if God is as big as most religious traditions claim, God has the option of being on everyone's side. That little piece of logic soon gets swept under the rug, for it wreaks havoc with the human penchant for sanctifying divisions and enmities with claims to divine favor.

Images of God prevalent in one religious tradition inevitably overlap with those of another, but each tradition has its distinctive tone and emphasis. Christians, for example, who find it quaint and dangerous that Muslims believe God has prepared rewards in paradise for those who die a martyr's death, might well recall that Christianity too has had its own tradition of martyrdom from the beginning. If Jews and Christians take offense at the idea that the God of Islam sanctions certain forms of violence, they would do well to recall not only the Just War theory but also the shockingly bloody images of God in Deuteronomy and other early sections of the Hebrew Scriptures, and even in the New Testament (NT) (cf. Lev 20:9–14; 26:7–8, 21–39; Deut 20:10–14; 21:10ff; 21:18–21; 22:20–21, 23–24; Ps 58:6–9; 64:7–10; 69:22–27; 139:19–22; Matt 10:34; Luke 12:49; 20:9–18). Religious persons understandably gravitate to those images of God already embedded in their traditions that help explain the circumstances in which they find themselves. Similarly, if asked to reflect on the matter, most religious people would likely assume that their most cherished (or dreaded) images of God are very close to those of the person next to them on the synagogue bench or the church pew. They might be surprised to discover that, in fact, their images of God bear a greater likeness to those of the Muslim in the mosque across town than to some of their coreligionists.

Most Jews and Christians are convinced their God is loving and kind, provident and generous, as well as thirsty for justice and equity; most Muslims believe the same. Of the "Ninety-Nine Most Beautiful Names" of God, the two by far most frequently invoked are "Gracious or Compassionate" and "Merciful." All but one of the Qur'an's 114 *suras* (chapters) begins with the phrase, "In the name of God, the Gracious and Merciful." One might say these two names are as important for Muslims as are the names Father, Son, and Holy Spirit heard in so many Christian invocations. Virtually every Muslim public speaker begins with that Qur'anic phrase and goes on to wish the audience the blessings and mercy of God.

The opening chapter of the Qur'an sets the tone of prayer for Muslims and lays the foundation for our present consideration:

In the Name of God, the Compassionate and Merciful: Praise to God, Lord of the Universe.
The Compassionate, the Merciful,
Master of the Day of Judgment.
You alone do we serve; from you alone do we seek help.
Lead us along the Straight Path,
the path of those who experience the shower of your grace,
not of those who have merited your anger
or of those who have gone astray.
(Qur'an[Q] 1:1–7)

Here, we find clues to several of the principal divine attributes. Compassion and mercy top the list and receive an emphatic second mention. In addition, God rules the "two worlds" (seen and unseen, i.e., the universe), takes account at Judgment, offers aid and grace, and manifests a wrathful side to those who prefer arrogant independence from the origin of all things. At the center of the prayer, the Muslim asks for guidance on the Straight Path, a path laid out and marked as the way of divine graciousness.

Not one of the Ninety-Nine Names of God, on which Muslims meditate as they finger the thirty-three beads of the rosary, will sound a dissonant note in the ear of Christian or Jew. All of those names conjure up images of God. Islamic tradition has divided the names into those that express an awareness of God's beauty and approachability (*jamal*) and those that evoke a sense of the divine majesty and awe-inspiring power (*jalal*). These references to the two sides of God recall the theological distinction between immanence and transcendence. God is both near and accessible—closer even than the jugular vein, according to Qur'an 50:16—and infinitely beyond human experience and imagining. Rudolf Otto's classic definition of the "holy" can further clarify the matter. The great German thinker calls the "sacred" or "holy" "the mystery both terrifying and fascinating" (Otto, 1958). *Mystery* refers to irreducible, unanalyzable meaning, before which one can only stand silent. Paradoxically, one who experiences mystery cannot but be filled simultaneously with intimations of both irresistible attractiveness and sheer dread (Otto, 1958). Think, for example, of Moses' curiosity at the sight of the burning bush and of his terror at finding himself in the presence of the Living God. He is riveted between the desire to flee and wanting to stay forever. Or think of Peter, James, and John, who go to the mountain and are frightened to find Jesus transfigured in

Shown here from the archway of a surrounding portico is the seventeenth-century Congregational Mosque in Delhi, India. Note the reflecting pool in the courtyard and the three domes over the prayer hall.

glory before them, speaking with Moses and Elijah, yet in their fear is the awe that results in Peter wanting to build three tents to keep the sanctity of their presence earthbound.

Though all religious traditions ultimately strive to give expression to the total experience of divine mystery, each has its distinctive ways of emphasizing one or the other aspect. Whereas Christianity's central doctrine of Incarnation tips the scale toward divine immanence, Islamic imagery tends to interpret the experience of God rather in terms of transcendence and majesty. This is only a rough and relative characterization, however; Christians also view God as beyond human grasp, and as we shall see later, Islamic tradition has also known God as an intimate companion. It is fair to say that most images of God both enjoy seasons of prominence and suffer periods of relative disuse in the history of every religious tradition. On balance, however, the Islamic tradition has generally preferred images of divine majesty.

One fascinating image that is both highly instructive and easily misinterpreted is that of the divine trickster. One occasionally hears non-Muslims characterize Islam's God as wily or cunning, as though God delighted in cruel hoaxes. Not so. The Qur'an refers to God as the "best of those who devise schemes" (e.g., Q 3:47, 8:30, 13:42, 27:51) to indicate that no human being can know the mind of God. Al-Ghazali (d. 1111), one of Islam's greatest pastoral theologians and one of the most famous citizens of medieval Baghdad, develops the idea further. Partially because of its shock value, Ghazali sees in the divine stratagem (*makr*) the ultimate reminder that human beings are better off not trying to second-guess their creator. Ghazali tells the story of how once when the angel Gabriel was with Muhammad, the two acknowledged to each other that they felt stark terror in the presence of God. God then spoke to them to reassure them; they need not be afraid, for he had made them secure. Should they indeed be unafraid, Muhammad wondered? Had not God himself told them not to tremble? Gabriel cautioned that they ought not banish their fear too casually, regardless of the apparent meaning of God's words; they were, after all, in the presence of *God*. There, only a fool would know no dread (McKane, 1962, 57ff.). This arresting image is meant to emphasize God's utter transcendence of human imagining. A human being who thinks he or she has God down to a pattern has wandered from the Straight Path into the realm of presumptuousness. Let no one imagine that God is so boring as to be predictable.

Numerous verses of the Qur'an emphasize God's sovereignty and power. Two such texts come to mind. The first, called the "Throne Verse," appears as an inscription around the interior of domes in dozens of major mosques across the world:

> God—there is no deity but He; the Living, the Everlasting. Neither slumber nor sleep overcome Him. To Him belong all that heavens and earth encompass. Who can intercede with Him, except by his leave? He knows all that surrounds [created beings], while they can grasp nothing of what He knows, except as He chooses. His Throne stretches across heaven and earth; sovereignty over them tires him not, for He is the Exalted, the Magnificent. (Q 2:255)

God is thus the beginning and end of all things, the Creator, the Sustainer, the Provider, the Lord of space and time. According to a saying of Muhammad (part of a body of literature called "Hadith"), the Throne Verse, like all the Qur'an, has existed eternally in the mind of God and was known to earlier prophets. Anas ibn Malik (c. 612–712), a well-known companion to the Prophet Muhammad, said:

> God revealed to Moses, "Whoever continues to recite the Throne Verse after every prayer, on him will I bestow more than that granted to those who are ever thankful. His reward shall be as great as that of prophets and that granted the righteous for their good deeds. I shall spread over him my right hand in mercy. Nothing would hinder him from entering Paradise." . . . Moses said, "My Lord, how can anyone hear this and not continue to observe it?" God said, "I grant this to no one except a prophet, a righteous person, a man I love. . . ." (Ayoub, 1984, p. 248)

Later in this chapter, we will return to this text briefly to discuss some issues related to the interpretation of scripture.

One of the great writers who have elaborated on the theme of God's transcendence is the Persian Sana'i of Ghazna (d. 1131, in what is now Afghanistan). Addressing God, he writes in the preface to his mystical didactic epic, the *Garden of Ultimate Reality*:

> O you who nourish the soul and ornament the visible world,
> And you who grant wisdom and are indulgent with those who lack it;
> Creator and sustainer of space and of time,
> Custodian and provider of dweller and dwelling;
> All is of your making, dwelling and dweller,
> All is within your compass, time and space.
> Fire and air, water and earth,
> All are mysteriously within the scope of your power.
> All that is between your Throne and this earth
> Are but a fraction of your handiwork;
> Inspirited intelligence acts as your swift herald,
> Every living tongue that moves in every mouth
> Has but one purpose: to give you praise.
> Your sublime and exalted names
> Evidence your beneficence and grace and kindness.
> Every one of them outstrips throne and globe and dominion;
> They are a thousand plus one and a hundred less one.
> But to those who are outside the spiritual sanctuary,
> The names are veiled.
> O Lord, in your largesse and mercy
> Allow this heart and soul a glimpse of your name! (From the Persian of Sana'i's *Hadiqat al Haqiqat*, I:2–11)

A second Qur'anic text, perhaps even more important as an architectural inscription than is the Throne Verse, offers a magnificently imaginative glimpse of the unimaginable. The "Verse of Light" provides another ingredient in our complex of imagery:

> God is the Light of Heaven and Earth. Picture His light as a niche within which there is a lamp, and the lamp is within a glass. And it is as though the glass were a glittering star lit from a sacred olive tree neither of east nor west, whose oil would fairly radiate even without the touch of fire. Light upon light, and God guides to his light whom He will. (Q 24:35)

That text has inspired marvelous designs on prayer carpets and on the niches (*mihrab*, a recess in the wall that orientates the worshiper toward Mecca) of mosques all over the world. It suggests several relevant issues in this context. First, it recalls the symbolism of the revelatory cosmic tree, one that glows without being consumed and is so large it spans the universe (being, therefore, exclusive of neither east nor west). On the level of imagery, the text has functioned as a kind of summary, like the Throne Verse, of divine qualities.

Second, the last line brings to mind a question that has been significant in shaping Islamic intellectual history, namely, the matter of divine ordination of events or predestination. If God guides whom he will, then does he also not will to guide others? And if so, could those others truly be held responsible if they lose their way? The issue is complex. Suffice it to say for the moment that Islamic tradition has generally striven to strike a balance between God's unlimited power and the human person's limited freedom and commensurate accountability. It is useful to think of the apparent predilection for some form of divine predetermination as an analogy to the Biblical phenomenon of God's "hardening the heart" of Pharaoh and of even some of the people of Israel.

Finally, the Verse of Light alludes to that crucial divine function of guidance, which in turn brings us back to the image of journey. "Guide" is one of the Ninety-Nine Names, and the Qur'an often speaks of God in that capacity. Just after the Throne Verse, the scripture continues: "God is the Guardian of those who believe; He brings them forth from darkness into His light. Those who choose not to believe in their arrogance will be led from the light into darkness, there to become companions of the fire forever" (Q 2:257). The irony, in view of the Verse of Light, is striking. Those who rely on themselves cannot discover the authentic light but come only to that fire that is darkness itself.

According to some interpreters, God's relationship to journeying goes beyond the function of guidance. A widely influential and prolific thinker named Ibn Arabi (born in Spain, d. 1240) elaborates on the connections. He discerns sixteen journeys in the Qur'an. God begins by taking the primordial journey from the utter transcendence and inaccessibility of Sublimity downward to his Throne. From there, God dispatches Creation on its journey from nonbeing into being and sends down the Qur'an. God sends Adam on the Journey of Calamity from paradise to Earth. Noah embarks on the Journey of Safety, and Moses on the Journey of Divine Appointment to meet God. (We will shortly recall how Moses' chief attribute is that he conversed with God).

In Ibn Arabi's view, and in that of other important mystics before and since, every spiritual journey is one of three types directly related to God. There are journeys away from, toward, and in God. The first occurs when God banishes a fallen angel, when shame drives a sinner away, or when God sends a prophet or messenger into the world. Second, though all beings travel toward God, not all reach their goal. Unrepentant sinners experience the frustration of endless wandering; those who have obeyed but remain imperfect in their acknowledgment of the absolute unity and sovereignty of God arrive in the divine presence but are veiled from the divine vision; and the elect find the ultimate goal. Of those who journey in God, some (known as philosophers) falter along the way because they rely on the rational faculty; the elect, saints, and prophets make easy progress (Ibish, 1971, 441–46). (For more on the subject and on Ibn Arabi's "prophetology," see Chittick, 1990; and Austin, 1980.)

As we will see shortly, the essential mediating role of prophets is to lead people from darkness to light. Speaking of the mission of Moses and his brother Aaron, Qur'an 37:117–18 says: "We [God speaking] gave them the Book that clarifies, and led them to the Straight Path." We turn now to consider first, Islam's scripture within the context of the larger history of revelation, and second, the place of Muhammad within the history of prophethood.

THE QUR'AN AND THE HISTORY OF REVELATION

> It is He [God] who sent down [revealed] to you the Book, confirming in truth all that preceded it; and before that He had sent down the Torah and the Gospel as guidance to humankind.(Q 3:3)

Among the many foundations of Islamic religious tradition that intrigue and often puzzle non-Muslims, the Qur'an surely ranks high. First-time readers with some knowledge of Biblical narratives are invariably struck by the frequent allusions to familiar tales of Adam and Eve, Abraham, Moses, David and Solomon, and Jesus and Mary. Christians, especially, marvel that an entire chapter (sura 19) is named after Mary and that Jesus' mother is actually mentioned more often by name in the Qur'an than in the Greek Testament (the Christian Scripture).

More careful examination of the scriptures, such as a comparison of the story of Joseph in sura 12 with the account in Genesis 37–50, inevitably raises numerous questions for Muslims and non-Muslims alike. When Christians and Jews discover a Qur'anic Moses or Joseph, or Jesus or Mary, who do and say things evidently at variance with the Biblical narratives, they often conclude that the Qur'an must be a slightly modified "borrowing." Muslims, on the other hand, explain discrepancies as evidence that Jews and Christians have obviously tampered with the original revelation to make it more palatable and less demanding. In fact, some argue, had the earlier "Peoples of the Book" not altered the record, God would not have needed to restore the revelation to its pristine purity by sending Muhammad with a corrective message. Besides, Muslim tradition adds, Muhammad was illiterate and therefore could not have plagiarized Biblical material.

Neither point of view is helpful, for both conclusions arise out of a spirit of partisan competition rather than out of a desire to deal openly with the data of history. The arguments seek only to defend the integrity of one scripture at the expense of the other. True, a great deal is at stake here, but only to the degree that one is unable to take the larger view of God's communication with humankind.

One possibility Christians and Jews might profitably explore is this: just as stories of the great religious figures do not belong exclusively to any people or culture, so their capacity to reveal divine truth belongs to all whom God wishes to have access to them. Stories are a free-floating possession of humanity. If variations on narratives that some associate with the Bible occur in the Qur'an, they are there for an important purpose that transcends the rights of Christians and Jews to claim exclusive ownership of "their" stories and truths.

Muslims, for their part, might well understand the Qur'an as bringing a new perspective, reinforcing the ancient message, and enhancing and multiplying the opportunities for human beings to respond in faith. More than one Muslim author has suggested that Muhammad's "illiteracy" functions in Islamic theology much the way Mary's virginity functions in Christianity. In neither case does the human being strive to initiate. In both instances, it is God who effects the wonder of sending His word into the world. For Christians, Mary is the medium for the Word made Flesh; for Muslims, Muhammad serves as the instrument by which the Word is made Book. (See, for example, S. H. Nasr, *Ideals and Realities of Islam* [London: Allen & Unwin, 1966] for related observations.) The "Inlibration" thus parallels the "Incarnation."

The Qur'an itself suggests an explanation for the controversy at hand here:

> Humankind were once a single community. God sent prophets with news and warnings,

> and through them revealed the Book in truth that He might judge between people when they disagreed with one another. But, after the clear indicators had come to them, it was only out of self-centered stubbornness that they differed among themselves. God guided those who believed to the truth over which they argued, for God guides to the Straight Path whom He will. (Q 2:213)

Before considering further such important issues as the place of the Qur'an in Islamic life and various modes of interpretation, it will be helpful to sum up briefly some of the Qur'an's most important formal qualities and themes.

As a historic event, the revelation of the Arabic Qur'an defined a community of faith as its fundamental source of authority. Unlike either the Hebrew or the Greek Testaments, the Qur'an unfolded over a relatively short period of time, and its articulation is attributed to only one human being. Beginning in about 610 CE, when he was about 40 years old, Muhammad began to experience, in mostly auditory but occasionally visual form, what he would come to identify as divine revelations. Muhammad initially delivered the message orally, somewhat in the form of homiletical material. Not until more than two decades after the Prophet's death would a definitive text be compiled and written. Tradition has divided the text into two main periods, the Meccan and Medinan, corresponding to the years before and after the Hijra, the move to Medina in 622 CE. Scholars have more recently further divided the Meccan period into early, middle, and late periods, on the basis of the form and content of the suras.

During the Meccan Period (610–621), five themes appear most often in the earliest suras: (1) Evidently presuming belief in some deity on the part of their hearers, they emphasize God's creative power, providence, and guidance. There was at first no emphasis on belief in only one God. (2) They speak of accountability at judgment in a rather general way, without specific reference to particular reward or punishment as motivation for upright behavior. In view of these two, the suras suggest that the appropriate response for the individual is a combination of gratitude and worship. (3) This response flows out of an inner recognition of one's total dependence on God expressed formally in prayer. (4) Two parallel social consequences are also acknowledged in the need for generosity, as expressed in giving to those in need and seeking a just distribution of wealth. (5) Finally, the early message includes the theme of Muhammad's dawning awareness of his own prophetic mission and all that it would demand of him.

During the middle Meccan period, both the tone and the content of the suras began to change. Stories, first of indigenous Arabian and then of Biblical prophets, illustrated graphically the disastrous consequences attendant upon refusal to hear the prophetic message. Here, one finds a growing insistence on monotheistic belief and forthright condemnation of idolatry.

Toward the end of the Meccan period, emphasis on the rejection of past prophets grew apace with Muhammad's own experience of local opposition.

During the Medinan period (622–632 CE), both the style and the content changed dramatically. Whereas the Meccan suras tended to be poetic in tone, a quite dramatic form called rhymed prose (*saj'*), the later message became more prose-like. Its content reflected the growing need to regulate the daily life of the expanding community of Muslims, and the reality of increased contact with Christians and Jews (of whom several large tribes played a major part in the life of Medina) (see Watt, 1953, 1956).

Over a period of twenty-three years or so, the divine interventions would come upon Muhammad in a variety of circumstances, often at times when he was struggling with a particular

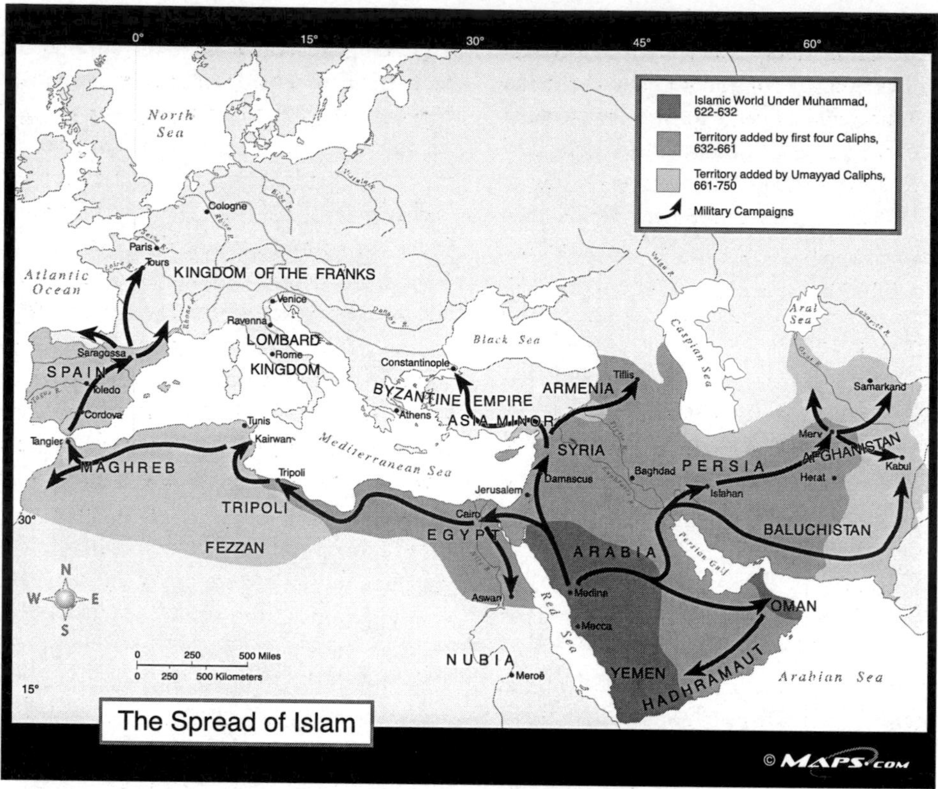

The Spread of Islam

problem or issue. For example, for a while after the Hijra, the Muslims faced Jerusalem when they prayed, as did the local Jews. Apparently, some friction caused a falling out with the Jewish community, causing Muhammad concern over the continued symbolic statement of the prayer orientation. Thus came the revelation, "We have seen you turning your face about toward the heavens. We shall now turn you toward a direction (*qibla*) that you will find satisfying. Turn your face toward the Mosque of the Sanctuary [site of the Ka`ba in Mecca]; wherever you are, turn your faces toward it" (Q 2:144). That verse sometimes serves as a decorative inscription over the *mihrab* (niche) in mosques.

The Qur'an forms the core of all Islamic worship and devotional activity. As part of the daily ritual prayer, Muslims regularly recite the opening sura quoted earlier, as well as several other short pieces. An example is the very brief sura 112 *al-Ikhlas* (Sincerity or Purity of Faith): "Proclaim: He is One God, God the besought of all; He does not beget; He is not begotten; and there is none like Him." It is an unmistakable reminder to Muslims that they are different from Christians with their belief in Father, Son,

KA`BA

One of the sacred sites of Islam, situated in Mecca in present-day Saudi Arabia, the city of the pilgrimage (one of the five pillars of Islam), this one-room, cube-shaped stone structure is believed to have been built by Abraham and his son Ishmael, and the nearby well called Zamzam is believed to have been used by Ishmael's mother, Hagar. Each year, millions of pilgrims come to visit Mecca and the Ka`ba as part of their spiritual journey.

and Spirit. However, perhaps just as important as the theological content is the sheer physical experience of reciting and/or hearing recitation of the Qur'an. The effect on listeners is often profound, for the mode of delivery combined with the extraordinarily earthy sound of Arabic make for an intensely moving experience. One commentator has likened the recitation to the Christian practice of Communion, in that in both instances, one has the Word on the tongue (Cragg, 1973, 1971).

Qur'an recitation is also part of many religious occasions outside the five daily prayers. After a funeral, families of the deceased often hire a reciter to come and grace the time for condolence with appropriate scriptural texts. During the fasting month of Ramadan, Muslims make a special place for recitation. They commemorate the twenty-seventh day of that lunar month as the "Night of Power," when Muhammad received the first revelation. In addition, the entire Qur'an is recited during the thirty nights of Ramadan. For that and other such "liturgical" purposes, the text of the scripture has been divided into thirty sections, each of which is further halved, and those halves further quartered, yielding a total of 240 divisions. One can easily keep track of how far one has to go during each period of recitation.

There are social dimensions to be considered as well. All across the Islamic world, the art of Qur'an recitation is highly prized. One can almost always tune to a radio station that broadcasts recitation and commentary all day. In some places, such as Malaysia and Indonesia and even on a smaller scale here in the United States, the art has become very competitive. National contests draw huge crowds to sports stadiums, and winners look forward to going to a grand final meet in Mecca. In virtually any large mosque, for example, one can find people sitting alone and chanting their recitation quietly to themselves or engaging in lively discussions about the text.

On the level of individual devotion too, the Qur'an functions prominently. Some Muslims still strive to memorize the entire book, whose approximately six-thousand verses make it roughly the length of the NT. Memorizing the text means having it in one's heart and "keeping" it there. Paralleling the memorization of the Qur'an is what has been called the Qur'anization of the memory. The phrase originally referred to the intensely scriptural way of thinking manifested by some of the great Muslim spiritual writers and mystical poets, but there are further implications as well. Especially throughout the Arabic-speaking world, phrases from the Qur'an have become so much a part of ordinary speech, particularly among traditional-minded Muslims, that many people no longer know where the sacred ends and the profane begins.

Methods of Exegesis

Islamic tradition has known several important varieties of scriptural interpretation, or exegesis. In the last section, we looked at two of the Qur'an's premier texts, the Throne Verse and the Verse of Light. We shall return to them shortly for some insight into how Muslims have interpreted their scripture. The Qur'an itself makes a foundational observation as to the two principal ways human beings might understand its verses:

> He it is who has revealed the Book to you. Some of its verses/signs are categorical in meaning. They are the mother [i.e., essence] of the Book. Others are open to interpretation [i.e., metaphorical or allegorical]. Those whose hearts harbor ill-will pursue its metaphorical verses, in their desire for disharmony and esoteric interpretation [ta'wil]. None but God knows the inner meaning. (Q 3:7)

That short text is remarkable in its succinct articulation of the central difficulty all scripture-based traditions must face. The text clearly comes down on the side of clarity and literal meaning. Unfortunately, it leaves unanswered the question of why it contains the ambiguous at all.

Legal

We will call the first type of interpretation the "legal" or juristic. For all Muslims, Qur'an is at the heart of all religious law, followed in short order by sayings attributed to Muhammad, called Hadith. It is the task of the legal scholar to search the text for the clearest, least ambiguous references to a given regulatory matter (from dietary law to family inheritance to criminal sanctions). What the jurist wants is to interpret the scripture so as to extend its applicability to present needs and circumstances, even if those were not obviously foremost at the time of the revelation.

Theological

A second type of exegesis is the theological. Ever since at least the late seventh or early eighth century, Muslims have been asking difficult questions about how the sacred text communicates the divine mystery. The imagery of God seated on the Throne has been at the center of much discussion in classical Islamic theology, for it raises the question of whether and to what degree one ought to interpret scripture literally. Taken literally, the text conjures up anthropomorphic pictures of the deity: there is a Throne and God actually sits upon it, and so forth. Taken metaphorically, the text becomes a colorful reference to divine sovereignty and transcendence. Islamic tradition has on the whole considered the latter option a dangerous invitation to water down the meaning of the sacred text.

Two of the principal positions in the theological debate are those of a group called the Mu`tazilites (emerged in the eighth century CE, literally means "those who keep themselves apart") and the school of a man named al-Ash`ari (d. 944). A fundamental tenet of the Mu`tazilites was that the Qur'an was not uncreated, as the traditionalists argued, but created and therefore subject to the critique of human reason. It sounds perhaps like so much hair splitting, but it had the import of Christian theological debate around the divinity and humanity of Jesus. Basing all their arguments on reason (doing theology from below, one could say), the Mu`tazilites believed that taking literally such texts as the Throne Verse made no sense at all, for the anthropomorphism thus entailed would bring God down to human scale. It was simply not rational to speak that way about the transcendent. In his classic Mu`tazilite commentary, Zamakhshari says of the *kursi*, or footstool, attached to the Throne, "It is no more than an image expressing God's greatness. In reality, there is neither *kursi*, an act of sitting, nor one who sits" (Ayoub, 1984, 251). The verse therefore uses a "fanciful image" to communicate the idea of God's extensive power, knowledge, and sovereignty (Gatje, 1976, 146–47).

Al-Ash`ari had been a member of the Mu`tazilites in his youth and became disaffected with their inability to rein in their own rational arguments. He countered that, on the contrary, what made no sense was any attempt to limit God in any direction whatsoever. He concluded that one simply ought not to speculate about what God has in mind. If the Qur'an says God sits on a throne, one must take the statement at face value and let it be. He quotes, with utmost approval, the Hadith of Muhammad, "The *kursi* is the place of the two feet [the footstool of God]. It has a squeaking sound like that of a new saddle" (Ayoub, 1984, 249). His now-famous methodological formula, *bila kayf* ("without a how"), sums up the notion that one simply ought not to speculate on these things. Ash`ari's opinion has carried the day, for the most part, with its emphasis on divine mystery.

Allegorical

The Shi`a or Shi`ite Muslims were especially partial to a third type of exegesis. Just as the jurists read scripture with any eye for regulatory items and the rationalists went for the anthropomorphisms, Shi`ite interpreters have been keen to focus on any text that might support the religious and political legitimacy of Muhammad's son-in-law Ali and his descendants. Shi`ite exegesis is therefore highly allegorical. Recall, for example, the Verse of Light. One classic reading of it likens God's light to Muhammad, the niche to Muhammad's breast, the lamp to the knowledge of prophecy, and the glass to Muhammad's prophetic knowledge passed along to Ali. That the tree is of neither east nor west means Ali was neither Jew nor Christian. Just as the tree nearly glowed even untouched by fire, so Ali would nearly utter the prophetic knowledge, even if Muhammad had not passed it on. And the phrase "Light upon light" refers to the succession of one Imam (spiritual descendent of Ali) from the previous Imam (Gatje, 1976, 243–45).

Mystical

Finally, the fourth type is mystical exegesis. Islamic mystics have read the sacred text for any hint of the possibility of an intimate relationship between human and divine. Traditionalists often found such talk at least slightly blasphemous, and rationalists regarded it as sentimental at best, but the rich mystical tradition has mined every reference to divine love and concern, every suggestion of divine immanence, discerning at least two levels of meaning in each tidbit. The outward meaning is apparent to most everyone: to arrive at the hidden meaning requires *ta'wil*, the very thing some would say the Qur'an counsels against (see Q 3:7, quoted previously).

Some examples of the Qur'anic phrases dearest to the mystics include the following:

> To God belong the East and the West; wherever you turn, there is the face of God. (2:115)

■ ■ ■

> I am truly near: I answer the prayer of the petitioner who beseeches me. Therefore let them respond to me and have faith in me, that they might receive guidance. (2:186)

■ ■ ■

> Everything on earth perishes; but the face of your Lord remains, majestic and most revered. (55:26–27)

While the mystical tradition was not loathe to interpret such texts metaphorically, they did so without in any way deflating them of their mystery, as the Mu`tazilite approach ran the risk of doing. In his reading of the Throne Verse, for example, the mystic Ibn `Arabi considers the *kursi* to be the center of knowledge on the cosmic scale, as is the human heart on the microcosmic level. He goes on to say that God does not tire of keeping all things in existence, "because they have no existence without Him. . . . Rather the realm of the ideal form is His inner dimension and the realm of forms is His outer dimension. They have no existence except in Him. Nor are they other than He" (Ayoub, 1984, 250–51). Such statements, liable as they may seem to the charge of pantheistic monism, that is, where everything is one and is God, were the sort of utterances for which many a mystic ran afoul of more traditional thinkers.

Before we move on to the Prophet, two other beautiful short texts will help to reinforce the sense of power and inexhaustible grandeur that Muslims experience in their scripture.

The first text and its parallel emphasize the infinitude of God's revelation, extending impossibly beyond creation's capacity: "If all the trees

IMAGE: © JOHN RENARD

The Taj Mahal is a seventeenth-century tomb built by Mughal Muslim ruler Shah Jahan as a burial place for his favorite wife in Agra, North-Central India. Passages from the Qur'an are etched throughout the tomb and surrounding buildings.

on earth were pens and all the oceans ink, with seven more seas besides, they would not suffice to record the words of God" (Q 31:27; see also 18:109). Christian readers may be reminded of the text with which John's Gospel ends: "But there are also many other things that Jesus did; if every one of them were written down, I suppose that the world itself could not contain the books that would be written" (John 21:25). The second is reminiscent of a theme associated with Mount Sinai. Sinai swooned when God gave Moses the Torah and, according to the mystics and rabbis, exploded into many pieces, each of which fell upon and blessed a part of the earth. "If we had sent this Qur'an down upon a mountain, you would have seen it crumble to pieces and humble itself for fear of God" (Q 59:21).

MUHAMMAD AND THE HISTORY OF PROPHETHOOD

> Say "We believe in God and what has been revealed to us and what was revealed to Abraham and Isma`il and Isaac and Jacob and the tribes, and what was given to Moses and Jesus and what was given to the prophets from their Lord. We make no distinction among them and to Him do we surrender gratefully [lit., "we are Muslims to Him"]." (Q 2:136; see also 29:46)

Jewish and Christian readers will already have some familiarity with the notion of prophets and prophetic mission. Since time immemorial, prophet-types have played a major role in the religious history of the Middle East. In the Hebrew Scriptures, prophets receive a mandate to speak on God's behalf. Their mission often requires that they stand up to the high and mighty, posing the divine challenge of justice for the powerless of the earth. The problem of how to discern true prophets from charlatans has exercised religious minds for millennia as well. In addition to the full-fledged prophets, lesser characters have also played a part. These include sages, oracles, and soothsayers.

All of these religious types were familiar to many people in the Arabia of Muhammad's day, but as Muhammad would discover, the majority of the populace welcomed the advent of a prophet no more enthusiastically in the seventh century CE than they would have in the seventh century BCE. A brief summary of the major events of Muhammad's life will provide the necessary immediate context for our consideration of his paradigmatic role in the life of the Muslim community.

Muhammad was born in the trading town of Mecca around 570 CE to a rather poor family of the clan of Hashim, one of the branches of the

Quraysh tribe. His father died before Muhammad was born, and the boy's mother died when he was 6 years old. According to Arabian custom, the youngster was sent to be reared among the Bedouin tribes of the desert regions. Tradition names his nurse Halima. After his mother's death, Muhammad grew up first in the custody of his grandfather, Abd al-Muttalib, and later in the house of his uncle, Abu Talib, whose son Ali we have already mentioned briefly. Tradition has it that the young Muhammad traveled with his uncle on business. One story tells how in Syria they met an old Christian monk named Bahira, who discerned the marks of prophetic greatness in the boy.

At this time, pre-Islamic Arabian religion was mostly a kind of "polydemonism," with multiple spirits, mostly associated with natural features such as stones (e.g., the Black Stone in a corner of the Ka`ba), springs, groves of trees, and so on. When Muhammad was about 25, he married a widow fifteen years his senior. Khadija ran her own caravan business, and Muhammad went to work for her. Apparently, Muhammad liked occasionally to retreat to mountain solitude to meditate and seek within the source of life. Around 610 CE, when Muhammad had reached 40, the age long considered in the Middle East a necessary precondition for the imparting of wisdom and ministry, he began to experience troubling visitations that sent him, in turmoil, to ask Khadija's counsel.

On the "Night of Power" now commemorated on the twenty-seventh day of Ramadan, the earliest message commanded him to "Recite!" (lit., "make qur'an, recitation") that which no human being could know unaided. The encounter left him confused and uncertain. Not until as much as a year later did Muhammad hear a follow-up message of confirmation: "Indeed your Lord is the one who best knows who has strayed from His path, who best knows those who are guided" (Q 68:7). Assured that he was not losing his sanity, Muhammad persisted in his attitude of attentiveness to the messages from the unseen world. From then on, revelations came more frequently. During the next several years, Muhammad slowly gathered a circle of converts who would form the nucleus of a faith community. Leaders of the Quraysh (rulers of Mecca) grew increasingly unhappy at the effects of Muhammad's preaching on caravan and pilgrim traffic to the Ka`ba and at the prospect of a rival leader in their midst. Around 615 CE, under growing pressure and amid threats to the safety of his community, Muhammad sent a group to seek asylum across the Red Sea with the Christian ruler of Abyssinia (Ethiopia). Muhammad remained in Mecca.

Tradition reports that on the twenty-seventh night of the month of Rajab (late August) in the year 621 CE, Muhammad underwent a two-fold mystical experience. In the first part, God "carried his servant by night, from the Mosque of the Sanctuary to the Farther Mosque" (Q 17:1). Later interpreters would equate the first site with the shrine of the Ka`ba in Mecca, the second with the southern end of the temple platform in Jerusalem, where now stands an early eighth-century structure called "the Farther Mosque" (*al-masjid al-aqsa*). This "Night Journey" (*isra'*) was already clearly a kind of otherworldly experience, for ancient narratives place Muhammad in the company of earlier prophets in the Farther Mosque, who naturally asked him to lead them in the ritual prayer. The second part of the journey, however, called the "Ascension" (*mi`raj*), finds the Prophet riding a winged human-faced steed named Buraq and led by Gabriel toward the very throne of God. Marvelously embellished tales have developed around this experience. Vivid descriptions of Muhammad's excursion follow him through the various levels of heaven, where he meets all of his major prophetic forebears, down to the dark circles of hell, where Gabriel shows him the horrors of the damned. This is truly the picture of a heroic journey of initiation in the mysteries of the unseen world. Many Muslims believe the journey involved physical locomotion, but a strong tradition of nonliteralistic interpretation has always regarded it as a spiritual and inward experience. It is considered a paradigm of the individual Muslim's spiritual path.

During the year of the Night Journey and Ascension, and perhaps also during the previous year, Muhammad had been investigating the possibility of moving his community from the increasingly hostile environment of Mecca to a safer haven. Hopeful prospects arrived in 621 CE with a delegation from Yathrib, a city several hundred miles north of Mecca. Looking for someone to help them negotiate a peaceful settlement to factional problems in their city, the representatives invited Muhammad to come and apply his already renowned talent for arbitration. Arrangements were finalized, and in 622 CE, the Muslims headed north to Yathrib, whose name would soon change to Medinat an-Nabi ("City of the Prophet"), or simply Medina. That crucial journey was called the *Hijra* or Emigration. It marked the birthday of Islam, so to speak, and the beginning of the Muslim calendar (with dates marked AH, "after the Hijra"). This journey developed in Islamic piety and as a metaphor for the Muslim community's relationships with the world at large.

Muhammad's years in Medina, as reflected in the text of the Qur'an as well as in later historical writing, witnessed major changes in his style of leadership and in the shape of the community of believers. Muhammad's prominence in the new setting gave prestige to the community. As the group increased, so did the demands on Muhammad's administrative time and skill so that what began as spiritual leadership gradually grew into a more comprehensive oversight. During the Medinan period, the Muslims also took up arms against the Quraysh, who had carried on a continuous campaign against the Muslims after the Hijra and fought a number of serious military engagements with the Meccan forces. After nearly eight years of bitter conflict, the two sides struck a truce. Muhammad returned there in 630 to claim the city for the Muslims, and by that time, the Quraysh had decided not to resist, so the city was taken without significant military effort. In 630, Muhammad led a triumphal band to claim the city for the Muslims. Two years later, Muhammad returned to Mecca for what would be his farewell pilgrimage to the Ka`ba: the *Hajj* ("pilgrimage"), as a religious symbol and experience of return to the center and as a metaphor around which to understand Islam as a unique community of faith.

Given this brief overview of the key events in Muhammad's life, it remains for us to try to understand how Muhammad saw himself within the larger sweep of God's use of prophets to reveal the Word to humankind. Both the Qur'an and the Hadith are replete with references to earlier prophets, from Adam to Jesus. Islamic tradition numbers over two-dozen figures sent to particular peoples, including David, Solomon, Noah, and Jonah, as well as the Arabian figures Hud, Salih, and Shu`ayb. All of them are "prophets" (*nabi*, pl. *anbiya'*) commissioned to warn their people; some are in addition "messengers" (*rasul*, pl. *rusul*) to whom scriptures are revealed. All of the prophets and messengers experienced rejection at the hands of their people, and some were killed. In every instance, God dealt harshly with the people.

Muhammad readily identified with several of the prophets in particular, especially with Abraham, the "Friend of the Merciful" (*Khalil ar-Rahman*), and Moses, "God's Conversant" (*Kalim Allah*). In Islamic tradition, Abraham was neither Jew nor Christian but a *hanif*, a seeker after the one true God. As the Qur'an says:

> Truly Abraham was a model [lit., an *umma*], obedient to God, and a seeker [lit., *hanif*] who assigned no partner to God. He responded

> in gratitude to the bounty of the one who chose him and guided him to the Straight Path. . . . So We have revealed to you [*Muhammad*] that you should follow the believing ways [lit., *milla*] of Abraham the seeker. (Q 16:120–121, 123)

It was Abraham who had prayed that God would "send among them a messenger from their midst who will unfold to them your signs and teach them the Book and the wisdom" (Q 2:129).

Moses' importance in the Qur'an is equal to that of Abraham:

> We sent Moses with Our signs: "Bring your people out from profound darkness into the light and make them mindful of the days of God." Truly in that are signs for all who are long-suffering and grateful. (Q 4:5)

Qur'an 73:15 likens Muhammad especially to Moses. Islamic tradition likewise sees a reference to Muhammad in the words of Deuteronomy 18:18, in which God says to Moses, "I will raise up for them a prophet like you from among their own people; I will put my words in the mouth of the prophet, who shall speak to them everything that I command" (Corbin, 1978, 121ff.). Curiously, one text of the Qur'an (7:155–57) has God speaking approvingly to Moses of "those who follow the Apostle, the unlettered Prophet [i.e., Muhammad] whom they find written of [in their own] Torah and Gospel. . . ." The allusion is apparently first to the text of Deuteronomy just mentioned, and second, to references in the Gospel of John (14–16) to the Paraclete.

Medieval Muslim theologians interpreted the Johannine text in a fascinating manner. This is an important opportunity to exemplify how languages differ. Speakers of Semitic languages such as Arabic become accustomed to finding basic meanings in consonantal roots of words that, when written, are without their vowels. Transferring that way of thinking to Greek, scholars reasoned that Christians had misread Jesus' term as *paraklētos*, "advocate or counselor," interpreted by Christians as the Holy Spirit. A simple insertion of the correct vowels would yield *periklytos*, "the highly praised one," and thus a meaning more acceptable to Muslims. The name *Muhammad* in Arabic derives from the root *HaMaDa*, "to praise." To intensify a root meaning, Arabic doubles the middle consonant, hence *HaMMaDa*, "to praise highly." In order to express the idea that a particular individual has been praised highly, Arabic forms a passive participle by prefixing *mu-* and producing the word *muHaMMaD*, the "highly praised one."

What is most important to note in all this is the Muslim conviction that God sends a message to suit every circumstance perfectly. As the Qur'an says, "We (God) have sent no messenger except with the language of his people, that he might give them clarity. God allows to wander off whom He will, and He guides whom He will" (Q 4:4).

All prophets have been wayfarers, as have all human beings. But what distinguishes prophets, from Adam to Muhammad, from the rest of wandering humankind is that God's messengers come with the explicit mission of helping the rest find their way amid the confusion, the maze of possible paths and goals, the plethora of markers and way stations. Islamic tradition offers a wide range of imaginative models of spiritual progress. One model associates various stages along the way with individual prophet-guides. The latter are in turn associated with particular colors, degrees of spiritual achievement, levels of the cosmos, and such human faculties as heart, spirit, and innermost secrets. Using such a model, one can speak of spiritual progress as a process of encountering a succession of the "prophets of one's own being" as the traveler proceeds upward through the spectrum of colors and from the gross to the subtle.

DISTINCTIVE SCRIPTURAL THEMES IN ISLAMIC SPIRITUALITY

Qur'anic themes are central to any appreciation of Islamic spirituality. It is to such thoughts as these that Muslims instinctively advert as they reflect on their deepest religious values. This section will begin with (1) the theme of prayer in the Qur'an and Qur'an as prayer, then (2) move to several of the fundamental interior attitudes Muslims are called to cultivate, and finally (3) cover the outward responsibilities where the tradition challenges believers to put those attitudes into action.

Prayer in the Qur'an and Qur'an as Prayer

One of the principal difficulties non-Muslims encounter in reading the Qur'an is that of finding a focus that can help them trace the scripture's basic message. The foregoing section on Qur'anic interpretation has noted that what one sees in the Qur'an depends a great deal on what one is looking for. For our purposes, it is essential to bear in mind that the Qur'an, as all sacred texts, seeks to communicate an experience. One way to focus on the heart of that experience is to read the Qur'an as both a sourcebook of prayer and as a prayer in itself.

As a sourcebook of prayer, the Qur'an lays the conceptual and practical foundations for all subsequent developments in the history of Islamic spirituality. Here I am speaking of the scripture as a word spoken by God and addressed to human beings. As a prayer in itself, the Qur'an becomes a divinely initiated word addressed back to God. I will return to the latter aspect later in this chapter, in the context of experiencing the Qur'an in memory and recitation. For the moment, let us look at prayer as a theme in the sacred text, both as divine instruction in how humans ought to respond to God and as concrete prophetic example.

Some of the earliest texts suggest that night vigil and recitation were at the heart of the matter. References to "prostration" and to various daily times for prayer also occur in early suras. For example, a sura dated to about 615–616 CE says: "Therefore glorify God when evening comes and when you awake; for to Him belongs praise in the heavens and on the earth; and in late afternoon and as dusk begins to fall" (Q 30:17–18). Such suggestions of what eventually developed into the five daily prayers receive more detailed attention in later suras, especially those of the Medinan period, when the growing Muslim community needed increasing communal discipline and instruction.

Examples of personal prayer, or what would come to be known as the prayer of invocation or supplication (*du`a'*), also abound in the Qur'an. During the middle and later Meccan periods, when Muhammad was experiencing growing opposition from influential members of the Quraysh tribe, stories of previous prophets and the enmity of their peoples toward them become crucial to the scripture's message. Those prophets naturally serve as models of prayer, suggesting both when and how one ought to address God from the heart. The years 615–622 were times of particular hardship for the small Muslim community, and the praying of the pre-Islamic prophets reflects and comments on that experience. Abraham's extended prayer at the core of sura 14 is a prime example. He intercedes for the people of Mecca:

> My Lord, make this city secure, and protect me and my children from worshipping idols. My Lord, truly have they misguided many people. One who follows me is with me, but the one who rebels—but You are the Forgiving, the Merciful. . . . My Lord, cause me

> and my descendants to be given to regular communal prayer, O our Lord, and receive my supplication. Our Lord, be forgiving to me and my parents and all believers on that Day of Reckoning.

From the Medinan period comes another, more generic prayer as an example of the sentiments a community of believers such as the one by then more firmly established might express:

> Our Lord, not in vain have You created this, may You be glorified! . . . We have heard the call of one inviting to faith, "Believe in Your Lord," and so we have believed. Our Lord, forgive our sins, cover our evil deeds, and let us die among the righteous. Our Lord, give us what You have promised through your Messengers and let us not be put to shame on Resurrection Day. (Q 3)

The Qur'an and the Inner Life

Among the various essential attitudes the Qur'an recommends, the following four deserve special mention: attentiveness, intention, striving, and gratitude. The theological equivalent of the attitude of attentiveness is uncompromising monotheism—belief in and acknowledgement of one God only, called *tawhid* in Arabic. Its opposite is carelessness, laziness, a spiritual torpor born of self-absorption, a most basic and destructive form of denial. Attentiveness means seeing things as they really are, with the eyes of faith; it means discerning in creation and in oneself, as well as in the revealed scripture, the "signs" of the Creator and Revealer.

Without that mindfulness and heedfulness, no divine–human relationship is possible. Directly related to that attentiveness is right intention. Any action merely performed by rote loses its fully human character and hence produces no spiritual benefit. I will discuss later some of the more subtle aspects of intention in relation to the performance of religious observances and in relation to the need for high vigilance regarding one's general state of soul and motivation. Suffice it to note here that explicit intention precedes all fully human acts.

At the center of the human condition lies the need to struggle, to strive against one's baser tendencies and against the spiritual entropy born of the heedlessness endemic to the human race. Here lies the core of that most misunderstood of Islamic themes, *jihad*. The Arabic root *JaHaDa* (with the three consonantal root letters in upper case) means "to exert oneself." Believers must struggle against whatever stands between the self and its origin and goal, and strive to overcome injustice and oppression. Battle against the fiercest of all enemies, the enemy that resides "between one's two sides," as Hadith puts it, ancient tradition calls the Greater Jihad. To the Lesser Jihad, combat against outward foes, we will come shortly.

What could possibly motivate the hard work of rigorous spiritual discipline? One often hears Islam characterized as a religion of submission, whose adherents operate largely out of fear of a cold, capricious deity. While the Qur'an's emphasis on divine majesty and power has indeed sometimes given rise to a resigned fatalism, the scripture in no way recommends passivity. Prayer for forgiveness occurs often in the Qur'an, but a sense of gratitude to God is at least as significant a motive for ethical action as is fear of punishment. "God has given you all you have asked for; and were you to attempt to add up the kindnesses of God, you would fall short. Indeed, humanity is prey to injustice and ingratitude" (Q 14:34).

All positive virtues flow from the awareness that God is the beneficent and unstinting source of all good, who expects that those most blessed will in turn share their gifts most generously with others. As a means to the attainment of gratitude, one must be purified of any delusions of grandeur or self-sufficiency, as well as of selfish motivation in giving. The term that came to mean "almsgiving," *zakat*, derives from a root meaning "to purify oneself."

> If you give alms in public, for others to see, it is well; but if you conceal your alms, and give them to the poor, it is better for you. . . . Whatever of good you spend in alms shall be for your souls and you should not spend except out of longing for the face of God. (Q 2:271–72)

Gratitude ultimately flows over into praise of God, an attitude that suffuses both the Qur'an and ordinary Arabic speech. We turn now to the implications of these interior qualities for human action.

The Outward Dimensions of Qur'anic Spirituality

The human spirit does not suffer isolation gladly; it naturally seeks expression in relationships to other persons and to the world. Generosity, personal responsibility, and diligence in the Lesser Jihad are three manifestations of healthy engagement of the individual with his or her surroundings. (1) Generosity is the outward result of inner gratitude: one can be truly generous only to the degree that one acknowledges God's primacy in giving.

> Give to kin, to the poor and the traveler what they need; that is best for those who seek the face of God. . . . What you give in the hope of profiting at the expense of other people will gain you nothing in God's sight; what you give as purifying alms [zakat] as you seek

THE FIVE PILLARS OF ISLAM

The following is a summary of the basic minimum beliefs and practices that are part of a larger religious reality.

Daily Practices

1. The profession of belief (Shahada): "There is no deity but God and Muhammad is the Messenger of God." God is otherness yet oneness; God relies on the truth-telling of human messengers who are called "prophets."
2. Five brief but regular ritual prayer times from early morning to late evening (Salat): The prayer can be performed anywhere but must be oriented toward the Arabian city of Mecca. Before the prayer itself, one begins by ritual cleansing with water, but if necessary, sand, or even earth, is acceptable.

Occasional practices

3. Almsgiving (zakat): One's wealth, which is of this earth and temporary, comes from Allah, and almsgiving is meant to purify oneself of any sense of ownership, so this act is to remind the donor of the source of all good gifts.
4. Fasting: While most religions recommend fasting in some form, Islamic practice is more rigorous partly because the ninth lunar month of Ramadan rotates through all the seasons. Abstaining from food, drink, and sexual gratification from dawn to sunset every day for thirty days is a sharp reminder to focus on the more important dimensions of life, a need that only God can fill. Among the desired effects is a deepened compassion for the poor and hungry, the will to counter one's own baser tendencies, and a clearer sense of one's relationship to the Creator.
5. Pilgrimage (hajj): While some other major world religious traditions emphasize pilgrimage, the practice is perhaps more central to Islam than to others. Muslims are enjoined to visit Mecca once in a lifetime, thus maintaining a strong sense of being members of a community on pilgrimage, and they formally fulfill their duty of the Hajj only between the eighth and thirteenth days of the twelfth lunar month.

> the face of God—that will produce abundant return. (Q 30:38–39)

All beneficence thus points not to the individual, who serves really as a broker, but to God. Generosity in turn is linked to a heavy emphasis on social responsibility (see, e.g., Q 2:177). The scripture condemns those who hoard their wealth in the hope that it will save them from their mortality (Q 104:1–3). Equally condemned are those "who do not treat the orphan with dignity nor encourage each other to feed the poor . . . [and who] greedily devour their inheritances" (Q 89:17–19).

One of the Islamic ethical and theological issues most discussed over the centuries, from the earliest times, has been that of the (2) tension between divine omnipotence and human responsibility and moral freedom. In attempts to preserve God's transcendent sovereignty from the slightest hint of dilution, parties to the debate have sometimes gone to the extreme of virtually denying human freedom. On the other side, an overriding concern to safeguard individual moral responsibility has led some to the opposite extreme of suggesting that it is God whose choices are limited. As we have seen, one can interpret the Qur'an in a wide variety of ways, but it maintains a paradoxical balance. God's power knows no bounds, but human beings both enjoy a wide array of options and must shoulder responsibility for their choices. Repeatedly, the scripture makes it clear that "God does not change a people's condition until they change the thoughts of their own hearts" (Q 13:11).

That responsibility leads to the final outward dimension, willingness to engage actively in the hard work of (3) stewardship over creation. Acceptance of the divine charge of accountability for the shape of things here on earth, Islamic tradition calls the Lesser Jihad. One cannot authentically enter into this often-mundane striving without first joining the battle within, the Greater Jihad. In practice, the struggle involves acting on one's convictions about everything, from the environment to human rights to local school board elections. Muslim authors speak of the jihad of the pen, of the tongue, and, more recently, of the ballot box. Wherever human beings work for peace and justice, there is jihad. There is also the jihad of the sword. As a last resort, when all other means have been exhausted, jihad may also include the use of force, but the use of violent means is carefully hedged with prohibitions against terrorism, mistreatment of prisoners, and wanton destruction of natural resources. War against an aggressor is justifiable because "aggression is more despicable than killing" (Q 2:193).

Questions about the Text

1. What are the root words and name for God in Islam?
2. What is a sura?
3. How long did it take for the Qur'an to be written? How did the tone of the Qur'an change from the Meccan to Medinan period?
4. What are the four exegetical types used to interpret the Qur'an? What does each emphasize?
5. What is the "Night of Power"?
6. What is the Hijra?
7. What does the name Muhammad mean?
8. What are the four "essential attitudes" for the inner life?
9. What three qualities are needed for the "outward" relationships to persons and the world? Explain them.

Questions for Discussion

1. How can a religious person's images of God influence the individual's overall approach to life? Do you have a dominant image of God? If so, what is it?
2. How can the divine names offer insight into Islam and other traditions? What names do you find most helpful?
3. After reading the chapter, what aspects of Islam were new to you? What would you like to know more about, and why?
4. From the reading of the text, in what ways have you found that Muhammad's life served as an exemplar for Muslims?
5. What similarities and differences do you see in the essential attitudes and outward relations between Islam and your religious experience?

For Further Study

Austin, R. W. J., trans. *The Bezels of Wisdom*. Mahwah, NJ: Paulist Press, 1980.

Ayoub, M. *The Qur'an and Its Interpreters*. Albany: State University of New York, 1984.

Bloom, Jonathan, and Sheila Blair. *Islamic Art*. London: Phaidon, 1997.

This text is a beautifully illustrated and engaging introduction to the various visual expressions associated with major Islamic societies for nearly a millennium and a half.

Chittick, William. *The Sufi Path of Knowledge*. Albany: State University of New York Press, 1990.

Corbin, Henry. *The Man of Light in Iranian Sufism*. Boulder, CO: Shambhala, 1978.

Cragg, K. *The Event of the Qur'an*. London: Allen & Unwin, 1971.

———. *The Mind of the Qur'an*. London: Allen & Unwin, 1973.

Ernst, Carl W. *Following Muhammad: Rethinking Islam in the Contemporary World*. Chapel Hill, NC: University of North Carolina Press, 2003.

This is an excellent approach to unmasking some of the prevalent stereotypes about Islam and Muslims.

———. *The Shambhala Guide to Sufism*. Boston: Shambhala, 1997.

This text is a very readable introduction to the literary, social, and institutional dimensions of a phenomenon often identified as the "mystical" approach to Islam.

Gatje, H. *The Qur'an and Its Exegesis*. Berkeley and Los Angeles: University of California Press, 1976.

Ibish, Yusuf. "Ibn Arabi's Theory of Journeying," in *Traditional Modes of Contemplation and Action*, edited by Y. Ibish and P. L. Wilson, 441-46. Tehran: Imperial Iranian Academy of Philosophy, 1971.

McKane, William. *The Book of Fear and Hope*. Leiden, MA: Brill, 1962.

Nasr, S. H. *Ideals and Realities of Islam*. London: Allen & Unwin, 1966.

Otto, Rudolf. *The Idea of the Holy*. New York: Galaxy, 1958.

Renard, John. *Seven Doors to Islam: Spirituality and the Religious Life of Muslims*. Berkeley: University of California Press, 1996.

The author provides a thematic look at the vast range of literary and visual expressions of the Islamic tradition.

Renard, John, ed. *Windows on the House of Islam: Muslim Sources on Spirituality and Religious Life*. Berkeley: University of California Press, 1998.

This is an anthology of primary source material translated from a dozen languages and organized according to the major thematic categories of *Seven Doors to Islam*.

Sells, Michael. *Approaching the Qur'an: The Early Revelations*. Ashland, OR: White Cloud Press, 1999.

This text offers beautifully translated texts of the scripture, along with a CD illustrating various styles of formal recitation by professional Qur'an reciters from across the globe.

Watt, M. *Muhammad in Mecca, Muhammad in Medina*. Oxford, UK: Oxford University Press, 1953, 1956.

from the REFERENCE LIBRARIAN

Synoptic Outlines of Contents for all Topics—Islam

Students sometimes have difficulty identifying a research topic, especially in a subject in which they are likely to have no prior knowledge. In this section, we will look at how an encyclopedia can assist you in identifying research topics. Since many students are likely to have little prior knowledge of Islam, we'll use that as our test case.

The "synoptic outline of contents" described in a previous chapter is one potential source of topics. Fortunately, the major English-language encyclopedia for the study of all religion(s), the fifteen-volume *Encyclopedia of Religion* (first ed., 1987; second ed., 2005, also available in an electronic version) contains such an outline in volume 15.

The synoptic outline in the *Encyclopedia of Religion* is organized into forty-four broad divisions, including major world religions ("Christianity," "Jainism," etc.), as well as historical (e.g., "Greek Religion," i.e., ancient Greek religion), geographical (e.g., "Caribbean Religions"), and ethnographic (e.g., "African American Religions") categories. Within each of these broad divisions are listings of "Principle Articles," "Supporting Articles," and "Biographical Articles." Certain categories have unique lists: The entry for "Islam" also lists articles under the heading "Schools, Groups, and Communities." Thus it is possible to tell at a glance what is contained in the encyclopedia about a particular religious tradition.

Simply browsing through the list of articles is one way of identifying a research topic. In this case, the various kinds of topics for which the encyclopedia facilitates research include biographical and conceptual articles. Conceptual articles would include such topics mentioned by Dr. Renard as "Free Will and Predestination (Islamic Concepts)," "Shiism," or "Qur'ān: Tradition of Scholarship and Interpretation." You may also discover such unexpected topics as "Islamic Calligraphy" or "Ecology and Islam." The list of biographical articles is also helpful, especially because systems of transliterating Arabic names into English can vary. For example, the author identified by Dr. Renard as Ibn Arabi appears in the list as "Ibn al-`Arabī," while Al-Ghazali appears under "Ghazālī, Abū Hāmid al-."

As useful as the synoptic outline is, it may not tell you everything you want to know. For example, the synoptic outline in its list of articles under "Islam" tells you that there is an article on "God in Islam." As we have already seen, "God" is a very large topic, too large, in fact, to provide a focus for research (in most cases) at the undergraduate level. In a case like this, it might be helpful to turn to the encyclopedia's index. In fact, the index entry for "Islam," in addition to the sub-entry "God in," has a number of sub-sub-entries pertaining to various aspects of God in Islam. For example, there are numerous entries for "names of [God]," which reminds us of Dr. Renard's reference to the "Ninety-Nine Most Beautiful Names (of God)." Other entries include "creation by," "friends of," "knowledge of," "power of," etc. any of which might suggest a way to focus your research topic. Here is one to try on your own. How would you find information in the *Encyclopedia of Religion* (or some similar reference work) regarding Islamic views of non-Muslim figures such as Abraham, Moses, or Jesus?

Such synoptic outlines as contained in the *Encyclopedia of Religion* are included in the following reference works:

Gordon D. Newby. *A Concise Encyclopedia of Islam*. Oxford, UK: Oneworld Publications, 2002.

This work offers a "Thematic Index" on pp. 233–44, that is, entries are grouped by categories such as "Beliefs," "Terms and Concepts," "Persons," "Places and geographic locations." However, it includes no detailed index.

John L. Esposito, ed. *The Oxford Encyclopedia of the Islamic World*. 6 vols. New York; Oxford, UK: Oxford University Press, 2009.

See "Topical Outline of Entries," "Index" in vol. 6.

Richard C. Martin, ed. *Encyclopedia of Islam and the Muslim World*. 2 vols. Woodbridge, CT: Macmillan Reference USA, 2004.

See "[alphabetical] List of entries," "Synoptic outline of entries," "List of maps," "Glossary," "Appendix: Genealogies and Timelines," "Index."

The following titles are all useful for quickly looking up terms, definitions, and basic factual information; that is, they fall into the category of "concise" dictionary:

Ludwig W. Adamec. *Historical Dictionary of Islam*. Lanham, MD: Scarecrow Press, 2001.

E. van Donzel. *Islamic Desk Reference: Compiled from The Encyclopaedia of Islam*. Boston, MA: Brill, 1994.

John L. Esposito, ed. *The Oxford Dictionary of Islam*. Oxford, UK: Oxford University Press, 2003.

Ian Richard Netton. *A Popular Dictionary of Islam*. Atlantic Highliands, NJ: Humanities Press International, 1992.

The most extensive reference work on Islam in English is the twelve-volume *Encyclopedia of Islam*. However, the following title is more likely to be useful for undergraduates:

Cyril Glassé. *The New Encyclopedia of Islam*. Lanham, MD: Rowman & Littlefield, 2001.

This work contains a number of helpful features, including color photographs, several appendices containing maps, historical synopses, charts, genealogical tables, chronology, and so on.

The following reference works are useful for research focused on the Qur'an:

Oliver Leaman, ed. *The Qur'an: An Encyclopedia*. Oxford, UK: Routledge, 2006.

Jane Dammen McAuliffe, ed. *Encyclopaedia of the Qur'ān*. 5 vols. Boston, MA: Brill, 2001–2006.

SKILL KEY #1

Use the library's reference collection to begin your research.

a) Use a subject-specific encyclopedia to acquire specialized knowledge about a subject.
b) Use a subject-specific encyclopedia whose scope is appropriate for both your topic and the approach you want to take to that topic.

continued

continued

c) Use encyclopedia bibliographies to identify subject headings for your topic.
d) Use a concise subject-specific dictionary to look up the specialized vocabulary of a particular field.
e) Use an encyclopedia's index to locate information on subjects (including persons) for which there is no separate article.
f) Examine the synoptic outline of contents (or however it is designated) in an encyclopedia (1) to get a quick overview of the contents and (2) to get topic ideas for research.
g) Use an encyclopedia's index to get ideas for research topics.
h) Use cross-references to locate additional relevant material in an encyclopedia.
i) Use an encyclopedia's index to locate all (or as much as you want) relevant material on your topic. Note especially how detailed the index is and whether the editors of the encyclopedia make any special comments about it.

SKILL KEY #2

Use the library's catalog to locate sources of information.

a) Use subject headings to locate precisely books on your topic.
b) Use subject headings whose scope fits your topic as closely as possible, then adjust your search with a broader or narrower subject heading as necessary.
c) As an alternative to using encyclopedia bibliographies, use keyword searching to identify subject headings for your topic.
d) Combine one or more subject headings in a search to retrieve books on a topic for which no single subject heading exists.
e) Use the floating subdivision "encyclopedias" in combination with a keyword to identify encyclopedias on a subject.

continued

continued

f) Use the floating subdivision "moral and ethical aspects" to identify material, whether "pro" or "con," related to the ethical aspects of a subject.
g) Use the floating subdivision "religious aspects" to search for religious/theological aspects of nonreligious/nontheological subjects.
h) If necessary, use all the subject headings assigned to a book to identify material on a particular subject.
i) Use the name of an organization or group as an author to search for documents produced under the aegis of that group. Be aware of the possibility of changes in the group's name over time.

Student Tasks

1. Do a keyword search on "Islam AND encyclopedias" in your library catalog. If your library does not have any encyclopedias specifically on Islam, try a broader search: "religion AND encyclopedias."
2. If your library owns the *Encyclopedia of Religion*, look at the entries under "Islam" in the synoptic outline of contents in volume 15. Then look at the index entries under "Islam." How does the list of articles in the synoptic outline compare with the index entries? Is there a topic that looks interesting and that you would like to pursue?
3. If the library does not have the Encyclopedia of Religion, find an alternative (using the technique given in #1). If you can, find an encyclopedia with a synoptic outline (or however it may be designated).
4. Choose one of the persons mentioned in the chapter by Dr. Renard, and find an encyclopedia article on that person. Now, look at the index entry for that person. Is there more in the encyclopedia about the person than in just the article you looked up?

5. Choose a conceptual topic from the chapter, and use an encyclopedia index to locate information on that topic throughout the encyclopedia.
6. Search the Internet for information on the same person you looked up in #4. Do the same for the conceptual topic you looked up in #5. Did you find information you would regard as authoritative? What leads you to think so? How many different ways can you search for this kind of information on the Internet?

CATHOLIC THEOLOGY IN A GLOBAL CONTEXT

Catholic Theology in a Global Context: A World Church

Angelyn Dries, OSF

from the EDITOR

To love God implies that one can expect many surprises in one's life. As a classic humorous remark puts it, "If you want to make God laugh, just tell God your plans." I sometimes think of a "God of surprises" this way: just when I think I have all the answers, when I have put them in a box, closed the flaps, and neatly and tightly tied it with a pretty red bow, God smiles, unties the bow, opens the box, takes out the answers I have packaged so nicely—and gives me a bigger box! This chapter explores some of the questions that need a bigger box.

After the Resurrection, Jesus' "final command" to his disciples is "Go, therefore, and make disciples of all nations" (Matt 28:19). So the church, as the community of disciples, did precisely this; they went out into the world, spreading the good news.

Twenty centuries later, the church is still preaching this good news. The world, however, keeps changing and presenting new opportunities to follow Christ. This chapter will explore some of the new challenges the church faces as it has moved from a predominantly western Eurocentric population to a fast-growing, global population. With this globalization, the necessary functions of the church, such as decision-making, theology, liturgy, and governance, will be done on a wider scale, in different ways, with different insights, and with increasing global awareness—in sum, a new way of being the church.

This chapter introduces many Christian communities around the world. It does not attempt finished answers. It is as if God has untied the church's bow, opened its little box, and handed the church a bigger box, telling it that the workings of the Holy Spirit cannot be easily contained. The church discovers in this a mandate to realize in a new way again that God really is the God of all people and loves universally.

This chapter finishes our book with a realization of the future that is occurring before our eyes. In the Reference Librarian's section, more skills are introduced to probe this world context and to find resources to help in understanding it. As always, a skill needs to be used and reused. The skills that have been introduced in this book can be applied to any academic discipline, for one's own wonder, or for curiosity. We encourage the reader to practice them often; a world of knowledge and education can be opened for a lifetime.

OVERVIEW

How is it that we hear, each of us, in our own native language . . . about God's deeds of power? (Acts 2:8–11)

For much of the nineteenth and twentieth centuries, the theological "greats," such as Karl Rahner, Yves Congar, Hans Küng, Edward Schillebeeckx, and David Tracy, grew up, were educated, and taught either in Europe or in North America. North Americans often studied in Germany, France, Rome, and Belgium to learn from these and other theologians. During the same time period, many of the immigrants to North America were from Europe, Eastern Europe, or the Mediterranean countries. However, since at least 1970, the theological picture has opened in new geographic directions, as is true for immigrants coming to North America.

We often find ourselves working or attending class with Asians, Africans, Europeans, Latin Americans, and even Oceanians. The U.S. census in 2000 highlighted the diversity of ethnic and racial backgrounds in this part of North America. At the same time, global statistics indicate a numerical shift in Catholic and Christian populations from Europe and North America to Asia and the southern hemisphere. We also once again became aware of the worldwide scope of the church with CNN's almost nonstop coverage of the events following the death of Pope John Paul II. The cameras panned over the many faces of Catholics in India, Kenya, and the Philippines. In the last twenty years, scholars began to use the term *World Christianity* or *world church* to characterize a new awareness of the church's diversity. However, a world church is more than geography.

Growth in Catholicism by Continents, 1975–2000

Continent	*Catholic Population 1975*	*Catholic Population 2000*	*Change*
Africa	48,528,000	130,018,000	168%
America	341,290,000	519,391,000	52%
Asia	52,589,000	107,301,000	104%
Europe	261,924,000	280,144,000	7%
Oceania	5,227,000	8,202,000	57%

Source: Froehle and Gautier, 46, 71, 86, 103, 116.

MEANING OF TERMS: WORLD CHRISTIANITY, WORLD CHURCH

The fall of the Berlin Wall and the massacre of students in Tiananmen Square, both happening in 1989, drew our attention to globalization as one of several megatrends that affect us all. We are impacted by a "world culture," which has been developing due to the growth of capitalism, free-trade agreements, instant communications, economic interdependence, and technology, among other things. The idea of a church reaching to the "ends of the earth" has been part of Roman Catholic history, beginning with the apostles and with Saint Paul. More recently, several theologians have used the term *World Christianity* or *world church* as a way to speak about the impact that local churches are having on all Catholics.

In 1945, a Maryknoll, New York, priest named John Considine wrote a small book, entitled *World Christianity*. Considine had many years of experience working in Rome, where he interacted with missionaries and local church leaders from all over the world. He also traveled extensively in Latin America and Africa to see firsthand the Catholic peoples in what at that time were considered mission countries. He observed that the immense post–World War II changes had made it imperative that Catholics have a knowledge, an understanding, and a regard for the peoples of the church universal.

DEFINITIONS OF GLOBALIZATION

"Convergence of a multipolar world, global capitalism, and communications technologies." (Robert Schreiter, *The New Catholicity*, 8)

"The intensification of worldwide social relations which link distant localities in such a way that local happenings are shaped by events occurring many miles away and vice versa." (Anthony Giddens, quoted in *Magesa*, 2004, 150–51)

At the Second Vatican Council (1961–1965), bishops from all over the world gathered in Rome, where, for the first time, they themselves realized in a graphic way the diversity and particularity of the Church, represented by indigenous Church leadership. This included the presence of bishops from the Eastern Rite Churches, which historically were shaped in a different theological culture than the Roman Catholic Church. Karl Rahner, a *peritus* (theological expert) at the Council, noted the gathering as "the Church's first official self-actualization as a world Church" (Rahner, 1979, 717). He noted that, to some extent, the theology that had been exported from Europe carried with it a particular culture and civilization, which Europe considered superior to others. Such exportation had practical as well as theoretical problems. For example, in African cultures where polygamy was the practice, did a man need to give up all his wives except one to be baptized as a Catholic? What would become of his other wives, who would thereby lose their social and economic identity in the close-knit community?

Rahner's experience of the Second Vatican Council led him to identify three theological eras in the Catholic Church:

1. The period of Jewish Christianity, when the proclamation of the saving message of Jesus was first given among the Jewish people.
2. The period of the church in the distinct cultural region of Hellenism and Europe. The apostle Paul introduced a radically new direction for the church in the context of the "pagan," "Gentile," or Roman religion. At the same time, however, Eastern Christianity took its own path with a different philosophical and theological emphasis.
3. The present period, after the Council, when "the sphere of the Church's life is in fact the entire world." (Rahner, 1979, 721)

Rahner suggested, "Either the Church sees and recognizes these essential differences of other cultures for which she should become a world Church and with a Pauline boldness draws the necessary consequences from this recognition, or she remains a Western Church and so in the final analysis betrays the meaning of Vatican II" (Rahner, 1979, 724).

That the gospel is "translatable" within cultures is itself an important consequence of the doctrine of the Incarnation. This point has been made by Lamin Sanneh, a Gambian-born Yale professor who first converted to Islam and then to Catholicism. Christianity "translated itself out of" Aramaic and Hebrew into Greek and Latin and eventually into most of the languages of the world (Sanneh, 1). Islam has proven itself adaptable in many places, but it holds Arabic as central to its prayer, sacred literature, and law. Christianity, however, has seen new cultures and languages as potential sources for the expression of the central Christian message. This concept is identified theologically in the expression called "inculturation." Inculturation is the interaction and adaptation of the gospel in various contexts, a practice modeled on the Incarnation, the Christian belief that the Word of God become flesh in Jesus, revealing God's saving love to all. This reality is dynamically and critically "incarnated" in specific cultures and situations and involves both a critique and affirmation of a culture.

THEOLOGICAL ASPECTS OF A WORLD CHURCH

Just before the Second Vatican Council, voices of local churches and of missionaries around the world were beginning to find expression, not just in vernacular languages in Eucharistic liturgies but also in the area of theology. Women and men in Latin America, Africa, and Asia were highlighting new emphases, themes, and methods in theology.

All theology, according to Saint Anselm (1033–1109), is "faith seeking understanding," but theology unfolding in different parts of the world has a different context. Theology in western countries came to rely heavily upon scholastic philosophy for the clarification of revelation and religious truths. Scholastic methodology tended to rely on reason and to work deductively; that is, general principles were logically applied to specific issues or questions. By the 1960s, "emerging subaltern voices," as Sri Lankan theologian R. S. Sugirtharajah has called them, began to be heard (Fabella and Sugirtharajah, 2000, 2). In general, much of this theology developed in an ecumenical environment and was based strongly on the Bible, with men and women theologians noticeably connected with their local church communities.

Much of world theology is being done in communitarian fashion. That is, theologians are crossing denominational boundaries to work together to shape a theology that explores the gospel in their particular cultural context. Nevertheless, we will briefly note two representative theologians from three areas and identify their context, methodology, sources for theology, and major themes/issues. We will see that local contexts affect the reception of the gospel and interaction with various Catholic traditions and thus give a particular "flavor" to a specific theology.

Latin American Theology

Catholic life and teaching entered Central and South America as part of Spain and Portugal's colonial empire, beginning in 1492. Some of the theological issues of that time with respect to the colonial empire centered on the development of international law, the identification of the "others" (i.e., indigenous peoples) as persons in their own right, and establishing whether Native Americans could be admitted fully into the Church through baptism. Latin America remained an "official" Catholic region politically, culturally, and religiously for most of its post-1492 history.

In the 1960s, theologians from Latin America addressed the great economic and social disparity they found in most of their countries. They were assisted by a large body of Catholic social teaching, beginning with Pope Leo XIII's *Rerum Novarum* ("On the Condition of Workers," 1891) and supported by the Vatican Council II's *Gaudium et Spes* (1965) and later, the World Synod of Catholic Bishops' statement, *Justice in the World* (1971).

> The joy and hope, the grief and anguish of the people of our time, especially those who are poor or are afflicted in any way, are the joy and hope, the grief and anguish of the followers of Christ, as well. (*Gaudium et Spes* 1)
>
> Action on behalf of justice and participation in the transformation of the world fully appear to us as a constitutive dimension of the preaching of the Gospel, or, in other words, of

> the Church's mission for the redemption of the human race and its liberation from every oppressive situation. (*Justice in the World* 6)

Many people suffered because of oppressive governments, the presence of crushing poverty, the murder and disappearance of citizens, a chasm between the poor and the rich, and widespread illiteracy. Oftentimes, Catholic Church leaders tended to side with the political leadership. Communism and Marxism seemed a viable alternative for people, especially those who were poor. Within this situation, local church leaders and some missionaries from abroad began to form small groups where people reflected upon their lives and poverty in light of the Jewish and Christian Scriptures. They then took action to rectify injustice, as they saw it. The method was a "liberative *praxis*" (Gk., "action"). The groups came to be known as *communidades de base* ("base communities"). In the 1960s and 1970s, many such groups sprang up in Latin America, forming one of the foundations for liberation theology.

Rather than using a philosophical framework to analyze religious truth, liberation theology tended to rely on social sciences to critically reflect upon social and political realities. Theologians worked inductively, rather than deductively, starting with people's experience and then examining the scriptures and Church teachings in light of them. Theologians based their theology on the experience of many poor people, so liberation theology was sometimes thought of as "theology from below," in contrast to "theology from above" (i.e., theology done by "experts").

Several themes surfaced, all of them scripturally based. Jesus is portrayed as the liberator not only from personal sin but also from the structural sin of poverty and conditions that kept people oppressed. The exodus paradigm highlights God as the God of the poor and the work of the people as hastening the reign of God. Reflecting upon the words of the Jewish prophets, especially Isaiah and Micah, liberation theologians challenged the Church to be a church of the poor.

The growth of liberation theology, the strength of the base communities, the development of literacy programs, and the criticism of unjust government or Church structures together began to have social and political consequences. Lay people were gaining confidence and new skills and demanding justice. Some politicians and other groups that perceived these developments as a threat to their power began murdering their own people and missionaries who were helping to "conscientize" the people. Probably the best-known are those in El Salvador: Archbishop Oscar Romero, the four U.S. Catholic women (1980), and the six Jesuits teaching at the University of Central America and their housekeeper and her daughter (1989).

Some North Americans heard about liberation theology from missionaries who wrote back home to tell family and friends what was happening in Latin America, but Gustavo Gutiérrez, a Peruvian theologian, presented the first full treatment in his groundbreaking *Theology of Liberation: History, Politics, and Salvation* (1973). Theology is a critical reflection upon praxis. The starting point for theology is engagement with people in their situation, which is where the Word of God is revealed. In particular, situations need to be judged from the perspective of those who are on the margins of society and the Church. He highlighted key biblical themes:

a) The exodus—a passage to liberation in order to make them a holy people
b) The eschatological promise of the reign of God—how the vision of God informs the present
c) The prophetic—both denounces injustice and transforms the present reality to reflect the values and reality of the reign of God

Gutiérrez sees Jesus Christ as the liberator and salvation as liberation from the broken relationships found personally and structurally in society. Several of the key themes of liberation theology found their way into the Latin American bishops' pastoral statement when they met in Puebla, Mexico, in 1979. Gutierrez writes:

> The most important instance of [the process of human liberation] in our times, especially in underdeveloped and oppressed countries, is the struggle to construct a just and fraternal society, where persons can live with dignity and be the agents of their own destiny. It is my opinion that the term *development* does not well express these profound aspirations. *Liberation*, on the other hand, seems to express them better. Moreover, in another way the notion of liberation is more exact and all-embracing: it emphasizes that human beings transform themselves by conquering their liberty throughout their existence and their history. The Bible presents liberation—salvation—in Christ as the total gift, which, by taking on the levels I indicate, gives the whole process of liberation its deepest meaning and its complete and unforeseeable fulfillment. Liberation can thus be approached as a single salvific process. This viewpoint, therefore, permits us to consider the *unity, without confusion*, of the various human dimensions, that is, one's relationships with other humans and with the Lord, which theology has been attempting to establish for some time; this approach will provide the framework for our reflection. (p. x)

Theologian Maria Pilar Aquino, whose parents were Mexican immigrant workers, emphasizes many of the same themes of early liberation theologians from Latin America, but she particularly focuses on the theological contributions of women's lives and perspective in the process, highlighting the strong role Mary, mother of Jesus, continues to hold.

Her methodology arises from the centrality of the faith of the people, the option for the poor and oppressed, a close relationship between spirituality and theology, and a "liberating praxis" of accompaniment with people in their struggle for dignity, peace, and humanization (see Aquino, 1993). Women's experience corrects an androcentric (or "male-centered") position of liberation theology and provides a sense of realism for theology. Theology is "realist," treating human nature with its conflicts, contradictions, hopes, and struggles, so that those situations and tendencies that create death might be transformed into life.

African Theology

Catholic life in Northern Africa traces itself back to almost the beginnings of Christianity. The apostle Mark influenced the Coptic Church in Alexandria, Egypt, a church that continues today. The Acts of the Apostles tells the story of the Ethiopian who was converted by Philip the apostle (see Acts 8:29–39), and there has been a consistent Christian presence in Ethiopia (the area was called Abyssinia at the time), since at least 500 CE, after the arrival of nine Syrian missionaries twenty years earlier. North Africa was well represented in the theological formulation of key aspects of the relationship of the members of the Trinity and Jesus' nature. In the twentieth century, many African countries are postcolonial nations, which also have a history of Muslim and Christian slave trade and Muslim and Catholic interaction, especially in sub-Saharan Africa. Africans retain a strong community orientation, tribal identity, and oral traditions. The spirit world is present and active, intervening in daily life. Africans still widely practice polygamy and retain traditional sacrificial rites.

Africans have been reclaiming their early church and patristic roots, as well as their cultures. Several theologians employ "narrative" theology, using the dynamics of African proverbs, songs, myths, African rituals, and life experiences as the basis for reflecting upon current experience and the gospel. With a vibrant song tradition among many tribes, it is not surprising that Africans are calling for more vibrant liturgical rituals, which encompass or intersect African rituals, worldview, and spontaneity. Themes and issues theologians address are inculturation, peace, and reconciliation between and among tribes, as well as a criticism of "anthropological poverty," an internalization of the mentality of dominated and exploited peoples. African ecclesiology suggests strong and active participation of all members of the Church.

We will look at two theologians who explore what inculturation means for Africa. A biblical scholar from Nigeria, Teresa Okure plumbs the meaning of New Testament (NT) passages that show Jesus among the people of his day. A key concept she notes is his "self-emptying" (Gk.: *kenōsis*; see Phil 2:6–11; John 1:1c, 14) in the Incarnation. In his humanity, Jesus emptied himself of a "divine mode of operating" and took on our humanity. Jesus was born into a Jewish culture in the eastern part of the Mediterranean, when Israel was dominated by the Roman Empire, but he also critiqued his culture, especially its attitudes toward riches, the impoverished, socially unacceptable people, and religious practices and laws, which were seen as ends in themselves. Okure cites the resources Jesus drew upon in his inculturation:

- His certainty that he was doing the will of the One who sent him
- His conviction of his mission to transform people's lives and cultures
- His own personal integrity

Okure challenges the Nigerian Church, in particular, to be self-emptying: to examine new theological paths arising from the experience and fabric of African lives, rather than to cling to those inherited theological and liturgical structures foreign to African life. The Church needs to be "self-emptied" of a kind of tribalism that excludes some people and discriminates, to the detriment of the building up of the body of Christ. Self-emptying means addressing the personal fears people might have as they work to transform the African Church and society.

> In the Incarnation, therefore, it is not only humanity that tends towards God in Christ and becomes one with God, but it is God also, who tends towards humanity and becomes one with humankind. Paul would regard this as a great mystery (see Eph 5:32).
>
> Our effort to understand inculturation in the Nigerian and other African contexts, thus requires us to identify the two realities, that must needs be united and mutually enriched. These two realities are our Christian faith—the Good News of Jesus Christ, and our African reality of peoples in their different cultures. (Okure, 1990, 57–58)

Tanzanian priest and theologian Laurenti Magesa combines a pastoral sensitivity, theological sharpness, and a social science methodology to examine and challenge elements of Catholic life, such as moral traditions and marriage, in Kenya, Tanzania, and Uganda.

He follows the now-familiar methodological path of an examination of the experience of African Catholics in the three countries mentioned. He brings to light the process of "religious-

The painting of The Pentecost shown here is by Tanzanian artist Charles Ndege. Fr. Joe Healey and other Maryknollers have commissioned a number of Ndege paintings, and Christmas cards with his paintings are published by Paulines Publications Africa.

cultural symbiosis," that is, how the faith has actually been received by Africans, and considers what the Church of the future might look like, especially in liturgy and pastoral practice. Of particular note is the description of Jesus, common among other African theologians. African sensitivities see Jesus as the Brother-Ancestor-Healer in the Church as Family. Each of the nouns arises not only from scripture but also from important African values. Much of indigenous African worship bonds the present generation with their ancestors. Ancestors share blood with descendants, are viewed as sacred, mediate the visible world and that which is unseen, and possess spiritual powers. So, too, does Jesus. This "ancestral ecclesiology" flows over into sacramental and moral life, healing, and hospitality.

Asian Theology

Asia includes a vast amount of territory and almost two-thirds of the population of the earth, so it is difficult to generalize about so many groups. There is a longstanding tradition that Christianity has been in India since the preaching of the Apostle Thomas, who came to the Malabar coast of South India in 52 CE, though more probably a sustained Christian presence has been in that area since the fourth century. Nestorian missionaries, followers of an early bishop of Constantinople, brought Christianity to China in 635 CE. Franciscan missionary John of Monte Corvino traveled from Persia to India in 1291, where he preached and baptized a number of people and then proceeded to Beijing, where he was joined by another Franciscan and spent many years in Cathay (the name for China at the time). John noted at the time the strong presence of Nestorian Christianity in the area.

Asian Catholics continue to live among followers of the ancient religions of Hinduism and Buddhism. These religions see no disconnection between "religion" and the rest of life, as people in North America often do. Catholics are a significant minority in all Asian countries, except the Philippines, where Catholicism is the predominant religion. Catholics are making their theological way partially in dialogue with those religions. Asian philosophical traditions differ from the reason and logic of western philosophy in that they assume that a harmony undergirds all of daily life. The *Yin* and *Yang* of Taoism, for example, are "true" together, sometimes in different practices or perhaps in opposite realities (i.e., hot and cold). Harmony is the constant balancing of these unifying forces. These traditions understand the nature of truth as being multiform, rather than monoform.

Asian theological methodology and sources are related, as we find in the poetry and dramas of a Catholic South Korean layman, Kim Chi-Ha, imprisoned, tortured, and in solitary confinement for many years between 1960 and 1970. The experience of unjust suffering and oppression forms the basis of *Minjung* ("the Korean people") theology, which uses folk tales and community identity to reflect upon the gospel as it intersects with a fundamental Korean concept of *han* ("suffering"). *Han*, a complex Korean word, describes a basic "suppressed vitality" or existential pain arising from suppression (cf. Ahn, 1997).

Jesuit Aloysius Pieris, a Sri Lankan theologian, also employs an Asian "style" as he explores theology against the backdrop of Buddhism and within the fundamental concept of harmony in Asian culture and thinking. For example, he suggests that a harmony exists between the Word and Silence. In a dialectical relationship, Silence is the unspoken Word and the Word is Silence heard. Theory and praxis are one and the same for Asian theologians.

Shown in this photo is the Nestorian Monument (or Stele), which was discovered in 1625 in Xi An. The inscribed Chinese characters tell us that the monument was built to commemorate the introduction of Christianity in China in 781 CE, and they note the arrival of a Nestorian missionary in the, then, capital city of China. Photo: Thierry Ollivier. Musée des Arts Asiatiques-Guimet, Paris, France.

> Here let me refer to the current trend of using "Buddhist techniques" of meditation in "Christian Prayer" without any reverence for the soteriological [salvific] context of such techniques. For the naïve presupposition is that the (Buddhist) *Way* could be had without the (Buddhist) *Truth*. It is time to impress on our theologians that in our culture the *method* cannot be severed from the *goal*. . . . *Technē*

> [the Greek word from which derives the English word, *technique*] is not a mechanical action, but a skill, an art. In our traditions, the art of doing a thing is itself the thing done. The *goal* of life, in Buddhism, is the *art* of living it. The perfection to be achieved is the style of achieving it! The obvious corollary is that the Asian method of doing theology is itself Asian theology. *Theopraxis* is already the formulation of Theology. (Pieris, 1979, 447)

Karl Rahner, in his *Theological Investigations* (1971, 8:66, 86), and more recently the Asian Synod of Bishops (1999) have drawn attention to the critical role that women have in addressing significant social, political, and cultural problems in Asian countries. Prostitution, trafficking in women and children, and violence against women are identified as key realities affecting women's dignity and worth. Such horrendous situations are often supported by myths and proverbs related to women. These and other pastoral concerns form the basis of much of the theological development in Asia. In 2002, fifty-five Asian Catholic women theologians met to reflect theologically upon the 1999 Asian Bishops Synod meeting. The theme of their gathering, "Ecclesia of Women in Asia: Gathering the Voices of the Silenced," highlighted six major areas affecting women: violence, the Bible, Church structure, spirituality, ecofeminism, and world religions. If a practice toward women denies their dignity or voice, the result will affect how we see their role in the community and in the Church, but it will also be revealed in an implicit Christology. We see this clearly in this excerpt from the keynote address given by Evelyn Monteiro at the conference:

> **Women and the Bible**
>
> The Bible has been one of the most misused books against women. The silence, invisibility and trivialization of the role and experience of women within the Bible are misread as divine principle rather than recognizing it as the work of men written in an ethos of patriarchy. The image of women as the "weaker vessel" "created for the sake of man," as "inferior," "temptress," "gateway to hell," etc., is misinterpreted as deigned by the Creator rather than recognizing her as a being created in the image and likeness of God. Consequently, not only are women silenced but also the biblical notion of gender equality remains hidden within the pages of Scriptures.
>
> **Women and Church Structure**
>
> Does the Church structure lend itself to be supportive of the place and role of women in the life and governance of the Church? Is the Church of Asia women-friendly? Is the Church, the Body of Christ, in solidarity with women through participatory opportunities and through empowering and entrusting women with full and creative leadership responsibilities? These are some questions that perhaps need to be addressed especially in view of the Synodal document that states, "[T]he Church should be a participatory Church in which no one feels excluded, and judge the wider participation of women in the life and mission of the Church in Asia to be an especially pressing need." (Monteiro, 2005, p. xxi)

The World Church in North America

About the same time the world theologies were developing, major ethnic or racial groups in North America (some of whom had been here prior to the colonial empires) developed a consciousness about their specific religious and theological identities. In the late 1960s, James H. Cone began to develop a "black theology," and

AN OVERVIEW OF SELECTED THEOLOGIES IN THE WORLD CHURCH

	Latin America	Africa	Asia
Context	Colonial remnants remain in culture; large gap between rich and poor; situations of violence, especially in the 1970s and 1980s	Animism, tribal cultures, strong community orientation	Catholics live as a minority among Buddhists, Hindus, Confucianists; in some countries, Catholicism is considered a foreign religion
Theological emphases	Liberation; situations need to be judged from viewpoint of marginalized people	Inculturation	Inculturation
Method	Observe, judge, act; done in "base communities"; use of social sciences	Use of symbol (i.e., sacramental), narrative, music	Ecumenical; done in dialogue with other religions
Emphases in sources	Scriptural passages that highlight liberation, release from injustice: exodus, prophets in the Jewish Scriptures	Attention given to tribal myths, music, ceremonies, "folklore," and indigenous traditions	Interaction with Asian philosophy or harmony

by the early 1980s, Hispanic theology developed against the background of Cesar Chavez, Dolores Huerta, and the Farm Workers' boycott movement. Theologians Cone and Diana L. Hayes critiqued racism, the residual effects of slavery, and unjust social and ecclesial structures.

In the 1970s, Asian immigrants began to enter North America in large numbers, especially from Vietnam and Laos. Peter Phan, a Vietnamese priest and theologian, draws on the cultural and spiritual riches of Asian American immigrants and Asian culture to suggest a Vietnamese American theology.

The U.S. Catholic bishops have been aware of intercontinental connections in the world church in their pastoral letters on "Call to Solidarity with Africa" (2002) and on immigration (written in conjunction with the Bishops of Mexico, 2003). Thus we can see that each local church needs to think globally as well as locally.

SOME COMMONALITIES IN THEOLOGIES FROM AROUND THE GLOBE

Theology being done by local churches throughout the world exemplifies the rich ways in which Catholic faith is "seeking understanding." Several commonalities in theological development are easily discernible. Theology and a world church have been impacted by women's voices and by particular situations that create injustice or affect the dignity and worth of human beings. The theologies have a strong biblical base and are done in a context of living in longstanding, multireligious relationships. Almost all start with praxis or experience, rather than with theory, and pursue transformation of individuals, society, and the Church. The theologies tend toward the practical but seek "the face of Christ" in a particular cultural context. The areas of greatest theological exploration are found in the chapters and topics we have discussed in this book: scripture, Christology, ecclesiology, sacraments, morality, social justice, and religious traditions of Judaism and Islam.

Diversity and Unity, a World Church Theological Issue

Several broad theological questions are raised in the experience of a world church: What is the relationship between unity and diversity? What holds everything together if we have so much difference? Wouldn't it be easier if Catholic theology were the same all over the world?

From its origins, Christianity has had diversity, beginning with multiple gospel traditions and varieties of church structures in the patristic period. Eastern Rite Churches, including the Ukrainian Church (Byzantine Rite) and the Maronite Church (both of which are also found in North America), have tended to highlight the mystery of God, the need to entrust oneself to that mystery, and a harmony between the mind and experience. We do need to "test the spirits to see whether they are from God" (1 John 4:1), but perhaps it is not a matter of either diversity or unity, but of *both* diversity and unity. As Laurenti Magesa and others have noted, the Incarnation is the model. Jesus Christ, like us in everything but sin, is the point or nexus of unity and diversity for us all. As noted in the beginning of this chapter, Catholicism is a world church: one body with many members but with the differences that inculturation invariably brings.

The theological constructions, which we have examined in various ways through this chapter and this book, are not ends in themselves but are gifts for the growth of the Body of Christ, as the Church continues its journey as pilgrim people. In many ways, world church theology is the act of preaching the gospel of Jesus, or evangelization.

> Theological language contains much that is approximate; it must therefore always be open to renovation from new perspectives, further precision of concepts, and the correction of formulations. Similarly, there is the permanent emergence of new paths in our speech about God which seeks to express revealed truth in appropriate terms. All this is required along with the clear conviction that—according to a traditional affirmation—no theology can be identified with the faith. Theological pluralism within the unity of faith is an old fact in the church. In this context different theologies are useful and important efforts but on condition that they do not consider themselves unique or indispensable and they be aware of their role of modestly serving the primary tasks of the church. (Gutierrez, cited in Nickeloff, 1996, 271–72)

Questions about the Text

1. What are Rahner's three theological eras in the church? What are his reasons for these divisions?
2. What is inculturation? Give an example.
3. What is globalization? Give an example.
4. What is one characteristic of Latin American theology?
5. What is one characteristic of African theology?
6. What is one characteristic of Asian theology?

Questions for Discussion

1. What situations, events, or media have made you aware of a "world church" or "world Christianity"?
2. Compare the samples of theologies from around the world. What do they have in common? What is unique to each?
3. Suggest specific ways in which different socioeconomic, religious, and cultural contexts around the world affect how one does theology.
4. What contributions do you think these diverse theologies make to the world church?
5. Do any of the theologies mentioned in this chapter find a resonance with you? Why or why not? What difference would they make in the world?

For Further Study

Print Sources

Ahn, Byung-Mu. "Korean Theology." In *Dictionary of Mission: Theology, History, Perspectives*, edited by Karl Muller, Theo Sundermeier, Stephen B. Bevans, and Richard H. Bliese, pp. 246–250. Maryknoll, NY: Orbis Books, 1997.

Alangaram, A., SJ. *Christ of the Asian Peoples: Towards an Asian Contextual Christology*. Bangalore, India: Asian Trading Corporation, 1999.

The author explores what Christology looks like in "Asian clothes," using as a background the documents published by the Federation of Asian Bishops Conference.

Amaladoss, Michael, SJ. *Making All Things New: Dialogue, Pluralism, and Evangelization in Asia*. Maryknoll, NY: Orbis Books, 1990.

A leading Jesuit from India explores the issues of the Church in Asia as it intersects with long-established religions older than Christianity.

Aquino, Maria Pilar. *Our Cry for Life: Feminist Theology from Latin America*. Maryknoll, NY: Orbis Books, 1993.

Bellagamba, Anthony. *Mission and Ministry in the Global Church*. Maryknoll, NY: Orbis Books, 1992.

A missionary with experience in several countries provides a challenge to Christians who have an interest in understanding and living a sense of mission, even though they never leave their own country. Two chapters especially provide an overview of the changing social and political realities that impact the Catholic Church worldwide: "Megatrends Affecting the Church" and "The Emerging Global Church."

Bosch, David J. *Transforming Mission: Paradigm Shifts in Theology of Mission*. Maryknoll, NY: Orbis Books, 1991.

See also the companion volume with primary sources: Norman Thomas, ed. *Classic Texts in Mission and World Christianity*. Maryknoll, NY: Orbis Books, 1995. This now-classic text provides a synopsis of mission from historical and thematic perspectives.

Considine, John Joseph, *World Christianity*. Milwaukee, WI: Bruce, 1945.

While Protestants had begun in the 1920s to think in terms of the *missio Dei* as the foundation for mission, Roman Catholics did not identify this emphasis until the Second Vatican Council. Considine was a forerunner in suggesting the idea among Roman Catholics.

Gutiérrez, Gustavo. *Theology of Liberation: History, Politics, and Salvation*. Maryknoll, NY: Orbis Books, 1973.

The classic text on liberation theology became a significant way for American Catholics to learn about the theological response of the Latin American Church to the problems of poverty and oppression.

Irvin, Dale, and Scott Sunquist. *History of the World Christian Movement*. 2 vols. Maryknoll, NY: Orbis Books, 2001, 2007.

This history provides a picture of the Western Roman Catholic Church, the Eastern Rite Churches, and the churches of the southern hemisphere, several of which date back to the first decades of Christianity.

Magesa, Laurenti. *Anatomy of Inculturation: Transforming the Church in Africa.* Maryknoll, NY: Orbis Books, 2004.

Monteiro, Evelyn. "Ecclesia of Women in Asia: A Forum for Catholic Women Doing Theology in Asia." In *Ecclesia of Women in Asia*, edited by Evelyn Monteiro, SC, and Antoinette Gutzler, MM., pp. xvi–xxiv. Delhi, India: ISPCK, 2005.

National Council of Catholic Bishops. "Strangers No Longer: Together on the Journey of Hope." A pastoral letter concerning migration from the Catholic Bishops of Mexico and the United States, January 22, 2003. Available online at *http://www.uscc.org/mrs/stranger.htm.*

Nickoloff, James B., ed. *Gustavo Gutiérrez: Essential Writings.* Minneapolis, MN: Fortress Press, 1996.

Okure, Teresa. "Inculturation: Biblical/Theological Bases." In *Inculturation of Christianity in Africa*, edited by Teresa Okure, Paul van Thiel, et al., pp. 55–88. Eldoret, Kenya: AMECEA Gaba Publications, 1990.

Phan, Peter C. *Many Faces, One Church: Cultural Diversity and the American Catholic Experience.* Lanham, MD: Rowman & Littlefield, 2004.

The author explores the implications of global Catholicism as immigrants made their way to the United States.

Pieris, Aloysius, SJ. *Love Meets Wisdom: A Christian Experience of Buddhism.* Maryknoll, NY: Orbis Books, 1988.

———. "The Asian Sense in Theology," *Dialogue* 6, nos. 1, 2 (January–August 1979): 447.

Rahner, Karl, SJ. "Towards a Fundamental Theological Interpretation of Vatican II," *Theological Studies* 40, no. 4 (December 1979): 716–27.

Sanneh, Lamin. *Encountering the West: Christianity and the Global Cultural Process; The Africa Dimension.* Maryknoll, NY: Orbis Books, 1993.

U.S. Catholic Bishops. "A Call to Solidarity with Africa." November 14, 2001. Available online at *http://www.usccb.org/sdwp/africa.htm.*

Reference Works

Froehle, Bryan T., and Mary L. Gautier. *Global Catholicism: Portrait of a World Church.* Maryknoll, NY: Orbis Books, 2003.

See selected charts for comparison of statistics on Catholicism across the continents.

Fabella, Virginia, MM, and R. S. Sugirtharajah, eds. *Dictionary of Third World Theologies.* Maryknoll, NY: Orbis Books, 2000.

Selected Websites

U.S. Catholic Conference of Bishops. Available online at *http://www.usccb.org.*

Sixteen percent of the departments relate to some aspect of the diversity of North American Catholicism or to the relationship between U.S. Catholics and people around the world. See especially the following departments: African American Catholics, Catholic Relief Services, Church in Latin America, Hispanic Affairs, Migration and Refugee Services, Social Development and World Peace, World Mission.

Africa Faith and Justice Network. Available online at *http://www.afjn.edu/.*

U.S. Catholic China Bureau. Available online at *http://www.usccb.net.*

Dictionary of African Christian Biographies Project. Overseas Ministries Study Center, New Haven, CT. Available online at *http://www.dacb.org/.*

Videos

Voices of Women. Available from Mission Education Office, Columban Fathers. St. Columbans, NE.

This video shows a good example of liberation theology with women in the Philippines in a "base community" setting.

In the Shadow of Dabajian Mountain. Available from Mission Education Office, Columban Fathers. St. Columbans, NE.

This video shows the interaction between missionaries and the indigenous Atayal in the mountains of Taiwan, both working to conserve the local culture.

Walking from the Shadows. Available from Mission Education Office, Columban Fathers. St. Columbans, NE.

This shows the work of missionaries among exploited migrant workers in Taiwan, most of them women. It also illustrates some of the effects of globalization.

from the REFERENCE LIBRARIAN

Geographical Descriptors— World Christianity

In one sense, everything you have learned throughout this book about reference sources and research techniques has prepared you for researching Christianity in its global context. For example, as Sr. Dries states, globalization raises issues of social and economic justice, the status of women, "liberation," and so on, so much of what you learned in the chapter on social justice will also be applicable for researching these issues in their global setting. Viewing Christianity in its global context also raises new issues for more traditional theological topics such as Christology and ecclesiology, so the resources and techniques described in the chapters on those topics will also be of use. You have been prepared to research the encounter of Christianity with other world religions by your previous study of Judaism and Islam. The effects of indigenous contexts on the Church's liturgical life can be studied using the resources of the chapter on sacraments. Even the issue of "inculturation," so much discussed in connection with the global setting of Christianity, is the modern version of what took place in the encounter of ancient Christianity with its own "global" setting: Hellenistic, Greco-Roman culture. The chapters on the New Testament and Judaism have, among other things, prepared you for the study of inculturation in that ancient setting in which modern concerns are foreshadowed.

Several reference sources of varying scope are available that focus in some way on issues related to Christianity's global impact. These include encyclopedias and dictionaries relating to Christian missions (e.g., *Dictionary of Mission: Theology, History, Perspectives*), Christianity in a particular geographical area (e.g., *A Dictionary of Asian Christianity*), and particular theological issues (e.g., *Dictionary of Feminist Theologies*). Doubtless, more such reference works will be published in the future. (See the reference bibliography at the end of this section.)

However, one reference tool's scope is much broader than any of these and takes pride of place for researching global Christianity:

> Fahlbusch, Erwin, et al., eds. *The Encyclopedia of Christianity*. 5 vols. Grand Rapids, MI: William B. Eerdmans, 1999–2008.

The preface of this encyclopedia declares explicitly that it was written with the intention of "describing Christianity in its global context," that is, its scope is truly global. To that end, scholars from many countries and various cultural backgrounds have contributed articles, including articles about Christianity on every continent (including articles on "Asia," "Africa," etc.) and articles on Christianity in over 170 individual countries.

If your library does not own *The Encyclopedia of Christianity* (although it should; this is a standard reference source), *the New Catholic Encyclopedia*, first or second edition, is a good alternative.

The term *World Christianity* is perhaps a little misleading. The main point of Sr. Dries's chapter is the diversity to be found in the various expressions of Christianity throughout the world, a diversity created by the variety of indigenous customs, patterns of thought, cultural expressions, and so on. Rather than a single "World Christianity," there are, rather, "World Christianities." One way of studying "World Christianity," then, is to focus on a particular expression of it found in a specific geographical/cultural location.

To see how this works, let's start with the article on Brazil from *The Encyclopedia of Christianity*. After noting the titles in the bibliography at the end of the article, we might discover the following records in the library catalog:

Author	Bruneau, Thomas C.
Title	The political transformation of the Brazilian Catholic Church [by] Thomas C. Bruneau.
Published	[London, New York] Cambridge University Press [1974]
Bibliography	Bibliography: p. [253]–264.
Subjects	Catholic Church—Brazil. Church and state—Brazil.

Author	Mainwaring, Scott, 1954–
Title	The Catholic Church and politics in Brazil, 1916–1985 / Scott Mainwaring.
Published	Stanford, CA: Stanford University Press, 1986.
Note	Includes index.
Bibliography	Bibliography: p. [297]–319.
Subjects	Catholic Church—Brazil—History—20th century. Church and state—Brazil—History—20th century. Brazil—Church history. Brazil—Politics and government—20th century.

As you examine the list of subject headings for these two books, you will notice that the geographical designation "Brazil" is used in two ways. In the first record, "Brazil" appears after the subject headings "Catholic church" and "Church and state." These are two examples of subject headings that can be subdivided geographically. This works with many (though not all) subject headings, so one way to "particularize" your search (assuming you have a subject heading to start with) is to add a geographical descriptor as a subdivision.

In the second record, the geographical designation "Brazil" itself appears as a subject heading, which is then further specified by the addition of the subdivision "Church history."

Sometimes you can either use a geographical designation (like a country name) as a main subject or a subdivision of a heading and it will not make much difference. (See the subject headings in the second catalog record just shown.) The main reason for knowing both ways of using geographical descriptors in subject headings is that not all subject headings subdivide geographically. But you can still give a geographical focus to your search using subject headings that cannot be so subdivided in combination with a search using a geographical descriptor that may appear in another subject heading for the same book.

Let's say you are interested in ecclesiological structures in Africa. From what you learned in the chapter on ecclesiology, you know (or could find out) that the subject heading for ecclesiology is "Church." But "Church" does not subdivide geographically; you cannot use "Church—Africa" as a subject heading. However, if you begin with a search on "Church" and then combine that with a search on "Africa" as a subject term, you might retrieve a record such as the following (if you do not know how to combine searches in this manner, ask your librarian to show you):

Author	Rweyemamu, Robert.
Title	People of God in the missionary nature of the church: A study of concilian ecclesiology applied to the missionary pastoral in Africa.
Published	Rome, 1968. (Delivery: Neue Zeitschrift für Missionwissenschaft, Schöneck/Beckenried.)
Bibliography	Bibliography: p. v–xiii.
Subjects	Church. Mission of the church. Christianity—Africa.

Notice that "Africa" appears as a subdivision of "Christianity," which does subdivide geographically (giving you another potential subject heading to use). You might also be able to find records where "Africa" is the main subject heading.

Let's try another one. This time you are interested in researching Christological views in Latin America. One subject heading for Christology you may have learned in the chapter on Christology is "Jesus Christ—Person and offices," another subject heading that does not subdivide geographically. Beginning with this subject heading and combining it with a search for "Latin America" as a subject term might produce a record such as the following:

Uniform title	Jesús, ni vencido ni monarca celestial. English.
Title	Faces of Jesus : Latin American christologies / edited by José Míguez Bonino ; translated from the Spanish by Robert R Barr
Published	Maryknoll, NY: Orbis Books, c1984.
Note	Translation of: Jesús, ni vencido ni monarca celestial.
Bibliography	Bibliography: p. v–xiii.
Subjects	Jesus Christ—Person and offices. Theology, Doctrinal—Latin America—History—20th century.

"Latin America" appears after another subject heading, "Theology, Doctrinal," and this gives you an additional point of access for researching this topic.

A final word about research: library collections are complex, and even librarians sometimes need to spend time locating what they are looking for. It would be a poor library indeed that did not have anything on your topic. Usually it is just a matter of finding the right key to unlock the door to the library's riches. There are many keys available for your use because there are many ways of gaining access to your library's collection. In this book, you have been introduced to some of them. There are other keys, such as using periodical indexes and databases to locate articles, with which your librarian can assist you. If you have used up all your "keys," don't be afraid to ask librarians to share their "key rings." That is why they are there.

Reference Bibliography

Fahlbusch, Erwin, et al., eds. *The Encyclopedia of Christianity*. 5 vols. Grand Rapids, MI: William B. Eerdmans, 1999.

Müller, Karl, SVD, Theo Sundermeier, Stephen B. Bevans, SVD, and Richard H. Bliese, eds. *Dictionary of Mission: Theology, History, Perspectives*. Maryknoll, NY: Orbis Books, 1997.

See the "Contents" on pp. vii–xii for a list of articles. Also contains extensive bibliographies.

Sunquist, Scott W., ed. *A Dictionary of Asian Christianity*. Grand Rapids, MI: William B. Eerdmans, 2001.

This volume contains no index, but see the alphabetical list of entries on pp. ix–xix. Contains bibliographies and focuses on one of the three major "areas" mentioned by Sr. Dries. Unfortunately, there is no equivalent (yet) for either Africa or Latin America, but the *Encyclopedia of Christianity* mentioned previously provides excellent coverage of all such areas.

U.S. Catholic Mission Handbook. Washington, DC: U.S. Catholic Mission Association.

The U.S. Catholic Mission Association publishes data gathered from U.S. Catholic "sending organizations" roughly every two years. Several recent handbooks are available in pdf. format from the association's website: *www.uscatholicmission.org*.

Library Skills

Here is our final list of library skills. You may want to copy them and keep them handy with you as you master the ins and outs of research. You can use them for any subject—the skills are transferable—so put them in a notebook, written or electronic, that is readily accessible and with you. There are many other library skills besides these, but if you have mastered these, you are well on your way to becoming an expert library user. Remember, practice makes perfect, and these skills can help you for a lifetime. Use them wisely and well.

SKILL KEY #1

Use the library's reference collection to begin your research.

a) Use a subject-specific encyclopedia to acquire specialized knowledge about a subject.
b) Use a subject-specific encyclopedia whose scope is appropriate for both your topic and the approach you want to take to that topic.
c) Use encyclopedia bibliographies to identify subject headings for your topic.
d) Use a concise subject-specific dictionary to look up the specialized vocabulary of a particular field.
e) Use an encyclopedia's index to locate information on subjects (including persons) for which there is no separate article.
f) Examine the synoptic outline of contents (or however it is designated) in an encyclopedia (1) to get a quick overview of the contents and (2) to get topic ideas for research.
g) Use an encyclopedia's index to get ideas for research topics.
h) Use cross-references to locate additional relevant material in an encyclopedia.
i) Use an encyclopedia's index to locate all (or as much as you want) relevant material on your topic. Note especially how detailed the index is and whether the editors of the encyclopedia make any special comments about it.

SKILL KEY #2

Use the library's catalog to locate sources of information.

a) Use subject headings to locate precisely books on your topic.
b) Use subject headings whose scope fits your topic as closely as possible, then adjust your search with a broader or narrower subject heading as necessary.
c) As an alternative to using encyclopedia bibliographies, use keyword searching to identify subject headings for your topic.

continued

continued

d) Combine one or more subject headings in a search to retrieve books on a topic for which no single subject heading exists.
e) Use the floating subdivision "encyclopedias" in combination with a keyword to identify encyclopedias on a subject.
f) Use the floating subdivision "moral and ethical aspects" to identify material, whether "pro" or "con," related to the ethical aspects of a subject.
g) Use the floating subdivision "religious aspects" to search for religious/theological aspects of nonreligious/nontheological subjects.
h) If necessary, use all the subject headings assigned to a book to identify material on a particular subject.
i) Use the name of an organization or group as an author to search for documents produced under the aegis of that group. Be aware of the possibility of changes in the group's name over time.
j) Use geographical descriptors either as subject headings or as subdivisions to focus research on a subject as it relates to a particular geographical area, such as "local" expressions of Christianity.

Student Tasks

1. Choose a country. Find out if your library has a dictionary or encyclopedia on Christianity in that country. If it does not, find an encyclopedia that does tell you about Christianity in that country.
2. Using the same or a different country, search your library catalog using the name of the country as a subject heading. Scroll through the list of subject headings. What subdivisions do you see after the name of the country that would be relevant for studying theology or Christianity in that country?
3. Use the name of the country you selected for #2 as a subdivision following the subject heading "Church history" or "Christianity" (e.g., Church history—Brazil; Christianity—Great Britain). How do the results compare with what you found in #2?
4. Choose a country or region. Try to find a website for the organization of Catholic bishops for that country or region. What problems do you encounter in trying to do this?

INDEX

F

G

H

I

J

O

P

Q

R